Path of the Soul

How Jesus Attained Christ Consciousness

Al Florey

BALBOA
PRESS

A DIVISION OF HAY HOUSE

The astrological charts of Jesus were generated by the WinStar Pro 6 program manufactured by Matrix© Software, Gainesville, Fl. 32653.

Balboa Press books may be ordered through booksellers or by contacting:

Balboa Press
A Division of Hay House
1663 Liberty Drive
Bloomington, IN 47403
www.balboapress.com
1 (877) 407-4847

Print information available on the last page.

ISBN: 978-1-9822-1303-9 (sc)
ISBN: 978-1-9822-1302-2 (e)

Library of Congress Control Number: 2018911400

Balboa Press rev. date: 09/28/2018

Table of Contents

Part 3 — The Mission

Diagrams, Charts, and Tables

Dedication

Path of the Soul is lovingly dedicated to Barbara J. Briner, DO. Thanks to her pioneering work in Esoteric Healing and the healing treatments I received, I was physically rejuvenated and spiritually renewed. This changed the course of my life from serious health issues to one of discovery—the discovery of Jesus as a man, a soul, and a spirit.

Acknowledgements

I am especially grateful to Bonnie Dysinger, Carole Shaheen, and Jan Newlove for the many hours they devoted to proofreading *Path of the Soul.* Their comments and suggestions were very helpful and greatly appreciated. I am also grateful to Diana Censoni and Joanne Christenson for the assistance they provided.

I would like to also acknowledge my first spiritual teacher, the Rev. F. Reed Brown. His guidance firmly placed my feet upon the spiritual path some forty years ago and set me on a lifelong spiritual quest.

To the many spiritual teachers and authors who have inspired me throughout my life, I say thank you. I especially want to thank Alice Bailey who devoted her life to presenting the teachings of the beloved Master Djwhal Khul (DK).

Last but not least, I would like to acknowledge my students. Many of them have been with me for more than twenty years. Their dedication has been an inspiration year after year.

Prologue

Discovery of the Birth Chart of Jesus

I had recently installed astrological software on a computer at a friend's office in Champaign, Illinois. The new software could generate a natal chart for anyone born between 600 BC and 2,400 AD. My hope was to pinpoint when the messenger of the Aquarian Age was likely to appear. I knew I was searching for the proverbial needle in a haystack, but I had to try.

On a warm August evening in 1987, I drove down to the office to run a few astrological charts. Since Jesus was the messenger of the Age of Pisces, my thought was to find out where the planets were located in relation to the twelve signs of the zodiac at the time of His birth. In particular, I wanted to see where the outer planets were placed and whether the outer planets formed any major aspects to each other or to His personal planets.

Though the high-frequency energies of the outer planets seem to be relatively minor and often disruptive notes in people's lives, the outer planets have a profound effect upon the greater society and culture. People whose personal planets form major aspects to the outer planets in their charts often become the voice behind the revolutionary changes taking place in the society. I wondered if this was true of Jesus.

I entered Jesus Christ, Bethlehem, Israel, 12:01 p.m. (local time), December 25, 0001, into the data input fields of the astrology application to generate the chart. When I didn't see anything significant in the chart, I decided to generate charts using days between December 24 and January 5. Once the computer generated the chart, I clicked on the print button to send it to the dot matrix printer. When the last chart finished printing, I glanced at the large clock on the wall. It was 9:30 p.m. "Time to go home," I thought to myself.

The next thing I recall was hearing the clicking sound of the old dot matrix printer. Another chart was printing. The name in the upper right-hand corner of the chart was Yeshua. My first thought was that the pins on the printer (which pull the paper up from the box) had shifted, cutting off the right side of the chart.

As more of the chart appeared, I noticed that the placement of the planets had nothing in common with the charts I had been running. Plus, Neptune was at the Mid-heaven. That was significant. The chart slowly appeared pin by pin. As the date of birth printed in the center of the chart, the hair on my neck and arms stood up. The date of birth was March 7, -3,[1] 4:00 a.m. The name on the chart was Yeshua and the place of birth was Nazareth, ISRL.

I looked up at the clock. Somehow an hour and a half had passed in the span of a few minutes. Ever since my near-death experience in 1983, I had been experiencing a number of strange things that couldn't be explained. Stereo speakers screeched with static when I went near them. Burned-out fluorescent lights would flicker back on and would stay on for a couple of days. More than once, I felt as if I was slipping out of my body through the top of my head.

I wasn't trying to intuitively perceive the date of Jesus's birth. My objective at the time was to get a sense of where the outer planets were placed in relation to the personal planets around the time of Jesus's birth, knowing full well that His birth date was never historically recorded.

I then generated the ninth harmonic of the chart. Over the years, I had discovered that the ninth harmonic allowed me to tune in to a client at a deeper level. I often felt as if the ninth harmonic opened a window to their Soul. What I saw in the ninth harmonic chart often affected how I analyzed a client's chart. Once I looked at the ninth harmonic for the chart of Yeshua and compared it to the natal chart, I was sure I was looking at the birth chart of Jesus. But the only way to be sure was to conduct an in-depth analysis of the natal chart.

A few days later, I ran a number of astrological transit reports. Once I looked at the transit reports around the time of Passover in 30 CE[2] through 33 CE, I knew I was looking at the birth chart of Jesus. These reports revealed when Jesus was crucified. They also indicated when His ministry was likely to have started.

The longer I studied the chart, the greater my amazement. The degree to which the symbolism of the astrological factors in the chart seemed to reflect Jesus and His teachings was startling. More than anything, I wanted to do an in-depth analysis of the chart, but at the time I didn't have the concentration or stamina needed to conduct the analysis. I was still recovering from my near-death experience. I put the chart, the transit reports, and other research into a box and put it in storage.

Over the next twenty-five years, I moved nine times, mainly around the Lansing, East Lansing (Michigan) area, although I had also moved from Illinois back to Michigan, from

---

[1] The Gregorian calendar does not have a year 0. The March 7, -3 date is the historical date of March 7, 4 BC.
[2] CE stands for, Common Era, while BCE stands for, Before the Common Era.

Michigan to Virginia, and back to Michigan. Each time I moved, I moved the box containing the charts. At least that is what I thought. Countless times during those twenty-five years, I thought about analyzing the chart of Jesus.

I retired January 1, 2013, but it wasn't until I had some minor basement flooding in the summer of 2014 that I tried to find the natal chart of Jesus. I searched through a good number of boxes I had in storage. Most of them were filled with handouts I had developed for different classes and workshops over the years, but the natal chart of Jesus was nowhere to be found.

Each time I had changed my residence, I purposefully moved a small battered box that once contained paper for the dot matrix printer, thinking the chart was in there. I found the box, but neither the chart nor the transit reports were in it. I was disappointed, but so much time had passed since the chart first appeared that an analysis of the chart no longer seemed as important as it once did.

In the later part of 2014, my health started to decline. By May 2015, I had become so weak and off balance that walking was difficult. I could barely make it three feet without something to hold on to. I fell too many times to count. After sitting for a while, once I stood up and started to walk, I would find myself facing the opposite direction within three or four steps. My doctor suggested I get a walker or a cane to help steady me.

I often felt stabbing pin pricks, numbness, and burning sensations in my face as well as in my left arm and leg. In early June, I could no longer feel the gas or brake pedals of the car. Many times I thought I was slowing down and would come to a screeching halt, or I would step lightly on the gas pedal only to hear the tires squeal. Driving a few blocks to the store became more challenging than it was worth. I was deteriorating so quickly that I decided that my life was drawing to a close.

My 1983 near-death experience had left me with some neurological issues, but nothing as debilitating as what I was experiencing in 2015. My short-term memory had been rapidly declining for a while. By early June, I could no longer think clearly or make simple decisions. At the rate my body was neurologically shutting down, I knew I was about a month away from needing home health care and possibly less than a year to live.

I wasn't upset about dying. After all I had been living on borrowed time since 1983. At the last minute, I decided to make an appointment with Barbara Briner, DO. Dr. Briner is well-known for her pioneering work in Esoteric Healing and osteopathic manipulation. If anyone could tell me what was going on, I knew she could.

By the time of my appointment I could hardly walk across the floor of the small waiting room and down the hallway to the treatment room. The look on Dr. Briner's face said it all.

My half-hour treatment went on for an hour and a half. I noticed some improvement in my ability to walk and decided to have regular weekly treatments to slow the rate of decline.

You can imagine how surprised I was when I woke up the next morning feeling great. I felt better than I had felt in years. My strength and balance were back. I could walk straight and didn't need anything to hold onto. Just the night before, my leg muscles screamed with pain as I walked upstairs to go to bed, but that morning, I bounded down the stairs free of all pain.

I had barely finished my morning coffee when Dr. Briner called. She expressed her concern and indicated she was thinking about calling an ambulance to take me to the hospital. "No, I feel great. Really great! It's a miracle," I shouted into the phone.

I had the most wonderful day. I bounced around the house and went for a brisk walk—something I hadn't been able to do for months. I not only had energy and strength, but my thinking wasn't muddled and my memory was back. When I laid down that evening, I felt truly grateful for the wonderful day. But I couldn't help but wonder what condition I would be in when I woke up.

The next morning as I was opening my eyes, I clearly heard, "You must recreate the birth chart of Jesus." Startled, I jumped out of bed, tossed on some clothes, and barreled down the stairs. As I poured a cup of coffee, I repeated the words, "You must recreate the birth chart of Jesus."

Strangely, I remembered His time of birth, 4:00 a.m., but I couldn't remember the date and I wasn't sure about the year. I remembered the Sun was conjunct several planets in Pisces and that Neptune was conjunct the Mid-heaven. I had a vague recollection of Mars and Saturn seeming out of place.

I had an old version of the Matrix© Astrology software installed on a computer in the basement. After a cup of coffee, I went to the basement, turned on the computer, and clicked on the icon for the WinStar© application.

I entered March 7, -4, 4:00 a.m., Bethlehem, Israel, into the data entry fields and clicked OK. The chart that appeared looked similar to the chart of 1987, but it wasn't the same. Since I knew the Sun was in Pisces, I decided to run a chart for the different days when the Sun was in Pisces during the year -4. Although there were similarities, none of the charts seemed to match the chart I remembered.

After a short break, I went back to the basement. As soon as I sat down, I knew I was using the wrong year. I also recalled that the original chart of Yeshua listed Nazareth as the place of birth. But there is so little difference between the longitude and latitude of Nazareth compared to Bethlehem, I couldn't see how entering Nazareth would make a difference.

I entered March 7, -3, 4:00 a.m., and selected Nazareth, ISRL. Within seconds, the monitor displayed an exact replica of the birth chart of Yeshua that appeared during the time of the Harmonic Convergence in 1987. Only then did I recall that the Moon was in the sixth house in Cancer and that it formed one of the points of a grand trine configuration. The Sun, Venus, Uranus, Mercury, and Neptune formed the other two points.

I printed the chart, turned off the computer, and ran upstairs. I set the chart down on the dining room table. After getting a legal pad and pen from my office on the second floor, I returned to the dining room and sat down. For a while, I just stared at the chart.

On Saturday, June 20, 2015—almost twenty-eight years after the chart first appeared—I started to write. For hours I jotted down notes as I looked over the chart. The exhilaration I felt the day before continued as I thought about the symbolism and meanings of the astrological factors in Yeshua's chart. Without a doubt, I was looking at the most amazing birth chart I had ever seen.

For four weeks, the significances and meanings behind the astrological factors of the chart washed over me in waves. I scribbled notes as fast as I could write. Each day during those four weeks, I felt as if I were in some kind of altered state. I neither had a concern nor a need for anything to be different from the way it was at that moment. I truly had a profound sense of divine order and a deep sense of peace. For four weeks I was free of all distractions.

"Perhaps submitting to my impending death had something to do with the perfect peace I was feeling," I thought to myself. It was as if the slate of my life had been wiped clean. There was nothing more I needed to do. All personal desire and drive was gone. All I could do was be present in the moment, even though the moment was unlike any moment I had ever experienced. For the first time, I knew what the Yogis of the East meant when they spoke of bliss.

I started the analysis of the birth chart of Jesus with a lengthy discussion of the Sun in the sign of Pisces. I then jotted down a large number of thoughts in relation to each of the planets. I concluded the handwritten portion of the analysis with a discussion of the (angular) aspects that the planets formed to each other.

What was most surprising to me was how all three outer planets formed an aspect to each other and formed a close aspect to many of the personal planets in the chart. This was significant, even though the outer planets were unknown two thousand years ago. By the end of the analysis, I was convinced that the energies of the outer planets not only profoundly affected Jesus, but they were more important to His life and mission than the other astrological factors of the chart.

How Jesus became the messenger for the Age of Pisces had a lot to do with His sensitivity and conscious responsiveness to the influences of the outer planets. My sense of the importance of the outer planets in Jesus's life changed everything. Suddenly, it was as if Jesus was being revealed to me through a light that spread across the heavens, linking planet to planet and star to star. The birth chart became a beautiful mandala—a mandala of the life and spirit of Jesus.

Prior to that moment, I wasn't able to sense the deeper meanings and significances of the astrological factors of His chart. Nor did I have the intuitive sensitivity necessary to see the interplay, the exchange, and the blending of the different types and qualities of energies that impacted Jesus's life, uplifting Him into the light and realization of Christ consciousness.

It was four weeks to the day when I completed the handwritten portion of the analysis. For twenty-eight straight days, I felt a soft, wonderful peace. But when I woke up the morning of the twenty-ninth day, it was gone. I had fallen back to earth. After a cup of coffee, I grabbed the two legal pads that I had filled with notes and ran upstairs. I set the legal pads down on the desk in front of my office computer and turned it on.

"Time to begin," I shouted silently.

PART ONE

The Path

Chapter 1

Universal Path of the Soul

Jesus was born the son of Marium and Yousif in the early hours before dawn on the morning of March 7, 4 BC.[3] Once the baby was wrapped in swaddling cloths and placed in Marium's arms, did she look into the eyes of her newborn son and see the only begotten Son of God, the Christ, who would perform the works of the Father, be crucified, and be resurrected on the third day as Christianity proclaims? Probably not.

Now that we have the date and time when Jesus was born, it is possible to see Jesus's life from His birth to His Crucifixion in a new light, free of religion, theology, and dogma. This comprehensive analysis of the birth chart of Jesus shines a bright light upon Jesus as a person and a Soul and reveals how He unfolded, developed, and mastered His divine potential.

Using the symbolism of traditional astrology and Soul-centered esoteric astrology, the progressive unfoldment, development, and spiritualization of Jesus are presented in a way that helps people understand the nature and breadth of the path of the Soul. It is upon this path that people discover their own unique patterning and unfold their divine potential.

Path of the Soul tells the inspiring story of the life, the message, and the mission of Jesus and explains in great detail how Jesus mastered successively higher states of mind and attained Christ consciousness. Such lofty achievements as, enlightenment, bliss, at-one-ment with the Divine, and Christ consciousness are not states of mind that only a few people can achieve. Rather, they are states of mind that all people can attain when their vast potential is unfolded within the crucible of the human mind.

From step to step and stage to stage, the prodigal sons and daughters who have journeyed to a far land return home. This journey home is referred to as the path of the Soul. Upon this

---

[3] 4 BC is the historical year Jesus was born, since there wasn't a year zero in the calendar. In astronomy (which has a year zero), the astrological year Jesus was born is -3.

path, mankind journeys from darkness to light, from the unreal to the real, from revelation to revelation, and from realization to new realization, through the successively higher gateways of the mind onto the courtyard of the Divine.

There is a secret chamber in the planetary heart filled with a wealth of information about this journey and how people can unfold their divine potential. Unfolding this potential is the objective of all who step upon the path of the Soul. Although portions of these teachings have been revealed to the masters and initiates throughout history, these teachings have been purposefully withheld from the public. Since time immemorial, the guardians of the ancient wisdom teachings have been patiently waiting for the day when they could release these teachings to the public.

That day is now.

For more than two thousand years, the words of the Buddha and the Christ have spiritually fertilized and tilled the soil of the collective hearts and minds of humanity in preparation for this day. At last, a sufficient number of people are ready to begin their training for world service as co-creators of the Divine. It is they who will lay the foundation for a new heaven and a new earth.

The potential to become a divine co-creator is imprinted upon the Souls of all people, yet few have turned away from the outer world long enough to perceive their own divine patterning. Most people are oblivious to their own Soul.

Historically, the spiritualization of human consciousness has taken place at an exceedingly slow pace, but this is about to change. Today, the opportunity to speed up the rate at which people attain the higher states of mind is being offered to all who are willing to do the work. To take advantage of this opportunity, it is important to have a basic understanding of the human constitution and knowledge of how the mind and consciousness unfold in the seven planes of the evolutionary system of earth.

Though this information may seem abstract and esoteric at times, it is important to have a basic understanding of the nature of this journey into the planes of light and the higher states of spiritual realization. The evolution of consciousness involves the unfoldment, development, and mastery of the three aspects of the divine mind, first as the personality, then as the Soul, and finally as the Spiritual Triad.

The Constitution of a Human Being
The Personality, the Soul, and the Spiritual Triad

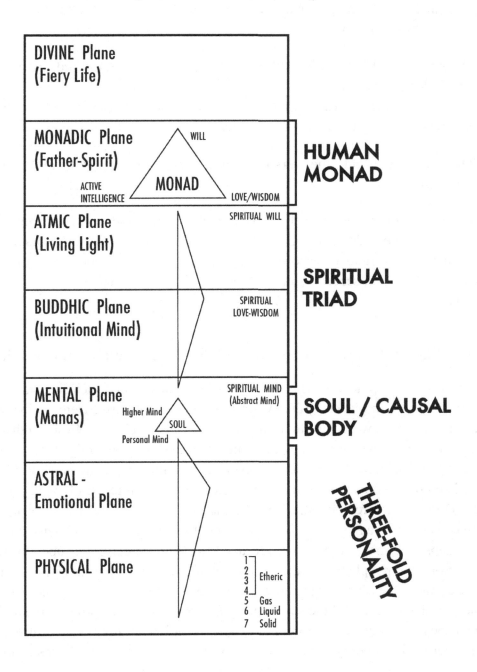

DIVINE Plane (Fiery Life)	
MONADIC Plane (Father-Spirit) — WILL, ACTIVE INTELLIGENCE, MONAD, LOVE/WISDOM	HUMAN MONAD
ATMIC Plane (Living Light) — SPIRITUAL WILL	SPIRITUAL TRIAD
BUDDHIC Plane (Intuitional Mind) — SPIRITUAL LOVE-WISDOM	
MENTAL Plane (Manas) — SPIRITUAL MIND (Abstract Mind), Higher Mind, SOUL, Personal Mind	SOUL / CAUSAL BODY
ASTRAL - Emotional Plane	THREE-FOLD PERSONALITY
PHYSICAL Plane — 1,2,3,4 Etheric; 5 Gas; 6 Liquid; 7 Solid	

3

Esoterically, the three aspects of the divine mind are referred to as: divine will-purpose, love-wisdom, and active intelligence. In consciousness, the unfoldment and development of these three aspects of the Divine at the level of the Monad (the Father Spirit) is referred to as the Spiritual Triad. At the personal level, these three aspects of the divine mind people unfold and develop are known as:

1. The physical-etheric instinctual mind: the physical appetites and drives, personal will and initiative (the will-to-be).
2. The astral-emotional desire mind: feelings, sentiency, love, and affections (the ability to psychologically relate to one another).

3. The concrete mind: the personal intelligence, rational, logical thought, and discernment.

All people begin this journey by developing the threefold personal consciousness, regardless of the stage of development the Soul had previously attained. At this initial stage of development, the (brain) consciousness is unfolded and developed in terms of skills, capacities, faculties, and senses. This development is preliminary to the work called for upon the path.

The Seven Planes, the Seven Rays, and the Seven Principles of Consciousness

The progressive development and mastery of more expansive and inclusive states of mind takes place in the seven planes of the evolutionary system of earth. Here, in the West, the seven planes (from the lowest plane to the highest) are referred to as the physical-etheric plane, the astral-emotional plane, the mental plane, the buddhic plane, the atmic plane, the monadic plane, and the divine plane. Each plane corresponds to a unique type and quality of energy.

There is no division of the evolutionary system of earth in terms of energy and divine life-force. Divine life-force streams from the human Monad (the Father Spirit) onto the physical-etheric body via the Soul. However, within the consciousness of mankind, there are significant gaps in terms of what people are able to sense or perceive. It is upon the universal path of the Soul that people bridge these seven planes in mind, consciousness, and being.

People attain successively higher states of mind as they sense and consciously respond to the energies and qualities of the successively higher planes. This progressive unfoldment of consciousness takes place regardless of people's religion, ethnicity, or culture.

All is energy! But energy is not uniform. Matter is energy at its densest, slowest rate of vibration, quality, and note, while spirit is energy at a higher vibratory rate and quality. Each plane has a unique type of energy that helps unfold one or other of the seven principles of consciousness. These seven principles exist in a state of potentiality. People develop their potential as they register and consciously respond to the ray-magnetized energies of successively higher planes.

Each of these seven principles corresponds to one of the seven rays of manifestation. The seven rays are the building forces of the universe. Each ray serves as an underlying magnetic field for a particular plane.

The processes whereby people unfold, advance, and master the threefold personal mind, the threefold mind of the Soul, and the threefold mind of the Spiritual Triad involve the transmission of energies magnetized by one of the seven rays of manifestation. Each ray in turn has seven qualities that correspond to one or other of the Seven Ray.

The Seven Rays of Manifestation[4]

Ray one corresponds to the first aspect of the divine mind—will-purpose.
Ray two corresponds to the second aspect of the divine mind—love-wisdom.
Ray three corresponds to the third aspect of the divine mind—active intelligence.
Ray four corresponds to the attribute—harmony through conflict.
Ray five corresponds to the attribute—knowledge and the concrete sciences.
Ray six corresponds to the attribute—devotion and dedication to an ideal.
Ray seven corresponds to the attribute—ceremony, ritual, and order.

In relation to the advancement of human consciousness, rays four through seven stimulate the unfoldment and development of the four attributes of the divine mind, while rays one, two, and three stimulate the unfoldment and development of the three aspects of the divine mind. Since each of the seven rays has seven sub-qualities, there are forty-nine different types of force in the evolutionary system of earth.

In consciousness, people become responsive to these different qualities of force one by one over the course of countless lifetimes. Each quality has its own vibration, note, color, and blend of ray forces, and each quality has a targeted purpose in terms of its capacity to advance some aspect of the mind and consciousness.

---

[4] The seven rays of manifestation represent a new field of study. In general, people know little about it, yet it is an exceedingly important subject in relation to the evolution of consciousness and the unfoldment of successively higher states of mind and consciousness.

Each of the seven principles of consciousness is unfolded by a specific type of energy as the forces of a particular plane impact the mind and (brain) consciousness. People progress as the consciousness shifts upward from a lesser quality to a higher quality in relation to a particular principle of consciousness (e.g., the principle of the mind), and from one principle to a higher principle.[5] The specific steps that people take to further their development in relation to a particular principle, however, can vary from one person to another.

By way of the forces of the physical-etheric, astral-emotional, and lower mental planes, people unfold, develop, and later master the threefold personal consciousness. This occurs as the forces of these three planes impact the brain consciousness. In this way, the threefold personality, the personal self, is advanced.

The personality is a great center of unfolding self-consciousness specifically charged with the unfoldment and development of the third aspect of the Divine, active intelligence. As people unfold and develop the threefold personal consciousness, active intelligence is advanced at the level of the personality. The Soul, on the other hand, is charged with unfolding the second aspect of the Divine (love-wisdom). The Soul is a great center of life and being whose nature is essential love untainted by any personal considerations or preferences. Though the Soul is individuated, it is self-less.

The mission of the Soul is to anchor the principle of love on earth and to express love-wisdom through the instrumentality of the refined personality. To accomplish this, the Soul prepares the individual in all areas of development of the personal mind and consciousness, so the full measure of the principle of love can be expressed on earth via the physical body.

The Three Subtle Bodies and the Silver Cord

The evolution of consciousness begins anew each lifetime as people unfold the three aspects of personal consciousness. Preparation for this activity begins the moment the Soul anchors the silver cord or sutratma in the fetus (sometime between the fourth and sixth month of pregnancy).

The silver cord connects the Soul (which resides in the upper mental plane) to the physical-etheric body. Two different types of energy stream through this cord: the stream of consciousness, which is anchored near the pineal gland, and the stream of life, which is anchored near the heart.

At the same time that the Soul anchors the silver cord in the etheric vitality body, it expands its field of influence from the upper mental plane into and through the three planes

---

[5] People can unfold and develop more than one principle of consciousness at a time.

of earth—the lower mental, astral, and physical-etheric planes. Within this expanded field of influence, the Soul creates the three subtle bodies that envelop and interpenetrate the physical body. The three subtle bodies are sheaths of different types and qualities of forces. Over the course of people's lives, various energies and forces stream through these force fields onto the physical-etheric body and impact the brain consciousness. These electromagnetic force fields are commonly referred to as the etheric vitality body, the astral emotional body, and the lower mental body. The lower mental body is where the personal mind resides.

The magnetism of these subtle bodies is first created when the Soul anchors two permanent atoms plus the mental unit in the aura of the fetus. The physical-etheric permanent atom is anchored in the first (the highest) sub-plane level of the physical-etheric body. From this placement, the physical permanent atom generates an electromagnetic field referred to as the etheric body. The astral permanent atom is anchored in the first sub-plane level of the astral body and generates the force field that is referred to as the astral body. The mental unit is anchored at the fourth sub-plane level of the mental body and generates the lower mental body.[6]

These force fields (subtle bodies) interpenetrate and envelop the physical body prior to one's birth. However, they tie into the physical body during different stages of people's lives. Once tied into the physical body, the forces streaming through the subtle body stimulate the (brain) consciousness in a way that advances the development of one or other aspect of personal consciousness.

Although the vital etheric body interpenetrates the physical body at birth, the streams of light that tie the etheric body to the physical body is not completed until sometime between the ages of four and seven. Initially, the survival and viability of the newborn depends on the life-forces streaming from the Monad to the Soul and from the Soul to the physical body via the silver cord. Life-force enters the etheric crown center at the top of the head.

The etheric body is composed of meridians of etheric light. These meridians underlie the nervous system. When a large number of meridians of the etheric body cross each other, they create a chakra or center through which energy streams from the etheric vitality body into the physical body. There are seven major chakras or centers of the etheric body: the basic center, the sacral center, the solar plexus center, the heart center, the throat center, the ajna center, and the crown center. Additionally, there is an important center at the top of the spine referred to as the alta major center. Each of the etheric centers magnetically attracts a different sub-ray quality of force.

---

[6] At the higher level of the Spiritual Triad, the mental, buddhic, and atmic permanent atoms are anchored in the first sub-plane level of the mental plane, buddhic plane, and atmic plane respectively. These three permanent atoms electromagnetically generate the light bodies or sheaths of the Spiritual Triad.

The astral body ties into the physical-etheric body via the solar plexus center. As a rule, the linking of the astral body to the physical body is completed sometime between the ages of seven and fourteen. By way of the astral body, the forces of the astral plane express in people's lives. As a rule, the lower mental body ties into the physical body between the ages of fourteen and twenty-nine.

These subtle bodies are magnetized force fields comprised of the forces of the three planes of earth that the permanent atoms magnetically attract. These matter forces, in turn, attract and repel different qualities and types of energy and forces of the three planes that envelop the earth. The forces that the subtle bodies electromagnetically attract are drawn into one or other of the etheric centers, depending on the quality of the force. Each chakra or center is magnetized receptive toward a particular quality of force.

The development of threefold personal consciousness takes place as the energies and forces of the etheric, the astral-emotional, and the lower mental planes impact the mind and consciousness via the subtle bodies and etheric centers. The quality of people's consciousness depends on the quality of forces attracted into the subtle bodies that stream through the chakras.

When people are consciously focused in the lower etheric centers,[7] the traits and characteristics of the little self dominate people's lives. The little self is a product of the influences of the cellular intelligences and drives of the physical body. Identifying your selfhood with the needs, nature, drives, and appetites of the physical body greatly affects the quality and vibration of both the astral-emotional and the lower mental aspects of personal consciousness that people bring forth.

Since people's development of threefold personal consciousness is the result of the cellular intelligences of the physical and subtle bodies, people's actions and behaviors are initially more characteristic of the nature of the physical body than they are of the Soul. This is the human condition as long as people consciously respond to the unrefined forces that express via the three lower centers: the solar plexus, sacral, and basic centers.

The immediate evolutionary goal of mankind is to shift the consciousness upward from the lower etheric centers into the upper centers of the etheric body: the heart, throat, ajna, and crown centers. Once the self-consciousness begins to shift into the heart center and throat center, the brain consciousness starts to respond to a higher quality of forces.

---

[7] The seven centers are equally important to the health and well-being of the physical body. In relation to the evolution of consciousness, however, there is a great difference between the upper centers and the lower centers of the etheric body. In terms of self-consciousness, the basic, sacral, and solar plexus center relate more to the nature, drives, and appetites of the physical body, while the upper centers (the heart, throat, and crown centers) relate more to the unfolding qualities and values of the Soul.

Centering the consciousness in the upper centers awakens a sense of personal and social responsibility, honesty, ethical behavior, human decency, and a drive to learn how things work on earth. During this advanced phase of personal development, people's consciousness and their actions and behavior begin to conform to the laws that govern humanity, rather than the laws of nature that govern the activities and behavior of the animal kingdom.

The evolutionary goal set before humanity is to achieve a polarization of the consciousness at the mental-plane level. This is necessary in order to become a rational thinking human being. The purpose behind the evolutionary forces that impact mankind is to free people from an entanglement of their consciousness with the unenlightened physical qualities. This, in turn, transforms the consciousness from the limiting selfishness people exhibit as a result of the influences that the physical body has upon the consciousness during the early stages of development.

By transferring the atoms of self-consciousness from the lower etheric centers to the upper centers (especially from the sacral center to the throat center), the mental aspect of personal consciousness is developed. This results in the polarization of the personal consciousness at the midrange of the mental plane. When the consciousness is polarized at the mental-plane level, people usually have a strong sense of self, a more advanced concrete mind and intellect, and an ability to rationally think for themselves. The consciousness of roughly half the population of the world is still polarized in the lower astral-emotional plane, not in the concrete mind.

As the energy streams along the outer petals of the etheric heart center, throat center, and crown center, people unfold and start to exhibit the personal behavior, characteristics, and traits that are more in line with the universal laws that govern humanity. When this is the case, people demonstrate love for their family and associates, integrity, creativity, philanthropy, kindness, ethical behavior, honesty, personal responsibility, self-discipline, and fairness.

At this higher level of personal development, the quality of people's lives sharply distinguishes them from those who are only responsive to the forces expressing through their lower centers. When people are mainly responsive to the forces streaming through the lower etheric centers, they tend to exhibit selfishness, greed, jealousy, vengeance, bigotry, and a preoccupation with sex. Their lives are filled with the emotional drama, personal passions, and self-indulgences that serve no purpose in relation to the evolution of consciousness.

Only when the uplifted atoms of self-consciousness are magnetically captured by the upper centers do people become truly decent, ethical, moral, and trustworthy. This development is preliminary to the development of the higher mind and spirituality. When people respond to the laws of humanity, they innately interact with others in a respectful, considerate way and willingly shoulder personal and social responsibility. Over time, such people demonstrate an unwavering ethical and moral character based on universal human rights, standards, and values. They are no longer driven by a self-referencing consciousness that responds primarily to the forces that stream through the lower centers.

The objective of the laws of humanity is to bring about right relations between all people and to cultivate personal and social responsibility. The universal laws of humanity apply to all people regardless of the society, religion, familial relations, nation, race, or gender.

Final Phase of Development of the Threefold Personality: the Integrated Personality

In lifetime after lifetime, people unfold and develop the various components of the threefold personal consciousness: The physical instinctual mind, the astral-emotional desire mind and sentiency, and the concrete mind, logical rational thought. This development involves advancing skills, capacities, faculties, and senses. Here, people are on the path of human evolution, not the path of the Soul. The evolutionary goal set before mankind at this stage is to unfold the threefold personal consciousness and to polarize their consciousness at the mental-plane level by focusing on the development of intellect and rational, logical thought.

Once the consciousness is mentally polarized, people can begin to integrate the three aspects of personal consciousness into a unified whole. This development precedes the spiritualization of human consciousness. Before the threefold personal consciousness can be integrated and unified, however, many of the forms of duality and conflict within the personal consciousness must be resolved.

During the developmental stage of the threefold personal consciousness, the physical instinctual mind, the astral-emotional feeling nature, and the personal mind and intelligence are relatively independent of each other. This results in people wanting to do one thing and thinking they should do something else. In general, people do not realize the extent to which the elements of their personal consciousness are relatively independent of each other until they try to orient their lives to the higher values, qualities, and nature of the Soul.

As people resolve the conflicts within and between the three aspects of their personal consciousness, they integrate and unify them. Only then can the three aspects of the personal consciousness work together harmoniously. This stage of development is referred to as the stage of the integrated personality.

The stabilization of the consciousness at the mental level and the resolution of the conflicts within the personal consciousness (represented by the hard aspects in the natal chart) are needed in order for people to the reach this final step of development of the threefold personal consciousness. As an integrated personality,[8] the physical-etheric, emotional, and mental aspects of the personal consciousness work well together.

People who have reached this point of development and function as an integrated personality are usually quite successful and socially prominent as a result of the three aspects of the personal consciousness working together. However, there is no spiritual vision that governs them. This is important.

Since the threefold personal consciousness is unfolded and developed via the forces of the three matter planes, even the integrated personality is considered a form or vehicle, since it is composed of the subtle matter forces of the three planes of earth. This includes people's instincts, feelings, desires, and thoughts. The threefold personal consciousness, itself, is not a product of the Soul or the human Monad. For this reason, the self-referencing nature of the threefold personal consciousness is referred to as the little self or not-self.

At the stage of the integrated personality, people continue to be preoccupied with their own desires, interests, and needs, not those of others. In addition, they still have a significant amount of personal karma that must be resolved. Also, people who function as an integrated personality are more likely to violate universal law than they were prior to this achievement. This is due to the enhanced empowerment of the personal mind that takes place when the three aspects of the personal consciousness are unified. Becoming personally whole as a result of the unification of the three aspects of personal consciousness strengthens the personal will and ego. For this reason, people at this stage are an even greater force in society for good or ill.

Many people function as an integrated personality for lifetimes and enjoy great material and social success, but with little if any spiritual growth. Advancement beyond this stage of the integrated personality involves the unfoldment and development of the threefold higher mind. This higher level of development is entirely self-initiated. The evolutionary forces of earth do not compel people to achieve a state of mind higher than that of the integrated personality. People's Soul or spirit guides may encourage them to advance, but neither the Soul nor the Monad can force them to do the work necessary to attain a higher state of mind.

---

[8] As an integrated personality, the consciousness is mentally polarized and the faculties, capacities, and skills of each of the three aspects of personal consciousness are interrelated with each other. As a result of the unification of the threefold personal consciousness, the individual exhibits a strong sense of self. The integration and unification of the threefold personal consciousness polarizes the consciousness in a new field of forces (a new subtle body) referred to as the personality body. The personality body is on its own ray. The subtle personality body of the integrated personality envelops and interpenetrates the physical body and the three subtle bodies from the fourth sub-plane level of the mental body.

The unfoldment, development, and the eventual mastery of the three aspects of the human Monad (first as a personal self, then as the higher self (the Soul), and finally as the Spiritual Triad) take place as the successively higher types and qualities of energy stream through the upper centers of the etheric body. Mankind's potential to unfold successively higher states of mind gives credence to the Psalmist's statement, *"I say, 'You are gods, sons of the Most High, all of you.'"*[9] Human beings are truly gods-in-the-making. For this reason, it is important to understand the steps and stages of the path of the Soul.

---

[9] Herbert G. May and Bruce M. Metzger, The New Oxford Annotated Bible: An Ecumenical Study Bible (New York: Oxford University Press, 1977). Psalms 82:6. (RSV) (Italics added)

Chapter 2

Initiations, Stages upon the Path

Once the three aspects of the personal consciousness are integrated and working together, and the faculties, abilities, and capacities of the personal consciousness have been developed, people are ready to step upon the path as a probationer.

As a probationer, people begin the work necessary to unfold and develop the three aspects of the Divine at the level of the Soul. As the energies radiating from the causal body stream into the upper centers of the etheric body and stimulate the brain consciousness, people unfold and advance the higher mind—the consciousness of the threefold higher self.

The causal body envelops the Soul at the second and third sub-plane levels of the mental plane. When perceived intuitively, this field of light has the appearance of a lotus flower. The causal body is a great field of different qualities and sub-qualities of upper mental-plane energy. It is this higher quality of energy that stimulates the development of the three aspects of the higher mind. This occurs as the energies of the Soul stream into the upper etheric centers via the petals of the lotus (the causal body).

Over the course of many lifetimes, the causal energies are organized into twelve petals (symbolically speaking). These petals unfold one by one from the innermost jewel of the lotus located at the first sub-plane level of the mental plane. The impulses of the Soul stream across the petals of the lotus into the upper etheric centers: the heart, throat, ajna, and crown centers.

Once a substantial amount of the self-consciousness has been transferred from the lower etheric centers into the upper etheric centers, the upper centers magnetically attract the energies of the Soul by pulling the petals away from the inner jewel of the lotus. These twelve petals unfold one by one over many lifetimes. Once unfolded, the ray-magnetized energies of the petals stream through the awakened upper centers of the etheric body. This activity stimulates the (brain) consciousness with the ray, frequency, and quality of energy needed in order to unfold the intelligence, love-wisdom, and will aspects of the Divine at the level of the Soul.

Allegorically, the lotus is comprised of four tiers of petals, each with three petals. The outermost tier of petals is referred to as the knowledge tier of petals. The middle tier is referred to as the love tier of petals. The inner tier of petals is referred to as the sacrifice tier of petals. The three petals of each tier represent the ray three (intelligence), ray two (love), and ray one (sacrifice-will) sub-qualities of each tier of petals.

The three sub-qualities of the petals in the (fourth) innermost tier of petals are referred to as manas, buddhi, and atma, which conceal the jewel of the lotus. The three sub-qualities or energies of the three innermost tier of petals are involved in the unfoldment of the intelligence aspect of the Spiritual Triad, while the energies streaming from the intelligence, love, and sacrifice tiers of petals impact the consciousness in a way that helps people unfold and develop the higher mind.

The mind of the Soul is brought forth in people's lives as the energies of the Soul stream through the upper centers of the etheric body and impact the consciousness. Here, the ray-magnetized energies of the Soul stream along the petals of the intelligence, love, and sacrifice tier of petals into the upper centers of the etheric body.

Most people have yet to open the upper centers of their etheric bodies to the energies of the Soul (via the petals of the lotus). The awakening of the upper centers is brought about by the kundalini as it rises up one or other of the three channels of the spine of the etheric body. These three channels are referred to as the ida, pingala, and sushumna.

As the kundalini rises up the pingala channel, it opens the throat center to the radiating energies of the knowledge tier of petals. The kundalini rising up the ida channel opens the heart center to the energies of the love tier of petals. The kundalini rising up the central sushumna channel opens the crown center to the energies of the sacrifice tier of petals. The threefold kundalini fire rises up one channel or another in response to people's spiritual activities, interests, and service work.

It is the energies and sub-qualities (knowledge, love, and will) of the three petals of the knowledge tier that stream into and through the upper centers of the etheric body. This occurs in response to people's search for greater knowledge and understanding. Soul energies via the knowledge tier of petals stream into the field of the personal mind and brain consciousness. Besides increasing people's understanding of physical-plane life and the nature of human beings, the influx of Soul energies from the knowledge tier of petals intensifies the light of the personal mind. This enables people to apply the Soul-infused light of the mind to control and later master their physical appetites, drives, and instinctual nature.

The Twelve Unfolded Petals
of the Lotus (Causal Body)

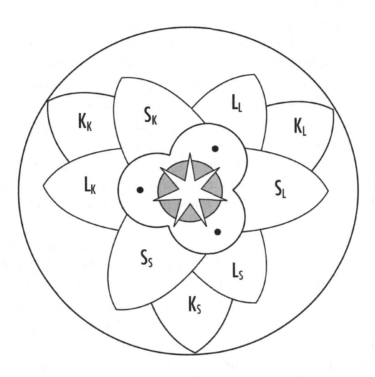

1. Outer Circle = Knowledge Tier of Petals (K_K, K_L, K_S)

2. Middle Circle = Love-Wisdom Tier of Petals (L_K, L_L, L_S)

3. Inner Circle = Sacrifice Tier of Petals (S_K, S_L, S_S)

4. Innermost Circle = Sacred Petals of the Lotus

   (Atma, Buddhi, Manas)

5. Jewel of Life in the center of lotus

The three sub-qualities of the love tier of petals stream through the upper centers of the astral body into the upper centers of the etheric body. These energies correspond specifically to the etheric heart center. The energies radiating from the love petals begin the spiritualization of human consciousness. The influx of Soul energies via the love tier of petals enables people to apply their Soul-infused mind to control and later master their astral-emotional, feeling nature.

The three sub-qualities of the sacrifice (will) tier of petals stream into the upper centers of the mental body, through the upper astral centers, into the upper centers of the etheric body. As the energies and qualities of the sacrifice tier of petals stream through the upper centers, they centrifugally expel many of the lower forces present in the three subtle bodies. This activity results in a transformation of people's consciousness, resulting in the unfoldment of a higher state of mind. The influx of the energies and qualities of the Soul (via the causal body) slowly transforms the integrated personality into the higher self.

The influx of the energies and qualities streaming from the petals of the lotus into the upper etheric centers enables people to attain the first three initiations. With each successively higher initiation, the rate at which people can achieve a higher state of mind is accelerated.

Like all of us, Jesus moved forward in mind and consciousness from step to step and stage to stage upon the universal path of the Soul. To understand how Jesus attained Christ consciousness, the path of the Soul must be considered in relation to the various stages of the path. Each stage of development of the higher mind and then the mind of the Spiritual Triad corresponds to one of the five major initiations that people must attain to achieve human perfection.

The path of the Soul is the same for everyone and yet perfectly unique. Upon the path of the Soul, people first unfold, develop, and master the threefold personal consciousness, then the threefold higher mind, and much later the threefold spiritual mind of the Triad. Slowly, people realize successively higher states of mind and attain successively higher levels of initiation.

The unfoldment, development, and mastery of the mind and consciousness of the personality, the Soul, and the Monad involve the unfoldment and development of successively higher principles of consciousness. Once a principle is sufficiently developed and mastered, it is stabilized at an initiation ceremony that takes place in the spirit side of life.

The Masters of the Spiritual Hierarchy (located in the higher planes of light) adopted initiation[10] as a way to accelerate the rate at which mankind could progress. During an initiation ceremony, the Masters of Love-Wisdom solidify a person's development and mastery of a particular principle of consciousness. For example, the principle of love-wisdom is the principle of consciousness that people unfold as the energies of the buddhic plane impact the brain consciousness. When love-wisdom is unfolded, developed, and mastered, it is referred to as Christ consciousness.

During the initiation ceremony, the Hierophant of the ceremony applies the rod-of-initiation to a particular chakra or center. This stimulation of one of the upper centers opens the doorway of the mind to a new plane of experience and experimentation. This event sets the processes into motion that unfold a higher principle of consciousness.

THE FIVE INITIATIONS - ATTAINMENT OF HUMAN PERFECTION

The Stage of Spiritual Probation: The Goal Is to Attain the First Initiation

The first initiation is symbolically referred to as the birth of the Christ, the birth of love-wisdom within human consciousness. Once people have attained the stage of the integrated personality, the next step upon the path involves anchoring the principle of the will-to-be and mastering the forces that express in their lives as the drives and urges of the physical body. This becomes important to a person once love-wisdom begins to unfold. The ability to impose mental discipline upon the physical body enables people to master the type of forces that stream through the lower etheric centers.

Becoming consciously sensitive and responsive to the physical body is very important during the early stages of development, but at some point, people need to develop a consciousness that is responsive to the life and qualities of the higher planes.

The work involved in attaining the first initiation includes activities and studies that draw down the energies and qualities radiating from the unfolded petals of the intelligence tier of the lotus. This is when people consistently demonstrate their obedience to the universal laws of humanity.

As a result of the influx of energies from the outer knowledge tier of petals, the faculties of the mind and intellect are strengthened and the light of the personal mind is intensified. Only then can people exercise enough mental power and discipline to free themselves

---

[10] Each initiation involves mastering ray one, ray two, and ray three in relation to a particular plane. Since there are three minor initiations for each major initiation, there are fifteen initiations people must achieve to attain human perfection at the fifth initiation. In total, the evolutionary system of earth offers nine major initiations for a total of 27 initiations.

from the influences of the cellular intelligences of the physical body and attain the first initiation. The influx of energies from the intelligence tier of petals advances people's mental creativity, knowledge, and understanding.

The primary driving force in the life of a probationer is a desire for greater knowledge and understanding, both in relation to oneself and in relation to the world. Here, the focus is on learning how things work on earth socially, politically, and culturally. In response to this desire, mankind has established colleges and universities to teach the concrete sciences. This stage is secular, not spiritual, and corresponds to higher education.

Once people become as a probationer, they enter the Hall of Knowledge. In the Hall of Knowledge, people's focus is on learning their life lessons and gaining the understanding needed to progress, first in relation to the physical body and the physical-etheric plane, then in relation to the emotional feeling nature (via the energies of the love tier of petals), and finally in relation to the lower mental plane (via the energies of the sacrifice tier of petals). The light of the mind is increased as the light of the Soul streams across the unfolded petals of the lotus into the upper etheric centers and impact the consciousness.

Once a sufficient amount of the ray three energies and its three sub-qualities that radiate from the knowledge petals have impacted the consciousness and advanced the intelligence aspect of the higher mind, people are ready to master the instinctual appetites and drives of the physical body and attain the first initiation. It is the influx of the energies from the three petals of the knowledge tier that awakens the knowledge and willpower that people need to master the physical body and its nature. (Mastery is not a denial or repression.)

The first initiation is a stage preliminary to the spiritualization of human consciousness, but it cannot be achieved until the threefold personal consciousness has been sufficiently developed. This includes the development of the faculties, capacities, skills, and capabilities of all three aspects of the personal consciousness.

In summary, in order to attain the first initiation, people need to function as an integrated personality and demonstrate mental control over their physical appetites and drives. Without the knowledge and willpower that the energies of the knowledge tier of petals bring forth, people are unable to consistently demonstrate mental control of the physical body and its instinctual drives and appetites. Mastery over the appetites and drives of the physical body is necessary before the essential love of the Soul can unfold in people's hearts and mind. Until people have achieved the first initiation, they are likely to behave inappropriately from time to time, regardless how intelligent or kind they are.

The Stage of Discipleship: The Goal Is to Attain the Second Initiation

Once spiritually oriented people have attained the first initiation, they step forward upon the path as disciples. The focus of disciples is on awakening love-wisdom. This calls for controlling and then mastering the selfish, astral-emotional desire nature.

The Gospel story begins with the birth of Jesus, the incarnation of love on earth. It, therefore, speaks to the disciple. Discipleship is advanced as the energies of ray three, ray two, and then ray one sub-qualities radiating from the three petals of the love tier impact the mind and consciousness.

Knowledge of the birth of Jesus symbolizes people's knowledge or awareness of essential love that is beginning to impact their minds and consciousness. Knowledge of this higher quality of love arises as the energies of the first (the knowledge petal) of the love tier of petals stream through the astral body into the upper etheric centers.

The unfoldment of love-wisdom within these physical bodies of earth is a lengthy process involving the influx of energies from the love tier of petals. By way of prayer, meditation, spiritual studies, and service, people draw the energies from the love tier of petals into and through the astral body into the upper etheric centers, the heart center in particular.

Initially, the stage of discipleship represents a lengthy period of the gestation of love-wisdom within these human forms. This occurs as the principle of love is anchored within the mind. Here, love-wisdom (the Christ Spirit) is hidden within the heart center until it has been adequately nourished by the essential love of the Soul. This gestation period can last lifetimes.

The sign Virgo represents the principle of Mother-matter in relation to human consciousness. For this reason, Virgo is known as the sign of the hidden Christ. The ray two energies of Virgo are quite active during this gestation phase when love-wisdom is being anchored in human consciousness. Once essential love is sufficiently built up, it rises from the heart center onto the ajna center and impacts the brain consciousness.

Except for the brief mention of a twelve-year-old Jesus in the book of Luke (when He stayed behind in the Temple at Jerusalem after the Passover), Jesus doesn't appear in the Gospel story until He shows up at the Jordan River, where John is baptizing people for the repentance of sins. To Judeans, it was a sin to violate the Mosaic Law or dishonor the covenant agreement the ancient Israelites had entered into with their Lord. In terms of the evolution of consciousness, however, the term sin represents a shortcoming or failure to demonstrate obedience of the laws of humanity. Basic human decency, honesty, truthfulness, equanimity, faithfulness, fairness, respect for others, and integrity demonstrate such obedience.

The universal laws of humanity call for the elimination of selfishness, greed, hatred, separatism, bigotry, and the tendency to control or manipulate others. By definition, the egocentric nature of the little self violates these universal laws and interferes with people's ability to consistently demonstrate the type of behavior that is expected of all human beings. Regular alignment and attunement to the indwelling Soul via meditation and prayer mitigate the selfish tendencies of the little self.

Esoterically, the second initiation is referred to as the baptism in the Jordan River. Since water is a universal symbol for the astral feeling, sentient aspect of the personal consciousness, John's reluctance to baptize Him indicates that Jesus had successfully attained the second initiation prior to His baptism:

> *Then Jesus came from Galilee to the Jordan to John, to be baptized by him. John would have prevented him, saying, 'I need to be baptized by you, and do you come to me?' But Jesus answered him, 'Let it be so now; for thus it is fitting for us to fulfill all righteousness.' Then he consented. And when Jesus was baptized, he went up immediately from the water, and behold the heavens were opened and He saw the Spirit of God descending on Him like a dove, and alighting on Him.*[11]

Up until the second initiation has been attained, the inner Christ child is in danger of drowning due to the watery torrents of people's own selfish emotions and desires. For this reason, the work of disciples involves stilling the personal waters (the emotional desire nature). This stage involves mastering the personal emotions, feelings, desires, and self-indulgent tendencies. The work required involves transforming the personal desires into spiritual aspirations and cultivating a spiritual idealism. This occurs as people dedicate themselves to devotional activities and impose discipline upon their selfish indulgences and emotions.

To attain the second initiation, people must open their heart centers to the essential love of the Soul. The influx of the essential love of the Soul occurs as the energies radiating from the three petals of the love tier of the lotus stream through the astral body into the upper etheric centers. Over time, the consciousness is stimulated by this higher quality of love in a way that brings forth a more loving, compassionate, and forgiving nature. This influx of the ray two qualities of the Soul brings forth spiritual aspiration, idealism, the faculty of the higher creative imagination, and a degree of clairvoyance.

The second initiation is not easily attained until people dedicate themselves to regular spiritual studies, service activities, meditation, and prayers for the health and wellbeing of

---

[11] Matt. 3:13–16. (RSV) (italics added)

others (not just close friends and family members). Most of all, people need to shift their attention away from their own personal desires and begin to focus on the needs of others.

During this second stage of the path, people become aware of the great duality that exists within their own consciousness between their selfless, loving qualities, and spiritual values (a product of the energies of the love petals) and their own selfish feelings, affections, and desires. At this time, disciples are called on to systematically remove the selfish elements of the not-self that are tied to their lower astral emotional aspect of their personal consciousness. This involves relinquishing things that the disciple is emotionally attached to and identifies his or her selfhood with.

The entire threefold personal consciousness (including people's thoughts, emotions, and instinctual nature) is permeated with the ray three factor of crystallization. It is this factor conditioning the personal consciousness that gives rise to separatism within the consciousness. Esoterically, separatism is mankind's greatest shortcoming, for separatism leads to division, prejudice, racism, and a sense of superiority or inferiority. Ray two (love-wisdom), on the other hand, carries a magnetic factor that unifies, not separates.

The spiritualization of human consciousness begins once the second petal (the love petal) of the love tier of petals unfolds, allowing the love of the Soul to stream into the awakened heart center of the etheric body. As the energies magnetized by ray two stream through the etheric heart center, they impact the consciousness in a way that stimulates the unfoldment and expression of the loving qualities and higher values that are characteristic of the Soul.

Mastering your emotional desire nature is possible once sufficient energies radiating from the love tier of petals have impacted the consciousness and brought forth the love aspect of the higher mind. This results in the ability to truly love one another, not just the members of one's family and close friends.

Even today, the attainment of the second initiation can be emotionally exasperating, painful, and exhausting, especially when this is the first time the Soul has attained the second initiation. People often rest for a number of years, sometimes for lifetimes, once they attain the second initiation.

Since Jesus had resolved many of the tests, challenges, and struggles of the second initiation in a recent past life, He was able to demonstrate a mastery over His astral-emotional nature early in His life. Attainment of the second initiation is easier when the second initiation had been previously attained. When this is the case, the karmic cords attaching people's atoms of self-consciousness to the lower astral-emotional forces have already been severed.

The first and the second initiations are referred to as threshold initiations. They represent a level of mastery that is preliminary to the spiritual path. These two initiations are necessary because of primitive man's misstep during the ancient civilization of Atlantis. Many of the primitive Atlanteans unfolded a desire for the things of earth and started to identify their selfhood with their desires, rather than with the spirit. Correcting this misstep involves orienting oneself to the Soul and eliminating all emotion-based attachments to the things of earth. This can take lifetimes to accomplish and is exceedingly difficult, especially when people continue to violate the universal laws that govern humanity.

The work involved in attaining the second initiation eliminates the not-self in terms of the emotional aspect of the personal consciousness. The mental aspect of the not-self, on the other hand, is dealt with as people approach the third initiation.

All influences of the not-self must be eliminated before people can achieve oneness with the Soul at the third initiation. When people no longer identify their selfhood with the physical body or with their astral-emotional, feeling nature, or with their self-aggrandizing thoughts and beliefs, the path is cleared for significant spiritual growth and development.

The spiritualization of the threefold personal consciousness involves blending the energies and qualities of the love and will of the Soul with those of the integrated personality. This usually takes place over the span of a number of lifetimes. Though people may be religious and abide by the beliefs, dogma, and tenets of their faith, they usually are uninterested in their spiritual growth on a daily basis until the love aspect of the higher self is reasonably well developed.

Once the second initiation has been attained and people are dedicated to expressing the higher qualities, character, values, and nature of the Soul, the individual becomes a pledged disciple.

The Stage of the Accepted Disciple: The Goal Is to Attain the Third Initiation

According to the book of Mark, after the baptism of Jesus in the Jordan River,

> *The Spirit immediately drove him out into the wilderness. And he was in the wilderness forty days, tempted by Satan, and he was with the wild beasts, and the angels ministered to him.*[12]

This verse indicates that once the second initiation has been attained, the disciple is confronted with the untamed wilderness of the mind. The concrete mind represents the

---

[12] Mark 1:12. (RSV) (italics added)

untamed wilderness when it is filled with thoughts of how to acquire personal power, name, and fame (self-glorification), or is filled with greed, prejudice, narrow-minded thoughts, and mental or spiritual arrogance. Most of all, the mind is untamed in the sense that people lack concentration, one-pointed focus. The mind typically flits from one thing to another.

At this stage, Satan as the tempter is synonymous with the esoteric concept of the dweller-on-the-threshold,[13] which people confront as they approach the third initiation. The personal mind does not have the capacity to master itself. Only the light of the higher mind can master the mental aspect of personal consciousness. For this reason, the third initiation is the first truly spiritual initiation upon the path of the Soul.

As the energies of the sacrifice (will) tier of petals stream through the upper centers of the etheric body, they advance and strengthen the will of the higher mind. This brings forth one-pointed focus and an awareness of the need to sacrifice oneself for others through service to God and mankind. Here, the focus shifts away from the personal self and its preoccupation with personal preferences, indulgences, and biases. The work to attain the third initiation involves denying the little self and taking up your cross, so to speak. Astrologically, this is the fixed cross of the heavens comprised of Taurus opposite Scorpio and Leo opposite Aquarius.

Greater spiritual disciplines and capacities are needed to endure the tests and trials people experience as they approach the third initiation. This includes the development of the faculty of discrimination and the ability to discern to between the will of the Soul and the personal will.

Once a pledged disciple demonstrates a willingness to engage in the work necessary to attain the third initiation, one of the Masters of Hierarchy offers to train the disciple in the Master's Ashram. Once spiritually-oriented disciples accept the training, they become an accepted disciple.

The realized Masters of the Spiritual Hierarchy will not work with disciples until they have attained the second initiation and are approaching the third initiation. Prior to this time, people (often unknowingly) misuse the understanding and skills gained from the training that the Masters provide.

In the wilderness of the mind, the disciple meets the tests and trials that correspond to his or her mastery of the forces of the mental plane. Once the voices of the instinctual nature of the physical body and the voices of the astral-emotional desire mind have been stilled, accepted disciples begin to hear the ministrations of the angels free of distortion. The inner

---

[13] The symbolism of the dweller-on-the-threshold is discussed in detail in Chapter Twenty, Dweller on the Threshold.

Christ child (love-wisdom) reaches its maturity once the accepted disciple approaches the third initiation.

By successfully resisting the temptations in the desert, Jesus demonstrated His mastery of the three types of life lessons that pertained to the mental aspect of personal consciousness. This involved demonstrating a disinterest in achieving name, fame, and personal power. Such mastery is necessary in order to transcend the personal consciousness and shift the consciousness into the realm of the Soul. Since the Soul is group conscious (not ego conscious), once Jesus functioned from the level of the Soul (biblically referred to as the Son of God), it was imperative for Him to gather disciples to teach.

There is a point in the spiritualization of human consciousness when the disciple is more oriented toward the Soul and its nature than to the outer world of the integrated personality. At this stage, the desire to do the will of God typically drives people forward. As people work to embody and express the nature, qualities, and mind of the selfless Soul and willingly sacrifice their time, interests, and concerns to help others, they attract the energies from the sacrifice tier of petals into the mental body. The energies of the sacrifice tier of petals subsequently stream into the upper etheric centers, the crown center in particular. This cannot take place, however, until the kundalini (via the sushumna) has opened the crown center to the will of the Soul.

As the energies of the sacrifice tier of petals stream into the upper centers, people begin to respond favorably toward the will of the Soul. It is at this time that the second-degree initiate becomes an accepted disciple. The primary objective of the accepted disciple[14] is to achieve a union of the concrete mind with the mind of the Soul.

As the third initiation is approached, the accepted disciple expresses more of the values, qualities, and character of the Soul and innately responds to the universal Laws of the Soul. At this stage, people no longer need the rules and laws of society to keep them from behaving inappropriately. Nor do they need a religious commandment to keep them from (so called) sinful behavior. Accepted disciples are governed by the Laws of the Soul once the energies of the love tier and sacrifice tier of petals have awakened the essential love and will of the Soul within the disciple's mind.

The work involved in attaining the third initiation relates to the unfoldment of a consciousness and character that expresses the values, standards, nature, and qualities of one's own selfless

---

[14] When a disciple is approaching the third initiation, a master of the Spiritual Hierarchy often accepts the disciple into his or her Ashram for training. The focus of the masters in these Ashrams involves implementing the divine plan on earth in an effort to help advance the evolution of human life, consciousness, and being. This includes the establishment of universal spiritual principles within the collective minds of humanity. Training of accepted disciples who are incarnate on earth usually takes place at night during sleep.

Soul. As disciples approach the third initiation, they begin to sense the inner sacred space deep within them, especially during meditation and periods of deep contemplation. This sacred space is often infused with the auric emanations of the Angel of the Presence.

According to the ancient wisdom teachings, the Angels of the Presence came forth from the heart of God (the Solar Logos) millions of years ago to serve as a bridge or intermediary between the mind of the human Monad (located in the monadic plane) and the burgeoning, primitive minds of humanity.

The causal body, which envelops the Soul and retains the essence of the past-life development, was created out of the light substances of these Angels. This angelic substance has been imprinted with people's potential and with the essences of the emotional and mental patterns of thoughts, feelings, and behavior of the personalities of countless lifetimes. Today, the Soul and the Angel of the Presence are so intertwined that it is nearly impossible to differentiate between them.

By way of the Angels of the Presence, the individuated human Soul became the first manifest vehicle for the incarnating human Monads. The Soul is untainted by the intelligences of cellular life. All of its work is devoted to bringing forth an integrated personality through which the human spirit can actualize its potential and divine purpose. The ultimate goal of the human Monad is to bring forth a perfected loving-intelligent instrument that can begin to manifest or objectify the unfathomable purpose of the Logos on earth. As a group, mankind is not likely to comprehend this divine purpose until far into the future.

The Angels of the Presence do not serve the individual; rather, they serve the Planetary Logos and its purposes, even though they are an intermediary between the incarnating human Monad and the integrated personality. For eons, the Angels of the Presence have been constrained by the limited capacities of mankind.

These beautiful Angels have sacrificed their cosmic evolution for millions of years to advance the life, consciousness, and being of mankind. Imprisoned within the upper mental realm, they unceasingly work to bring forth and advance creative loving intelligence within mankind. This involves the unfoldment, development, purification, and transformation of the personal mind and consciousness. Their initial goal is for the Soul to bring forth a form vehicle (the integrated personality) that has the particular qualities and capacities that the Soul needs in order to fully express love on earth.

The Angels of the Presence are unceasingly committed to this work. They are freed from their service only when the development of the personality vehicle has been completed. Until that time, these Angels bridge the gap in consciousness between the Monad and the integrated personality.

By way of the Soul and the Angel of the Presence, the human Monad gives life to the physical and subtle bodies of mankind and gives life to the consciousness that is unfolding through them. The capacity and quality of the physical and subtle bodies and the unfolding consciousness are advanced as the Soul projects its impulses and impressions upon the burgeoning human consciousness. Slowly, the three aspects of the higher mind are brought forth, developed, and mastered.

People on the path are required to sacrifice many things in their lives. This is in accordance with the universal laws that govern the evolution of consciousness. In relation to the first three initiations, people are called on to sacrifice successively greater aspects of the not-self. The elimination of people's identification with the characteristics and traits of the not-self must be finished before people can attain the third initiation.

Throughout this stage of development of the higher mind, the energies of the Soul stream onto the threefold integrated personality and uplift and transform the consciousness. Slowly, the Soul supplants the integrated personality as the ruler of one's life. This occurs once the nature, qualities, values, and character of the personal self have been transformed into the nature, values, and character of the Soul.

Again, it is the light of the personal mind that people use to master the first two aspects of the personal consciousness and attain the first two initiations, but it is the intensified light of the higher mind (not the personal mind) that masters the mental aspect of personal consciousness.

At the third initiation, the threefold integrated personality is transcended and the individual attains at-one-ment with the Soul. Union of the integrated personality and Soul was the ultimate goal of disciples two thousand years ago. Today, attaining human perfection at the fifth initiation is the goal set before disciples and initiates.

Once the third initiation is attained, people realize how the physical body is nothing but an outer garment that is needed in order to live on earth, but it has nothing to do with their selfhood. They also realize that their former beliefs, ideas, feelings, relationships, status, possessions, profession, religion, and so forth were just tools used to bring forth greater understanding, knowledge, and wisdom.

In preparation for the third initiation, it is important for disciples to engage in the higher forms of spiritual activities that can reveal the world of the Real. The world of the Real lies deep within or behind the world of the Soul. Here, disciples must project streams of the conscious light from the unfolded petals of the lotus to the three centers of the Spiritual Triad. These three higher centers are referred to as the manasic center, buddhic center, and atmic center, which are located in the higher planes of light.

The three streams of mental light that connect the mind to the three knowledge petals of the lotus are extended from the knowledge petals to the higher manasic center. The streams of light connecting the astral heart center to the love tier of petals of the Soul must be extended from the three love petals to the higher buddhic center. The streams of light that connect the mind to the unfolded petals of the will tier must be extended to the atmic center.

These streams of light are referred to as the rainbow bridge since they are comprised of mental-plane energy that is magnetized by any one of the seven rays. In consciousness, the bridge between the personal mind, the higher mind, and the unfolding mind of the Spiritual Triad is stabilized once the consciousness is polarized at the level of the Soul at the third initiation. Esoterically, the third initiation is referred to as the transfiguration initiation.

> *And after six days Jesus took with him Peter and James and John and led them up a high mountain apart by themselves; and he was transfigured before them and his garments became glistening, intensely white, as no fuller on earth could bleach them. And there appeared to them Elijah with Moses; and they were talking to Jesus.*[15]

To attain the third initiation, the disciple must complete the development of the threefold higher self. This involves the unfoldment of a higher level of understanding and realization that arises as a result of the energies radiating from the sacrifice petals of the lotus. It is by way of the higher mind that people become responsive to the world of original ideas and the world of meaning and causation. The world of meaning and causation underlies the outer physical world and is the precipitating cause of the physical and subtle forms of earth. This includes thought forms and desire forms.

The third initiation represents a time when the Soul gains command of one's life. In effect, the mind of the Soul supplants the concrete mind. Once the third initiation is attained, the Soul mounts the cardinal cross of the heavens comprised of Aries opposite Libra and Cancer opposite Capricorn. The cardinal cross is the cross of world service to God and mankind.

Each initiation opens up a new plane of experience and experimentation. Once Jesus transcended the threefold personal consciousness, He became responsive to the divine plan and aware of His responsibility to teach others. Though Jesus was probably unaware of the specific details, His mission was to present a new approach to the Divine, the path of the heart.

Although the personal self is transcended at the third initiation, it still exists as a center of life through which the Soul serves mankind on earth. Here, the refined and purified Soul-infused unified personality is naught but the instrument of the Soul. At this stage, the integrated personality is no longer the instrument of the egocentric personal self.

The energies of the Monad (the Father Spirit) start to impact the consciousness directly

---

[15] Mark 9:2-9:4. (RSV) (italics added)

once the third initiation has been attained. The impulses of the mind of the Monad reach the initiate via the rainbow bridge that links the three centers of the Spiritual Triad to the corresponding three centers of the higher mind. This bridge is self-generated and strengthened by the disciple's selfless thoughts and prayers and invocations of divine light and love on behalf of the planet and all life thereon. By way of the rainbow bridge, initiates begin to unfold and develop the three aspects of the Monad via the light of the three centers of the Triad. This activity unfolds the threefold mind of the Spiritual Triad.

The Stage of the Initiate—The Goal Is to Attain the Fourth Initiation

Esoterically, the fourth initiation is referred to as the crucifixion initiation which is taken on the cardinal cross. In relation to the evolution of consciousness, this is the true crucifixion. The fourth initiation calls for the sacrifice of something even greater than the sacrifice of the threefold personal self to the Soul. At the fourth initiation, initiates sacrifice the Angel of the Presence.

Jesus is said to have experienced the fourth initiation when He was crucified. Due to His great love for the Father, Jesus fully accepted His impending death in the Garden of Gethsemane. At that moment, an immense amount of the will-to-love poured through Jesus as a result of His willingness to sacrifice His life. This, in turn, shattered the causal body.

> *And He said, 'Abba, Father, all things are possible to Thee; remove this cup from me; yet not what I will, but what Thou wilt.'*[16]

The shattering of the causal body sets the Angel of the Presence free to return to the cosmic heart center of the Solar Logos (who embodies the entire solar system). The release of the Angel is why the initiate can feel forsaken at the fourth initiation.

Throughout the evolution of consciousness, there are occasions when people feel as if they have touched the presence of God. In all likelihood, however, they have sensed the loving presence of the Angel of the Presence, not the presence of the Logos. With the departure of the Angel, the fourth-degree initiate can feel utterly forsaken.

> *And about the ninth hour Jesus cried with a loud voice, 'Eli, Eli, láma sabach-tháni?' that is, 'My God, my God, why hast thou forsaken me?'*[17]

---

[16] Mark 14:36. (RSV) (italics added)
[17] Matt. 27:46. (RSV) (italics added)

Once the force field of the causal body is destroyed, the fourth initiation is attained. The destruction of this force field severs the last remaining cords that link the atoms of people's self-consciousness to the things of earth. The shattering of the causal body not only frees the Angel from its obligations to the Planetary Logos (its purpose having been served), it destroys a force field that has veiled and concealed the Monad from the awareness of the initiate.

At this time, the remaining life energy expressing via the physical-etheric, astral, and lower mental permanent atoms is transferred into the respective manasic, buddhic, and atmic permanent atoms of the Spiritual Triad. The initiate's atoms of self-consciousness no longer operate in the three planes of earth.

The opposition of the planet earth to the Sun in people's natal chart symbolizes this slow, methodical transfer of the life energy from the physical and astral permanent atoms and mental unit to the manasic, buddhic, and atmic permanent atoms. This transfer is not completed, however, until the divine life-force in the basic center (the kundalini) has been fully transferred into the crown center. This transfer eliminates all need to incarnate on earth.

At the fourth initiation, the higher mind is transcended. The gap in consciousness between the integrated personality and the Father Spirit is finally bridged. This results in the attainment of one of several states of pure spirituality, such as enlightenment or Christ consciousness. Once the fourth initiation is attained, the initiate is referred to as a master.

Individuality is not lost at the fourth initiation even though the master's conscious life and being are now sensitive to the impulses of the universal, all-inclusive Spirit. The type of individuality that exists at this stage, however, has little similarity to the individuality that exists at the levels of the integrated personality and Soul.

Every erg of force of the causal body (which had purposefully obstructed the divine light from impacting the personal consciousness) is removed from the fourth-degree master at this time. This allows the divine light to pour directly from the Monad onto the conscious life and being of the new master.

Gone is everything that creates differentiation within the consciousness—all that separates and divides. Gone is every element of the world of form. Not even the subtle patterning of the world of ideas creates separation or differentiation within the mind of the master. There is only an unfathomable and relatively incomprehensible sense of oneness with all life.

Just as there are three subtle bodies that envelop and interpenetrate the physical body at the level of the integrated personality, earth itself is enveloped by the three planes of subtle matter. These planes are comprised of the collective subtle bodies (etheric, astral, and lower mental subtle bodies) of the four kingdoms of nature. As a result of the training necessary to attain the fourth initiation, the master gains command of the planetary forces of the physical-etheric, astral, and mental subtle bodies of the planet.

Fourth-degree initiates have command over the matter forces of the three planes of earth, while third-degree initiates have command over these same three types of forces but only in relation to their own subtle bodies. They have a limited ability to command the planetary forces of the three planes of earth.

Command over the forces of the three planes of earth requires extensive occult training by the Masters of the Spiritual Hierarchy. This involves command of the wind and rain, as well as command of the cellular intelligences of the physical-etheric, astral, and mental subtle bodies. This means that a master also has command over evil spirits.[18]

Once the fourth initiation is attained, masters only incarnate on earth at the request of the Chohan[19] of the ray that their Soul is on. The incarnation of a fourth-degree master takes place in order to correct some adverse condition that has arisen within the consciousness of mankind, or to anchor a new divine principle within the human mind, or introduce a new approach to the Divine.

The efforts of the Soul to perfect the integrated personality instrument continue right up until the moment the fourth initiation is attained. Once the fourth initiation is attained, there is nothing in the human consciousness or in the causal field that responds to the vibrations of matter. Nor are there any forces that can electromagnetically draw the Soul back into incarnation. All personal karma and past-life karmic patterns have been eliminated. The master may accept a mission to incarnate on behalf of mankind, but in terms of development, the three planes of earth have nothing more to offer the master.

The Stage of the Master: The Goal Is to Attain the Fifth Initiation

The fifth initiation is esoterically referred to as the resurrection initiation. That which the master is called on to sacrifice at the fifth initiation is so sublime and deeply veiled that people are unaware of its existence prior to the fourth initiation.

The work involved in attaining the fifth initiation is to embody the will and purpose of the Divine which the Monad embodies. When masters approach the fifth initiation, a link is created between the mind of the master and the mind of the Monad in its aspect of

---

[18] Two thousand years ago, the term evil spirits often referred to unevolved disincarnate spirits who attached themselves to individuals who had yet to sufficiently individuate.

[19] Chohan is the term for a sixth-degree master who oversees the masters, senior disciples, and disciples of a one of the seven Ray Ashrams of the Spiritual Hierarchy, e.g., the Ray One Ashram or Ray Two Ashram.

will-purpose. The dissemination of divine will-purpose in the evolutionary system of earth is regulated by the universal Laws of Life that govern the human Monad. Only masters who have demonstrated their unwavering obedience to the Laws of the Soul and have served the divine plan without hesitation respond to the higher Laws of Life.

At the fifth initiation, the master attains human perfection and is resurrected into a quality and light substance of pure life that far exceeds anything known on earth. Here, the master begins to experience the cosmic principles of freedom and abundant life. For two thousand years, these last two initiations (the crucifixion and resurrection initiations) have been too esoteric and sublime for all but a few masters to comprehend. By way of these two initiations, Jesus became the way shower for mankind and the messenger for the teachings of the dawning Age of Pisces.

The enlightening wisdom perceived by a fourth-degree initiate removes all sense of ray differentiation by which their Souls had been previously oriented and grouped. The fourth initiation opens a doorway of the mind that leads the master into a realm of the atmic living light. By way of this living light, the self of the Spiritual Triad experiences the will of the Logos emanating from Shamballa, the planetary center of divine will.

Once the fifth initiation has been attained, there are no forms or light substances that envelop the master. Rather, the master exists in a state of pure being that is free of all substances of the seven planes of the cosmic physical plane.[20] Masters can generate a form to use when working with mankind, but they are no longer enveloped in substance.

Since the fifth initiation is always taken on ray one, the resurrection of Jesus from the tomb of matter on the third day was brought about via the power of ray one. Jesus's Resurrection was a demonstration of His mastery of the second sub-aspect of ray one, the builder sub-aspect. Mastery of this builder sub-aspect of ray one results in an ability to transform light into matter and matter back into light. For this reason, Jesus was able to transform the physical cellular matter of His physical body into light.

At the fifth initiation, the master becomes the perfected human being. Once attained, the master's attention shifts toward developing complete identification with the Monad. Identification with the Monad is a deeper, more profound state of at-one-ment with the Divine. Identification with the Monad strengthens the master's attunement to the Planetary Logos, whose life streams through all life of the seven planes of earth. A state of identification with the Monad is a state of mind far beyond mystical oneness with God that was experienced at an earlier stage. It is the loftiest state of mind that can be attained in the evolutionary system

---

[20] The cosmic physical plane is the lowest of seven cosmic planes, just like the physical plane is the lowest of the seven planes of earth.

of earth. This identification is realized at successively greater and more inclusive levels of initiation (from the sixth initiation to the ninth initiation).

As their progression continues past the fifth initiation, masters progressively envision the fullness of Creation as it is envisioned within the mind of the Planetary Logos. This begins an even higher level of training by which a master becomes a creative god capable of wielding the seven rays to manifest life within its field of influence, depending on the cosmic path the ascended master chooses to pursue.

In summary, these steps and stages of the path of the Soul lead to the attainment of such lofty states of mind as, enlightenment, bliss, Christ consciousness, and human perfection. They represent the stages of spiritual growth people experience, regardless of their religion, philosophy, ethnicity, gender, or culture.

The key to understanding the universal, yet unique, path of the Soul is an in-depth analysis of the natal chart. To solve the mystery of Jesus and discover how He attained Christ consciousness, we must turn to the birth chart of Jesus.

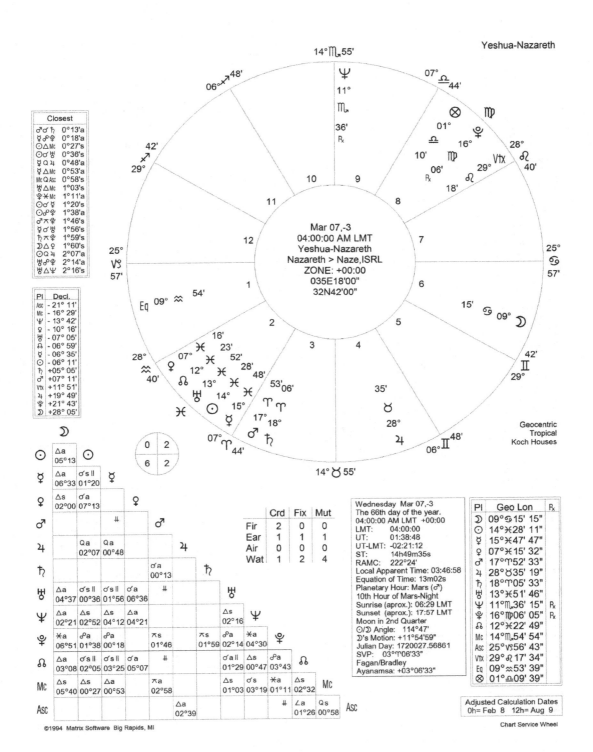

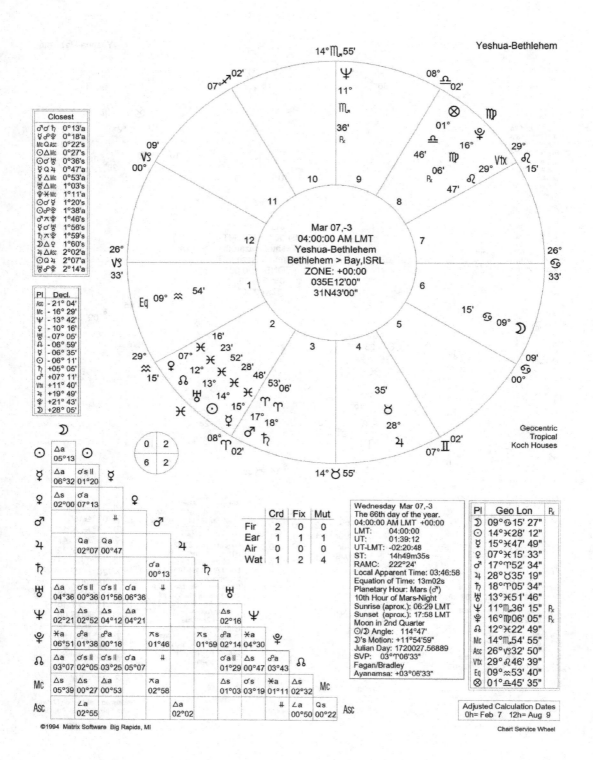

Yeshua-Bethlehem

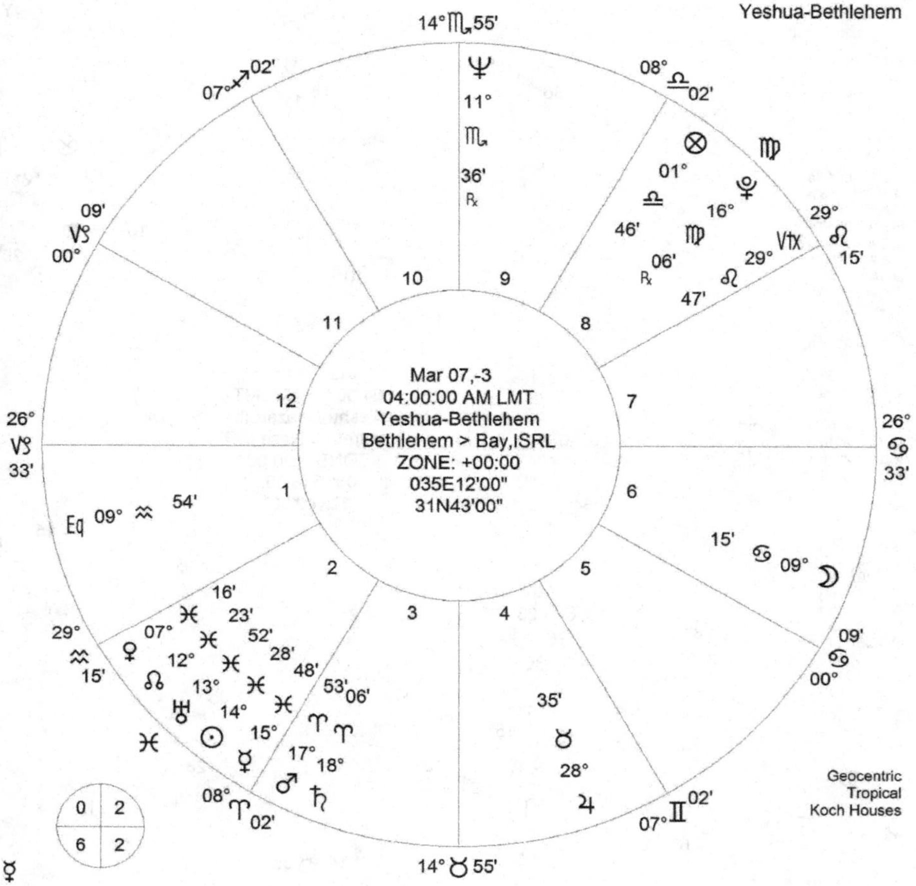

14°♏55'
07°♐02'
08°♎02'
09'
♑
00°
29°
♌
15'
26°
♑
33'
26°
♋
33'
29°
♒
15'
09'
♋
00°
08°♈02'
07°♊02'
14°♉55'
10
9
11
8
12
7
1
6
2
5
3
4
Mar 07,-3
04:00:00 AM LMT
Yeshua-Bethlehem
Bethlehem > Bay,ISRL
ZONE: +00:00
035E12'00"
31N43'00"
♆ 11° ♏ 36' ℞
⊗ 01° ♎ 46'
♇ 16° ♍ 06' ℞
Vtx 29° ♌ 47'
Eq 09° ♒ 54'
♀ 07° ♓ 16'
☊ 12° ♓ 23'
♅ 13° ♓ 52'
☉ 14° ♓ 28'
☿ 15° ♓ 48'
♂ 17° ♈ 53'
♄ 18° ♈ 06'
♃ 28° ♉ 35'
☽ 09° ♋ 15'
Geocentric
Tropical
Koch Houses
0
2
6
2

Closest	
♂☌♄	0°13'a
☿☍♇	0°18'a
Mc Q Asc	0°22's
☉△Mc	0°27's
☉☌♅	0°36's
☿Q♃	0°47'a
☿△Mc	0°53'a
♅△Mc	1°03's
♇⚹Mc	1°11'a
☉☌☿	1°20's
☉☍♇	1°38'a
♂⚻♇	1°46's
☿☌♅	1°56's
♄⚻♇	1°59's
☽△♀	1°60's
♃△Asc	2°02'a
☉Q♃	2°07'a
♅☍♇	2°14'a

Pl	Decl.
Asc	- 21° 04'
Mc	- 16° 29'
♆	- 13° 42'
♀	- 10° 16'
♅	- 07° 05'
☊	- 06° 59'
☿	- 06° 35'
☉	- 06° 11'
♄	+05° 05'
♂	+07° 11'
Vtx	+11° 40'
♃	+19° 49'
♇	+21° 43'
☽	+28° 05'

	☽	☉	☿	♀	♂	♃	♄	♅	♆	♇	☊	Mc
☉	△a 05°13											
☿	△a 06°32	☌s ∥ 01°20										
♀	△s 02°00	☌a 07°13										
♂			∥									
♃		Qa 02°07	Qa 00°47									
♄					☌a 00°13							
♅	△a 04°36	☌s ∥ 00°36	☌s ∥ 01°56	☌a 06°36	∥							
♆	△a 02°21	△s 02°52	△s 04°12	△a 04°21				△s 02°16				
♇	⚹a 06°51	☍a 01°38	☍a 00°18		⚻s 01°46		⚻s 01°59	☍a 02°14	⚹a 04°30			
☊	△a 03°07	☌s ∥ 02°05	☌s ∥ 03°25	☌a 05°07	∥			☌a ∥ 01°29	△s 00°47	☍a 03°43		
Mc	△s 05°39	△s 00°27	△a 00°53		⚻a 02°58			△s 01°03	☌s 03°19	⚹a 01°11	△s 02°32	
Asc		∠a 02°55				△a 02°02				∥	∠a 00°50	Qs 00°22

	Crd	Fix	Mut
Fir	2	0	0
Ear	1	1	1
Air	0	0	0
Wat	1	2	4

Wednesday Mar 07,-3
The 66th day of the year.
04:00:00 AM LMT +00:00
LMT: 04:00:00
UT: 01:39:12
UT-LMT: -02:20:48
ST: 14h49m35s
RAMC: 222°24'
Local Apparent Time: 03:46:58
Equation of Time: 13m02s
Planetary Hour: Mars (♂)
10th Hour of Mars-Night
Sunrise (aprox.): 06:29 LMT
Sunset (aprox.): 17:58 LMT
Moon in 2nd Quarter
☉/☽ Angle: 114°47'
☽'s Motion: +11°54'59"
Julian Day: 1720027.56889
SVP: 03°♈06'33"
Fagan/Bradley
Ayanamsa: +03°06'33"

Pl	Geo Lon	℞
☽	09°♋15' 27"	
☉	14°♓28' 12"	
☿	15°♓47' 49"	
♀	07°♓15' 33"	
♂	17°♈52' 34"	
♃	28°♉35' 19"	
♄	18°♈05' 34"	
♅	13°♓51' 46"	
♆	11°♏36' 15"	℞
♇	16°♍06' 05"	℞
☊	12°♓22' 49"	
Mc	14°♏54' 55"	
Asc	26°♑32' 50"	
Vtx	29°♌46' 39"	
Eq	09°♒53' 40"	
⊗	01°♎45' 35"	

Adjusted Calculation Dates
0h= Feb 7 12h= Aug 9

©1994 Matrix Software Big Rapids, MI

Chart Service Wheel

Chapter 3

The Epic Grand Trine

The natal chart of Jesus is truly remarkable, befitting of the great Soul who anchored the principle of love on earth. Neptune stands at the highest point in Jesus's chart conjunct the Mid-heaven. From this vantage point, Neptune served as the pole star of Jesus's life and the planetary apex of several grand trines.[21] This feature alone is quite remarkable, since the esoteric symbolism of Neptune at its deepest level represents the cosmic principle of love-wisdom.

To understand your own path to ascension, the place to begin is an overview of your natal chart. In Jesus's chart, Neptune, the ruler of Pisces, formed a beneficent trine to each of the four planets in Pisces (Venus, Uranus, Sun, and Mercury) plus the North Node and the etheric planet Vulcan. Neptune also formed a trine to the sixth-house Moon in Cancer which, in turn, formed a trine to His four planets in Pisces, creating a number of grand trines in the chart of Jesus.

Traditional astrology refers to a grand trine as a triplicity. A triplicity groups the twelve signs of the zodiac by one of four elements: earth, air, water, and fire. The three signs conditioned by the same element trine each other when they are separated by 120 degrees.

There are at least nine unique grand trines in the chart of Jesus. For example, one grand trine is created by Venus trine Moon, Moon trine Neptune, and Neptune trine Venus. Another grand trine is created by Uranus trine Moon, the Moon trine Neptune, and Neptune trine Uranus. Due to the conjunction of Venus, the North Node, Uranus, the Sun, Mercury, and the esoteric planet Vulcan, plus the conjunction of Neptune and the Mid-heaven, there

---

[21] A trine aspect is formed when two planets are 120 degrees apart, plus or minus six degrees. Planets that trine each other are usually in the same element and must be within an orb of influence. The orb for the Sun and Moon can be as much as plus or minus eight degrees. When three planets are 120 degrees apart from the other two planets, they form an equilateral triangle in the chart. This configuration is known astrologically as a grand trine.

were nine grand trines in the chart of Jesus. Together, they formed one phenomenal epic grand trine. This greatly intensified the creative power that a grand trine confers.

Although it is unusual to have a grand trine in a chart, it is not unheard of. What is exceedingly rare and auspicious in the chart of Jesus is the large number of planets that formed this epic grand trine. There were seventeen trines in the natal chart of Jesus. Sixteen of them involved the planets, luminaries, house angles, and the North Node that comprised the epic grand trine configuration.

Having seventeen trines in a birth chart is exceedingly rare and auspicious. However, it was the cumulative interplay, exchange, and blending of the rays[22] of the planets and luminaries that formed the epic grand trine that conferred something far greater than the meanings and significances that astrologers assign to each trine. The profound effect this combination of rays had on the mind and consciousness of Jesus awakened something that had yet to awaken within these forms of earth—the second aspect of the Divine (love-wisdom).

Since the sixteen trines of the planets, angles, and luminaries in Jesus's chart that formed the epic grand trine were in water signs, much of the development of His consciousness involved the unfoldment and development of love-wisdom, first at the level of the integrated personality and then at the level of the Soul.

A trine relationship formed between two planets in water signs can transform the qualities of the emotional, feeling, sentient aspect of the personal consciousness into the higher qualities of love. This occurs as the energies of the love tier of petals stream through the astral body into the etheric heart center.

In relation to the evolution of consciousness, triplicities pertain specifically to the growth in consciousness that occurs as a result of shifting the consciousness upward from a lower sub-plane gradient to a higher sub-plane level and quality within a plane (either the physical-etheric, the astral, the mental, or buddhic plane), depending on which of the four elements condition the grand trine.

Trines specifically relate to people's temperament, personality traits, and tendencies. They correspond to the personality qualities and characteristics that people unfold and exhibit in their lives as a result of the forces transmitted by the planets that trine each other. In particular, trines relate to the steps upon the path that lead people to develop a high quality of consciousness in relation to one of the three aspects of personal consciousness, depending on which element is involved.

The energies of two planets that are trine blend together with relative ease and little effort on the part of the individual. Each planet trine another planet is advancing two dynamics

---

[22] The energies each planet transmits is on one of the seven rays. See addendum, Table One.

of the psyche in relation to an aspect of consciousness (i.e., the astral-sentient or the mental aspect of personal consciousness).

Regardless of whether the element of a grand trine is earth, air, fire, or water, the interplay of energies of a trine relationship stimulates the development of people's creativity. This occurs as the energies of the three planets forming a grand trine blend with each other. The specific nature of the creativity depends on the planets, signs, and houses involved. The interplay, exchange, and blending of the energies represented by the trine impact the consciousness directly without clashing with the forces of resistance that the hard aspects (squares and oppositions) generate.

Think of each planet as a receiving and transmitting center of different types and qualities of energies magnetized by one of the seven rays. Again, the seven rays are the seven magnetic building forces responsible for creating the manifest world. This building activity includes bringing forth the three aspects of personal consciousness. When the energy being transmitted by a planet is registered by the mind, it stimulates the unfoldment and development of the dynamics of the psyche that the planet represents. Since people are at different steps and stages of the path and are influenced by the seven rays in different ways, people demonstrate a wide range of responses to the various qualities and types of energy that impact the consciousness.

A grand trine combines the ray three creative powers with the ray one power of the will. Thus, a grand trine represents a rather dynamic creative power in people's lives. The addition of this ray one quality of the will brings in a power that people often use to obtain that which they desire. When the consciousness is polarized at the mental level, however, the creativity and willpower a grand trine confers results in a heightened mental creativity. People find it easier to reach the goals that they establish.

The effect of the interplay of the energies of a grand trine is greater insight, vision, high idealism, and creativity. The exact nature of this creativity, idealism, and insight depends on the particular planets forming the grand trine, the houses involved, and the level of development a person has attained, i.e., where the consciousness is polarized.

Typically, a grand trine confers a degree of optimism and hope, and a very real sense of satisfaction. People with a grand trine often feel that they are divinely blessed, guided, and protected. Surely Jesus felt this way.

The planetary energies and ray influences of grand trines are usually beneficial, regardless of the level of evolvement the individual has attained. People who have grand trines in their charts tend to have an overall sense of well-being, especially in those areas of life (represented by the twelve houses) where the planets of the grand trine are placed. They often feel as if they are divinely inspired. Typically the interplay of the energies of a grand trine contributes a positive influence that significantly mitigates stress and tension.

When people have a grand trine in their charts, it is as if their wishes and desires are fulfilled without having to exert much effort. This is why people who have a grand trine often think of themselves as being lucky or blessed in some way. The reason for this is the heightened power of ray one. Ray one willpower moves into people's lives through a point equidistant from the three planets forming a grand trine configuration.

Ray one intensifies the magnetic attractive power of people's desires. The interplay and exchange of energies that take place when three planets form a grand trine greatly increase the likelihood that people's desires are fulfilled. However, this can lead to an excessively self-indulgent nature and self-absorption. When people are self-absorbed, they often feel, think, and act in ways that violate universal law. Self-absorption leads to difficult and often painful karmic lessons that must be learned before the person can step upon the universal path of the Soul. Self-absorption and self-indulgent tendencies interfere with people's ability to master the threefold personal self.

A grand trine represents an ability to easily materialize one's desires, but people must be careful what they wish for. Grand trines present the subtlest tests of all of the tests and trials of life. What people manifest in their lives is greatly affected by what they desire, and what people desire depends on their point of evolvement and stage of development. From the Soul's perspective, the problem with a grand trine is that its strong attractive power allows people to glide through life on the bounty that a grand trine brings to them. This can result in a pleasant, happy life, but little growth.

Since the average person is usually focused on satisfying personal desires and acquiring the things of earth, the energies generated by a grand trine flow into one's life in a way that readily manifests the things that are desired. People do not have to work as hard in those areas of life where the planets of the grand trine are placed to get what they want. Why strive when much of what you desire seems to magically appear?

A large number of trines in the natal chart can also diminish people's initiative and drive, especially in those areas of life (houses) where the planets are located. Grand trines do not stimulate people's initiative and drive since they stimulate mental creativity, not physical action.

Another danger is that when people selfishly misuse the energies of a grand trine, they greatly intensify a rhythm of selfishness in their lives. When this occurs, instilling higher spiritual values and standards and mastering the physical and emotional aspects of personal consciousness become significantly more difficult and challenging.

People with grand trines often have an attitude that the world owes them. Such feelings of entitlement are common when people have a large number of trines. When the grand trine is in water, people's preoccupation with their feelings and with the more pleasurable, indulgent things of life is usually more pronounced.

Universally, water symbolizes the fluid, unformed, and unstructured emotions. Just as something must provide water with structure, the emotions need something to contain them. As people mature, it is the concrete mind and intellect that provides the emotions with the structure, direction, and purpose they need.

Although the energies of water grand trines naturally correspond to the astral plane, you alone decide whether to use the energies of the grand trine to fulfill your personal desires or to use them to bring forth the essential love of the Soul and its values. In particular, the energies of water grand trines lend themselves to the unfoldment of mystical vision, spiritual aspiration, and high idealism. They can be used to accelerate the rate at which people achieve a union of the integrated personality and Soul.

When people with a large number of water trines are at the stage of personal development, their strong emotional desire nature can interfere with their ability to align and attune to the Soul, as well as interfere with their ability to relate to the physical body and to life in a healthy, constructive way. When people are preoccupied with their personal feelings and emotions, they often find it difficult to accomplish the goals and objectives they set for themselves. Rather than prepare themselves for something they need to do tomorrow, they go to the bar to be with their friends.

It would be extremely harmful—even disastrous—for the average person to have as many trines as Jesus had in His chart. Until the astral-emotional aspect of personal consciousness has been mastered (at the second initiation), people who have a large number of water trines are easily overwhelmed by their feelings and preoccupied with their desires. When this is the case, little personal growth and even less spiritual growth can be achieved. This preoccupation with one's feelings and desires is intensified when the Moon, Venus, Neptune, and the signs of Pisces, Scorpio, and Cancer are involved in the grand trine. Sensitivity to the emotions and feelings of others is especially pronounced when Pisces is involved—as it was in Jesus's life.

The combination of the planetary influences of a water grand trine can make it difficult to take charge of one's life, especially in those areas represented by the houses where the planets of the water grand trine are placed. It is not unusual for people with a water grand trine to feel victimized by minor slights or to have a crucifixion complex, especially when the Moon is involved. People often compensate for their extreme sensitivity to the feelings and emotions of others by isolating themselves.

Due to their extreme emotional sensitivity, people with a water grand trine are frequently psychic and are naturally attuned to the astral world. Psychic abilities are an extension of the physical senses into the astral and the lower mental planes. This includes clairvoyance (astral sight), clairaudience (astral hearing), clairsentience (touch), and clairgustience (smell). Clairvoyance, the higher creative imagination, and idealism are the three highest astral-plane senses that people can unfold and develop as energies build into the upper sub-plane levels of the astral body.

The Epic Grand Trine and Jesus

Because of the profoundly harmonizing, creative effect that the epic grand trine had on Him, Jesus was able to experience God as love, formulate the path of the heart, and serve as the divine messenger for the dawning Age of Pisces.

These accomplishments are more significant than what people realize. Two thousand years ago, love-wisdom had yet to awaken within the consciousness of mankind. The level and caliber of consciousness and understanding that mankind had attained back then was significantly lower than it is today. The shroud of ignorance was great!

When Jesus incarnated on earth, people did not approach the Divine through selfless, unconditional love. There was no path of the heart. Jesus developed this path within His own heart and mind and then presented it to mankind. Jesus was not born as the messenger of the Piscean Age. He earned the right to serve in this capacity as a result of the great spiritual heights He attained.

Although Jesus was not fully realized, He was much farther along the path than others. Jesus attained Christ consciousness when He experienced the Divine in the aspect of love-wisdom. Before Jesus, no one who became self-conscious in the evolutionary system of earth had ever experienced love-wisdom free of all distortion.

Without this epic grand trine, it is unlikely that Jesus would have been able to attain Christ consciousness two thousand years ago. This does not mean that people need to have an epic grand trine in their charts to attain Christ consciousness—far from it. However, if you are interested in attaining human perfection according to your own divine patterning, it is important to understand the steps and stages of the universal path that led Jesus to this lofty state of mind.

Twenty-five hundred years ago, the Buddha pierced the matter veils that entombed human consciousness, brought forth the light of wisdom, and attained enlightenment. Two thousand years ago, Jesus pierced the three matter veils of earth and brought forth the love-wisdom aspect of God. In so doing, Jesus attained Christ consciousness. To accomplish this realization two thousand years ago, the exchange and interplay of the energies that took place as a result of this epic water grand trine were exceedingly important. Without them, Jesus could not have anchored love-wisdom within the third planetary center (collective humanity).

The teachings that Jesus developed represented a new spiritual path—a path that called for an unwavering dedication and devotion to the God of love. God in its aspect of love is very different from the Judean Father of the covenant agreement—the God of law. The God of love corresponds to the ray two aspect of the Divine, while the God of law corresponds to the ray three aspect of the Divine, active intelligence. Over the past two thousand years, love-wisdom has ever so slowly unfolded within the hearts and minds of humanity.

The path of the heart is not the path of personal affections and love. Affectionate love is an expression of the attractive astral forces of the fourth and fifth gradations of the astral body. These forces express via the solar plexus and the sacral center (the consciousness in relation to sexuality and physical movement). The path of the heart involves the unfoldment and expression of the essential love of the Soul. This occurs as the energies of the love petals of the lotus stream into the heart center and impact the consciousness.

On the path of the heart, people's mind and consciousness are stimulated by the magnetic unifying qualities of the Soul, which are infused with essential love. Essential love is unconditional, inclusive, and universal, and when it impacts the consciousness, it brings forth unconditional love, compassion, forgiveness, humility, thankfulness, and mercy. The essential love of the Soul unfolds once the personal consciousness is reasonably purified of its negative and self-centered tendencies and traits.

This purification of the personal consciousness was especially important in Jesus's life since the interplay of the energies of water grand trines stimulate the astral-emotional aspect of consciousness. As long as people entertain negative and selfish emotions, they are repeatedly pulled into the emotional drama of life, away from the harmony and peace of the higher realms.

Jesus, on the other hand, did not express the emotional characteristics and tendencies that are common among those who have a water grand trine, since He had achieved control and mastery of self-centered and self-referencing emotionalism early in His life. Most likely, the patterns of personal desire had been transformed into spiritual aspirations long before His current life. As a result, Jesus was open to the uplifting, magnetism of His Soul at a young age.

The epic grand trine suggests that the patterns of responsiveness to the lower astral-emotional desire forces that plague most people had been eliminated in a recent past life. Without these patterns, Jesus wasn't easily swept away by the strong astral currents that a grand trine in water so often generates. In fact, Jesus seems to have been relatively oblivious to the lower astral forces. The type and quality of energies and forces people are consciously responsive reflect the point of evolvement the Soul has attained.

This epic grand trine in water intensified Jesus's extreme sensitivity. Undoubtedly, Jesus was sensitive to the emotional currents that swept through the society and was quite sensitive to the feelings of His family and friends at an early age. Without a doubt, Jesus was able to walk in other people's shoes and feel their pain. Given the degree of His sensitivities, He felt their frustrations and pain deeply, but He didn't react to the emotions of others in a personal way or take them on as His own, which sensitive people often do.

Most likely it was difficult for Jesus to separate Himself from the feelings of others prior to His twenty-first birthday. Though His extreme sensitivity may have been overbearing at times when He was young, His Capricorn Ascendant shielded Him from being completely overwhelmed by the feelings of others.

Saturn, as the ruler of His Capricorn Ascendant, supplied Him with the ray three mental energies and stability needed to contain His emotions. In other words, His Capricorn Ascendant provided the quality of energy Jesus needed to create the structures within His mind necessary to deal with His extreme sensitivity constructively. Also, due to the individuating influences of Uranus, especially in His early twenties, Jesus developed a strong enough sense of self that He was able to clearly differentiate between His own feelings and the feelings of others.

Undoubtedly, Jesus's extreme sensitivity to the feelings of others resulted in His desire to heal, to comfort, and to relieve others from their suffering. Jesus so empathized with people that He felt their anguish, but rather than languish in despair, He ardently prayed for them. His sincere prayers, in turn, resulted in the unfoldment of substantial healing abilities.

Jesus's desire to heal and comfort others indicates that He had attuned to the Soul prior to His incarnation as Jesus. This resulted in an ability to respond to the essential love of His Soul from a young age. This attunement to His Soul prevented Him from acting selfishly or responding to others in a negative, emotional way.

The pain and suffering of others didn't have a disruptive effect upon Jesus personally. Rather, Jesus responded to the suffering of others with compassion and a heart-felt desire to become an instrument of the Father to heal, to bless, and to uplift humanity. Only those who are responsive to the impressions of their Souls respond in such a way.

The work of disciples is to transform personal desire into spiritual aspiration and to cultivate a determination to help improve the quality of life of others. This is in line with the nature and values of the Soul. Attunement to the Soul brings forth a genuine interest in healing and comforting others and a willingness to sacrifice oneself for others. Such impulses of the Soul are only registered in the consciousness once people shift away from their preoccupation with the concerns of the little self to the needs of others.

The essential love of the Soul awakens unconditional love for others. This occurs as the energies of the love petals stream through the heart center of the etheric body. When people do not love one another, there is no need for the essential love of the Soul to stream into their lives. The desire to love and heal others is what builds up the magnetic power needed to draw the energies of the love petals of the lotus into one's life.

The energies of the Soul awaken the higher senses, faculties, and capacities, and stimulate the unfoldment of the inclusive, selfless values and qualities of the Soul. In particular, the energies of the love petal of the love tier of the lotus unfold the faculty of the higher creative imagination, which enables people to sense the higher spiritual planes of life and light. It is the higher imagination that gives form to the light patterns and seed ideas of the higher realms. By way of the higher creative imagination, sublime truth is perceived and spiritual inspiration arises within the (brain) consciousness.

A grand trine configuration of planets is known for bringing forth a powerful imagination. This is especially true of a water grand trine. But whether the imaginative capacity is of any value depends on the vibratory rate, the ray, type, and quality of energies that people sense and respond to within their consciousness. When the consciousness is still polarized at the mid-astral plane level, the imagination is stimulated by the patterns of personal emotions and desire forms that mankind has generated throughout history.

When the psychic imaging involves the forces of the lower astral plane, what is psychically imaged usually corresponds to the desire forms of mankind, not to the impressions of the Soul or the universal mind. There is a great difference between the psychic images that the imagination envisions when people are stimulated by the midrange astral forces and what they envision when the upper astral- and buddhic-plane energies and rays activate the higher creative imagination.

Historically, mankind has created a world of glamour and illusion by imprinting the matter of the astral plane with selfish patterns of force (emotions, desire forms). For this reason, the lower emotional aspect of human consciousness resonates with the ancient rhythm that primitive mankind first generated. Today, many of the events of daily life are still precipitated by people's responsiveness to this ancient rhythm. Slowly, humanity is replacing this ancient rhythm with the higher rhythm of wisdom, inclusive love, peace, and harmony.

For disciples, a grand trine becomes an important vehicle for the transmission of ray one (will) into the disciple's life, regardless whether the grand trine is in earth, air, fire or water. The specific element conditioning the grand trine merely indicates the aspect of threefold consciousness where the creative will expresses. Again, the water element corresponds to the second aspect of the Divine and therefore relates to the astral-emotional aspect of personal emotions, desires, and love. For those on the spiritual path, however, it relates to the love aspect of the higher mind and to the heart center of the Soul.

As a result of the epic water grand trine, once Jesus attained the third initiation, the interplay and exchange of the rays that took place in His life helped to unfold and develop the pure love-wisdom aspect of the Spiritual Triad, which, in turn, advances the intuitional mind. This corresponds to the heart center of the Monad. By extension, it also corresponds to the emanations of the planetary heart center—the heart of God.

The willpower that this epic grand trine generated throughout Jesus's life so intensified the attractive power of His prayers and invocations, and so deepened His moments of contemplation and meditation that Jesus was able to easily manifest that which He prayed for. Here, ray one combined with the magnetic power of the water grand trine to pierce the veiling forces of His subtle bodies. This enabled Him to directly touch into the light and essential love of His Soul at an early age.

For disciples, when the rays and principles of three planets are linked together in a balanced, harmonious way by a grand trine configuration, a vortex or portal is created in the very center of the grand trine through which the energies of the higher planes stream into the consciousness. By way of this vortex, people can shift their consciousness upward to a higher plane more easily. With so many planets involved in the epic grand trine in Jesus's chart, the creative willpower in Jesus's life was tremendous.

Initially, this vortex extended from the upper mental world of the Soul to the consciousness of Jesus, but once He attained the third initiation, this vortex extended from the Monad (via the buddhic center) onto His brain consciousness. This enabled Jesus to consciously enter the planes of light, where He experienced the Divine in both its second aspect of love-wisdom and in its first aspect of will-purpose. This was unheard of prior to the incarnation of Jesus. By the time of His ministry, this epic grand trine formed a portal from the Monad through the planes of light onto His brain consciousness of earth. This enabled Jesus to truly know the will and purpose of the Father Spirit.

Ultimately, the powerful effect ray one had as it poured through the vortex of the epic grand trine throughout Jesus's life generated a force that pierced the veils of the three planes of earth.

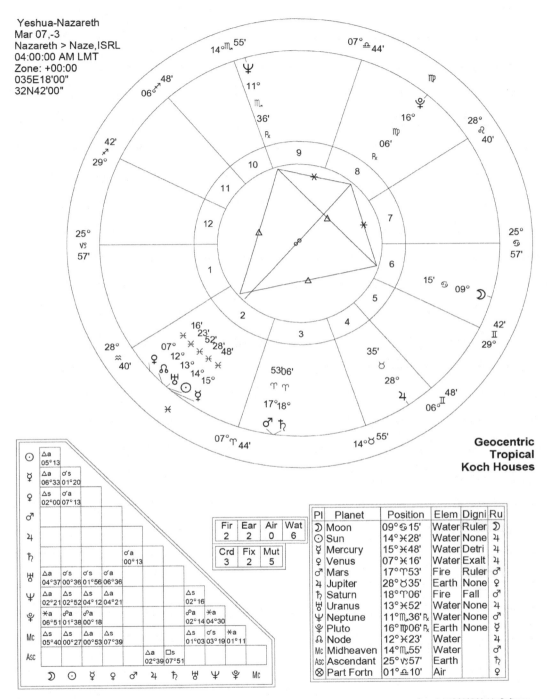

Yeshua-Nazareth
Mar 07,-3
Nazareth > Naze,ISRL
04:00:00 AM LMT
Zone: +00:00
035E18'00"
32N42'00"

Geocentric
Tropical
Koch Houses

Fir	Ear	Air	Wat
2	2	0	6

Crd	Fix	Mut
3	2	5

Pl	Planet	Position	Elem	Digni	Ru
☽	Moon	09°♋15'	Water	Ruler	☽
☉	Sun	14°♓28'	Water	None	♃
☿	Mercury	15°♓48'	Water	Detri	♃
♀	Venus	07°♓16'	Water	Exalt	♃
♂	Mars	17°♈53'	Fire	Ruler	♂
♃	Jupiter	28°♉35'	Earth	None	♀
♄	Saturn	18°♈06'	Fire	Fall	♂
♅	Uranus	13°♓52'	Water	None	♃
♆	Neptune	11°♏36'℞	Water	None	♂
♇	Pluto	16°♍06'℞	Earth	None	☿
☊	Node	12°♓23'	Water		♃
Mc	Midheaven	14°♏55'	Water		♂
Asc	Ascendant	25°♑57'	Earth		♄
⊗	Part Fortn	01°♎10'	Air		♀

	☽	☉	☿	♀	♂	♃	♄	♅	♆	♇	Mc	Asc
☉	△a 05°13											
☿	△a 06°33	♂s 01°20										
♀	△s 02°00	♂a 07°13										
♂												
♃												
♄							♂a 00°13					
♅	△a 04°37	♂s 00°36	♂s 01°56	♂a 06°36								
♆	△a 02°21	△s 02°52	△s 04°12	△a 04°21			△s 02°16					
♇	*a 06°51	♂a 01°38	♂a 00°18					♂a 02°14	*a 04°30			
Mc	△s 05°40	△a 00°27	△a 00°53	△s 07°39				△s 01°03	♂s 03°19	*a 01°11		
Asc					△a 02°39	□s 07°51						

45

Chapter 4

The Kite Configuration

From the eighth house of transformation, endings, and regeneration, Pluto divided the Moon-Neptune side of the epic grand trine in half. Pluto is sextile Neptune and the Mid-heaven and is widely sextile the Moon in Cancer. It is opposite the eastern point of the grand trine where Venus, the Sun, Mercury, Uranus, and the North Node were located. This placement of Pluto transformed the epic grand trine into a configuration known as a kite.

When a planet opposes one of the three points of a grand trine and sextiles the other two, it adds an intense dynamic quality to a person's life. The opposing planet acts as a lens that focuses the creative powers generated by the interplay of the planetary energies and rays of the planets of the grand trine.

Great success is often achieved when the planets in a chart form a kite configuration. The opposition planet represents a highly stimulated aspect of the mind that focuses the power and creativity generated by the planets of the grand trine. The exact nature of this creativity and power depends on the planets, signs, and houses involved.

Although a kite configuration only requires three planets to form a grand trine configuration and a fourth planet to oppose one of the three points of the grand trine, the kite configuration in Jesus's chart involved seven planets linked together by fifteen trines, ten conjunctions, three sextiles, and four oppositions. The large number of interconnected planets exponentially intensified the creative drive, power, and concentrated focus of the mind of Jesus and endowed His life with intrigue and mystery.

The reason for this great intensity was due to the large number of planets that were conjunct in Pisces: Venus, Uranus, the Sun, Mercury, plus the esoteric planet Vulcan and the North Node. When three or more planets conjunct each other in a sign, they are referred to as a stellium of planets.

A stellium indicates that the dynamics of the psyche represented by the planets forming the stellium are able to work closely together to accomplish some objective. In and of itself, a stellium of planets results in success of a unique and profound nature, but when another planet opposes a stellium that is part of a grand trine, failure is not an option. It is exceedingly auspicious that Pluto opposed this stellium of planets in Jesus's chart and acted as the focusing lens for the energies of the epic grand trine. Undoubtedly, this kite configuration of planets greatly intensified the power potential Jesus needed to successfully complete His mission as the teacher, way shower, and the messenger for the Age of Pisces.

To astrologers, the ideal chart has a balanced number of hard and soft aspects. The hard aspects precipitate difficult life lessons and growth experiences, while the soft aspects provide ease and relief from the difficulties that the hard aspects cause. When people have a large number of soft aspects (especially trines) in their charts, they often lack the drive needed to succeed. For Jesus, the opposition of Pluto to His planets in Pisces nullified this general rule.

Jesus did not have a balanced number of hard and soft aspects in His chart. Given His level of evolvement and the powerful opposition of Pluto to the stellium of planets in Pisces, He did not need such. Even when the angles and lunar nodes are taken into consideration, there were few hard aspects in the chart of Jesus. There were no squares, sesquiquadrates, or semi-squares.

Jesus had an unusually large number of non-challenging aspects: seventeen trines, three sextiles, and eleven conjunctions. The absence of squares in His chart indicates that Jesus was born into one of two conditions: either the bounty the earth has to offer readily flowed onto Him due to the merit earned in recent past lives, or there were no force patterns within His causal body that represent selfish conflicted traits and tendencies. This situation suggests that much of the duality within the threefold personal consciousness had been resolved prior to incarnation. As a result, Jesus had few life lessons and developmental needs in terms of the threefold personal consciousness. The focus of His life was not on personal growth.

The natal chart of Jesus indicates that many of the dynamics of His psyche were unified and functioned harmoniously in relation to each other. There were no major conflicts within His emotional aspect of personal consciousness or between the emotional and mental dynamics of the psyche. Most likely these issues had been resolved prior to His incarnation.

Pluto, as the opposing planet of the kite configuration, was the agent that sharply focused the energies of the planets that comprised the epic grand trine configuration, concentrating their energies through a single point in the mind of Jesus. This placement of Pluto greatly empowered and focused His mind.

Because of the rays transmitted by the particular planets involved in the epic grand trine, Pluto (as the focusing lens) unified all seven rays into one beam of light. This means that much of the threefold personal consciousness of Jesus was unified in purpose and intent. In this way, the substantial benefits (faculties, skills, capacities, etc.) that the planets of the epic grand trine brought forth were directly funneled into the kind of activities that Pluto compelled as the agent of divine will. When Pluto is the planet that focuses the energies and qualities of a grand trine, the power potential is intensified considerably (for good or bad, depending on the stage of development the individual has attained).

The ray three creativity and the ray one dynamism that the epic grand trine contributed to Jesus's life were intensified by the ray one power potential which Pluto conferred as the opposition planet. Pluto expresses the power of the will and is associated with the occult (hidden or concealed). Generally, what is hidden is the knowledge and understanding that allows a higher principle of consciousness to unfold.

At a deeper level, the term occult refers to the great secret that has been hidden from mankind since primitive Atlanteans caused the destruction of Atlantis. This secret pertains to the knowledge of how to use the mind and voice to create that which is needed.

Primitive mankind caused the destruction of the ancient civilization of Atlantis through its misuse of the understanding given to them by the god-men. This occurred at a time when primitive mankind was just beginning to unfold sentiency and feelings within the physical body. Ever since then, the collective unconscious of mankind has harbored a great fear of the occult. Today, the understanding as to how to access the power-to-create is concealed deep within all human beings. Since mankind will serve as divine co-creators one day, this knowledge must be rediscovered once the fifth initiation is attained.

Many of the miracles Jesus demonstrated— such as the multiplication of substance (the loaves of bread and fish at the Sermon on the Mount), stilling the waters, and the transubstantiation of water into wine—involved exercising power and control over the matter of the three planes of earth. It is not surprising that Jesus demonstrated great occult powers in His life and performed miracles. Given His chart, it would have been surprising if He had not.

Neptune was the pole star and the emissary of the second aspect of the Divine (love-wisdom) that guided Jesus across the sea of life, but Pluto was the engine that propelled Him forward. As the focusing agent for the energies and qualities of the epic grand trine, Pluto was the factor of power that drove Jesus from initiation to initiation onto Christ consciousness.

As the agent of the will of the Divine, Pluto is associated with transmutation, regeneration, transformation, and death. In Jesus's life, the force of the will didn't impact just one area of life or one aspect of His consciousness. Being the focusing agent for the energies of the epic grand trine, Pluto's laser-like beam pierced the force fields of all three subtle bodies and directly impacted His consciousness. This resulted in a number of difficult, challenging, and often unpleasant experiences. The positive and constructive ways in which Jesus responded to these events, however, is what quickly moved Him along the path.

As the vehicle that transmits the ray one power of the will, Pluto awakened divine will and purpose within the mind of Jesus, but for a price. Initially, Pluto triggered a number of conflicts in His life that involved His personal will. When resolved, these conflicts brought about major transformations of the self. It was these that led Him to the experience of rebirth as the Soul.

With the Sun (the personal self and its will) in Pisces opposite Pluto (the ruler of Pisces at the Soul level) in Virgo, most likely Jesus felt as if He was compelled to sacrifice His personal will to the will of God (the will of the Soul). However, the personal will of Jesus that He needed to sacrifice to the will of the Soul was not the typical self-aggrandizing willfulness of the little self that many people exhibit.

For Jesus, the personal will that He needed to sacrifice involved the type of willfulness that disciples face and relinquish at the third initiation. The egocentric willful nature that many people exhibit had been transcended prior to His incarnation. As Jesus approach the third initiation, He needed to evaluate His allegiance to the Judean commandments, laws, dietary and behavioral rules, beliefs, and overall worldview, and decide which ones had become obsolete in His life.

This clash between His personal will and the will of the Soul generated points of tension in Jesus's life that forced Him to address a number of issues. Jesus had to work through and resolve all differences that remained between His personal will and the will of His selfless Soul. The sacrifice of the personal will to the will of God (the will of the Soul) is the foremost sacrifice people make as they approach the third initiation.

The struggle and conflict between the will of the personality and the will of the Soul resulted in episodes of endings and new beginnings, especially in Jesus's teenage years. Each time Jesus successfully resolved the points of tension that such incidents generated, the powers of transmutation, transformation, and regeneration were released into His life.

Since Pluto establishes the eighth-house issues that people face in life, this eighth-house placement of Pluto in Jesus's chart opposite the eastern point of the epic grand trine further intensified Jesus's drive to succeed. But this wasn't to achieve personal success or to gain personal power. Again and again, Pluto triggered a crisis in Jesus's life, the effect of which was to bring forth meaningful transformations of the self. With the resolution of each crisis, the command of the will of the Soul was strengthened.

Ray one Pluto (in its ray three sub-aspect) is the planetary agent that expresses the destroyer forces of divine will. People may find it difficult to believe that the will of God could cause death and destruction, but it does. The death and endings Pluto brings about, however, never touch the indwelling life within the physical body. Ideally, Pluto destroys the structures within the mind that have become obsolete and are currently interfering with one's progression. This involves the elimination of different patterns of emotions, feelings, and beliefs, as well as the end of certain relationships and the loss of property and possessions. Its effects can also result in one's death, for the death of the physical body is merely an opportunity for the indwelling life to grow, experiment, and experience in a new, more appropriate vehicle.

In the chart of Jesus, the three outer planets (Uranus, Neptune, and Pluto) formed major aspects to each other. This is significant due to the worldwide effects that the outer planets have upon mankind as a group. When a major angular relationship is formed between the outer planets, mankind is forced to address larger social issues. Since the outer planets represent the cosmic agents that transmit new types and ray qualities of energies onto the earth, they have significant worldwide implications in terms of the advancement of mankind as a group.

The higher the level of development people achieve, the greater the likelihood that they can register and constructively respond to the high-frequency energies of the outer planets. These energies stimulate the mind in ways that bring forth new systems of thought, ideas, beliefs, new inventions, scientific discoveries, and so forth.

Although Jesus was not aware of Uranus, Neptune, or Pluto, or aware of the effect they had upon His life and consciousness, He most definitely responded to the influences of the outer planets as evidenced by His life, mission, and message. Throughout His life, Jesus demonstrated a sensitive responsiveness toward the high-frequency energies of the outer planets. This in itself is indicative of someone on the path of initiation. Even today only a small number of people are able to respond to the high-frequency energies of the outer planets in a healthy, constructive way.

Historically, only the collective minds of mankind had the capacity to register the energies of the outer planets. The personal light (held in the etheric body) tends to be too undeveloped and disorganized to register the high-frequency energies of the outer planets. For the most part, this is still true today.

When the outer planets form major aspects to each other in the natal chart and to the personal planets, people have an opportunity to become consciously responsive to the effects that the outer planets have on society. This can trigger significant changes in their thoughts, beliefs, and interests, resulting in new discoveries and systems of thought and belief. When this is the case, the individual often becomes an agent for change within the society.

People who become agents for constructive, progressive change in the minds of humanity must first experience and resolve the conflicts that arise between their own thoughts, ideas, and beliefs and the new thoughts and ideas brought forth as a result the energies of the outer planets.

People often become the inventors and agents for revolutionary social changes, providing they are advanced enough in mind and consciousness to register the high-frequency energies of the outer planets. This is especially true for old Souls when their personal planets form an aspect to the outer planets. Thus, when the outer planets form a major aspect to each other and to a person's inner planets, the individual often becomes the voice behind a new system of thought. This was definitely true in Jesus's case.

When Jesus was born, Pluto was sextile Neptune, Uranus was trine Neptune, and Pluto was opposite Uranus. These outer planets also formed aspects to all of the planets in Jesus's chart except Jupiter. Due to the major aspects these outer planets formed to His personal planets, Jesus was strongly impacted by the high-frequency energies of the outer planets throughout His life.

The three sextiles and four oppositions that Pluto formed to the planets in Jesus's chart conferred a dynamism to His life that systematically transformed Jesus from a self-contained individual lacking personal initiative (due to the sixteen trines) into an exceedingly dynamic individual caught up in the revolutionary changes taking place in the Judean society and the collective minds of humanity.

Jesus was born in the latter days of the five-hundred-year transition period between the waning Age of Aries and the dawning Age of Pisces. As a rule, during the latter years of the transition between two Ages or the early years of a new Age, masters usually incarnate on earth to deliver the teachings for the new Age and to establish certain new ideals.

The possibility that Jesus could serve as the messenger for the new teachings of the Age of Pisces is certainly indicated in His chart. The interplay and exchange of the energies between His personal planets and the outer planets strongly suggests that Jesus incarnated for a great purpose. The close relationship of the personal planets of Jesus to the outer planets of Uranus, Neptune, and Pluto opened the door for Jesus to become the messenger for the teachings of the dawning Piscean Age.

The inner and outer planets in Jesus's chart were so closely tied together that it is difficult to separate Jesus the person from His mission. Jesus's mission involved anchoring the new principles and seed ideas of the Piscean Age within the collective mind of humanity.

It was the energies of the new Age of Pisces two thousand years ago that were beginning to impact mankind in a way that activated deep profound changes, disruption, and uncertainty, especially in Judea. (The mental aspect of personal consciousness was more developed in Judea than it was in many parts of the world.) As the principles of the Age of Pisces were brought forth, a conflict arose between the future and the forces of the past.

As these high-frequency energies of the outer planets impacted Jesus, they stimulated new areas of His mind and consciousness, resulting in successively higher spiritual revelations. As He responded to the rays and principles of the outer planets, new thoughts, beliefs, and a higher level of spiritual understanding arose within His mind that resonated with the Piscean Age, but not with the waning Age of Aries. It was this new Piscean understanding that initially clashed with many of the beliefs and ideas that Jesus had accepted as truth earlier in His life.

Since the personal planets in His chart were closely linked to the outer planets by aspect, Jesus personally experienced this clash between the spirituality of the Age of Aries and the spirituality of the incoming Age of Pisces. This means that He had to resolve the conflicts that arose between His feelings, thoughts, ideas, and beliefs associated with the outgoing Age of Aries and the new spiritual revelations and realizations that arose within His mind due to the influences of the Age of Pisces. Only when Jesus adapted His thoughts and beliefs to Pisces was He able to mentally formulate and subsequently present the teachings for the Piscean Age.

Fortunately, Jesus had relatively few astral-emotional or lower mental patterns of consciousness that resisted this new Piscean influence. With a lack of hard aspects between His personal planets and a strong emphasis in His chart on ray two (love-wisdom) and ray six (devotion and dedication), the task of transitioning from the religious worldview of Aries to a Piscean worldview was not as difficult for Jesus as it was for many. In Judea, this transition from Arian thought to Piscean thought was especially difficult, since Judeans had canonized the teachings of the outgoing Age of Aries.

During Jesus's life, the social and religious institutions, laws, and rules were all Arian in terms of vibration, ray, note, and quality. However, the energies that had supported the Age of Aries for two thousand years were being withdrawn. A new Age is always built upon the ashes of the obsolete structures of the former Age.

The lifeless shell of the old Age is subjected to the transmuting fires of the new Age. Ashes represent the matter residue of what is left once the divine life-force has withdrawn from the knowledge, understanding, feelings, beliefs, social structures, and institutions of the past. This is true culturally as well as at the level of the individual. Once the mental structures and other forms of matter have served their purpose, the life-force within them escapes. Once the life-forces of the Age of Aries vacated the institutions, thoughts, practices, and beliefs of the culture, they were subjected to the initiating fires of the new Age. This does not usually occur all at once; rather, the old way of life is subjected to the burning ghats of life over an extended period of time.

This clash between the Arian past and the Piscean future involved the cultural institutions, systems of thought, beliefs, and so forth, across the earth. A clash between two

Ages is not something that is resolved quickly due to mankind's innate resistance to change. Additionally, that which a new Age has to offer is presented progressively over the course of the two thousand years of the Age. However, there always is someone who serves as the messenger for the incoming new Age.

The messenger sets the basic note and tone for the Age and presents a new way to approach the Divine. This does not mean that all that a new Age has to offer is brought forth during the first few years of the Age. There are many sub-principles of the Age that are activated at different periods of times within the two thousand years of the Age.

Jesus served as the voice for the Age of Pisces. Although His chart indicates that He incarnated with the potential to become the messenger for the Piscean dispensation, it wasn't until He registered and constructively responded to the energies, qualities, and principles of the Age of Pisces that He became the messenger. Importantly, He personally was subjected to the energies needed to counteract many of the institutionalized forces of the Age of Aries that interfered with the establishment of the teachings of the new Piscean Age. This resulted in a conflict between the teachings Jesus brought forth and the teachings of the Arian Age that the ruling authorities upheld and defended.

To understand how Jesus was able to serve as the teacher and messenger of the Age of Pisces, it is important to understand the effect that the respective outer planets had on His development and spiritual progression. As the apex of His epic grand trine and the ruler of Pisces, the effect Neptune had was exceedingly important. The energies of Neptune awakened the principle of unconditional love within the heart and mind of Jesus and transported Him to new heights of spiritual understanding.

Simultaneously, the opposition of Pluto to Uranus, the Sun, and Mercury in Jesus's chart, along with the inconjunction of Pluto to His Mars-Saturn conjunction in the third house, helped free Jesus from many of the thoughts and beliefs of the passing world of Aries. However, His conscious awakening to the principle of love-wisdom and His ability to transcend the obsolete Arian-based beliefs and ideas did not take place all at once; rather, they occurred over the course of Jesus's life.

Undoubtedly, the outer planetary influences triggered a number of clashes between the two Ages within the mind of Jesus. This clash between the past and the future resulted in a series of personal crises that challenged Jesus and His thoughts, ideas, and beliefs. Such internal conflict would have been prominent from His late teenage years until His Soul assumed command over the threefold personal consciousness at the third initiation. It was necessary for Jesus to personally experience the death of the Age of Aries and the birth of the Age of Pisces within His own consciousness before He could serve as the divine messenger of the new Age.

More than anything, the dawning Age of Pisces represented a point upon the continuum of the eternal-moment-of-the-now when the second aspect of the Divine (love-wisdom) was beginning to impact the burgeoning consciousness of mankind.

Uranus is always the agent of change and its trine from the sign of Pisces to Neptune brought forth the new impulses and impressions that helped to establish the Piscean theme of loving devotion in Jesus's life. This influence also helped to soften the major disruptions that the opposition of Pluto to Uranus caused, especially in relation to the clash between the entrenched worldview of the Age of Aries and the new unfolding worldview of the Age of Pisces.

Here, it is helpful to consider the entire Uranus-Pluto cycle (from their conjunction to an opposition, back to a new conjunction). This Uranus-Pluto cycle often causes the destruction of the old and obsolete institutions of the society and culture, and prompts the creation of new institutions. For this reason, the major aspects that Uranus forms to Pluto have a great effect upon the government, society, and culture. As to be expected, Uranus's opposition to Pluto two thousand years ago created powerful destructive forces that caused many of the institutions and aspects of the society to be challenged.

The hard aspects that Uranus forms to Pluto as they transit the twelve signs of the zodiac are always fraught with disruption and change. The Uranus-Pluto opposition in Jesus's chart tied Him directly into the exceptionally disruptive Uranus-Pluto cycle that began in 69 BCE and concluded in 74 CE. The destruction of the Temple in Jerusalem and the Diaspora of Judeans (70–73 CE) occurred at the conclusion of this particular Uranus-Pluto cycle. This cycle was especially destructive because it was the last Uranus-Pluto cycle of the five-hundred-year transition period between the Age of Aries and the Age of Pisces. When the cycle concluded, the world had entered the Age of Pisces, free of the energies and ray influences that had supported and advanced the Age of Aries for two thousand years.

The Sun (the personal self) conjunct Uranus, along with its opposition to Pluto, tied Jesus directly into the great struggle that was taking place within mankind. This struggle was between the crystallized forces and institutions of the outgoing Age of Aries and the new spiritual ideas and beliefs that arose due to the energies of the incoming Age of Pisces. During Jesus's life, the personal and social disruption and destruction that the Uranus-Pluto opposition caused were intensified by the energies of the incoming Age of Pisces and incoming ray six. The sharp contrast between the dawning Piscean Age and the waning Age of Aries heightened the conflict, chaos, and turmoil of the already tense region of the Middle East.

The opposition of Uranus to Pluto dominated the life of Jesus in a number of ways. Undoubtedly, its influence generated intense crises and cataclysmic events in His life. When people resolve such crises constructively (by applying the light of their minds to the crises), they accelerate their personal and spiritual growth. In this way, the Soul is advanced.

Undoubtedly, Jesus was an old Soul when He incarnated on earth. The right to incarnate at the exact moment Jesus was born suggests that His Soul had attained great spiritual heights prior to His incarnation. As a result, He responded to these crises in a somewhat impersonal way and was not traumatized by them.

During this overview of the chart of Jesus, it should also be mentioned that all of the planets, the major angles, and the signs in Jesus's chart were of a negative polarity except for Mars and Saturn. (Six signs of the zodiac have a negative polarity, while six signs have a positive polarity.) This means that Jesus's basic disposition was overwhelmingly reflective, contemplative, and receptive.

Such a preponderance of the receptive, feminine polarity magnetizing the various dynamics of His psyche conferred an inward, meditative focus which intensified Jesus's psychic sensitivity and intuition. The receptive and reflective negative polarity of Jesus's basic disposition was significant.

With the completion of this overview of the chart, we are now ready to paint a more detailed portrait of Jesus.

PART TWO

Portrait Of Jesus

Chapter 5

Ascendant in Capricorn, the Mount of Initiation

The three most important astrological factors in the natal chart are the Ascendant, the Sun, and the Moon, but for very different reasons. The Ascendant of Jesus's birth chart (at Nazareth) was 25 degrees Capricorn 57 minutes.[23] This makes Saturn (which rules Capricorn at both the personality and Soul levels) the ruler of His birth chart. The effects that Capricorn and its ruler, Saturn, have on initiates are very different from the effects they have on people who are still functioning at the stage of development of the personal consciousness.

The Ascendant is the cusp of the first house and the most potent field of energy of the twelve houses. When functioning at the personal level of development, the houses restrict the expression and growth of a psychic dynamic to a particular area of personal life and experience, depending on the house where the planet is placed, i.e., in the first house area of life or the second house area, etc. At this stage, the twelve houses of the natal chart represent the twelve areas of life where the development of the various dynamics of the psyche (which the planets represent) takes place and where the psychic dynamics sound their note.

The Ascendant represents a potent field of energies through which people express themselves in the outer world. The sign on the Ascendant and the aspects formed to the Ascendant, therefore, greatly affect the quality and character of people's self-expression. For this reason, the Ascendant is often thought of in terms of the persona. The astrological factors associated with the Ascendant also affect the image that other people have of the individual. Someone's sense of self is often different from the image they project to others, since the persona is filtered through the planetary forces and influences of the sign on the Ascendant.

---

[23] If Jesus was born at Bethlehem at 4:00 am, the Ascendant would have been 26 degrees 33 minutes.

People look at the outer world through the lens of the Ascendant. The sign on the Ascendant and the aspects formed to the Ascendant condition people's perceptions of their environment and surroundings. These astrological forces can limit what people notice in the outer world and skew their perceptions. The sign on the Ascendant can also affect the quality of people's observations.

Due to this astrological conditioning of the Ascendant, people respond to certain things in the outer world, but not to others. The Ascendant is a great conditioner of the consciousness since it colors the events in people's lives and affects the type of reactions people have to their experiences. The Ascendant also greatly affects what people choose to share and not share with others.

In relation to the evolution of consciousness, however, the potent Ascendant has an even greater importance than what traditional astrology assigns to it. The Ascendant is the portal through which the Soul expresses itself in the lives of disciples and initiates. The extent to which the Soul is able to express itself depends on the stage of evolvement the individual has attained.

The astrological factors associated with the Ascendant provide important clues about the Soul's goals and objectives and the ease or difficulty people are likely to experience as they work to achieve them. Although the initial intent of the Soul relates to the growth of the threefold personal consciousness, once people are spiritual disciples, the astrological factors conditioning the Ascendant provide clues as to the Soul's intent as it pertains to their spiritual growth and achievements. Prior to this time, the Ascendant relates more to the physical body than to one's spiritual growth.

At the stage of discipleship when the ray energies and qualities of the love tier and sacrifice tier of petals impact the consciousness, people begin to identify with the values, qualities, and character of the Soul. This changes everything. It is at this stage that the Ascendant starts to represent the Soul and its expression. In effect, the Ascendant becomes the conduit through which the inner Soul begins to express itself in people's lives.

At this higher stage, the ray-magnetized energies that the ruling planet and sign on the Ascendant transmit become the dominant astrological factors impacting the consciousness, not the forces of the planet that rules the Ascendant.

This development alters the meanings and significances that the houses represent. The rays transmitted by the signs on the house cusps do not generate a constricting field of force like the planetary forces do when the threefold personal consciousness is being developed. This expands the development of a particular dynamic of the psyche beyond the area of life that a house traditionally represents.

Traditional astrology assigns meaning and significances to the houses appropriate for those who are at the stage of personal development. However, the traditional meanings of the houses are inadequate in relation to the developmental concerns of the advanced disciple. Though the twelve houses of the natal chart represent the twelve areas of life and experience in terms of the growth and development of the three aspects of personal consciousness, they have little to do with the processes involved in the Soul's unfoldment and development. The Soul's unfoldment involves the rays that the signs and ruling planets of the sign transmit.

Since the personality is brought forth anew each incarnation, all people need to unfold and develop the faculties, skills, and capacities of the threefold personal consciousness. Thus, the traditional meanings assigned to the houses are valid in everyone's life while the threefold personal consciousness is being developed. But the symbolic meanings assigned to a house changes as people progress.

Once the disciple has attained the third initiation and becomes an initiate, the twelve houses represent the twelve mansions of the Soul. Here, the emphasis is on the ray influences transmitted by the signs on the house cusps, not on the planetary forces, which had previously limited the expression of a psychic dynamic to a particular area of life. The traditional issues and meanings of the houses continue to affect the personality in relation to one's service activities (as an instrument of the Soul), but the planetary forces themselves are no longer important in relation to the initiate's growth and development.

Once the disciple approaches the third initiation, the purified personality becomes an instrument that the Soul uses on earth to accomplish its service work. This involves service to God and mankind along the lines of the ray of the Soul. This is in sharp contrast to the average person, who is minimally influenced by the ray their Soul is on. From the time when the consciousness is mentally polarized up until the time when the individual becomes an accepted disciple, the ray that the personality is on is the dominant influence.[24]

In the chart of Jesus, the Ascendant was in Capricorn. With a Capricorn Ascendant, Jesus's day-to-day experiences were filtered through His Saturn-ruled Ascendant. How He expressed Himself (His persona) and what was important to Him in the outer world were both conditioned by the practical, somber, and often serious tone of Capricorn. Fortunately, Jupiter (which transmits ray two, love-wisdom) formed a trine to Jesus's Ascendant.

When Capricorn is the rising sign, life is taken seriously. There is little time to play. A sense of duty and responsibility often quells the typical frivolity of youth. Capricorns tend to be mature-acting and serious when they are young, but less somber as they get older.

---

[24] Each subtle body, as well as the integrated personality and the Soul, are on their own ray. The specific ray each subtle body is on electromagnetically attracts certain forces moving through the subtle body. Neither the ray of the personality (which unifies the personal consciousness into the integrated personality), nor the ray of the Soul is prominent during the early stage of personal development, due to the influences of the planetary forces in people's life.

Starting around the time transiting Saturn squares natal Saturn for the first time (five to seven years of age), Saturn becomes the dispenser of karma and a maturing influence. When transiting Saturn opposes natal Saturn (fourteen years of age), Saturn's objective is revealed. Saturn compels people to unfold the mental aspect of personal consciousness. This includes the development of the concrete mind and rational, logical thought. It is at this time that Saturn becomes the enforcer of the universal laws of humanity. Interestingly, the Lord God of the Old Testament often appears saturnine in nature, especially in His role as the dispenser of justice.

The sign Capricorn helps to polarize the consciousness at the mental level and encourages people to develop their mental faculties and capacities. People's ability to constructively respond to the influences of Capricorn is indicated by their willingness to shoulder personal and social responsibility. Throughout this period, while the mental aspect of personal consciousness is being developed, the focus is on the material world and on personal achievement, which comes as a result of the development of the personal mind and intelligence. Interestingly, Capricorn represents the gateway that leads initiates into the world of the Real. During the stage of personal development, however, the gateway of Capricorn is shrouded in clouds of self-referencing feelings, emotions, thoughts, and beliefs.

According to traditional astrology, the Ascendant is closely associated with the physical body and people's identity. What people identify their selfhood with, however, changes as people mature and spiritually advance. Children identify their selfhood almost exclusively with their physical bodies. Once the astral body is linked into the physical body, young people start to develop atoms of self-consciousness that correspond to the astral-emotional desire aspect of personal consciousness. This development of the astral-emotional aspect of personal consciousness usually takes place between seven and fourteen years of age.

It is at this time that people identify their selfhood with both their physical body and with their feelings, emotions, and personal desires. Once the mental body is linked into the physical body (for most people, this occurs sometime after the age of thirteen), people begin to identify their selfhood with their ideas, thoughts, and beliefs, while continuing to identify their selfhood with the physical body and their feelings and emotions. In terms of unfolding and developing the mental aspect of consciousness, ray five (concrete sciences, knowledge) and ray three (active intelligence) are especially important.

The rays the sign Capricorn transmits include ray one, ray three, and ray seven. These three rays are on the line of the mind and power, which is very different from the ray line that dominated much of Jesus's life. As a personality, Jesus was on the ray two, ray four, and ray six line of manifestation. This line corresponds to the love aspect of the Divine, not to the mind or will aspect of the Divine.

The sobering influence of Capricorn on the Ascendant provides us with our first glimpse of Jesus as a man. He was serious, disciplined, and at times rather somber. When He was young, He was mature well beyond His years. Due to the influences of Capricorn and the deeply religious influences of His family, Jesus had a strong drive to obey the Word of God and to strictly adhere to Jewish law when He was young. To Him, the words of the Torah were the inviolable Word of God. The influences of Capricorn and its ruler Saturn strengthened Jesus's resolve to strictly obey the letter of the law, the rules, and the commandments of Judaism.

To Jesus, life was a serious proposition that demanded a great deal of self-discipline and strict obedience to the ever-present Lord God of Israel (Yahweh). In His early years, He never questioned the laws, rules, regulations, and commandments as recorded in the Torah. The Torah governed every aspect of His early life. Not only did its proscriptions govern His diet and daily religious practices, it also regulated His behavior and relations with other people.

As a teenager, Jesus consciously responded to both the mystical influences of Pisces and the sobering influences of Capricorn. He took Judaism seriously and was rather rigid in terms of His religious beliefs. Most likely He regularly fasted, often prayed, and lived a disciplined life.

At some point, Jesus knew He was to fully sacrifice His will to the will of God. The concept of sacrifice, which is a Law of the Soul, enters the consciousness via Capricorn. Initially, people awaken to the principle of sacrifice in relation to the sacrifices they feel obligated to make to fulfill their duties and responsibilities to their family, their ethnic group or tribe, the society, or the nation. As people progress even higher, the need to sacrifice one's own concerns and interests to help others becomes prominent. This occurs as the energies of the sacrifice tier of petals stream through the upper centers.

Due to the factor of crystallization that permeates the energies of Saturn, people with a Capricorn Ascendant often have a rigidly held image of the self that changes little during their lives. If Uranus (which breaks up the crystallized patterns of identity and selfhood) wasn't conjunct the Sun in Jesus's chart, He would have exhibited a stern, rigid self-image that would have been hard to change as He progressed.

When Jesus was in His early twenties, the energies of Uranus became active in His life and awakened an independent, rebellious streak. The status quo is never acceptable to Uranus. There is always change that is needed both in the society and in one's own life. In its purest sense, Uranus activates the principles of liberty and freedom. This dynamic, in turn, gives rise to mental curiosity and a drive to learn how things work on earth and in the heaven.

Curiosity is the key that opens the door to the Hall of Knowledge. All seekers of knowledge enter the Hall of Knowledge to begin their studies. A desire and drive to obtain greater knowledge and understanding is the first indication that the influences of the Soul are being registered in the brain. Specifically, it is an indication that the energies emanating from the outer knowledge tier of petals are impacting the mind and consciousness.

By way of the energies of Uranus, people begin to think for themselves. They individuate. This development is prerequisite to people's inherent obedience to the universal laws of humanity. There are a number of nations, religions, and cultures that have yet to honor people's universal right to think and choose for one's self. When people do not have the right to make important choices in their own lives, there is little growth.

Thinking for oneself leads to individuation, and individuation leads to acts and behavior that separate people out from the masses. This involves differentiating oneself from the beliefs, ideas, prejudices, and biases of the family, tribe, ethnic group, society, or nation.

People use the forces of Saturn and Capricorn to establish the norms and institutions of society and formulate the mental structures, norms, and rules of conduct for the individual. To Saturn, individualism poses a threat to the continuity and stability of the individual and the society. The greatest fear of Saturn is social disruption and chaos, especially the type of disruption that the energies of Uranus precipitate.

Individuation is possible once the consciousness is polarized at the mental level and the threefold personal consciousness is reasonably well integrated. But when people exhibit extreme independence and rebellion prior to their third initiation, they often create unhealthy disruptions in the society. During the early stages of personal development, people typically express their rebelliousness in a narrow-minded, self-serving, destructive way that serves no purpose in terms of the greater good. Nor do the changes they demand advance the group, the society, the nation, or the whole of mankind. Often, they set the society or nation back in terms of individual rights and freedoms which, in turn, adversely impacts people's ability to advance.

Very few people were able to respond to the high-frequency energies of Uranus two thousand years ago, but Jesus did. Jesus was able to respond to the interplay and exchange of energies of Uranus since He was in His early twenties. Uranus was the strongest planetary influence impacting Jesus due to its tight conjunction with the Sun (36 minutes from an exact conjunction).

People who respond to the high-frequency energies of Uranus tend to rebel against the establishment and its authority figures in a number of ways. Jesus was no exception. His strong independence and tendency to rebel against the status quo (especially in His early twenties) were exacerbated by the tension that the opposition of Pluto to Uranus generated in His life.

The stabilizing, maturing influences of His Capricorn Ascendant were very much needed in Jesus's life to offset His tendencies toward rebellion, and to direct the mentally liberating forces of Uranus constructively.

The stabilizing influence of His Capricorn Ascendant gave structure to His mind and communications. It also helped Him to deal with the strong currents for change that coursed through His life (and through society two thousand years ago) without being overwhelmed or becoming excessively zealous.

Undoubtedly, the ray three qualities of Capricorn grounded Jesus in the here and now, and conditioned His life and teachings with an earthy practical quality. Capricorn presented the type of energy Jesus needed in order to anchor the principle of love, first within His own heart and mind and later within the collective minds of humanity. It also provided Him with the quality of energy He needed in order to discuss His profound spiritual realizations with others in a practical, earthy way.

In spite of the exceedingly strong emphasis in His chart on the astral-feeling, love-wisdom aspects of consciousness, Jesus was able to focus His thoughts in the highest heavens while keeping His feet on the ground, so to speak. Only the sign Capricorn allows for such extremes. Jesus approached His life with a serious, deliberate determination as a result of the sure-footed, stabilizing influences of Capricorn.

With a Capricorn Ascendant, the intentions of the Soul naturally stream into people's lives through the Ascendant on ray one, ray three, or ray seven, depending on the Soul's intent and objective. Although Saturn always transmits ray three, the nature of Jesus's mission suggests that His Soul probably expressed in His life on ray one, divine will. This would have been the ray one sub-quality of His ray six Soul.

Once the third initiation has been attained, the Ascendant (as the conduit for the Soul) becomes more important than the Sun. Prior to this time, the Sun represents the personal self, while the entire birth chart represents the unfolding aspects of the threefold personal consciousness. Once people become accepted disciples, however, they embody the values and qualities of the Soul and identify with and express the Soul via the Ascendant. As an accepted disciple, the Sun in their natal charts becomes a point through which the cosmic ray two energies of the Solar Logos start to pour into one's life. This is true regardless of the Sun's sign.

Again, during incarnation, the Soul enters people's lives by way of the Ascendant. Its influence is minimal, however, until people become a disciple. By way of the Ascendant, the Soul becomes the dominant influence in disciples' lives as they approach the third initiation and start to identify their selfhood with the Soul.

Although the sign on the Ascendant does not indicate the ray that the Soul is on, it does represent one of the seven sub-ray qualities that the ray the Soul is on. The Soul unfolds the seven sub-ray qualities of the ray the Soul is on over the course of many lifetimes.

Chapter 6

Jesus Was a Pisces

Initially, it was a surprise to see the Sun in Pisces in the natal chart of Jesus. After all, the birthday of Jesus that Christians have celebrated for centuries places the Sun in Capricorn. Still, the placement of the Sun in Pisces shouldn't surprise anyone familiar with the teachings of Jesus and the symbolism of astrology.

Of the twelve signs of the zodiac, the symbolism of Pisces fits the life, the message, and the mission of Jesus better than any other sign. To state that the teachings of Jesus demonstrate the characteristics, qualities, and overall symbolism of Pisces is an understatement.

Not only was the Sun in Pisces in the chart of Jesus, but Venus, the North Node, Uranus, Mercury, and the etheric planet of Vulcan were also placed in Pisces, while Neptune, the ruler of Pisces, formed a trine to Venus, the North Node, the Sun, Mercury, Uranus, and the Moon. This emphasizes the immense importance of Pisces and Neptune in Jesus's life.

Undoubtedly, such a strong Piscean influence was necessary in order for Jesus to fulfill His divine mission as the messenger for the teachings of the dawning Age of Pisces. This required Him to first, unfold and develop both the ray two and ray six expressions of the principles of Pisces—unwavering devotion to the God of love.

Today, this doesn't seem to be of tremendous significance, but approaching the Divine through unconditional love was a brand new way to approach the Divine that Jesus brought forth. Two thousand years ago, the second aspect of the Divine (love-wisdom) had yet to be anchored in the third planetary center of life, humanity. This new approach to the Divine is called the path of the heart. The path of the heart is the path of all World Saviors and it always runs through Pisces.

To understand the influence Pisces had on Jesus, it is necessary to understand what the Sun represents. The Sun represents that unifying factor within the consciousness that contributes a sense of selfhood. In relation to the evolution of consciousness, the Sun represents first, the personal self and later, the integrated personality. Again, the self when functioning at the stage of the integrated personality integrates the elements of the psyche (the physical-etheric, emotional, and lower mental aspects of personal consciousness) into a unified whole. The extent to which the three aspects of personal consciousness are integrated and unified varies significantly from one person to another.

The personal self holds the various aspects and facets of the threefold personal consciousness together in a loosely held federation. Just as the planets are held in orbit around the Sun by its electromagnetic influence, the personal self holds the elements of the threefold personal consciousness within the circumference of its light and influence.

The nature, characteristics, and disposition of the personal self are significantly affected by the astrological factors associated with the natal Sun. For this reason, we must look to the meanings and significances of the Sun for clues as to how people approach life and how they can best approach the Divine.

Each planet in the chart represents an aspect of the threefold personal consciousness that is developed over the course of a lifetime as the energies and forces impact the consciousness. The quality of the threefold personal consciousness that is unfolded and developed depends on the degree to which the brain is able to register the different types and qualities of energies and forces. It is by way of these energies and forces that the potential indicated in the natal chart is actualized. This includes skills, capacities, capabilities, behavior, faculties, modes of action, and so forth. As people become responsive to successively higher-frequency energies and qualities in a positive constructive way, they progress.

According to the symbolism of traditional astrology, the Sun is the directing force of will in people's lives—the personal initiative—which is the motivating force associated with the ego (the primary umbrella complex of the psyche). The Sun also represents the subjective factor within the consciousness referred to as the will-to-be.

At the stage of development of the threefold personal consciousness, people think of the personal self as the all-powerful initiating self that acts, feels, and thinks. However, once people attain the stage of discipleship and seek to express higher spiritual qualities, standards, and values, they realize just how little power the self actually possesses. People lack the power to make many of the changes that they would like to make. One moment they are able to take the proverbial high road and the next moment they act in selfish, habitual ways. The reason for this is the basic nature and structure of the personal self.

The personal self is brought forth as different types and qualities of energies impact the consciousness and express through people's lives. In effect, the personal self is a product of the interplay and exchange of the energies and forces that stream through the ethers onto the earth. But this is only part of the story.

In an effort to create an instrument through which the fullness of the Soul can express on earth, the Soul brings forth a personal self in these physical bodies lifetime after lifetime which, in turn, reacts to the energies and forces of the matter planes. Just as the Moon is the reflected light of the Sun, the personal light is the reflected light of the Soul that shines in and through the physical body as the self.

Although the personal self typically believes that it is a light onto itself, it is really a reflection of the light of the Soul. The extent to which the light of the Soul is expressed through these physical forms, however, depends on the density of the matter forces in the aura through which the light of the Soul is transmitted.

The personal self of each lifetime has an opportunity to unfold and develop certain principles, skills, faculties, and capacities by actualizing the potential indicated in the birth chart. The Sun sign represents the primary conditioning quality impacting the personal consciousness and its development, and greatly affects not only the way people approach life, but also the types of behavior that people are likely to exhibit.

Each of the twelve signs of the zodiac transmits one or other of the seven rays. Which sign conditions the Sun is, therefore, important. The ray-magnetized energies of a particular sign affect the nature and qualities of the personality more than any other influence. The Sun sign conditions people's behavior and greatly affects the type of personal characteristics, tendencies, and overall disposition they unfold in their lives. It greatly influences the way people express both their potential and selfhood. The key to understanding Jesus and His teachings lies with Pisces.

Historically, astrologers have known less about the meanings and significances of Pisces and its ruler Neptune than they know about the other astrological factors. Only today are astrologers beginning to understand the purpose that the otherworldly influences of Pisces and Neptune serve. Both Neptune and Pisces are involved in the spiritualization of human consciousness. The type of spiritualization Pisceans experience involves the unfoldment and development of love-wisdom through devotion and dedication to an ideal. (The spiritualization of people's consciousness also pertains to the ray that the Soul is on. For example, when the ray of the Soul is ray four, the spiritualization of the consciousness and the ideal it advances often involves some form of artistic expression or creativity.)

The symbolism of Neptune and Pisces and the effects they have on the consciousness are difficult for people to understand. Both Neptune and Pisces represent influences that are antithetical to the threefold personal consciousness, especially the concrete mind.

In general, Neptune and Pisces are antithetical to all form life, including the human personality. In many ways, the understanding and realization they bring forth as their energies impact the consciousness are transcendent of the concrete mind. For this reason, people are unable to use their intellect or rational thinking capacity to understand the deeper meanings of the principles of Neptune and Pisces. Only the intuitional mind has the capacity to comprehend their significances.

Since the energies of Neptune and Pisces are antithetical to the lower concrete world, what frequently comes to mind when the forces of Neptune and Pisces impact the consciousness seems irrational. Yet, what comes to mind under their influences is perfectly rational to the higher intuitional mind and the pure reasoning of the buddhic plane.

What is remarkable is that from an early age, Jesus was able to respond to the strong Piscean influences impacting His life. This is significant, since the high-frequency energies and ray influences of Pisces and Neptune cannot be used to develop the basic faculties and capacities of the threefold personal consciousness, which is the focus of most people's lives up until the age of twenty-eight. This would be tantamount to using a flower petal to pound a nail into concrete.

Given what Jesus was able to accomplish in His life with such a strong Piscean influence indicates that His mental faculties and capacities had been sufficiently developed prior to His incarnation. It was this past-life development that enabled Him to unfold a one-pointed spiritual focus at a young age and to understand what he was spiritually experiencing. The ray-magnetized energies of Pisces and Neptune were so strong in Jesus's life and so overwhelmingly influential that there were few things in His life that would have distracted Him from His spiritual path and mission.

Both the energies of Neptune and Pisces correspond to the essential love of the Soul and to the pure love-wisdom of the higher planes of light. For this reason, the influences of Pisces are the most obscure and incomprehensible to most people. Only an initiate is capable of handling the strong otherworldly currents of Pisces and Neptune in such a positive, constructive way as Jesus.

This doesn't mean that people are unaffected by the energies of Pisces or Neptune. They are, but often in an unhealthy way. When people have yet to open the etheric heart center to the energies of the Soul, the energies of Pisces and Neptune are drawn into the lower astral-emotional region of the astral body. As long as there are lower, selfish emotional forces within the astral body, the higher frequency energies of Pisces and Neptune energize them. This generates unusual feelings and imaginings.

Though the energies of Neptune and Pisces relate primarily to the spiritualization of the consciousness, they do not have a spiritually uplifting effect on people until the energies of the love petals stream through the astral body into the etheric heart center. As the energies radiating from the love tier of petals stream into the heart center, the love aspect of the higher self is unfolded.

A strong influence of Pisces tends to mitigate people's willful nature and can adversely affect their physical vitality, stamina, and drive. When the Sun is in Pisces, the magnetic power that the forces of the three planes of matter exert upon the consciousness is diminished. As a result, people may exhibit an inchoate denial of the factual reality that exists, especially in those areas of life the influences of Pisces and Neptune affect.

Whenever the consciousness is identified with the physical body and with the self-serving and self-referencing emotions and thoughts, people with a strong Piscean influence are more susceptible to the physically debilitating effects that the energies of Pisces can have on the body. Often, there is a heightened sensitivity to the woes of life. This includes an extreme sensitivity to one's own sorrow, disappointments, tribulations, and pain, as well as sensitivity to the tribulations of others.

Pisceans sensitivity to the feelings of others is due to the effect that the energies of Neptune and Pisces have on the etheric force field enveloping the physical body. In general, the etheric body shields the consciousness from the environment and restricts people's sensitivity to the physical body and its senses.

Pisceans are more sensitive to the feelings of others are a result of their inherent sensitivity to the astral field of forces, both their own astral bodies and others. The quality of emotions and feelings they sense and how they react to what they sense, however, depends on the qualities of energies that are present in their astral body.

For many people, an extreme sensitivity to the astral world is a curse, not a blessing, due to the negative emotional forces present in the astral body. When people are at the stage of personal development and have a strong Neptune and Pisces influence in their charts, they frequently take on the astral-emotional tenor of the environment as their own.

Pisceans often hear a different note, one that leads them away from the things of earth and diminishes their desire for wealth, name, fame, success, status, and power. This frees up Pisceans to follow their inner voice—a voice that resounds in the sacred space deep within.

In general, people with a strong Piscean influence are not as materially minded as most people. Nor do they exhibit the usual personal drive and passion for life unless the fire element is strong in their charts. Consequently, Pisceans often feel lost and lonely, at least initially. This is especially true when the consciousness is polarized at the astral-emotional level.

People with a strong Piscean influence often feel different from others as a result of their super sensitivity to the emotional tenor of their environment and to the feelings of others, especially their sadness, grief, sorrow, and pain, since such emotions are so intensely felt. The sign in which the Moon is placed can mitigate or reinforce people's sensitivity and their sense of being different from others. Since the Moon was in the sign of Cancer in Jesus's chart, He undoubtedly felt very different from others and was acutely sensitive to other people's pain.

When Pisceans are at the stage of personal development, this sensitivity can be overwhelming and at times debilitating. Feeling victimized by others is common. Due to their super-sensitivity to the emotions of others, people with their Sun in Pisces frequently adopt unhealthy psychological defense mechanisms to protect them from the harshness of the world.

Today, people often respond to the otherworldly pull of Pisces by turning to drugs and alcohol as a way to escape from the material world and to dull their sensitivity. The materially denying factor found in the energies of Pisces and Neptune frequently results in a basic dissatisfaction with the mundane world. But escaping through drugs and alcohol is the worst possible way to respond to these energies.

When people are still functioning at the stage of personal development, the influx of Piscean energies pour into the astral body and stimulate the astral-emotional refuse. This includes negative emotions and feeling patterns, selfish desires, and fear. As a result, it is common for Pisceans to exhibit an emotional neediness and woefulness, and to complain about their suffering to others as if they are being martyred in some way.

People who have their Sun in Pisces often feel as if their desires are never met in a way that seems (emotionally) satisfying and enjoyable. This is especially true when their consciousness is still polarized at the mid-astral level. As a result, they are frequently doleful and consumed with self-pity and feel as if they are being victimized. When this is the case, the raging currents of the poor-me river run deep. Often they become fixated on getting others to acknowledge their pain and to commiserate with them.

Self-inflicted emotional pain is common when Pisceans resist the evolutionary impulses calling them higher. Becoming more inclusive by expanding people's sensitivities beyond the self is a thematic impulse of Pisces, but emotionally manipulating others to feel sympathy for them and their plight is not the best way to become inclusive.

People who have a strong influence of Pisces and Neptune in their charts but are not responsive to the essential love of the Soul typically experience confusion and deceiving feelings and are easily overwhelmed by their strange emotions and feelings.

Mankind has so polluted the lower sub-plane levels of the astral plane with negative emotions and selfish desire forms that people's emotions and feelings, as well as their emotion-riddled beliefs and ideas, are often an enigma to people whose consciousness is polarized at the mental-plane level. Such negative and often destructive emotions fill the unconscious realm of humanity and must be transmuted.

To the masters, people's desires for the things of earth and their overall emotionalism represent a completely invalid experience that has no purpose or basis in reality. People who are caught up in this unreality, however, believe they know the truth, even though their astral-emotional world distorts all semblances of truth and reality. The mental aspect of personal consciousness, on the other hand, reflects a degree of reality. Of concern is that the unreality of the astral plane is now distorting the mental world of humanity as well.

For countless millennia, mankind has misused the extremely malleable astral forces to create selfish desire forms and negative emotional patterns that have imposed a lower rhythm upon the forces of earth, one that deceives and deludes the mind and consciousness. This ancient rhythm has resulted in a lack of clarity of mind and purity of the heart. On the path, purity of heart is absolutely necessary in order to unfold the higher senses and faculties without distortion.

Because of this ancient rhythm, human consciousness has been submerged in illusion, glamour, and maya for a long, long time. Thus, the reality that is valid and true to many people actually obstructs the real and conceals the true nature and purpose of life.

The energies of the upper three sub-plane levels of the astral body, on the other hand, correspond to the love-wisdom aspect of the Divine that people are to unfold and develop at the level of the personality. This higher quality of love is enhanced once the three sub-qualities of essential love of the Soul (via the love petals) stream from the upper region of the mental body through the upper region of the astral body into the upper etheric centers. This allows people to unfold and express higher spiritual qualities, such as spiritual aspiration, empathy, compassion, mercy, humility, and love for one another. One day, the astral bodies of mankind will reflect the seven sub-qualities of divine love-wisdom on earth without any negative or selfish distortions.

Astrologically, neither Pisces nor Neptune can be mentioned without discussing the imagination. Since the energies of Pisces and Neptune impact people's lives via the astral body (not the mental body), people whose charts strongly emphasize Pisces are frequently described as having an overactive imagination.

In general, people dismiss the imagination and psychic sensitivity that many Pisceans exhibit as being mere imaginings that have no validity in terms of the factual-based reality, which is not necessarily true. The lower astral-emotional forces in people's astral bodies can distort what they imaginatively perceive and psychically sense, but the problem is not with the forces of Neptune or Pisces. The problem lies with the astral desire forms and the distorting astral forces that people electromagnetically attract into the astral body. Such lower astral forces interfere with people's ability to accurately interpret what is psychically sensed in terms of the astral plane.

The faculty of the higher creative imagination is brought forth as energies move into and through the upper three sub-plane levels of the astral body and impact the consciousness. The higher creative imagination is an important tool for perceiving the reality beyond the three matter planes. It is a faculty that generates images in relation to what is sensed in the higher formless planes.

Only when the astral-emotional aspect of personal consciousness is cleansed and purified of its selfish and negative forces can the faculty of the higher creative imagination be safely developed, free of emotional distortion. The extent to which the higher creative imagination and the inner mind's eye are developed determines whether people can accurately sense the life and reality of the spirit side of life or are merely caught up in personal imaginings.

Aligning and attuning to the Soul on a regular basis and becoming consciously responsive to the essential love of the Soul is necessary in order to unfold and develop the three aspects of the higher mind. This activity is exceedingly important for Pisceans, especially when they are attempting to unfold the higher creative imagination and psychic abilities. In general, daily meditation and prayer are important to all phases of spiritualization. The more people attune to the Soul and invoke divine love and light onto the earth and onto mankind, the greater the influx of energies of the Divine stream into upper three sub-plane levels of the astral body.

Opening the upper etheric centers to the energies of Divine and attuning the consciousness to the Soul are not easy for most people to accomplish. Humanity has been caught up in the false reality of glamour and illusion throughout history. But when the Sun is in Pisces, people have an opportunity to disrupt and dissolve the imprisoning walls of glamour and illusion. This frees the consciousness from the lower astral-emotional world. The type of freedom Pisces offers, however, does not take place all at once; rather, it takes place over the course of countless years, as people's love for one another dissipates the emotional-desire forms of the little self.

Initially, the vibrations, character, and quality of the personal self determine the type and qualities of forces that people respond to. All energy seeks to express physically. As long as people attract and allow the lower negative astral forces to express in their lives, people will continue to be responsive to the lower astral miasma of distorted feelings and glamour and will continue to express such things in their lives as hatred, greed, vengeance, jealousy, arrogance, superiority, anger, etc. At all times, people are responsible for the types and qualities of forces they express.

The primary effect that the Piscean energies have upon the consciousness is that they dissolve or dissipate the electromagnetism that holds the structures together, regardless of the type of structure, e.g., a way of life, a relationship, a profession, a belief, an organization, a nation, and so forth. The reason for this dissipating action is that all structures become obsolete and new structures are needed in order to advance.

By definition, structures restrict the personal self to a particular area of experience and experimentation. These structures are necessary while different components of the threefold personal consciousness are being developed. But as people progress and certain developments have been achieved, such structures limit further growth. When this occurs, they need to be removed. Neptune transmits the energies that slowly break down these structures, especially in relation to the astral-feeling world. The energies of Uranus, on the other hand, break down the concretized structures in relation to the mental aspect of consciousness.

This is why everything people personally identify their selfhood with, along with the things that they are personally attached to, must be eliminated once such things have served their purpose in terms of their growth and development. People's self-centered nature and their attachments to the things of earth skew or taint the capacities and mental faculties that people unfold (rendering them unusable to the Soul). As a result, people's attention is preoccupied with the lower personal arena of life. This becomes problematic upon the path.

The most common effect that Pisces and Neptune have involves a heightening of people's sensitivity to both the feelings of others and the overall emotional tenor of the environment. Due to this sensitivity, people become less focused on their own needs and more focused on the needs of others as they progress. As a result, people can more easily detach themselves from the material world. This involves severing the cords that tie the atoms of self-consciousness to the physical body and to self-centered emotions, considerations, and desires.

People have emotions, but they are not their emotions. Detaching the consciousness from the things of the three matter planes (which includes thoughts, beliefs, and feelings) spans lifetimes. Neither the physical body nor the emotions nor thoughts and ideas bestow selfhood, yet they appear to do so when people are at the stage of personal development.

Detaching the consciousness from lower, negative feelings and ideas is always appropriate, but renouncing the entire threefold personal consciousness and the things of the material world is appropriate only when people are psychologically ready to unify the integrated personality with the Soul as they approach the third initiation. Detachment and renunciation of the material world are part of the spiritualization process that all advanced Souls embrace at some point. When people have their Sun in Pisces or have a strong emphasis on Neptune in the natal chart, it is time to start letting go of the things of earth that they have used to define who they are.

The evolutionary intent of Pisces is to encourage people to liberate themselves from the things of earth by jumping off the perpetually spinning wheel of karma that binds their lives to the three lower planes of earth. The involutionary rotation of this wheel is caused by people's relentless desires for the things of earth and their need to satisfy them. As a rule, people do not seek liberation from the material world, however, until they hear the clarion call of the Soul to rise up from the planes of matter into the light.

Most people only hear the voices of the little self and are addicted to the sensationalism, emotionalism, and drama of their lives. The voice of the Soul can only be heard when the voices of the little self are sufficiently stilled. When stilled, the impulses of the Soul lead to sacrifice—the sacrifice of one's personal desires, preferences, and illusionary sense of being separate from others.

The desire to sacrifice and to serve others governs the Soul and its life, while the desire to serve oneself and one's own interests and preferences dominates the personality. At the stage of discipleship, people begin to register the impressions of the Soul calling them to serve and to sacrifice themselves for others.

When the Sun is in Pisces, people's sensitivity to mankind's suffering can be so overwhelming that the only recourse is for the individual to turn to some kind of sacrificing service to help relieve others from their suffering and misfortune. As long as the focus remains on one's own misfortune and emotional pain, pain persists.

The best way to awaken the heart center is through loving service to mankind. The increased sensitivity to the unifying qualities of the Soul that Pisces contributes, combined with a lessening of people's personal willfulness and drives, results in an expansive, more inclusive loving disposition. This desire to serve others becomes selfless and unconditional as a result of the otherworldly pull and the materially denying influences of Pisces. This results in an overwhelming desire to sacrifice the little self in service to God and mankind.

By way of the ray two energies of Pisces, people are slowly uplifted from the fog-bound astral-emotional world. As long as the consciousness remains polarized at the mid-astral, emotional level, however, the consciousness is caught up in a magnetic force field that distorts people's feelings and experiences. During the stage of personal development, all aspects of personal consciousness that people unfold are tainted with matter forces of the three planes of earth that limit, confine, restrict, and distort the consciousness.

Since mankind has generated a multitude of astral desire forms and patterns of negative emotions, and has consistently responded to the dark, obstructive astral forces that people have generated throughout history, everyone must individually overcome the power, influence, and control that these lower astral forces exert in their lives. Only when the astral body is sufficiently free of personal distortions can people use the energies of Pisces to move away from their age-long identification with the physical body and their attachment to egocentric feelings, thoughts, and beliefs.

Pisces represents the ending of one cycle of development of the psychic dynamics and the beginning of another cycle. Under the influence of Pisces, the dynamics of the psyche are synthesized and readied to begin a new cycle of development through the twelve signs. Once a capacity, faculty, skill, or capability has been developed in terms of the threefold personal consciousness and adequately applied and utilized in people's lives, the psychic dynamic that a planet represents is ready for the synthesizing experience of Pisces. The energies of Pisces synthesize the development of the dynamics of the psyche, as well as synthesize the capacities, skills, or faculties that have been developed over the course of countless lifetimes.

Although the development and subsequent Piscean synthesis of the various psychic dynamics take place cycle after cycle, there comes a time when the individual no longer needs to identify with the physical body or with some aspect of the threefold personal consciousness. When this is the case, the placement of the Sun in Pisces represents the moment in which all identification of one's selfhood with the egocentric integrated personality is eliminated. This enables the disciple to fully identify his or her selfhood with the Soul and its nature and qualities.

Jesus experienced this shift away from the personality as a young man once He had completed the development and purification of the threefold personality.[25] This is when the forces of Pisces extract the essences of the consciousness of the personalities of countless lifetimes and unifies them into a higher, more integrated state of mind and being. This allowed Jesus to shift (in consciousness) upward into the world of the Soul.

The little self is never uplifted into the world of the Soul by hatred, anger, or fear; rather, it is uplifted by holding the mind steady in the light of the Soul until such time when all that once appealed to the little self no longer has an appeal. It requires people to serve one another, to love, and to bless one another. It calls on people to invoke the divine light and love onto the earth and onto all mankind. This is the responsibility that the advance Soul with the Sun in Pisces comes to realize.

Attuning to the heart of God on a daily basis and invoking the love and light of God to bless all life—mineral, plant, animal, and human—is needed today more than ever. As more people are transformed into initiates and masters, the image of the perfection envisioned within the mind of God will materialize on the earth.

Just like the disciple, the earth must be reborn. Only then can perfect love, light, and peace appear upon the earth. Truly, the kingdom of heaven is at hand. Significant development is needed, however, before people are able to perceive the beauty, harmony, and

---

[25] Two thousand years ago, people's sense of selfhood and their identification with their feelings and thoughts was much weaker than it is today.

perfect love within them and all around them. This speaks to the work needed to awaken to that patterning of perfection that lies deep within them.

Sun in the Second House

At first glance, the Sun in the second house seems like an unlikely placement for the Sun in the chart of Jesus. The second house relates to that area of people's lives where they grow through their experiences involving material resources. The second house relates specifically to the methods people devise to satisfy their basic survival needs and to feel materially secure in life.

According to traditional astrology, the second house provides clues about people's material values and attitudes toward money, possessions, and those things they instinctively need to survive, such as their ability to earn a living and acquire the monetary resources necessary for supporting the lifestyle they desire. These statements reflect the symbolism of the second house, but only for people at the stage of personal development. At this initial stage, the Sun in the second house links people's identity with their ability to acquire monetary funds and material possessions. Identifying one's selfhood with materiality starts to fall away once people become a disciple.

Disciples reach a point in their progression when the second house no longer represents the kind of activities that further bind them to the material world. At this higher stage, the second house represents spiritual aspirations and values, rather than material values and desires. As the energies of the love petals stream through the heart center, disciples' desire to embody and express higher spiritual values and standards begins to shift their attention away from the material world. Although the second house continues to represent the disciples' possessions and their ability to obtain what they materially need, the second house starts to reflect what they spiritually value—acquiring *"treasures in heaven, where neither moth nor rust consumes and where thieves do not break in and steal."*[26]

The energies of the planets and the signs associated with the second house are always used to obtain that which is valued. As spiritual devotees progress, they become more interested in what they need to thrive spiritually. The exact quality and nature of what disciples tend to value depend on the sign, planets, and aspects formed to the planets in the second house and to the rulers of the sign(s) conditioning the second house.

As a disciple, the second house represents the magnetic qualities that help unify the personality with that which is spiritually valued. Since the Soul can be on any one of the

---

[26] Matt. 6:20. (RSV) (italics added)

seven rays, what a disciple values varies. Love is always valued since the essential nature of the Soul is love, regardless the Soul ray.

Taurus, the traditional ruling sign of the second house, establishes the issues of the second house. This means that Venus, as the personality ruler of Taurus (See Addendum: Table One), is involved in obtaining the material things of earth needed to feel personally secure. Initially, its energies are caught up in the world of glamour and desire at the personal level.

When people are unfolding the threefold personal consciousness, the signs and aspects formed to the planets in the second house and the planets associated with the second house by ruler-ship are suggestive of such things as earning ability, money, and possessions. They are also indicative of the type of efforts people put forth to satisfy their desires and needs. What people desire corresponds to the point of evolvement they have attained.

There is a point in mankind's development when using the energies of Venus to obtain the things of earth becomes a misuse of its ray five energies. For this reason, the second house in the chart of a disciple relates to that which is spiritually valued and to those things that help people unfold the values, qualities, and characteristics of the Soul. Disciples use the magnetically attractive power of ray five Venus to blend and unify the refined elements of the personal consciousness with the values and qualities of the Soul.

Once the disciple approaches the third initiation, the second house relates to the types of activities that destroy people's attachment to money and material possessions. At this point, disciples realize that their attachments to the things of earth interfere with attaining what they spiritually value. This occurs as the influence of the Soul-centered ruler of Taurus, Vulcan, begins to impact the consciousness of the accepted disciple. Vulcan rules Taurus at the Soul level.

By way of the energies of the planet Vulcan (which reach people on the waves of the light and will of the Soul), accepted disciples are able to construct the tools necessary to break the chains that attach their atoms of self-consciousness to the things of earth. Even though mastery of the astral-emotional aspect of consciousness is achieved at the second initiation, both emotion-based and mental-based attachments are not fully eliminated until people approach the third initiation. Vulcan specifically relates to the development of this ability to cut the chains that bind the consciousness of mankind to the three planes of earth.

Once the union of the integrated personality and Soul is attained, the second house relates to the attainment of enlightenment and to the will of the Divine (due to the influences of ray one Vulcan). This leads the initiate even higher and awakens a desire within the higher self of the unified personality-Soul to attain a union with the Atman, the Real Self, who resides in the living light and living waters of the world of the Real.

This eventually results in a lofty state of enlightenment. Enlightenment involves the higher expression of the ray five energies of Venus and the ray one energies of Vulcan in its second sub-aspect (the builder, creator aspect). Vulcan is an etheric sacred planet that disseminates the higher sacred ray one energies of divine will and purpose to those who have transcended the three planes of earth.

As an accepted disciple and then as an initiate, the ray(s) pouring into the second house via the signs of the zodiac represent the energies needed in order for people to fashion the faculties of the mind that both Jesus and the Buddha demonstrated.

At this higher stage, transcendent of the integrated personality, the planets placed in the second house and the astrological signs conditioning the second-house atmosphere provide clues as to how the initiate can shift the polarization of his or her consciousness from the world of the Soul into the world of the Real. This shift upward allows greater, more refined light to pour directly onto the mind. The influx of this sublime light results in pure reasoning and enlightenment. In terms of the buddhic-plane, Pisces relates more to the love aspect, while Taurus relates more to the wisdom aspect.

Throughout much of His life, what Jesus valued and felt He needed related to the higher spiritual symbolism of both the second house and Pisces. In other words, that which Jesus valued pertained to spiritual devotion and dedication. His intense spiritual devotion to the Father resulted in His realization that God was love. To Jesus, love was the basic nature of the Father. The large number of planets in Pisces in the second house in Jesus's chart intensified His dedication to God in its aspect of love and in its aspect of will and purpose.

In the early years of Jesus's life, the strong Piscean influences conditioning the planets in His second house so spiritualized Him and His life that it is unlikely He paid much attention to His basic survival needs and issues. Undoubtedly, He believed that the Father would provide everything that He needed. His epic grand trine repeatedly substantiated this belief. It is unlikely that Jesus felt any reason to even think about His material needs.

In the chart of Jesus, the sign on the cusp of the second house is Aquarius. Aquarius on the second-house cusp contributed a penchant toward the group consciousness of the Soul. When Jesus was young, the ray energy of Aquarius helped orient Him toward the needs and desires of others and instilled an interest in helping people fulfill their needs and aspirations. The group orientation of Aquarius affected all of the dynamics of the psyche represented by the planets in the second house. This influence made it easier for Him to transition from an individual orientation and consciousness into the group consciousness of the Soul once He attained the third initiation.

All thirty degrees of Pisces fell within the second house of Jesus's chart. This means that His Piscean Sun, Venus, Uranus, Mercury, and Vulcan were located in the second house. This stellium of planets in Pisces is a powerful combination of energies in one house.

The interception of the sign Pisces in the second house and the intercepted sign of Virgo in the eighth house shielded all of the dynamics of His psyche that His second- and eighth-house planets represented, preventing them from being subjected to the crystallization of feelings and thoughts. Many of the dynamics of three aspects of personal consciousness including His mental faculties and capacities were spared from becoming rigid. (Even thoughts are (crystalized) things of earth that the mind sets into motion.)

The interception of the signs Virgo and Pisces greatly reduced the distortion that the dynamics of the psyche are normally subjected to during people's lives. Due to this interception, the psychic dynamics represented by the planets in both Virgo and Pisces remained relatively free from crystallization. Also, since both Virgo and Pisces are mutable signs, the psychic dynamics represented by the planets in Virgo and Pisces were more amenable to change than the psychic dynamics represented by planets in fixed or cardinal signs.

The combination of the mutable influence of Virgo and Pisces and the interception of Virgo and Pisces in the second house prevented Jesus from being resistant to change in a number of important areas. Additionally, the placement of Uranus in the second house conjunct the Sun and Mercury also freed Jesus from the crystallizing influences of Saturn in terms of His identity, initiative, as well as His thoughts and ideas. Uranus is the great disrupter of saturnine crystallization.

It is only natural for young people to focus on satisfying their personal desires and to adopt the beliefs, ideas, opinions, and prejudices of their family, peers, and society. However, that which Jesus had assimilated from His family and society was quite susceptible to change due to the interception of the mutable Piscean planets in the second house. Thus, Jesus was more than willing to change His mind and change what He identified His selfhood with throughout His life. The mutable quality of Pisces and Virgo, along with the interception of Pisces and Virgo in the second house, impeded the usual processes that attach people to the things of earth. Thus, the combination of these influences freed Jesus to focus almost exclusively on the spiritual world.

At some point in His life, Jesus decided that His devotion and dedication to serving the will of the loving Father was all that mattered, not the material things of earth. Having such a belief is understandable given the placement of the Sun, Mercury, Venus, and North Node in Pisces:

Therefore I tell you, do not be anxious about your life, what you shall eat, nor about your body, what you shall put on. For life is more than food, and the body more than clothing.[27]

And do not seek what you are to eat and what you are to drink, nor be of anxious mind.[28]

Instead, seek his kingdom and these things shall be yours as well.[29]

These verses perfectly reflect the words of an initiate, especially when he or she has a Pisces Sun in the second house. Jesus valued the things of heaven, not the things of earth. This is true even though the focus of His early years was on establishing a close relationship with the Lord God of the Covenant who moved through the collective Judeans.

With this discussion of the Sun in Pisces, the epic grand trine, and the Ascendant in Capricorn, an image of Jesus is beginning to take shape. The next step is to add some color to this portrait of Jesus. This begins with a discussion of the aspects that the Sun formed to the planets and angles in His chart.

---

[27] Luke 12:22. (RSV) (italics added)
[28] Luke 12:29. (RSV) (italics added)
[29] Luke 12:31. (RSV) (italics added)

Chapter 7

The Coloring of the Personality (Part One)

Although the symbolism of each aspect and sign placement of the planets must be looked at individually in an analysis of the birth chart (since they have their own subtle note, vibration, color, and effect upon the consciousness), it is only when the meanings and significances of all the astrological factors are combined that we can hear the symphony of the self as a person and a Soul. The more times that a particular characteristic, trait, tendency, skill, or capacity is mentioned in an analysis of the natal chart, the greater the likelihood that the individual will exhibit it.

The aspects formed to the Sun in the natal chart confer additional qualities, capabilities, characteristics, and capacities in relation to the development of the personality. They also contribute additional coloring to the over-all disposition of the personality due to the exchange and interplay of rays each planet transmits. Each ray is clairvoyantly seen as a specific color.[30]

All people wear a multicolored coat comprised of different ray-magnetized fields of force. Each subtle body is on one or other of the seven rays and, therefore, naturally resonates with the planets that transmit the same or a complementary color. For example, the astral body is usually on ray six or on ray two. The purity of the coloring of these subtle bodies is what varies from one person to another. As people progress, the coloring of the subtle bodies becomes purer, brighter, and more translucent.

The Sun in the chart of Jesus was in Pisces conjunct Mercury, Venus, Uranus, the North Node and Vulcan. It was trine the Moon, Neptune, and the Mid-heaven, and was opposite Pluto and the earth. The Sun was also quintile Jupiter. The large number of planets to which the Sun formed an aspect is quite unusual.

---

[30] The color of a ray is different at the personality level than it is in the planes of light, since the higher planes are free of matter substances which affect the appearance of a ray.

The Sun (as the integrating, initiating factor of the personality) forms a strong bond to the Moon and to all of the planets in Jesus's chart except Mars and Saturn. This means that the various dynamics of the psyche of Jesus were well integrated and interrelated. Since ray two and ray six Pisces and ray six Neptune rules Pisces at the level of the personality, a large number of dynamics of the psyche of Jesus were conditioned by interplay and exchange of rays two and six.

These two rays in particular were involved in the spiritualization of the mind and consciousness of Jesus. With so many dynamics of the psyche conditioned by the same rays, note and sound, the mind of Jesus was uniform, harmonious, and powerful. When this is the case, the number of issues people must deal with before they can step upon the path is reduced—which, in turn, significantly accelerates the rate of progression.

The nature and quality of the interplay of planetary energies and the effects they have upon people's consciousness are always affected by the type of aspect (hard or soft) formed between two planets. Also, the closer a planet is to forming an exact aspect, the stronger the influence it has. The closest aspect that the Sun formed to another planet was its conjunction to Uranus. The difference between the Sun's position and the placement of Uranus was a mere 36 minutes of separation.

When two planets are conjunct, they come under the empowering influence of ray one will. The ray one force of will stimulates the inherent evolutionary forces that move mankind forward upon the path. Since the Sun was just starting to separate from an exact conjunction with Uranus in Pisces when Jesus was born, this conjunction indicates that a higher cycle of development of the personality was just beginning and the development of threefold personality that had taken place over a number of lifetimes had just concluded.

Sun conjunct Uranus in Pisces (36 minutes)

The extent to which people responded to the high-frequency energies of Uranus two thousand years ago is unknown. Almost universally, the structures of the intellect and mind were inadequately developed for people to sense the influences of Uranus except in a basic, emotionally reactive way. Even today, people are usually unaware of the effects that the forces of Uranus have on them, rarely assigning the sudden losses and pleasant surprises they experience as being precipitated by the often disruptive influences of Uranus.

Greek mythology indicated that the principle of Uranus (the Sky God) was just beginning to dawn upon the consciousness of humanity two thousand years ago; however, it had yet to be integrated into people's own consciousness. This is still true for many people. The principle of Uranus remains aloof and unintegrated in terms of the psyche of the average person.

The principle of Uranus relates to the intelligence aspect of the Triad—the abstract mind and its development. It is this intelligence aspect of the Triad that stimulates the mind in a way that gives birth to individuality and to new ideas. The liberating individuality that Uranian forces bring forth is the result of people registering the ideas originating in the world of ideas of the upper mental plane. These ideas are new, abstract, and foreign to the concrete mind and personal intellect. They are especially incomprehensible to those whose consciousness is polarized in the astral-emotional realm.

Uranus represents the principle of (mental) liberation, individuality, and freedom from matter conditioning. The concepts of freedom, liberation, and individualism arise within the personal mind as people register and consciously respond to the impulses and impressions of the mind of the Soul.

Two thousand years ago, people had yet to individuate. They had yet to separate out from the consciousness of the tribe or kingdom. The concept of individualism and the individuated self didn't arise within the consciousness of mankind in substantial numbers for another fifteen hundred years. Once individualism started to arise within the consciousness of mankind, it gave birth to a belief in the rights of the individual. This, in turn, gave birth to democracy.

Just as consciousness originates with the Soul and expresses in these physical bodies as self-consciousness, individuality originates with the manasic center at the first sub-plane of the mental plane. It has only been in the past few centuries that individuality has become important to the citizens of the industrialized nations. The women's movement is a modern-day expression of the efforts to individuate human consciousness.

The extent to which Jesus was able to respond to the high-frequency energies of Uranus is not known precisely, but He definitely responded and reacted to the influences of Uranus. Most likely the Uranian influences started to have a profound effect upon Him when He was around twenty-one years of age. Before Jesus could fulfill His mission as the messenger for the new Piscean Age, He needed to develop a strong sense of self that only the energies of Uranus can bring forth.

Jesus also needed to consciously register and respond to the influences of Uranus in order to maintain a strong, cohesive personal self that was distinct from the consciousness of the masses. Without this Uranian influence, He would have consciously floundered in the waters of the emotions and desires of mankind, unable to distinguish Himself from the tribe. A strong individuated selfhood must be developed before people can transcend the integrated personality at the third initiation.

Analysis of the birth chart of Jesus indicates that He was a warm, sensitive, kind young man during His early years, religiously devout, and relatively free of selfish tendencies. This doesn't mean He was always an angel. How could He have been? Pluto was opposite His Sun and Mercury. Jesus may have expressed the willful power of Pluto on occasion, but as He matured, Jesus learned to control the powerful forces of ray one Pluto that surged through Him.

With Uranus so close to His Sun and with both planets opposite Pluto, Jesus was definitely a rebel who held some pretty revolutionary ideas and beliefs, especially in the areas of religion and spirituality. This liberating independent streak Jesus expressed was necessary to liberate Him from the mass consciousness of the tribe. Once Jesus fully individuated and the link between the personal mind and the higher mind was strengthened, new spiritual ideas and ideals started to pour into His mind, thanks to the strong influences of Uranus and Neptune.

As He became more responsive to the Uranian influence that impacted Him, Jesus started to hear the beat of a different drum. He no longer resonated with the drumbeat of Judea. Practically all aspects of His consciousness were affected by this new, revolutionary spiritual impulse. Though the rebelliousness He felt in His early twenties was probably confusing initially, Jesus came to value His independent thinking and the clarity of mind that Uranus brought forth.

The conjunction of Uranus and the Sun was so close that the Uranian influences prevented the threefold personality of Jesus from ever becoming crystallized. This includes His feelings, as well as His thoughts, beliefs, and ideas. It is because of the energies of Saturn that people's sense of who they are as a person, along with their feelings, opinions, thoughts, and beliefs, become rigid and crystallized as they mature. This did not happen to Jesus, however, due to this close conjunction of Uranus and the Sun and the interception of Pisces and Virgo in the second and eighth houses.

More than any other astrological factor, Uranus is antithetical to the saturnine structuring of the concrete mind. The energies of Uranus would have repeatedly broken through any crystallized patterns of thought and behavior that might have formed in Jesus's life. At some point, Jesus realized that His life was not His own to personally enjoy. Even if He tried to live a normal life, the great needs of mankind repeatedly disturbed His peace and compelled Him to focus on others.

This does not mean that Jesus fully understood His mission once He started to respond to the influences of Uranus, but it does suggest that He exhibited a strong willful urge to freely express Himself. This was something that was unheard of two thousand years ago. This urge to freely express Himself became especially prominent once transiting Uranus squared each of the planets in Pisces (plus Pluto in Virgo) when Jesus was in His late teens and early twenties.

These hard transits of Uranus opened a door within Jesus's mind to the energies of the manasic center. As the higher qualities of the manasic center impacted His mind, Jesus unfolded the faculty of the abstract mind. This allowed Him to perceive the deeper meanings behind all things of earth. As the higher mind and abstract mind unfolded in Jesus's life, what He had heard in the synagogue and Temple in His younger years took on new meaning.

The energies of the manasic center are involved in unfolding and developing active intelligence at the level of the Spiritual Triad. The faculty of the mind that the manasic energies bring forth is commonly referred to as the abstract mind. It is this faculty of the spiritual mind that translates the extremely subtle light impulses of the higher buddhic-intuitional plane into universal symbolic images. The mind of the higher self is used to interpret these universal symbols into original ideas that the advanced concrete mind, in turn, intuits and translates into words.

The abstract mind is the mind of analogy, of parables, and universal symbolism. By way of the active intelligence of the Spiritual Triad, Jesus became aware of the underlying cause behind the outer dualistic world of the concrete mind. This capacity greatly strengthened His understanding of what He was intuiting. It also increased His independence from the mind-set of the Judean tribe.

During the first twenty-nine years of life, people are usually focused on the unfoldment and development of the faculties, abilities, skills, and capacities of the three aspects of personal consciousness. This includes the development of the concrete mind and rational thought. This would have been true of Jesus as well, but at some point as a young man, His progression started to accelerate at an exceptionally fast pace. As a result, He unfolded and then transcended the threefold personal consciousness at a young age.

It appears as if Jesus didn't need to focus on the development of the concrete mind; rather, He went from focusing on the development of the upper astral faculties and senses (spiritual aspiration, a sensitivity to the needs of others, psychic abilities, creative imagination, and idealism) to unfolding a knowledge of how to interpret the language of the abstract mind. This means His consciousness shifted from its polarization in the upper astral realm into the upper mental realm, skipping over the development of the divisive concrete mind to a large extent. The concrete mind separates, groups, and categorizes the things of the outer world as a result of the factor of separatism that permeates the lower mental-plane thoughts and ideas of the concrete mind.

Once Jesus had completed the prerequisite development of the threefold personal consciousness, He was able to receive and respond to the higher energies of the manasic center. The interplay of the energies of this conjunction significantly hastened the unfoldment of the intelligence of the Triad. It is the mind of the Spiritual Triad that perceives and understands the deeper meaning and causation behind that which becomes manifest on earth. This includes the concrete mind and intellect.

The acceleration of the development of these higher aspects of the mind and consciousness was due to the fact that Jesus had unfolded the intelligence and love petals of the lotus in recent past lives as evidenced by the epic grand trine. At a certain point early in His life, the energies radiating from the petals of the knowledge tier and the love tier of the lotus started to stream into the upper three sub-plane levels of His astral and etheric bodies. This allowed Jesus to link the personal mind to the manasic center of energies (via the petals of the intelligence tier) and subsequently unfold the abstract mind. With this development, Jesus learned how to interpret the impressions of the intuitional mind at an early age.

Esoterically, the concrete mind is the slayer of the real right up until the time when the disciple approaches the third initiation. Only then does the personal mind become the revealer of the real.

It appears that the concrete mind never became the slayer of the real in Jesus's life. Rather than focusing in the lower astral and mental areas of development, His focus was on activities that unfolded and developed the upper astral- and then the upper mental-plane qualities, senses, and faculties in His teenage years and early twenties. Nor did Jesus exhibit the power potential that the Sun represents in a personal way or express the usual egocentric characteristics and behavior that disciples must overcome upon the path. The little self never dominated His life. Jesus exhibited little if any egocentric willfulness.

From His early years, Jesus's focus was on the will of God, but it wasn't until His early twenties that His consciousness shifted from the upper astral world of clairvoyance, creative imagination, and idealism into the world of the Soul. As Jesus was unfolding the higher mind via the petals of the lotus, He also unfolded the abstract mind as a result of Uranus's influence. Uranus helped to link the manasic center to the concrete mind via the intelligence petals of the lotus.

The strong influence of Uranus meant that from a young age, Jesus was not subject to the limitations that people normally experience. Neither His personal will nor the effects His will had on others were limited in the usual ways. Due to the strong influence of Pisces and Neptune, combined with this strong liberating influence of Uranus, a unique transpersonal quality conditioned His behavior and actions at a young age.

Due to the point of evolvement Jesus had attained, this tight conjunction of Uranus to the Sun led to a large number of sudden changes in His life that transformed Him and intensified His sensitivity to the spirit side of life. From realization to greater realization, from revelation to greater revelation, Jesus was repeatedly transformed and renewed in body, mind, and spirit.

In His early years, people probably looked at Jesus as being unusual and erratic at times because of this strong Uranian influence. He was definitely unusual and a bit iconoclastic. Then, in His twenties, Jesus started to attune to the higher universal laws that are transcendent of both mankind's secular laws and religious laws. This attunement to the higher universal laws was necessary in order for Jesus to serve as the Piscean messenger. As a result, He was able to formulate a new approach to the Divine. This new approach was in line with the new impulses of the Piscean Age that were impacting the earth.

By way of this conjunction of Uranus and His Sun in Pisces, Jesus was able to perceive the seed ideas, the will, and purpose of God that were part of the divine plan two thousand years ago. This conjunction enabled Jesus to perceive and understand the intent behind the seed ideas that the Spiritual Hierarchy was depositing in the upper mental and buddhic planes during the early years of the Age of Pisces. This conjunction also brought forth the willpower necessary to shatter some of the crystallized patterns of thought within the society that were obsolete in relation to the dawning Piscean Age.

Once Jesus was consciously responsive to these Uranian influences, He no doubt found routine life to be boring and was in need of constant stimulation. With such a strong Piscean influence in His life, however, the type of stimulation that He sought was of a spiritual nature, e.g., a closer relationship to the Father or possibly a desire to know the will of God.

Due to the tightness of this conjunction of Uranus and the Sun, the energies of Uranus repeatedly created points of tension in Jesus's life. These points of tension helped to sharpen His focus and shift His consciousness upward into the planes of light, where He perceived new concepts and ideas and experienced successively greater realizations. Of especial importance is that this close conjunction led to a perfect alignment between the (brain) consciousness, the personal mind, the higher mind, and the manasic abstract mind of the Triad.

Sun conjunct Mercury in Pisces (1 degree 20 minutes)

The energies of Mercury are involved in the development of the mental aspect of the personal consciousness: the concrete mind, intelligence, and communication skills. The sign and house placement, along with the planetary aspects formed to Mercury, provide clues as to what people think about and how they process information.

Developing the concrete mind and studying the secular knowledge of the world were not emphasized in Jesus's life. Though Jesus was mainly focused on the development of the threefold personal consciousness, including His intellectual capacities, up until He was twenty-one, the energies impacting Him primarily emphasized the development of the love aspect of the Divine at both the personal and spiritual levels, not the development of the concrete mind.

At an early age, Jesus's development was so conditioned by the light and qualities of the Soul that His concrete mind operated very differently from those around Him. Most likely Jesus exhibited the qualities of the mind of the Soul at a relatively young age, not the self-referencing intellect that most people exhibit.

The Sun and Mercury were combust in Jesus's birth chart. When the Sun and Mercury are combust, the solar energies can overwhelm the thinking processes and communications, and interfere with people's ability to objectively observe their own behavior and thoughts. Here, the mind (located in the mental plane) isn't sufficiently separate from the radiations of the Sun to provide an objective perspective of the self.

When sufficiently developed, the inner personal mind (located in the mid-mental plane of forces) impresses the brain consciousness with its knowledge and understanding. (The inner mind continues after the change called death.) From its perspective, people can observe themselves and their behavior. This is not possible when the Sun and Mercury are combust.

When the Sun and Mercury are combust, there is no separate self to observe. The two dynamics of the psyche they represent function as one. This alone indicates that the personal mind and intellect of Jesus functioned in a way that was different from how the mind usually functions. There was no distance between the initiating self and the thoughts, beliefs, and ideas of Jesus; they operated as if they were one and the same.

Even more significant was the fact that the Sun, Mercury, Uranus, and Vulcan were all combust in the chart of Jesus. There was little if any factor of separatism to differentiate the initiating self of the integrated personality, the lower concrete mind, and the abstract mind (once it was brought forth). At a young age, these psychic dynamics functioned as one great dynamic of mental initiative, which operated primarily at the higher level of the abstract mind. Again, the abstract mind is the interpreter of the deep symbolic imagery and causal patterning that underlies and precipitates that which is manifest in the outer world.

This means that the dynamics of the psyche that Mercury, the Sun, and Uranus represent were closely integrated in Jesus's life. As a result of the close conjunction of these three, Jesus was able to unify the personal self, the personal mind, and the higher mind as a young adult. Then, in His twenties, the manasic intelligence of the Triad also became functional. The lower mind, the higher mind, and the spiritual mind of the Triad functioned in a harmonious, unified way in His life. This is extremely unusual. The symbolism of the tight conjunction of these three planets is emblematic of the ancient god, Mercury, in its role as the messenger of God.

As an adult, the higher mind and the spiritual intelligence of the Triad acted in Jesus's life as one unified field of intense electrified energy. Mercury no longer expressed in relation to the personal, self-referencing intellect. Instead, Mercury functioned in accordance with its buddhic-plane expression of pure reasoning. (The rhythm of the buddhic plane reflects and expresses the harmony of pure ray four.) This brought in the influences of the higher intuitive mind once the primary duality faced upon the path—the duality between the integrated personality and the Soul—had been resolved. As a result, the buddhic-plane quality of harmony conditioned the creative impulses of the higher mind of Jesus.

The conjunction of Uranus to the Sun indicates that Jesus had an opportunity to become the voice for change. The conjunction of the Sun, Mercury, and Uranus suggests that He was to formulate and then communicate His new understanding to others, while the strong Neptune and Piscean influences in the chart of Jesus indicate that the focus for these changes was in the area of spirituality.

Sun trine Neptune (2 degrees 52 minutes)

People with a Sun trine Neptune aspect often exhibit significant intuitive abilities and inspired creativity. Today, the combination of these energies is often expressed in relation to the arts or some form of humanitarian service activities. People with this aspect often express a love toward others that is transcendent of their own personal interests and concerns. They frequently are visionaries. This is due to their sensitivity to the higher, more refined spiritual energies emanating from the love aspect of the Soul, and later emanating from the buddhic center (the love aspect) of the Triad.

For many people, when the influence of Neptune is strong, the way they look at themselves is often problematic, especially during the early stages of personal development before they have unfolded a strong sense of self. Even though they may exhibit truly inspired, uplifting creativity from time to time, their personal lives are often in shambles due to the otherworldly influences of Neptune.

Again, Neptune is antithetical to all matter forces, including the integrated personality itself. Even the ego is vulnerable to the diminutive effect the energies of Neptune have. When the Sun and Neptune are trine, however, the diminution of the little self that Neptune causes is not as disruptive as when the aspect is a square or an opposition.

How people respond to this trine varies significantly, depending on their point of evolvement and their Soul ray. For all people, this trine helps spiritualize their consciousness and diminishes one's preoccupation with the material world. This trine is especially beneficial to those who have awakened their heart centers to the energies radiating from the love petals of the lotus.

With the large number of planets in Pisces in the chart of Jesus, Neptune, as the ruler of Pisces at the personality level, was the foremost conditioning influence upon the mind of Jesus, especially in relation to the dynamics of the psyche represented by the Sun, Mercury, Venus, and Uranus. Of even greater significance was that once Jesus approached the third initiation, the higher sacred quality of ray six (which is infused with cosmic ray two) poured onto Him.

Neptune was trine the Moon, conjunct the Mid-heaven, and sextile Pluto and the earth, as well as trine the North Node and planets in Pisces. The immense influence that ray six Neptune and ray two and ray six Pisces had in Jesus's life was especially prominent and important since His Soul was on ray six—one-pointed devotion and dedication to a higher ideal. The consequence of this influence was that the integrated personality Jesus brought forth in His life was innately attuned to the Soul. There wasn't a dissonance in ray qualities that He would have had to work through before the integrated personality and Soul could be unified.

Neptune did not form a hard aspect to any astrological factor in the chart of Jesus. If there were dynamics of the psyche of Jesus that still needed to be transformed into a loving devotional condition, there would have been hard aspects formed to Neptune. The easy exchange and interplay of divine love with the large number of the dynamics of the psyche indicate that it wasn't just one psychic dynamic that was infused with the quality of essential love; rather, His entire personality was constantly being transformed by the synthesizing action of love-wisdom as He took part in different spiritual activities.

The untainted Neptunian experience of being one with God that Jesus experienced early in His life cannot be adequately described in words. It can only be experienced once people let go of the limiting and restrictive saturnine reality of the personality.

In a mundane sense, the favorable interplay and exchange of energies between the Sun and Neptune heightened Jesus's sensitivity to the feelings of others. Most likely, Jesus appeared unusual, mystical, and otherworldly. As a young teenager He probably had prophetic dreams and displayed unusual psychic abilities. Never did the reality of the matter world supplant the spiritual world that Jesus sensed and knew from childhood. Jesus was liberated from the concrete world long before He was old enough to be hardened by it.

A Pisces Sun trine Neptune prevented Jesus from unfolding characteristics, traits, and tendencies that were oriented toward advancing egocentric behavior, concerns, and initiatives. It wasn't in His nature to seek name or fame or personal power. From an early age, Jesus was obedient to the Lord of Israel—the God of the covenant and dispenser of the law. But as the energies of Pisces, Uranus, and Neptune impacted Him, Jesus realized that the very essence of God was love.

Jesus believed that Yahweh, the Lord of the covenant, moved through the people of Israel and, therefore, through its history. He also believed that the Lord was ever present in the Temple. What was unique was that Jesus realized that He could have (and had) a close, intimate relationship with the God of love outside of the Temple.

This trine in particular contributed to the unfoldment and enhancement of the immense love and devotion Jesus felt toward God, the Father. This is due to the influences of both Neptune and Pisces. Neptune serves as the receiving center in our solar system for the highest quality of ray six. It functions as the planetary focalizing agent for the powerful radiations of ray two and ray six that emanate from the sign of Pisces and cosmic ray two that radiates from the Spiritual Sun—the heart center of the Solar Logos.

The otherworldly pull of Neptune and Pisces did not feel as foreign to Jesus as it does to most people. There wasn't anything in His consciousness that resisted the strong magnetic attraction of His Soul. His disposition naturally aligned with His Soul and was responsive to the impressions of the Masters who serve as the agents of the Divine.

Granted, Jesus did not experience the intense struggle between the personal egocentric forces and the mysterious energies of the Soul that people with a strong Pisces-Neptune influence usually feel. Long before His current life, the Soul of Jesus had turned its attention upward, seeking to advance its own progression; rather than being fixated downward upon the burgeoning threefold personal consciousness.

This trine of Neptune to the Sun represents the interplay and exchange of the quality of energies that spiritualize the consciousness, first in terms of the essential love of the Soul, and later in terms of the love-wisdom of the Spiritual Triad. This was especially true in Jesus's case, since He was an old Soul who had never separated out from the Divine. With the spiritualization of the consciousness of Jesus, the inner mind's eye (the eye of wisdom) was flooded with light—a light that revealed the presence of the Divine within and all around Him. It is the inner eye of wisdom that, when filled with light, reveals the world of the Real.

Once the eye of wisdom is filled with light, the one Spirit within all life can be seen and known. This realization takes place as divine purpose, love-wisdom, and creativity pour into the consciousness of the initiate. Lofty realizations such as this, however, do not shield the initiate from feeling the pain and tribulations of humanity. However, at this higher stage, there are no dynamics within the psyche of the initiate that experience the pain and tribulations of others in a personal sense.

By the conclusion of His life, Jesus had bridged the gap in consciousness from the personal level to the Soul, from the Soul to the manasic center, and from the Soul to the buddhic center of unifying pure love-wisdom. Jesus became consciously aware of the love that eternally streams out of the heart of God.

Like all of us, there was a time in the early part of Jesus's life, however, when He had to deal with the yearnings of the Soul that tugged on His heart strings to come up higher. But for Him, this period lasted only a few short years. Relatively quickly, Jesus moved from the personal world into the world of the Soul and from the world of the Soul into the pure love-wisdom realm of the world of the Real. The almost constant showering of ray six from Neptune and rays two and six from Pisces uplifted Him into the realm of pure love-wisdom.

The personality aspect of self-initiative had moved quickly through the evolutionary stages prerequisite to being able to identify oneself with the love-wisdom aspect of God. Being able to perceive the love-wisdom aspect of the Divine requires people to develop the higher senses and faculties capable of registering the refined energies of the buddhic plane. The higher senses and faculties of the intuitional mind must be unfolded and developed before people can register and respond to the impulses of love-wisdom of the Spiritual Triad.

The opposition of Pluto to the Sun ensured that Jesus would experience successively more intense transformations, while the trine aspects that Neptune formed to His planets and luminaries ensured that the goal of each transformation was to gain a greater understanding of the love-wisdom aspect of God. By the time of His ministry, Jesus was fully attuned to the Father in its aspect of love.

The higher formless world of the Real was revealed to Jesus once He was cognizant of the Father in its second divine aspect, love-wisdom. The rays transmitted by both the constellation of Pisces and the planet Neptune paved the way. As the way shower for the Piscean Age, Jesus demonstrated the most complete form of dedication and devotion to the God of love. But His ardent devotion did not magically appear. Rather, it was the constant influx of the ray two and ray six energies transmitted by Neptune and Pisces year after year that revealed the all-inclusive God of love to Him and all around Him. .

Even if Jesus had sensed the presence of the Father Spirit in a past life, He still needed to develop the faculties, capacities, and subtle senses within His brain consciousness that could register and respond to the higher impulses and impressions of the Divine. This is true for all incarnating Souls, including realized masters should they choose to incarnate.

All levels of development and states of mind must be attained in each new incarnation. The difference with Jesus was that He had already cleared the separating personality traits and characteristics in prior lifetimes and no longer had atoms of self-consciousness that responded to the negative and limiting astral and lower mental forces. The egocentric aspects of the personality had already been transcended prior to incarnation.

He still needed to consciously link the brain, the personal mind, and the mind of the Soul to each other, and then link the spiritual mind of the Triad to the brain consciousness. This means He needed to unfold each level of the mind up through the buddhic-plane intuitional mind before He could consciously register the impressions of the intuitional mind within His brain consciousness and demonstrate Christ consciousness.

This overwhelming emphasis upon Neptune and Pisces in the chart of Jesus led Him into the kingdom of heaven (the realm of pure light, love, truth, and wisdom). Sometime prior to His public ministry, He realized that this realm of light and enfolding love was His home, not the earth. This was especially pronounced in His life, due to the otherworldly influences of Neptune and Pisces, which had denied Jesus the opportunity to feel at home on earth.

As a result of the interplay and exchange of energies between the Sun and Neptune, along with the close relationship formed between the psychic dynamics represented by the planets of the epic grand trine, Jesus achieved one of the most important realizations attainable in the evolutionary system of earth: *"I am in the Father and the Father is in me."*[31] This mystical realization is so much greater than words can convey. It is not that the energies of Neptune and Pisces brought forth this realization; rather, they stimulated the type of spiritual activities (intense prayer and long periods of contemplation and meditation) that resulted in this profound experience and realization.

Jesus soon identified more with the spiritual world within than with the outer world. In the kingdom, He was embraced by a love that knows no bounds. Because of the effect this great love had upon Him, Jesus became increasingly more inclusive of others each day. Ultimately, His devotional love became so intense that it shattered the causal force field that enveloped the Soul. Upon the ray six path of the Soul that Jesus walked, the destruction of the causal body occurs when the force field of the causal body can no longer contain one's ever-expanding love and devotion. Once the causal body is eliminated, the new master becomes sensitive and responsive to even greater expressions of love-wisdom.

The causal body is shattered in different ways, depending on the ray that the Soul is on. Once the causal body is shattered, however, the consciousness shifts from the causal level into the buddhic, intuitional plane. At this higher level, there were no forces that obstructed Jesus's inclusive sensitivity toward life.

During His ministry, Jesus spent an immense amount of time talking about, describing, and indicating what people must do in order to enter into the kingdom. First and foremost,

---

[31] John 14:10. (RSV) (italics added)

this kingdom is not a location. *"The kingdom of God is in the midst of you."*[32] This is an esoteric concept that is difficult for the concrete mind to fully grasp due to its dependence upon the physical senses and brain. How can the kingdom be within, around, and all about? Such a realization must be experienced in the deeper states of meditation, prayer, and contemplation.

Jesus discovered this kingdom within Him and yet all around Him. He then devoted His life to telling others about it, exclaiming that it was at hand. It was (and is) accessible in the here and now of each moment since it is a state of mind. Terms like the kingdom of heaven and the Father were familiar words people could relate to two thousand years ago. But using such terms to describe a lofty, nonphysical state of mind and realization opens the door to misinterpretation and misunderstanding.

Jesus summarized the prerequisites for entering this kingdom when a man asked,

> *What must I do to inherit eternal life?*[33]

> Jesus replied: *You know the commandments: Do not kill, Do not steal, Do not bear false witness, Do not defraud, Honor your father and mother.*[34]

> When the individual replied he had obeyed these since His youth, Jesus added, *You lack one thing; go, sell what you have, and give to the poor, and you will have treasure in heaven.*[35]

All but the last commandment relates to the laws of humanity, which people must obey before they can achieve accepted discipleship. A willingness to sacrifice one's material possessions and serve the poor, on the other hand, corresponds to the Laws of the Soul and to the sacrifices that are required of people to attain the third initiation. This step was not something the individual was ready to take. This verse indicates that people enter the kingdom of heaven once the third initiation is attained. (The continuity of life continues once the physical body drops, but most people awake in their astral body or their lower mental body, depending on the level of development they had attained during their lifetimes. Others awake in the realm Jesus referred to as the kingdom of heaven.)

When Jesus was asked which commandment was the greatest, He replied,

---

[32] Luke 17:21. (RSV) (italics added)
[33] Mark 10:17. (RSV) (italics added)
[34] Mark 10:19. (RSV) (italics added)
[35] Mark 10:21. (RSV) (italics added)

You shall love the Lord your God with all your heart, and with all your soul, and with all your mind. This is the great and first commandment. And the second is like it. You shall love your neighbor as yourself. On these two commandments depend all the law and the prophets.[36]

These words of Jesus are a perfect example of an advanced ray six initiate attuned to the higher qualities of ray six Neptune and strongly influenced by the ray two and ray six energies Pisces transmits. This trine of Neptune to His Pisces Sun helped Jesus realize the importance of people's love for God and for one another. These biblical verses represent the truth that initiates realize on the path of the heart.

Divine truth can only be experienced when the initiate obeys the universal Laws of the Soul and is able to respond consciously to the impressions of the buddhic realm of love-wisdom and truth. As planetary transits and progressions heightened the exchange and interplay of the energies of Neptune and Pisces in His life, Jesus realized a much deeper mystical oneness with the Divine than anyone had previously realized. A sense of a relationship, and later oneness, with God which the energies of Pisces and Neptune brought forth resulted in Jesus's awareness of the presence of the God within Him and within others.

Though the Soul may experience a number of initiations prior to a new incarnation, the physical and subtle bodies are generated anew each incarnation. They, therefore, need to be prepared for initiation and readied to express greater aspects of the Soul and later express the qualities and capacities of the Monad.

Before Jesus could teach others how to approach the kingdom of heaven via the path of the heart, He needed to walk the path Himself. This He accomplished by unfolding the intelligence, the love, and the will of the Soul (the will of God), then the love aspect of the Spiritual Self or Triad. Through His attunement to the Soul, He was transformed into the nature and qualities of the Soul. This took place as He mastered the physical-etheric, the astral-emotional, and the mental forces that sought to express in His life via the lower etheric centers.

Jesus not only gained a mastery of His own three aspects of personal consciousness as a third-degree initiate, but attained the fourth initiation as well. This was accomplished as a result of Jesus's ability to respond to the influences of the rays that the signs and outer planets transmit, especially ray two and ray six.

Having completed much of the work preparatory to the path of the heart in a prior life and successfully retracing the steps of the initiate in His current life, Jesus was able to

---

[36] Matt. 22:37–40. (RSV) (italics added)

reach the last step upon the path of the heart. This step can only be taken when the initiate is strongly influenced by Pisces.

It is the Piscean unifying synthesis of all of the spiritual growth over countless lifetimes that enabled Jesus to complete the steps and stages of the path of the heart. The reward for this accomplishment was the right to serve as a World Savior. According to universal law, a World Savior comes forth on the energies of Pisces and is always sacrificed upon the earth. This event represents the final act of service and sacrifice in the lives of all initiates once the final step upon the path of the heart has been reached.

Chapter 8

The Coloring of the Personality (Part Two)

Sun opposite Pluto (1 degree 38 minutes)

The opposition of Pluto to the Sun is an extremely powerful aspect for a number of reasons. Pluto is the center for the transmission of ray one energy—the potent forces of life, purpose, and will. Unfortunately, most people only know the planetary forces of Pluto in its expression as the destroyer.

Most likely, Jesus experienced the forces of Pluto in its role as the destroyer, due to Pluto's opposition to the Sun, Mercury, and Uranus, and its inconjunction to Mars and Saturn. In effect, Pluto represented the world Satan that Jesus initially resisted but eventually conquered, just like the world heroes before Him.

Pluto represents a powerful outside force that impacted the life of Jesus. It would have seemed like an outside force since the dynamic of the will had yet to be fully integrated into His consciousness.

In general, the planetary forces of Pluto represent an evolutionary force or dynamic that lies deep within people's constitution, but not within the light of people's conscious awareness. The life forms of all things contain the seeds of their own death. It is these seeds that Pluto activates. Life and death are the two sides of the same coin in the created realms of the three planes of earth.

In relation to the evolution of consciousness, Pluto captures the light of the self (represented by the Sun) and transports it into the unpleasant, dank depths of the instinctual, lower emotional world of the unconscious, i.e., the underworld. As a result, people often feel afflicted or assaulted by the pain and sorrow they feel as a result of the events in their lives that Pluto precipitates. Pluto commonly activates ancient patterns of instinctual behavior and feelings.

Due to the prominence of Pluto in His chart, Jesus had to confront and systematically master the forces of darkness and evil, especially during His early years. What is important is that Jesus was willing to confront that which He thought of as evil and gain command of it. But He really didn't have much of a choice.

Pluto served as the focusing lens through which the planetary forces of the epic grand trine impacted Him. This resulted in intense and powerful periods of transformation. By way of the difficulties Pluto precipitated, Jesus gained control and then mastery over these planetary forces, i.e., over the various dynamics of His psyche. Most likely Jesus gained command over the dynamics of His personal consciousness at a relatively young age and unified them into one concentrated field, first as the integrated personality and then as the Soul. Once He attained the third initiation, however, Pluto became the lens focusing all seven rays that the planets of the epic grand trine transmitted, concentrating them into one beam of intense light. It was this multicolored beam of light that illumined the path of initiation before Him.

In a number of ways, the Sun and Pluto stand in stark contrast to each other, especially in terms of the evolution of consciousness. The Sun stands for the light, while Pluto represents that which is dark or hidden.

At a deeper level, Pluto serves as an agent of ray one spiritual prana, which is divine life-force that gives life to the consciousness and to the forms through which life expresses; while the rays of the physical Sun transmit the physical-etheric prana that the physical body absorbs via the etheric body and spleen.

Pluto represents the primal power of ray one within nature, itself—the divine life-force that streams onto all that exists. The ray one energies of the will also have an especially potent effect upon the astral-emotional forces. Ray one is the most powerful force found in our solar system and the most dangerous force to the uninitiated. When the Sun and Pluto form an opposition to each other, the two psychic dynamics they represent must form a relationship. Together, these two types of prana confer significant physical vitality, stamina, and regenerative powers once the Sun and Pluto are appropriately related to each other.

As the transmitter of ray one, the energies of Pluto initially stream into the crown center of the etheric body at the first sub-plane level and vitalize the physical body. The ray one energies of Pluto, therefore, have a great effect upon the physical body, its vitality, and its ability to act in life.

In a number of ways, Pluto and the Sun are the antithesis of each other. The Sun represents the personal self and its initiative, as well as the present moment. It represents the light of the conscious self. Pluto, on the other hand, awakens the deep psychological patterns of the past, especially the lower emotional-sentient aspects of the unconscious. This includes psychic remnants of the instinctual primitive man that still respond to the ancient rhythm of the earth and affect human behavior from the realm of the unconscious. For this reason, Pluto represents darkness.

Pluto in its aspect as the destroyer was quite active during the first year and a half of Jesus's life and again at the time of His Crucifixion. Analysis of the planetary transits supports the idea that Jesus's life was in danger during the first two years of His life. During the period in between infancy and just prior to His ministry, however, the energies generated by this opposition expressed mainly in terms of personal transformation, endings and new beginnings. Undoubtedly, Pluto triggered a number of intense transformations in His life.

Because of the frequency of these transformations, the rate at which Jesus progressed was greatly accelerated. This opposition of Pluto to the Sun, Mercury, and Uranus triggered the rapid transformation and renewal of the life, mind, and consciousness of Jesus right up through His attainment of Christ consciousness.

In general, the transformations people experience consequent to Pluto's influence arise from all kinds of experiences and events that challenge not only the way people express themselves as human beings, but also their beliefs, thoughts, feelings, goals, and objectives (depending on the signs, houses, and rays associated with the opposition).

Whenever Pluto opposes the Sun, there is an evolutionary need to completely transform all aspects of one's life; however, the specific goal behind a particular transformation varies from person to person, depending on the signs and houses involved and the point of evolvement that has been attained.

A high percentage of people with this opposition refuse to use this energy to transform their own behavior and actions. Instead, they project this energy onto the society or onto people around them and attempt to change them. Many of the difficult problems this tendency triggers arise because of the demands people with this opposition impose on others. To them, it is the other person who must change. Frequently, they insist that the government, the spouse, the boss, etc., must change to fit their own opinions of what is right or appropriate. In general, they exhibit a might-makes-right attitude and a determined willfulness that can have serious consequences. When this is the case, the opportunity to make the needed changes in one's life that this opposition calls for is lost.

In other words, people with this opposition who are still functioning at the level of personal development tend to misuse this ray one power of will to exert control, manipulate, and dominate both the people in their lives and the groups with which they are associated. Such people are often thought of as being controlling, authoritarian, and even despotic. Thus, people express the energies of this opposition as either a drive to radically transform one's own life or the life of others.

The average person with this opposition tends to express the energy generated by the opposition in a manipulative, domineering, and sometimes ruthless way to gain power over others. This is especially true of men. Here, Pluto energizes and intensifies the personal will which, when selfishly exerted, can have unpleasant consequences. In general, people are unable to handle the powerful forces of the will. They often use the energy generated to covertly control others, but such behavior releases powerful forces that precipitate chaos, disruption, and destruction in their own lives. Fortunately, Jesus did not have the willful emotional patterns that these potent forces can activate.

Those who have mastered the lower forces and transcended the integrated personality are able to express this plutonian energy constructively. As a result, they are able to bring forth the highest qualities of love-wisdom on the waves of divine will. This is possible once the disciple has first applied the forces that this opposition generates to transform his or her own behavior.

Pluto confers the deepest, most penetrating insights of all planetary influences. Such insights help people see their inappropriate patterns of emotions, feelings, and behavior so they can eliminate them. Thus, Pluto can activate patterns of negative emotions and feelings within the subconscious. This enables people to observe and work to eliminate them. Consequent to the elimination of the lower negative emotional patterns of behavior, people are transformed, regenerated, and renewed.

Pluto opposite the Sun demands periodic clearing and cleansing of the threefold personality. It calls for a clearing out of the inappropriate instinctual and emotional patterns of the little self. Often, people work to eliminate their lower instinctual habits, emotions, and behavior because of the painful and difficult experiences that Pluto precipitates. Such unpleasant experiences help people realize they need to make important changes in their lives. This cleansing of the mind and consciousness is ongoing in people's lives right up until that time when there is nothing left that separates the individual from the Soul.

People with a Pluto-Sun aspect in their natal charts frequently have an unusual ability to renew and regenerate themselves. Again, this is due the ray one aspect of life that Pluto transmits. With the opposition (and more so with the square), the regeneration, transformation, and reorientation of the self that is offered by Pluto is frequently resisted and unwanted. People often squander the opportunity for change and transformation that Pluto offers. Instead, they blame the government or something in the society or the people in their lives for the difficulties they experience. Some blame Satan. Yet, the difficulties they are experiencing originate with the evolutionary forces within them.

Pluto stimulates the forces within all three subtle bodies in a way that precipitate change, death and destruction in some area of life, resulting in personal transformation. Although such experiences can be unpleasant, plutonian forces can regenerate and renew one's life physically, emotionally, and mentally (depending on what planets or angles are involved).

Ideally, the tension generated by this opposition destroys the elements of the threefold personal consciousness that obstruct the light of the Soul and imprison the consciousness in the three matter planes of earth. This destruction is necessary in order to transform the threefold personal consciousness into the threefold higher self. The need to make significant changes in one's life and to let go of the past is central to the evolutionary processes that move humanity forward upon the path. Such transformative processes ultimately lead to the liberation of consciousness from the influences of the matter intelligences. This occurs once the prerequisite development of the astral-emotional and lower mental faculties, capacities, abilities, and senses has taken place.

At the personal level of development, the energies of Pluto encourage people to closely examine that which lies deep within them. But when people refuse to direct the deep, penetrating insights of Pluto to ascertain the cause for their difficulties, they tend to retaliate against people around them or blame the government and society for their difficulties.

Frequently, people with Pluto opposite the Sun become rather critical and attack the rules, norms, and taboos of society. As a result, the transforming forces that this opposition generates can be disruptive. Whether people's criticisms are constructive or destructive depends on the stage of evolvement the individual has attained.

Given the dominant astrological factors of His chart, Jesus naturally focused the penetrating light of Pluto on Himself first and then on the society, but not in a self-serving way. Jesus rejected many of the dietary rules and the inviolable laws that maintained the ethnic purity of the Judeans. He had contact with lepers and associated with known sinners. He forgave prostitutes and exhibited the psychic-intuitive powers that Judeans thought of as sorcery. This included the ability to see the past and the future of others.

He conversed with the unclean Samaritans and gathered food on the Sabbath. He closely associated with Jews and non-Jews, and with the most despised people in Judea, the Roman tax collector. At the same time, He criticized the holiest members of the Judean society, the Pharisees, for their feigned displays of piety.

Those with Sun opposite Pluto have an ability to unmask people and expose their hypocrisy. They can pierce the outer shell that protects the social norms and taboos of society, exposing the underbelly of society for all to see. Constructive criticism is fine as long as people do it impersonally and offer a better way to accomplish something, but when people use the energy generated by this opposition to critically attack others, rather than shine the penetrating light of Pluto upon oneself, they are missing a great opportunity for growth.

Why do you see the speck that is in your brother's eye, but do not notice the log that is in your own eye? Or how can you say to your brother, 'Let me take the speck out of your eye,' when there is the log in your own eye? You hypocrite, first take the log out of your own eye, and then you will see clearly to take the speck out of your brother's eye.[37]

Having clarity of mind and purity of heart—the product of lifetimes of work—Jesus saw the spiritual hypocrisy of people and frequently pointed it out to His disciples. As with all types of glamour, the glamour of being spiritually superior is just as egoistic as the glamour of arrogance and other forms of personal superiority. Needless to say, Jesus's habit of shining a light upon the Pharisees and pointing out that their righteousness as feigned piety was not well received.

By definition, Pluto opposite the Sun confers a tendency to express oneself in a powerful and extreme way. Overturning the *"tables of the money-changers and the seats of those who sold pigeons"*[38] in the Temple Court is a perfect example of the willful intensity that this Pluto opposition expresses. Overturning the tables, however, was not driven by personal anger or rage, but by the offense to God Jesus believed such activity to be. They *"have made it* (the Temple) *a den of robbers."*[39] The money-changers were profiting from their sales on what Jesus viewed as the sacred grounds of the Temple. True sacrifice is a sacrifice of something people value. When people can throw down a couple of coins and purchase their sacrifice for the Temple, it is not the kind of sacrifice that is required upon the path. Such activity is merely a commercial transaction that in Jesus's mind had no place on the grounds of the Holy Temple. This was the point Jesus was making.

In the chart of Jesus, this opposition serves a number of purposes. The opposition from Pluto to the Sun is an intense energizing factor that conferred the divine life-force and power of the will that Jesus needed to accomplish His mission. Without the influx of this intense willpower acting upon Him, He would have accomplished little that affected anyone other than those around Him.

Pluto, the planetary agent of divine will, precipitates all kinds of transformation on earth. Through its actions as the destroyer, the obstacles that interfere with attaining a higher state are destroyed. The removal and destruction of the things in people's lives that have run their course always takes place as a result of the influences of the outer planets, especially Pluto. This occurs even when people refuse to let go of something. But all plutonian destruction

---

[37] Matt. 7:3–7:5. (RSV) (italics added)
[38] Mark 11:15. (RSV) (italics added)
[39] Mark 11:17. (RSV) (italics added)

is followed by the actions of the will in its second sub-ray aspect of the builder. The ray one energies of Pluto and Vulcan are used to build a more appropriate form in one's life to replace that which has been removed or destroyed.

The regenerative power of Pluto brings the self (once identified with the old structure and ways of life) back to life in a new, more appropriate structure or form. Life is periodically renewed and regenerated whenever a portion of that life is liberated from an obsolete, confining structure. Ray one in its aspect of life gives life to the new forms and structures through which the consciousness can unfold and advance.

With Pluto opposing the Sun in Pisces in Jesus's chart, it was primarily the love-wisdom aspect that was cyclically regenerated and strengthened in the heart and mind of Jesus. The energy generated also strengthened His devotion and dedication to serving God and mankind.

Since this aspect is an opposition, however, many of the experiences precipitated by this opposition were unpleasant. The points of tension this opposition created shifted his consciousness higher, even when the experiences Pluto precipitated were unpleasant. This shift is possible when people do not react to adversity in negative personal way.

Because of this opposition, the intensity with which Jesus expressed Himself and the authority He conveyed would have been beyond that which the ruling authorities of Judea exhibited. By the time of His ministry, Jesus no longer demonstrated personal will or personal authority as in the case of most leaders. Rather, He embodied and emanated a light and power that originated in the higher planes. Since ray one rules governments and governance, it is understandable how the expression of this plutonian force precipitated conflicts between Jesus and the religious authorities.

This opposition in combination with Jesus's initiate status conferred a higher power and authority on Jesus that some people may have sensed but few understood. Those in positions of religious authority would have especially resisted His teachings and feared His commanding power. There were some open-minded Judeans who listened to Him on occasion, hoping He was the messiah who would save the Jewish people from the seemingly unending foreign domination; someone who would overthrow the dominion of Rome. But this was not the mission of Jesus.

The mission of Jesus was not secular in nature. He did not incarnate to overthrow the hegemony of Roman governance, so Judea could reclaim their sovereign theocratic state along the lines of King Solomon. Rather, His mission was to overthrow the rule of man so the essential love of the world of the Soul (the kingdom) could come forth on earth.

Of great significance is that this opposition pinpoints the step and stage of the path that Jesus had attained prior to incarnating. According to esoteric astrology, the Sun represents the initiating personal self who loosely ties the various dynamics of the psyche together. Throughout the stage of personal development, Neptune and Jupiter, as the co-rulers of Pisces, were the co-rulers of Jesus's life in relation to His evolution of His consciousness.

Since Pluto is the Soul-centered ruler of Pisces, an opposition of Pluto to a Pisces Sun indicates that when Jesus first incarnated, the will aspect of the Soul had yet to be fully integrated into His consciousness. Initially in His life, there was an aspect of the will of the Soul that still appeared to be outside of His consciousness that acted upon Him. Thus, the first truly new step upon His path involved relating the will of the Soul to the personal will.

Planetary oppositions require people to relate the two dynamics of the psyche represented by the planets opposed to each other. Since Pluto is a vehicle of ray one will, it was the personality (the Sun) in its expression of the personal will that needed to be related to the will of the Soul. (Pluto's opposition to Mercury indicates that the will of the Soul also needed to be related to the mental aspect of His personal consciousness.)

When Jesus incarnated, His Soul had yet to fully demonstrate a mastery over the personal will that disciples must demonstrate in order to attain the third initiation. The third initiation occurs once sufficient energies of the sacrifice (will) petals stimulate the mind and consciousness in a way that brings forth a complete sacrifice of the threefold personal consciousness. Until that time, the factor of separatism, which taints the threefold personal consciousness, still had a small degree of influence upon Him.

To attain the third initiation, all that separates the selfhood from the Soul must be sacrificed. This includes the sacrifice of both the things people love and those that they hate, for the Soul is self-less. All personally held ideas, beliefs, views, and opinions need to be sacrificed in order to transcend the integrated personality and function as a Soul. Only then is the consciousness polarized in the realm of the Soul.

The process whereby the various elements of personal consciousness are sacrificed usually spans lifetimes. Such sacrifice occurs repeatedly as the energies of the sacrifice petals stream through the upper region of the mental body into the crown center of the etheric body. This energy empowers the consciousness in a way that results in a complete sacrifice of the not-self.

Slowly, all elements of the egocentric self are transformed into the three aspects of consciousness of the higher self. In this way, the will of the Soul takes command over the personality instrument. Only then can the light of personal self be transferred into the light of the Soul.

It appears that the kinds of spiritual activities that help unify the integrated personality with the Soul had been taking place for lifetimes prior to Jesus's incarnation. During the most recent past life, the Soul-infused personality was about to experience the unification of the integrated personality and Soul when he or she died.

Since the will of the Soul was not in full command when Jesus incarnated, the final battle between the dweller-on-the-threshold and the Angel of the Presence had yet to take place. Jesus had already thrown his weight, so to speak, behind the Angel, but the dweller wasn't completely absorbed into the light of the Angel. This probably took place when Jesus was in his mid-twenties.

The three temptations in the desert represent Jesus's mastery over the three sub-aspects of the mental nature, resulting in the attainment of the third initiation. At the third initiation, disciples must demonstrate their ability to resist any temptation to selfishly misuse their advanced powers. Only when these tests are passed can the training by the Masters of the Spiritual Hierarchy begin in earnest. In Jesus's case, He started to receive occult training well before His ministry.

The ceremony in which the Masters of Hierarchy acknowledged that Jesus had attained the third initiation, however, didn't take place until His ministry. This event was recorded in the synoptic Gospels as the transfiguration on the mount. During the third initiation ceremony, disciple's mastery of the mental aspect of consciousness is sealed in the aura of the new initiate by the light of the rod of initiation that the Hierophant wields. Once the third initiation has been attained, the application of this rod opens the doorway of the mind to the life of the manasic or buddhic realms.

As a result of this opposition between the Sun and Pluto, the plutonian forces activated significant transformation of the personal will and consciousness of Jesus, readying Him for this final sacrifice of the personal will. This occurred as the plutonian power was integrated into His consciousness. As a result, Jesus unfolded a strong sense of will and purpose, which He accepted as the will of God. Fortunately, Jesus was beyond the stage in which He would have used these forces to overpower others for His own benefit.

By the time of His ministry, Jesus truly knew the will of God, although few people in Judea could accept that He did or believe that He was truly responsive to the will of God. The ruling authorities in particular could not fathom how Jesus had earned the right to state that He knew the Father and his will. They concluded that the authority He claimed and the powers He exhibited most likely originated with Beelzebub, since not even the Holy Council of the Temple (the Sanhedrin) demonstrated such powers and strength.

Once Jesus attained the third initiation, He only had a few more steps upon the path of the heart before He transitioned onto the path of power. These steps involved intensifying and further expanding the aspect of love-wisdom through devotion and dedication to God and mankind. This intensification of the power of love, along with a greater influx of the will of the Spiritual Self, shattered the refined field of energy enveloping the Soul (the causal body). Once this field of causal light was dispersed at the fourth initiation, Jesus stepped onto the path of power.

When an initiate attains the fourth initiation either by way of the path of the heart, as Jesus did, or by the path of the mind (loving intelligence), they step onto the path of power and become a full-fledged master. As a master, Jesus then turned His attention toward embodying and expressing the divine will. This calls for the development of an ability in which the master has command over the forces of nature that operate within and through the three planes of earth.

Jesus, as with all masters, first needed to demonstrate His mastery over the forces of the three planes of earth in terms of His own subtle bodies and threefold personal consciousness. This results in the third initiation. Initiates as they approach the fourth initiation, however, must demonstrate command over the collective planetary forces of the three planes of earth.

This level of mastery includes an ability to direct and command the forces within and expressing through the three subtle bodies of others. Since ill health is primarily caused by dense negative forces in the subtle bodies that block the life-giving forces of the Soul, this ability to have command over the forces of three matter planes endows a master with significant healing powers. (This does not grant the master the right to violate the karma of another person.)

During His life, Jesus reached that point in mind and spirit when He stepped from the path of the heart onto the path of power. When this occurred, the training Jesus received to command the forces of the physical-etheric, astral, and lower mental planes intensified. Any exercise of such occult power is dangerous prior to overcoming people's responsiveness to the forces of the three planes of earth.

Jesus is likely to have exhibited unusual psychic abilities from a young age, but it wasn't until His later years that He was trained in how to control the forces of the three matter planes. Training by the Masters of the Spiritual Hierarchy usually begins once an initiate approaches the third initiation, but occult training doesn't usually begin until an initiate approaches the fourth initiation.

In past lives, Jesus undoubtedly distributed the energies from the healing reservoir of light located in the world of the Soul to heal others. The healing powers Jesus unfolded in this lifetime, however, involved transmitting the healing life-forces located in the higher atmic plane of living light. These healing energies can regenerate and rejuvenate all living organisms. They represent a quality that has a commanding power over the twenty-one types of matter forces found in the three planes of matter.

At some time in His late twenties, once He had gained command over the energies generated by this Pluto-Sun-Uranus opposition, Jesus was taught how to work with these high-frequency energies of living light. Command over the forces of the three matter planes must be achieved before someone is able to serve as a World Savior. Such command requires a level of one-pointed concentration that only a master can achieve.

Since Jesus's consciousness was not polarized at the atmic plane level, atmic energies were still outside of His consciousness, not a part of it. To Him, these energies constituted the Father, which He invoked to still the winds and waters and expel the unclean spirits. Jesus believed that the Father healed physical maladies and calmed the winds. For this reason, Jesus prayed to the Father to accomplish such things. This is as it should be.

The miracles that a fourth-degree initiate is capable of performing are rarely seen on earth since, once the fourth initiation is attained, there are no elements of consciousness within the causal field of forces that can pull a fourth-degree master back into incarnation. All karma in relation to the three planes of earth has been eliminated.

Historically, the initiate has died shortly after taking the third initiation or the fourth initiation for the first time.[40] This is due to the nervous system's inability to handle the significantly higher-frequency energies and rays that pour onto the new third- or fourth-degree initiate.

Once the fourth initiation is attained, the Soul no longer has a need to incarnate on earth. All personal karma has been resolved and there is nothing within the mind, consciousness, or life of the fourth-degree initiate that could violate universal law. Henceforth, the master only incarnates for the purpose of fulfilling a divine mission, e.g., to transmute planetary karma or to anchor new teachings on earth.

By way of Neptune, Jesus was a mystic—a lover of God. By way of Uranus, Jesus was a divine messenger and occultist who delivered the teachings for the Piscean Age. By way of Pluto, Jesus was a miracle worker. More than any other astrological factor, this opposition of Pluto to the Sun enabled Jesus to unfold the occult powers necessary to perform miracles. Miracles involve the transformation of physical matter from one state or condition to another. (The intuition, as well as clairvoyance, clairaudience, etc., are subtle senses that do not involve the alteration or transformation of physical substances.)

Occultism is a faster way to attain higher states of realization than mysticism, but it is a

---

[40] The personality has never existed before the current lifetime; however, that which the Soul has achieved in a former incarnation is imprinted upon the causal field. The individual, therefore, benefits, as well as suffers, from the past-life activities of various personalities as they worked through their incarnations. Once an initiation has been attained, the future incarnations of that Soul would find it relatively easy to attain the initiation that a past life had achieved.

more dangerous path. People should not be involved in consciously manipulating the forces of nature before they are approaching the third initiation. Once the third initiation has been achieved, people are not likely to misuse these powers. There is still a portion of the spiritual ego, however, that must be transcended. This occurs at the fourth initiation. Technically, people can generate new karmic patterns up until the fourth initiation.

Jesus's occult training, in which He learned how to control and manipulate the physical, astral, and lower mental forces, and have command over evil spirits, appears to have started prior to His fourth initiation. This is understandable, given the potency of this opposition.

The probability that Jesus would unfold great occult powers during His life was quite high, due to the kite configuration in His chart and Pluto's role as the focusing lens of all seven rays that the planets of the epic grand trine transmitted. Once the forces generated by the oppositions Pluto formed to the Sun, Mercury, and Uranus had completed their transformative work upon the personality, ray one that Pluto transmitted carried the seven rays of manifestation directly onto the (brain) consciousness of Jesus, infusing Him with great power.

Demonstration of occult powers was not as unusual two thousand years ago as people might think. The masters of the mystery schools throughout the Mediterranean area, along with a large number of the masters of the East, have exhibited miraculous powers for millennia, but no one has ever demonstrated the breadth of powers that Jesus did.

Sun trine Moon (5 degrees 13 minutes)

Although the Sun trine Moon aspect is quite common and seems less significant than the preceding aspects, the importance of the Sun and Moon in relation to the development of the personality of Jesus and the fact that the Sun and Moon represent two of the three points of the epic grand trine makes the Sun trine Moon aspect exceedingly important. Since both the Sun and Moon have a large orb of influence, five degrees separation from an exact trine is reasonably close.

The Moon relates to the deep feeling patterns that people have unfolded over countless lifetimes. It therefore represents the past in a psychological sense as well as the past-life influences that greatly affect the type and quality of emotions, desires, and the emotional reactions people express in their lives.

The sign and house placements of the Moon and the aspects formed to the Moon provide clues about people's early childhood. They also affect the way they are likely to remember their childhood. As a rule, the Moon dominates the development of the personality up to the age of fourteen for males and has historically dominated the personality of women throughout their lives. Though this is less true today, women tend to be more in touch with their feelings than men.

The Sun trine Moon indicates that there was a harmonious interaction between Jesus's inner emotional nature and His personal will, initiative, and sense of self. And since the Moon formed eight major aspects of ease (primarily trines), there was little from His past that would have disrupted the harmonious exchange and interplay of energies between the planets of the epic grand trine.

Jesus was basically free of all self-referencing feelings, personal emotional patterns, and unfulfilled desires. This means that He was relatively free of all deep personal longings and desires that needed to be satisfied before He could integrate and unify the three aspects of the personal self. Being free of past-life personal habits, behavioral patterns, tendencies, and proclivities, Jesus wasn't distracted by the personal yearnings of the past as most people. In general, people have to deal with and experience the consequences of the patterns of personal behavior and emotions before they are able to perceive the path. Jesus was also free of both personal and familial karma. This indicates that there was nothing in His past and most likely nothing that occurred in His early childhood that needed to be addressed before He could pursue the opportunities before Him in His life.

As a result of the clearing and cleansing of His astral-emotional desire nature in recent past lives, His unconscious worked well with His consciousness. There were no patterns in the unconscious that usurped the divine life-forces streaming onto Him (via the silver cord). Nor were there any low vibratory forces in His astral body that would have obstructed or interfered with the influx of these divine life-forces emanating from the Monad (via the Soul). When this is the case, people exhibit significant vitality, stamina, and unusual recuperative powers.

People with a Sun trine Moon aspect in their charts often exhibit a harmony and balance between the masculine and feminine dynamics of the psyche. They are able to express their masculine side in terms of their ability to act in life and take the initiative, as well as express their more feminine, receptive, reflective, and sensitive side.

The exchange and interplay of energies between a Pisces Sun trine a Cancer Moon confer an inner peace, harmony, and optimism. With the Moon in Cancer (which it rules at the personality level), the inner emotional aspect of consciousness was not in need of additional conditioning. If the Moon had been in another sign, Jesus would have had to complete the development of the feeling-sentient aspect of consciousness that another sign would contribute before He could work on His mental-spiritual development.

The energies of the Sun energize the lower mental component of self-consciousness which, when integrated with the emotional component of self-consciousness, constitutes the core of the self of the integrated personality. Since the Sun was in Pisces and the Moon formed a trine to both the Sun and Moon, ray six Neptune conditioned both the emotional and mental aspects of His personal consciousness, not just the astral-emotional aspect. This enabled Jesus to attain the stage of the integrated personality at an early age and accelerated the spiritualization of all three aspects of His personal consciousness.

Esoterically speaking, the energies of the Moon are on ray four (harmony through conflict), while the Sun in Pisces is conditioned by ray two and ray six. This Sun-Moon trine further emphasized the ray two, ray four, and ray six line of influence that dominated Jesus's life. Today, this line is known as the path of the heart.

With a Pisces Sun trine a Cancer Moon and the Sun and Moon trine Neptune, it was only natural for Jesus to unfold and develop a strong devotion to the God of love. Pisces is the transmitter of both the higher qualities of ray two and ray six, while Neptune is a higher expression of ray six, which is infused with cosmic ray two at the higher levels. In addition, the epic water grand trine strongly emphasized ray six. Because of this heightened emphasis on the ray two, ray four, and ray six line, along with the quality of sensitivity and conscious responsiveness to these ray qualities that was innate to His disposition, Jesus was able to experience God as love.

The preponderance of these Piscean-Neptunian influences in His life accelerated Jesus's progression along the path of the heart and opened the door to a full realization of God in its aspect of love-wisdom. As a result of attaining this lofty realization, Jesus was able to shift His consciousness upward and experience the kingdom of heaven firsthand.

The kingdom of heaven is not some heavenly place where good people go once the physical body drops or when Gabriel blows His horn to awaken humanity from their graves. Jesus experienced the kingdom in the here and now. The quality of life in the kingdom of heaven is one of unbounded love, compassion, humility, and enlightened bliss. It is a realm of sacrificing service. By way of His loving, selfless service, Jesus expressed unconditional love. Esoterically, this center of sacrificing love is referred to as the planetary heart center.

Sun conjunct Venus (7 degrees 13 minutes)

In a simplistic sense, Venus relates to what people personally love. When people are at the level of personal development, it corresponds to the magnetic attractive force people use to connect themselves to the not-self. By way of this planetary force, people energetically bind themselves to one another and to the material things of earth.

At the personal level, Venus is associated with the desire nature. Its magnetic attractive forces have been used throughout history in a way that builds up a psychological attachment to the things of earth and to the people in one's life. Historically, this energy has been misused to link people to the past—to a moment of the eternal now that is no longer active. The sign and house placement of Venus indicates the types of relationships that people are attracted to and the kinds of material things they desire and attract to them.

At a higher level, Venus represents the component of the mind that reveals, especially in the sense that it is the light of Venus that reveals the second aspect of the Divine (love-wisdom). When people function at the stage of development of the threefold personal consciousness and are preoccupied with the material world, however, Venus reveals love at its lowest level of expression. Unknowingly, people are often drawn to both people and things that resonate with their past-life attachments and emotion-based attractions.

When the Sun and Venus are in Pisces and conjunct each other, people are often drawn to a deeper, mystical quality of love. A conjunction of a Pisces Sun and Venus brings forth a deep, mystical quality of love in people's lives. In Jesus's life, this placement of Venus and its conjunction with His Piscean Sun conferred an otherworldly quality to His life, a soothing, comforting voice, and a mystique that was especially noticeable when people looked into His eyes.

According to traditional astrology, the Sun conjunct Venus aspect often leads to a fondness for romantic trysts, social activities, and glamorous displays. But due to His mastery of the lower astral forces, which attract people to glamour, Jesus did not respond in such a way. Instead, the interplay of energies of this conjunction revealed a higher quality of love that enabled Him to connect to and express a higher quality of love than what was previously seen on earth. This higher quality of love is expressed as deep compassion, mercy, forgiveness, and unconditional love. Interestingly, this conjunction often manifests as a special fondness and love of children.

As a disciple, the conjunction of the Sun and Venus represents an opportunity to blend and unify ray two and ray five qualities. This may seem strange, given Venus's association with love and attraction at the personal level, but at the Soul level, it is Venus that bridges the two lines of the rays of manifestation. Thus, by way of this conjunction, the two lines of approach to the Divine were linked together in Jesus's life.

The linking of these two approaches to the Divine was especially important to Jesus, since His consciousness was so dominated by the feeling, love aspect. Once Jesus attained the third initiation and came under the influence of Pluto as the Soul ruler of Pisces, the linking of these two ray lines allowed for the development that was necessary in order for Him to transition from the path of the heart onto the path of power (and mind). Thus, Venus served a very important role in Jesus's life, even though it doesn't appear to be as significant as the other astrological factors in Jesus's chart. Once Jesus awakened the intuitional mind of the buddhic plane, it was incumbent upon Him to move in consciousness back and forth between the two ray lines of manifestation. Due to this conjunction, this movement between these two lines was possible.

By way of the ray five bridging energies Venus transmits, disciples are able to generate the rainbow bridge that links the personal mind first to the mind of the Soul, and then link the mind with the mind of the Spiritual Triad (via the Soul). Thus, Venus represents the revealing light and the bridging power that connects the mind and consciousness to successively higher centers.

Sun trine Mid-heaven (27 minutes)

Since the Mid-heaven is the highest point in the chart, it represents the nature and developed skills, abilities, and capacities of the self that people express in relation to their outer, professional life. Traditional astrology suggests that the Sun trine Mid-heaven aspect confers leadership abilities, professional prominence, and social stature.

With the Sun in Pisces, and Neptune conjunct the Mid-heaven in Jesus's chart, this trine provided the energy Jesus needed to express true spiritual leadership. This combination suggests that Jesus's spiritual leadership and authority were spiritually ordained once He had completed the work necessary to reach the summit of the mount of initiation the third time. In other words, His spiritual alignment and attunement to the Soul (and later His attunement to the Spiritual Self of the Triad) bestowed significant spiritual authority upon Him, but it was this trine of the Sun along with Neptune's conjunction to the Mid-heaven that provided Him with the opportunity to express true spiritual leadership in the outer world.

When the Sun is trine the Mid-heaven, people are better able to express their full capacity and capabilities as human beings. Since Jesus did not have a personal agenda to promote, however, He didn't express this energy to advance His own professional interests and stature, which is usually the case. In fact, Jesus didn't express the energy of this trine in the outer world until He had attained a union of the integrated personality and Soul, and the Soul was in command of His life, not the personality.

The Mid-heaven in Jesus's chart was in Scorpio. Scorpio represents the tests and trials of the first three initiations that disciples must pass before they can reach the summit of the mount of initiation. For Jesus, the spiritual tests and trials He experienced in relation to the first two threshold initiations were relatively minor since these had been attained in a prior life.

Although Jesus achieved a mastery of the ray one sub-aspect of the third initiation for the first time, even this initiation was not difficult for Him to achieve (as it is for most people), because of the favorable interplay and exchange of energies He experienced as a result of this trine of the Sun to the Mid-heaven and the conjunction of the Sun and ray five Venus. The third initiation is always taken on ray five. This helped to mitigate the adverse effects that the Sun-Pluto opposition had. (Pluto co-rules Scorpio at the level of the personality, but not at the level of the Soul.)

Sun conjunct North Node (2 degrees 5 minutes)

The North Node represents a field of forces that help orient people to the future in terms of the threefold personal consciousness and its development. The conjunction of the Sun and North Node indicates great leadership potential, due to favorable merit earned in past lives. Modern astrology suggests that this conjunction is common in the charts of people who had dedicated themselves in recent past lives to helping others.

The Sun conjunct North Node aspect indicates that the soul-infused personality of Jesus and the underlying evolutionary forces within His life were in sync with each other, resulting in a rather potent, cohesive, and singular message.

Chapter 9

Moon in Cancer, the Past

Just as the surface of the Moon reflects the light of the Sun, the screen of the mind reflects the emotional and mental patterns of the past, both those originating in the current life as well as in past lives. The patterns of the past enter into a new incarnation by way of the magnetism of the forces within the subtle bodies (especially the magnetism, of the astral body) that the Soul generates prior to birth. Such electromagnetic patterns greatly affect the quality, nature, and types of emotions, feelings, and sentiency people are likely to unfold and express in their lives.

Past-life behavior, character, qualities, emotional reactive patterns, habits, and tendencies—all greatly affect the quality of the personal consciousness the individual unfolds in his or her current life. Although past-life emotional characteristics and traits are often activated in the early years of an incarnation, people modify these emotional patterns throughout their lives and create new emotional patterns. Fortunately, the fluid psychic patterns of emotions, desires, and feelings are just one aspect of the more definitive and substantive threefold personal self.

Once the consciousness is polarized at the mental-plane level, the light of the mind becomes more representative of the solar light than lunar light, even though the personal light is a reflection of the light of the Soul.

Esoterically, the Moon is a decaying body. This means that there isn't any divine life-force pouring into the matter forms of the Moon. For this reason, no one on the path should ever be responsive to the lunar planetary forces emanating from the Moon. Even more significant is that the planetary forces of the Moon carry a life-denying factor that has an adverse effect upon the life of these physical bodies that can further ensconce the consciousness in matter. These lunar forces are not involved in the evolution of consciousness—quite the opposite. The decaying lunar forces are of an involutionary nature.

Unlike the Sun and planets of our solar system, the Moon has no embodied life. (Other Moons of our solar system are embodied.) Nor is there any evolution of consciousness taking place on the Moon, although there was prior to the evolutionary system of earth. Instead, the only forces emanating from our Moon are the forces of decay. For this reason, the lunar forces can adversely affect the lower emotional-feeling nature of mankind. This can result in dense, involutionary physical-astral forces that precipitate disease, disorder, and some forms of cancer. This occurs as a result of density and quality of the dense matter forces that can block the light and obstruct the influx of divine life-forces. For this reason, it is exceedingly important to forgive others. This helps to release the dense astral-emotional forces from the aura.

This decaying, life-denying factor permeating obsolete emotional patterns affects the physical body by denying life-sustaining energy to an etheric center that vitalizes a particular area of the body. All light and energy moves from the higher planes through the lower planes onto the physical plane. If negative, low-vibratory emotional or mental patterns of force are present in the subtle bodies, they can interfere with the influx of divine life-forces. This is why people need to forgive others on the mental, astral-emotional, and physical levels. This is also why people need to emotionally and mentally let go of that which is being removed from their lives.

The Moon is considered one of the three most important astrological factors in the chart. This is due to the fact that people's consciousness has been polarized at the emotional-feeling level lifetime after lifetime. Today, as a result of universal education, the consciousness of the average person in the industrial nations tends to shift back and forth between the astral and mental levels of personal consciousness. This tendency to shift back and forth throughout the day continues until the consciousness is finally polarized at the mental level.

This situation speaks to the power that the astral-emotional nature has had upon human consciousness for millennia. Only in the past few centuries has the consciousness of the average person included a prominent mental aspect of consciousness.

Again, the Moon represents the established, emotionally reactive patterns of consciousness within the psyche. The strength of these patterns is the contributing factor behind the tendency of people to react emotionally to the events of their lives, rather than mentally respond to their experiences. People often act upon, or react to, something before they think.

According to traditional astrology, the Moon and the astrological factors associated with the Moon can reflect the degree to which someone feels at home on earth. However, this traditional astrological interpretation is somewhat misleading. Although the Moon relates to the emotional patterns that are indicative of what people have loved, hated, feared, and desired for lifetimes, such things do not have any effect upon whether someone is grounded or connects to life here in the physical plane. Rather, the forces of the Moon by sign and aspect tend to reactivate familiar and similar emotions and feelings of the past.

Aside from the Moon's association with these familiar emotional feeling patterns, there is no reason for the Moon to indicate whether or not someone feels at home on earth. People may feel at home desiring the things of earth that were desired in recent past lives, but the linking of conscious life on earth is actually a component of the consciousness that corresponds to the basic center of the etheric body and the will-to-be dynamic of the psyche. The Moon and its influences, on the other hand, astrologically correspond to the solar plexus, not the basic center.

It has only been in the past century or two that a large number of people have achieved mental control over the astral-emotional aspect of their personal consciousness. To gain control of the astral aspect of consciousness (feelings, emotions, and desires), the consciousness must be mentally polarized and infused with the will of the Soul in order to add sufficient potency to the light of the mind.

By applying the light of mind upon the elements of the astral-emotional nature, people gain a degree of control of their astral-emotional nature. As people on the path achieve more control of the astral forces, the threefold essential love of the Soul is able to stream into the mind. Once the personal mind is adequately infused with the energies of the third petal (the will petal) of the love tier of the lotus, people can apply enough willpower to the light of the mind to gain a complete mastery of the astral-emotional aspect of personal consciousness.

Astrologically, the Moon serves as the container matrix that retains the emotion-based patterns activated during incarnation. These patterns are the product of the magnetism of consciousness of childhood and of past lives: old desires, emotions, feelings, habits, fears, passions, sensual pleasures, ways of being nurtured, etc. These patterns include both instinctual and emotional response patterns of behavior.

The Moon corresponds to the emotions and elements of astral-emotional patterning (including maternal nurturing patterns) that give rise to people's basic tendencies, proclivities, and desires. The Moon also corresponds to the age-long emotional patterns that bind the consciousness to the physical body. Such patterns comprise the basic strings of forces that attach people to the physical body and their feelings and preferences.

In terms of the evolution of consciousness, the development of the astral-emotional component of self-consciousness precedes the development of the mental aspect of the personal consciousness and individuation. The Moon, therefore, relates to the component of self-consciousness that is tied to the unconscious, e.g., people's fears, phobias, anxieties, jealousies, relational attachments, and so forth.

Esoterically, there are two types of self-consciousness that dominate the consciousness of mankind. Initially, the atoms of self-consciousness that people bring forth correspond to the astral-emotional aspect of personal consciousness. The second type of the atoms of self-consciousness that people bring forth corresponds to the mental aspect of personal consciousness and to the light of the mind.

The Moon represents the factor of self-consciousness that is imprisoned in astral darkness. Darkness and light represent the first duality perceived within human consciousness. This was not intentional. Nor is it a permanent condition. But it is the condition human consciousness is currently in, since practically every element of self-consciousness has been touched by this darkness. The astral plane has no light of its own.

The astral-emotional feeling nature is fluid and free of the restrictive boundaries and structures of the mental-plane world. Without boundaries, people's emotional nature naturally embraces the family's emotional patterns and behavior, as well as the patterns of the ethnic group, peer group, tribe, nation, or culture with which a person identifies. For this reason, people usually assimilate the family's feelings and emotions, especially in terms of the family's religious, political, national, tribal, and ethnic allegiances.

It is by way of the astral-emotional aspect of consciousness that people connect themselves to one another. Until a sense of self is firmly established within the mental aspect of consciousness, people function primarily in a familial group consciousness. This continues until the individuating mental component of self-consciousness that the Sun, Mercury, and Uranus bring forth has been developed.

During childhood, the astral force field is linked into the physical-etheric body between seven and fourteen years of age via a stream of energy or cord extending from the astral solar plexus to the etheric solar plexus. This allows people to activate feelings and emotions within the brain consciousness. This linkage of the astral force field to the physical-etheric body takes place during the precognitive period of development, roughly between the ages of seven and fourteen.

In most cases, up to the age of fourteen much of the patterning of the consciousness taking place is astral-emotional patterning of the (brain) consciousness. This patterning operates below the light of the mind and rational, logical thought. As a result, people entertain illogical and irrational emotions and patterns of feelings. Though stored in the subconscious, they greatly affect people's behavior and life in general. The light and forces of the mental plane cannot impact the (brain) consciousness directly until the mental body is tied into the physical-etheric bodies sometime after the age of thirteen.

Throughout the day, the quality of people's reactions to life and its events tends to be more representative of their astral-emotional patterning. People tend to be unaware of what is going on within the subconscious until these patterns become so disruptive that they seek professional help. Often, people become aware of their astral-emotional nature only when it bubbles up into the light of their conscious awareness due to a heightened stimulation of the astral forces. This astral-emotional excitation generates a number of vortices of swirling forces in the astral body. People express these energized astral forces as emotions, emotional reactions and outbursts. This speaks to the lack of control many people have over these astral forces. This situation exists until that time when the Soul-infused light of the personal mind supersedes the power of these astral forces. This involves gaining mental control over the astral-emotional forces sufficient enough to still the astral forces and quiet the emotions.

By way of this astral-emotional aspect of consciousness, people can absorb the emotional tenor of their environment. The degree to which the emotional environment is absorbed into people's lives depends on the sign and house placement of the Moon and the planetary aspects formed to the Moon. That to which the astral-emotional aspect of the personal consciousness responds is typically colored, diminished, or enhanced by the particular sign where the Moon is placed.

Most people readily absorb the emotional reactive pattern found within the environment in which they live, especially the emotional tenor and patterns of the people with whom they are personally associated, such as family members (especially the mother) and close friends.

As the emotional feeling nature and patterning are activated by planetary transits during people's lives, what the Moon symbolizes becomes an important component of people's disposition. This aspect of personal consciousness rises up from the emotional waters of life, the subconscious, into the light of day. The vibratory rate, color, and quality of the astral forces that people allow to express in their lives depend upon the stage of development the individual has attained.

The Moon and astrological factors impacting the Moon provide important clues as to people's ability to connect with other people, and the extent to which they feel comfortable around others. The astrological factors associated with the Moon also provide clues about the quality of emotions and feelings people express in their lives and how compatible their emotional feeling nature is with their own mental nature.

On the path, people become responsive to successively higher energies, qualities, notes, and vibrations. However, the effort to become responsive to higher energies, along with the ability to unfold and develop higher states of mind, takes place only when the egocentric emotional and mental patterns of consciousness have been eliminated. Such patterns energetically veil and obstruct the higher energies and draw the attention away from its focus upward. The greatest of all obstructions to experiencing the world of the Soul is the selfish negative content of the astral body.

Life, consciousness, and being are brought forth and advanced as different ray energies and forces are transmitted by the cosmically embodied Sun and planets. These rays are responsible for all expressions of life on earth. However, this vast and intricately interrelated system of energy exchange and interplay prompting the evolution of life and consciousness does not include the forces of the Moon.

The atoms of self-consciousness that the lunar forces activate are frequently representative of the ancient rhythm of glamour that distorts, deceives, veils, and materially glamorizes the human consciousness. For this reason, when people are responsive to and stimulated by the lunar forces, they tend to react in negative and self-centered ways. Greed, arrogance, jealousy, possessiveness, vengeance, and so forth have their origins in this ancient rhythm of glamour.

Thus, the astral-emotional forces further imprison the consciousness in a murky pool of drama and chaos that has nothing to do with the evolution of consciousness and divine purpose. The ancient patterns of glamour, along with the selfish emotional desire nature that the influences of the decaying lunar forces activate, need to be transmuted or centrifugally expelled from the aura by higher energies before people can attain the higher states of mind.

The fathers of the early Christian church referred to the lower region of the astral realm as purgatory, which is a relatively accurate description of this region. Esoterically, the lower sub-plane levels of the astral plane represent the dark unreal—a realm of glamour and deception—that blocks the upper mental-plane light of the Soul from freely expressing through the brain consciousness.

People on the path must eliminate their conscious responsiveness to the negative, selfishly conditioned astral forces. For this reason, people on the path must go through a period of cleansing and purifying the threefold personal consciousness of the lower astral forces. This cleansing process is accelerated once the streams of energy emanating from the three love petals of the lotus stream from the heart center of the mental body into the heart center of the etheric body. This higher quality of energy is used to transform selfish desire into spiritual aspiration and to stimulate the consciousness in a way that brings forth the loving, compassionate, and merciful nature of the higher self.

A high percentage of people are controlled by their personal desire nature and fixated on satisfying their constant desire for the things of earth. They tend to be unaware that the things of earth are tools that people can use to grow in consciousness and thereby learn how things work on earth.

In order to graduate from the school of learning on earth and enter the Hall of Knowledge (and later enter the Hall of Wisdom), people must let go of everything they are personally attached to and identify with once the prerequisite development of the threefold personal consciousness has been achieved. The development of the mind relates to actualizing the potential of the human spirit, not the unfoldment of the qualities of the involutionary life forms and their drives, appetites, and nature.

Mankind tends to behave as if what is permissible for the involutionary elementals lives of the physical and subtle bodies to behave is also permissible for them. Again, the evolution of human consciousness is not governed by the laws of nature that govern matter; rather, people are to be governed by the laws of humanity, and later governed by the Laws of the Soul.

The Moon symbolizes the fluid astral-emotional feeling self, which was the first to unfold within the physical body as people brought forth astral-emotional atoms of self-consciousness. The ancient emotional self-consciousness that the forces of the Moon stimulate originated with the primitive civilizations of mankind.

Today, most adults are focused on the development of the concrete mind and rational, logical thought. This means that the light and consciousness of the Soul are starting to illumine the lower mental aspect of the consciousness. At the same time, the emotional aspect of consciousness continues to operate in the darkness of the unconscious. This sets up the first duality for people to resolve as they progress: the duality between light and darkness within their own minds.

For many people, this emotional component of self-consciousness is still integrally associated with the polluted and distorted astral-emotional forces and desire forms. Such forces veil the light of the Soul and maintain the darkened world of the astral-emotional nature. These astral forces have been allowed to freely express through people's lives for millennia. As a result, people think, feel, and behave in ways that violate the values, qualities, and nature of the Soul as well as violate the basic universal laws of humanity.

Human consciousness should be able to perceive the divine light and love of the world of the Real, yet few have ever perceived such light during incarnation because of the multitude of dualities that exist within human consciousness. On the path, all duality must be addressed and resolved. One day far in the future, the entire astral plane will reflect the qualities of love and light of, first the Soul, and then the buddhic and manasic centers. Few people have cleansed the negative and selfish astral-emotional nature sufficiently for this astral-emotional aspect of consciousness to reflect pure love-wisdom.

The waters of the astral body must be cleansed and purified in order for the consciousness to reflect the love of the Soul and later reflect the love-wisdom of world of the Real. Until this cleansing takes place, there is darkness on earth to which the consciousness of mankind is attached. Once the light can shine through the seven sub-planes of the astral plane, the astral substances will perfectly reflect the love of God in its seven sub-ray aspects.

Moon in Cancer

In the chart of Jesus, the Moon was in Cancer. When the Moon is placed in Cancer, the astral-feeling nature is prominent. According to traditional astrology, this placement strengthens the ties between an individual and the mother and home environment. It also contributes a heightened sensitivity to the feelings of others, which often leads to the unfoldment of the astral senses. This includes clairsentience and clairaudience. In effect, the Moon's placement in Cancer establishes a natural resonance between the brain consciousness and the astral world. This placement also stimulates vivid dream imagery.

Again, the Moon is not a center of constructive energies; it is a center of decaying, lifeless planetary forces that stimulate old and often obsolete patterns of emotions, behavior, and forms of attachment to the things of earth that obstruct people's evolutionary progress and preoccupy them in the drama and chaos of the emotional, feeling world of personal relationships.

Analysis of the combined astrological factors in Jesus's chart indicates that prior to His incarnation He had successfully eliminated and mastered the personal emotional nature. As a teenager, He gained control of the lower astral forces seeking to express in His life, i.e., He had attained the second initiation. Of course, Jesus still needed to unfold the feeling-sentient aspect of personal consciousness in His current life; however, the quality of His astral body was purified and refined, not filled with selfish emotional patterns. The difficult work required to free the atoms of self-consciousness from the selfish emotional desire nature had already been completed in a past life. This is always accomplished through love.

In the chart of Jesus, the Moon formed seven trines. Metaphysically, trines represent good karma earned in past lives. Although this statement is a bit simplistic, this idea has merit. Of greater significance, however, is the fact the Moon did not form a square or opposition to any astrological factor in Jesus's chart. This means that there were no past-life astral-emotional patterns that disrupted His life.

Once the second initiation has been achieved, people are no longer consciously or unconsciously responsive to the lower forces emanating from this decaying planet. A high percentage of the pain and difficulties people experience is triggered by emotional reactions stimulated by the decaying planetary radiations of the Moon. The radiations of this center stimulate negative and often self-destructive emotional patterns of behavior. Two thousand years ago, people were generally more responsive to these lunar forces of decay than they are today.

Once people have attained the second initiation and start to approach the third initiation, they are no longer responsive to the decaying lunar forces. However, the Moon is still a center in the solar system. Esoterically, the Moon's placement in the chart is said to conceal a center of higher energy, usually Uranus or Vulcan, but on occasion, Neptune. Since Neptune is the Soul-centered ruler of Cancer, when the placement of the Moon is in Cancer, it acts as a portal through which ray six energy streams onto the initiate once the third initiation has been attained.

Once Jesus approached the third initiation, the energies of Neptune started to stream onto Him through this point in Cancer that the Moon concealed. Then, by way of a secondary center in the upper region of His astral body, the ray four (buddhic-plane) sub-quality of Neptune started to impact the consciousness of Jesus. From this center, the energies of Neptune streamed into both His ajna center and a corresponding secondary center of the etheric body deep within the heart center. This secondary center is involved in transferring the self-consciousness from the solar plexus into the heart center and from the heart center into the ajna.

As the essential love of the Soul poured through the heart center, it activated an inner meridian of light that links the solar plexus to the heart center. By way of this meridian, the atoms of emotional self-consciousness was uplifted in quality and then transferred from the solar plexus into the heart center—from darkness to light. As this transference took place in Jesus's life, He unfolded, developed, and more fully incorporated the principle of love into His consciousness.

Jesus unfolded an even higher expression of ray six Neptune via this secondary center within the etheric heart center. Since the solar plexus is the agent of feelings by which people become sensitive to the emotional tenor of the environment, transferring self-consciousness out of the solar plexus diminished Jesus's sensitivity to the personal emotions and feelings of others. This prevented Jesus from being overwhelmed by the feelings of others.

Thus, the higher sub-qualities and energies of ray six Neptune were active throughout His life. They were active by way of:

1) Neptune as the apex of the epic grand trine, which formed a trine to the Moon.
2) The planets in Pisces which Neptune rules at the personality level.
3) The Moon in Cancer, which is ruled by Neptune at the Soul level.

In this way, the Moon indirectly contributed to the unfoldment of a one-pointed loving devotion to God. In addition, Neptune's influences via the Moon's placement in the sixth house (the area of work and service) established a rhythm of devotional service to God and mankind.

This additional influence of the higher qualities of ray six (initially concealed by the placement of the Moon) further enhanced Jesus's love for others, strengthened His higher creative imagination, and heightened His compassion for humanity. The higher creative imagination, in turn, opened the inner mind's eye that reveals, first the world of the Soul, and later reveals the life of the higher planes of light. By way of His higher astral-sentient nature, Jesus developed impressive psychic abilities and a lofty idealism.

The Moon in Jesus's chart played an important role in terms of His ability to fulfill His mission. Since all personal responsiveness toward the astral forces and to the selfish emotional patterns had been mastered in a recent past life, the Moon's placement in the chart represented a very positive healing center of absorbing love that connected Him to others via His heart center without binding Him to others like the forces of the solar plexus do.

Jesus was not responsive to the forces of the personal astral-emotional desire world as a child or as an adult. This cleansing of the forces of His astral body and the liberation of His consciousness from astral influences prior to incarnating was exceedingly important, since the heart center is awakened and receptive to essential love only when the consciousness is no longer preoccupied with the emotional personal drama of life that the lower astral forces activate. This allowed the essential love of the Soul to pour freely through His upper astral centers (especially the heart center) into His upper etheric centers at an early age.

As the forces of the astral plane stream into the astral bodies of most people, they are electromagnetically drawn into the lower centers (especially the solar plexus) and express in people's lives as selfish emotions and desires. Since Jesus had eliminated all responsiveness to the lower astral forces prior to incarnating, however, the three sub-qualities of the love of the Soul entered His life via the upper centers of the etheric body, the heart center in particular. They were not pulled into the solar plexus. This influx of energies of the love petals awakened Him to the essential love of the Soul in His early years. Because His upper centers were open, the energies of the Soul did not stimulate the forces of the solar plexus as they so often do. There was little self-consciousness in the solar plexus that would have drawn Him into the emotional drama of life on earth.

Later, the love of the buddhic center freely streamed through the heart center in the greater crown center and awakened the pure love of the Triad within His (brain) consciousness. His conscious responsiveness to this pure love brought forth the revelations and realizations that led to the greatest of all insights—the essential nature of God is love.

From birth, Jesus wasn't reactive to the forces that streamed through the astral plane (and therefore through His astral body) below the third sub-plane level. In other words, He was born with the heart, throat, and crown centers of His astral body active and receptive to the light and love of the Soul. This resulted in a receptivity of, and a conscious responsiveness to, the essential love of the Soul in His early years and a conscious responsiveness to the qualities of pure love-wisdom in His later years.

Ray four buddhic-plane energies started to impact His consciousness once He attained the second initiation and then He extended the connecting spans of the rainbow bridge from the petals of the love tier to the buddhic center. This resulted in an influx of love-wisdom from the buddhic plane. This influx of love-wisdom, in combination with the influx of the essential love of the Soul via the love petals, enabled Jesus to unfold the principle of pure love-wisdom which, in turn, enabled Him to realize that God is love.

Since the astral-emotional aspect of consciousness had been purified of all personal taints, Jesus used the upper astral-plane energies in His early years to unfold clairvoyance and the higher creative imagination, and to enhance His spiritual idealism. Then, when His inner vision awakened, He was able to easily shift His consciousness from the love qualities of the Soul to the qualities of love-wisdom that are operative at the buddhic-plane level.

Chapter 10

Links between the Past and Present (Part One)

Moon trine Venus (2 degrees)

The Moon forms its closest aspect to Venus. This is important since young people become consciously responsive to these two planetary forces early in their lives. Esoterically, Venus represents the revealing light of the mind and is the agent that transmits ray five energies into our solar system. Ray five is the blending agent of the zodiac. Once two psychic dynamics are related to each other (via Mercury), ray five blends them together.

In aspect to the Moon, Venus's harmonizing revealing qualities had a positive influence upon the emotional, feeling nature of Jesus, especially in His early years. The blend and interplay of these two energies bring forth a warm, pleasant disposition.

In general, a trine between the Moon and Venus manifests in people's lives as a comforting love and concern for others, the breadth of which depends on people's point of evolution. When Venus is in Pisces, the Moon trine Venus aspect confers a heightened aesthetic sensibility, a soothing voice, and pleasant, harmonious relations with others.

The interplay of these two types of forces in Jesus's life conferred a gentle, empathetic approach toward others that helped Him establish right relations with those He encountered. The Jewish exhortation to repent was not just a call for people to return to the Judaic laws of the covenant agreement. It was a call for people to establish right relations with one another. More importantly, this Moon-Venus trine is a call for people to establish right relations between the past and the present within the consciousness and right relations between oneself and the Divine.

Initially, the Moon is an agent for the transmission of ray four qualities, especially in relation to the astral-emotional nature. This results in more relationship conflicts than any other influence during the early stages of development. Ray four energies are used to relate one element of the astral-emotional aspect of consciousness to another. This is necessary in order for people to perceive and then work to resolve duality within the consciousness. The Moon trine Venus aspect confers an ability to become consciously aware of, and subsequently harmonize, the conflicts that arise within the psyche, especially in terms of the emotional, feeling desire nature.

Esoterically, the Moon corresponds to the nurturing divine Mother Principle that must be related (via ray four energies) to the Father Principle. Harmoniously relating these two principles within the psyche is something mankind has failed to do. Harmoniously relating these two principles is not something that takes place within the psyche all at once; rather, it is ongoing.

Astrologically, the relationship between the Sun and Moon in the natal chart symbolizes the quality of the relationship that exists in the psyche between the Father Principle and the Mother Principle. These two principles must be related to each other at each level and then harmonized, unified. Once these two principles are related at the respective levels, the revealing, harmonizing influence of Venus helps unify them, the consequence of which is the birth of new atoms of self-consciousness.

Today, those on the path use the interplay of the energies generated by Moon trine Venus to harmonize the Mother Principle with the Father Principle within the psyche. This is important, since the ongoing relating and subsequent union of the Mother and the Father brings forth the Son, i.e., consciousness. In this way, greater consciousness is continually brought forth.

For people on the path, this act of first relating and then harmonizing two aspects of consciousness to each other (which this Moon trine Venus aspect represents) takes place at a higher level. Here, the threefold integrated personality is systematically related to, and then harmonized with, the Soul. Once the elements of the uplifted threefold personal consciousness are related to the corresponding elements of the Soul, Venus harmonizes the personal consciousness with the Soul. Eventually, this activity results in a union of the integrated personality and Soul.

Thus, the energies of this trine can be used to unify one aspect of consciousness to another aspect of consciousness. During the stage of personal development, they are also used to relate the individual to other people and to the material things of earth. Attraction to other people and to the material things of earth is brought about as a result of the way many people use the planetary forces of Venus in their lives. But, more importantly, Venus reveals love and awakens people to the second aspect of the Divine at each level from the physical plane to the divine plane.

When functioning at the stage of personal development, the lowest expression of love at is brought forth. People are attracted to others as well as to material things because they are responding to the quality of personal love that the other person or material object awakens within them. The other person or thing resonates with the quality of love and the aesthetic beauty and harmony they seek to in their lives.

When the consciousness is polarized at a higher level, however, the interplay of the energies of the Moon with those of Venus reveals great spiritual insight. This was especially true for Jesus, since He had so few lower astral-emotional patterns that needed to be related to each other. Nor were there any apparent dualities within the astral-emotional aspect of consciousness that He needed to resolve before love, light, beauty, and harmony was revealed to Him.

The blending of these two types of energies provided the psychic foundation upon which Jesus brought forth and expressed His love for God and for mankind. This combination related the consciousness of Jesus to successively higher planes and helped to harmonize the two planes of consciousness to each other as He progressed. In this way, the trine helped to relate and reveal the Soul to the personality, and later revealed the love of the higher self to the love of the Spiritual Self—the pure love-wisdom and truth of the Triad.

Moon trine Neptune (2 degrees 21 minutes)

The sentient feeling aspect of the self as represented by a prominent Moon typically manifests as an inner sensitivity and responsiveness to the feeling tenor of the environment. But when the Moon is also trine Neptune, the sensitive, receptive attribute of consciousness is of a much higher level of sensitivity and expression, one that manifests as empathy, humility, love, and compassion for others, and a fervent devotion to the Divine. In Jesus's case, this trine enhanced His devotion to the Father of love and intensified His spiritual sensitivity, first toward the world of the Soul and later toward the world of the Real.

Astrologically, the Moon, Neptune, Cancer, and Pisces are all associated with a strongly felt devotional nature. However, the object upon which people focus their devotion varies. When the Moon is in Cancer, the devotion people express is usually more personal and typically aligned with the mother and activities in the home (depending on the sign and house). When the Moon is trine Neptune, however, people's devotion tends to be focused on the higher spiritual worlds and on service activities to help improve the lives of others.

The interplay and blending of the energies of the Moon with Neptune frequently result in a discontent and restlessness with earthly life, which leads people on a quest for a better, more idyllic life. Many seek a heavenly realm of love and peace, harmony and beauty—a world free of the harsh vagaries of life. Throughout His life, Jesus responded to the divine discontent He felt as the spiritual fires within Him burned brightly, illumining the path before Him. Today, this compelling discontent with earthly life often encourages people to seek a closer relationship or mystical oneness with the Divine.

In Jesus's life, the influence of this trine most likely generated a deep idealization of His mother. Such idealization of the mother often interferes with men's ability to find a suitable mate, since no one can measure up to their ideal. The otherworldly pull of Neptune overwhelms the usually dominant physical-instinctual drives of most people. Undoubtedly, this Neptune-Moon trine diminished any interest in marrying and settling down Jesus might have had. This, in combination with the overwhelming negative polarity of the astrological factors in Jesus's chart, suggests that Jesus did not have a strong physical attraction to women.

Most likely, Jesus viewed His mother with unwavering devotion and respect. He probably celebrated her as being exceptionally devout and holy. This deep relationship with and appreciation of Mary may be why Jesus was willing to teach women, even though Judaism two thousand years ago prohibited women from receiving spiritual instructions.

The fact that Mary was the vehicle for the incarnation of a Soul like Jesus is supportive of the belief that Mary was second to none when it came to spiritual virtues. According to the ancient wisdom teachings, Mary entered the human kingdom from the angelic angle of consciousness, not the human angle. Angels embody perfect peace and have no desire other than to serve the purpose of the Logos.

Movement from the angelic angle to the human angle of development is unusual, but not unheard of. If Mary moved into the human angle of development, she would have been free of the sins (karma) of mankind, and been reasonably pure and untainted by personal desires.

To fulfill His mission, it was important for Jesus to be relatively free of many of the forms of karma people must face during their lives. This includes familial karma. With Mary shifting from the Angelic angle into the human angle of evolution, there wasn't the usual familial karma Jesus would have had to work through at some point in His life.

Like humanity, angels are at different stages of development within the angelic-devic angle of evolution. However, angels are serving agents of the Divine, while human beings are gods-in-the-making. The evolutionary objective of mankind is to achieve a level of development in which they function as divine co-creators. One day humanity will serve as the divine agents of the Logos capable of manifesting the perfection on earth envisioned within the mind of God.

At the stage of personal development, the energies in relation to the Mother Principle (which the Moon symbolizes) represent the receptive, negative polarity that is used to advance the vehicles through which human consciousness unfolds and expresses. The negative polarity and the Mother Principle, in particular, are integrally involved in the development of senses needed to perceive the life and being of successively higher planes. By way of these senses, the nature of life in the three planes of matter is registered, perceived, and consciously responded to via the mind. The development of the higher subtle senses and faculties of mind is what takes a long time to develop.

During incarnation, the respective senses and a conscious responsiveness to the qualities of life and mind must be unfolded and developed in terms of each of the seven planes of the evolutionary system of earth. For example, the astral psychic senses enable people to sense life in relation to the astral plane, while the physical senses provide information to advance the brain consciousness in relation to the physical plane.

By way of these physical-etheric senses, people slowly gain an understanding of how things work on earth. When people shift away from being reliant solely upon the physical senses, they become consciously aware of their sensitive feeling nature. People first extend their physical senses into the astral plane by unfolding and developing the psychic senses and higher creative imagination.

The astral psychic abilities of clairaudience (hearing) and clairsentience (feeling) are often the first subtle senses to be developed. Later, the upper astral sensory capacities of the higher creative imagination, clairvoyance (astral sight), and idealism are brought forth and advanced as the energies are drawn into the upper centers of the astral body.

In the West, the astral senses have been historically maligned as being unreliable, even evil. This is due to some disturbing impulses within the collective unconscious that date back to the latter days of the civilization of Atlantis. The collective unconscious of humanity still contains traumatized feeling fragments that date back to the destruction and sinking of Atlantis. This destruction occurred as a result of the great battle between two groups of primitive mankind—the forces of light and the forces of darkness.

Although both groups of Atlanteans relied on their astral senses (the intellect and concrete mind had yet to be unfolded), the forces of darkness used their psychic senses, along with the knowledge that the god-men given them, to acquire and possess the things of earth. This, in turn, brought forth personal desire, selfishness, patterns of negative emotional reactions, and egocentric glamour. The usage of the astral senses to procure and possess that which was desired became exceedingly problematic during the last half of the Atlantean Civilization.

The development of self-consciousness during the civilization of Atlantis preceded the unfoldment of the concrete mind and the cerebral activity of the brain. The Atlantean period predated spiritual vision. In addition, the intellect and other mental faculties had yet to unfold within these forms of earth. At that time, primitive mankind was more like a sentient animal than a modern human being.

During this ancient period when the astral-sentient aspect of personal consciousness was just beginning to unfold within these physical bodies, primitive mankind misused and distorted astral forces. For this reason, people need to cleanse and purify their astral bodies of selfish astral forces and gain a degree of control of their emotional nature before they should work on developing their astral senses. Otherwise, the lower astral forces will stimulate and distort much of what people sense. If the psychic capacity is developed too early, the astral senses tend to strengthen the ego which, in turn, makes it harder to achieve a union of the personality and Soul.

This Moon trine Neptune aspect had an exceptionally important influence upon Jesus in a number of ways. The interplay of these energies brought forth and advanced His psychic abilities and heightened His sensitivity to the feelings of others. Since the astral-emotional aspect of personal consciousness had been cleared, purified, and mastered prior to incarnating, Jesus was able to unfold and utilize His psychic sensitivity in a healthy constructive way. Jesus probably relied on His astral psychic senses in His younger years more than He relied on His burgeoning intellect.

The influx and blending of the higher ray qualities of the Moon trine Neptune aspect initially awakened the upper centers of the astral body of Jesus to the influx of the essential love of the Soul. As higher Soul energies poured through the upper centers, Jesus unfolded clairvoyance, clairaudience, spiritual idealism, and the higher creative imagination. This development took place as the three sub-qualities of the essential love of the Soul poured onto Him. At some point, the interplay of these two types of energies uplifted the remaining elements of self-consciousness within the solar plexus into His heart center.

Unfolding the astral and lower mental psychic abilities is prerequisite to unfolding the upper mental senses of the abstract mind (universal symbolism) and the intuitional mind. People must unfold and develop the senses of successively higher planes in order to perceive the life, qualities, and energies of those planes.

The strong influences of Pisces and Neptune significantly increased Jesus's natural sensitivity and heightened His psychic responsiveness to the spirit side of life. Later, these influences helped shift His consciousness from the upper astral realm into the buddhic realm of pure reasoning and free flowing love-wisdom.

During His ministry, Jesus did not depend on or rely upon His psychic abilities as He did in His early years. Rather, He relied on His senses and pure reasoning of the intuitional mind. The intuitional mind unfolds as the buddhic-plane energies of the Spiritual Triad pour into the heart, throat, and crown centers of the thousand-petal lotus—the greater crown center.

The buddhic plane is a realm of light, truth, and pure love-wisdom behind or dimensionally within the three planes of matter. As buddhic-plane energies impact the brain, pure reasoning is unfolded and developed. Pure reasoning does not involve the concrete mind or logical reasoning and thought. Rather, pure reasoning pertains to the wisdom and truth that spontaneously arises within the intuitional mind.

The buddhic realm is where all true prophecy originates as it relates to humanity. People with this trine who are on the path have the opportunity to become mystics guided by their inner intuitive impressions and sensitivities. By way of their intuition, they are able perceive the divine plan as currently constituted.

When incarnate, pure truth resounds in the stillness of the inner sacred space within. To perceive it, people must shift their awareness away from the multitude of voices of the outer world. The voices of the physical body, the emotions, and the chatter of the mind must be stilled in order to achieve the deeper states of contemplation and meditation wherein the disciple perceives truth. Most people are unable to hear the voice of the Divine that sounds in color and note through the immense light of the world of the Real.

Again, Neptune is the agent that calls for the sacrifice of the not-self. It calls for the elimination of all elements of the personal consciousness contrary in nature and quality to the Soul. The number of lifetimes that the past-lives of Jesus worked to sacrifice the not-self is unknown. It is possible that the Soul of Jesus was a leading voice for the forces of light in Atlantis. This group refused to separate themselves from divine purpose. Though they were just unfolding the astral-sentient aspect of personal consciousness at that time, those known as the forces of light never separated out from a state of group consciousness that was attuned to divine will.

Today, once the third initiation is attained and the initiate identifies with the Soul, he or she begins to think in terms of the group consciousness and interests of the Soul. Jesus demonstrated this unified group consciousness once He gathered His disciples together. Although it is natural to assume Jesus and the twelve disciples functioned as unique individuals, this is not how the consciousness of Jesus was functioning at that time.

Jesus expressed a consciousness of the group through His disciples in a way that demonstrated the first form of group consciousness on earth. This concept of group consciousness is very different from the herd consciousness of animals and the type of group consciousness mankind exhibits.

Since the astral body of Jesus had been cleared of emotional patterns prior to incarnating, the energies of this trine of Neptune to the Moon were not used to uplift the consciousness in terms of the threefold personal consciousness. Nor were these energies used to link the dynamic of personal love to the selfless essential love of the Soul. These two expressions of love had been unified prior to this incarnation.

Instead, the combination of these two energies was used to achieve a spiritual state of mind. For Jesus, the energies of this trine were used to unify the essential love of the higher mind with the pure love-wisdom of the Triad. This level of unification is necessary in order to attain Christ consciousness. The essential love of the Soul still contains an upper mental-plane element of the spiritual ego (which maintains a subject object perspective). As a Soul, the initiate is a lover of God. But at the higher level of the Triad, the initiate is love and expresses unconditional love in his or her life.

Once the fourth initiation has been attained, there is no self who loves, nor is there a loving higher self. There is only love. What is dropped is that factor of consciousness that differentiates the world of the Soul from the planetary heart through which the love of God eternally flows.

As the pure love-wisdom of the buddhic plane pours into the heart center in the greater crown, the initiate can attain the state of mind referred to as Christ consciousness. Christ consciousness is all-inclusive, unconditioned, undifferentiated love which is relatively free from those forces that limit or restrict the all-encompassing, omnipresent love of the Divine. This is the realization that initiates experience once the last step upon the path of the heart has been reached. The sacrifice called for at this stage shatters the causal body. Esoterically, a master then steps forth as the Planetary Savior—the Great Sacrifice.

Once the causal body of Jesus was destroyed, His consciousness expanded even further, and eventually encompassed the center called humanity. Functioning at the level of this more inclusive state of mind, Jesus was obliged to sacrifice Himself as the Son of God on behalf of the group called humanity. This involves a planetary sacrifice and service to mankind. At this stage, Jesus actually heard the voice of the Father. This is possible once there is nothing in the consciousness to obstruct the communications emanating from the heart and mind of the Logos.

Chapter 11

Links between the Past and Present (Part Two)

Moon trine Uranus (4 degrees 36 minutes)

The Moon and Uranus represent very different aspects of the consciousness. The Moon corresponds to the astral-emotional feeling aspect of consciousness and relates to ray four, while Uranus corresponds to the higher abstract mind and relates to ray seven. It is difficult to see how an aspect between these two planets could possibly advance people's development, but it can.

Although the basic center is initially magnetized receptive toward ray four, as people approach the second initiation, the magnetization of the basic center starts to shift receptive toward energies magnetized by ray seven. This begins the processes that ultimately relate the basic center to the crown center—personal will to divine will.

Once ray seven energies stream through the basic center, Uranian energies begin to stimulate the kundalini coiled within the basic center. Over time, this activates the kundalini and sets it on its journey up one of the three channels of the etheric spine.

As the kundalini rises up the pingala channel, it magnetizes the throat center in a way that draws down the ray three sub-qualities of the knowledge tier of petals. As the kundalini rises up the ida channel, it opens the heart center to the ray two sub-qualities of the love petals. As the kundalini fire-of-life rises up the sushumna, it opens the crown center and sensitizes the consciousness to ray one (will-purpose), first in relation to the Soul and later in relation to the Monad.

Once the disciple unfolds the petals of the knowledge tier and extends the linking strands of light from the knowledge petals to the manasic center, this Moon-Uranus interplay of energies unfolds the ability to perceive the world of causation and meaning that underlies the world of ideas. Creation itself is the mind-created world of manifestation that can trace its origins to the initiating impulses emanating from the world of causation and meaning.

Having established mental control of the astral-emotional aspect of consciousness and attained the second initiation, the ray four energies via the Moon (and Mercury) begin to express directly via the ajna center. This is in sharp contrast to the earlier stages of personal development when the intellect and concrete mind were being developed. At this earlier stage, the ajna center was magnetized receptive to ray five. The influx of ray five energies through the ajna resulted in the unfoldment of consciousness and the concrete mind within the apparatus of the brain.

Once the ajna center has been magnetized receptive to ray four energies, the different elements of the astral-emotional and mental aspects of consciousness can be systematically related to each other. The resulting mental awareness leads to the resolution of the duality within and between the emotional and mental aspects of personal consciousness. Later, this activity leads to the resolution of the duality between the integrated personality and the Soul, resulting in their subsequent unification.

When people are on the path and the planet Uranus forms a tight aspect to the personal planets, Uranian energies help people unfold the higher mind. Initially, this involves unfolding active intelligence via the energies of the intelligence tier of petals, but at the level of the higher mind, the energies of Uranus are used to unfold and express the abstract mind. This occurs as the energies of the manasic center pour into the throat center of the greater crown center, resulting in the unfoldment of the executive decision making capacity and the mental faculties of discernment and discrimination.

The subtle senses of the abstract mind are refined mental senses that perceive the formless patterns of light and interpret these light patterns into universal symbols. By way of the abstract mind, people begin to perceive the impressions of the intuitional mind and understand the consequences of their actions and activities. Most people are unable to see the cause-effect relationship between their words and actions and the events that transpire in their lives.

The development of these higher faculties and senses leads to the unfoldment of the inner mind's eye and the realization that all things in the three planes of earth are an outer manifest expression of an idea. They are a symbolic representation of a symbol. The energies of Uranus are integrally involved in awakening the inner mind's eye. By way of the inner mind's eye, accepted disciples and initiates register and perceive the subtle blueprints (seed ideas) of the higher planes.

The ajna is the etheric organ of vision of the inner mind's eye. As the petals of the lotus are unfolded, the ability to perceive the seed ideas and subtle impressions of the Masters of Hierarchy is unfolded. For this reason, the Moon trine Uranus aspect is associated with a disciple's ability to bring forth new, innovative, even revolutionary concepts and ideas. Unfortunately, people's personal interests and biases have historically distorted and misinterpreted much of what has been intuitively perceived. People's distortions of the meaning and intent behind these seed ideas have filled the mental plane with illusion.

As the spiritual development of disciples continues and the abstract mind is further developed, the interplay of the ray four and ray seven energies advance the capacity to intuit the subtle seed ideas of the planes of light. This higher level of development results in an ability to bring forth new, higher ideas, ideals, and systems of thought.

Since Uranus was in Pisces in Jesus's chart, the new, innovative thought that arose within the mind of Jesus centered on the teachings of the dawning Age of Pisces. As a result, Jesus was sensitive and consciously responsive to new, spiritual ideas, beliefs, and thought.

When combined with the lunar dynamic in the charts of disciples and initiates, Uranus confers an ability to perceive, interpret, and comprehend the impulses and impressions of the intuitional mind. This ability is due to the fact that the buddhic plane is on ray four. The interplay of the energies of the Moon and Uranus opens the door for people to sense the seed ideas of the world of the Real. This sensing does not result in the direct interpretation of these seed ideas into words; rather, they are first interpreted into symbols, analogies, and images that symbolically express the meaning and intent of the new principles and archetypes.

This was especially true for Jesus once He attained the third initiation and the energies of Neptune started to stream through the center in Cancer where the Moon was placed in His chart. After His third initiation, the influx of Neptunian energies through this ray four center of the Moon heightened His responsiveness toward the impulses of the intuitional mind. As a result, Jesus achieved a more universal and relatively inclusive mystical state of mind. This development also enabled Him to intuit the divine plan in relation to the dawning Age of Pisces.

Again, advanced Souls who have Uranus in aspect with the personal planets often become the voice behind social change, new systems of thought and innovation. This was especially true in Jesus's case, since Uranus was conjunct the Sun, Mercury, and Venus, and was trine the Moon in His chart.

The harmonious blending of ray four (Moon) and ray seven (Uranus) helped shift His consciousness upward to the mind of the Soul and helped unify the intelligence and love aspects of the higher mind. This is not the case, however, when people are still responsive to the lower astral-emotional forces.

This unification of the intelligence and love aspects of the higher mind is necessary in order to understand the world of the Real that is revealed at this higher stage when the focus is on the higher planes of light. Through the single eye, the life and light of the world of the Real is seen and the sublime beauty of truth is perceived. This development helped to revolutionize Jesus's awareness of truth and overall spiritual understanding. The interplay of the energies of the Moon trine Uranus also stimulated and advanced His higher creative imagination, conferring an electrical vibrancy to His creative imagination that enabled Him to perceive the worlds of the higher planes of light.

Through the mind of the Soul and the unfolding mind of the Triad, Jesus envisioned and accurately perceived the world of the Soul, which is the world of ideas, and later perceived the higher world of love-wisdom and truth. Because of His unfolding attunement to the love aspect of the Spiritual Triad, Jesus was able to comprehend His mission in terms of the divine plan. Although it is by way of the higher mind that Jesus perceived the impressions of God, it was by way of the faculty of the higher creative imagination that the teachings of the Piscean Age were revealed to Him.

The interplay and exchange of these two energies enveloped Jesus in an unusual sparkling effervescence, especially when He was young, but once His consciousness shifted upward into the manasic and then buddhic levels, this quality took on the electrical emanations of the Divine itself. Jesus became electrifying in speech and appearance.

With both the feeling and mental aspects of His consciousness attuned to this higher buddhic-plane reality, Jesus perceived the new principles of the Piscean Age and was able to anchor them within the planetary center of humanity for mankind to unfold and develop during the Piscean Age.

Moon sextile Pluto (6 degrees 51 minutes)

Although the orb of this sextile is wide, the Moon is sufficiently tied into the kite configuration of planets that a discussion of this sextile is important. In Jesus's life, both the Moon and Neptune acted as release valves for the tension generated by the Pluto opposition to the Sun, Mercury, and Uranus. This was especially important in the early years of Jesus's life.

Although people associate Pluto more with its destroyer sub-aspect, its ray one life-giving aspect is also important. Divine life-force moves directly into the etheric vitality body. For this reason, the Moon sextile Pluto aspect in Jesus's chart conferred a profound regenerating, rejuvenating power, especially in terms of the physical and astral-emotional aspects of life. People with this sextile often have a heightened vitality and stamina.

Pluto is always associated with transmutation, transformation, regeneration, rejuvenation, and occult powers. In general, the combination of the energies of the Moon (the past) and Pluto confers the energy people need to face and remove selfish, obsolete astral-emotional habits, and patterns of behavior. Pluto activates the physical-instinctual patterns of behavior buried within the unconscious and brings them into the light of people's conscious awareness to transmute.

Pluto represents a power that slices through the mental and astral force fields and impacts the physical body directly. As its energies move through the astral field, it shines its light into the dark caverns where the monsters of the unconscious reside and are sustained by the more primitive waters of self-consciousness. The patterns of behavior and feelings found there (in nature and quality) relate to a time when the astral-sentient aspect of human consciousness was first dawning within these physical forms. As a result, Pluto can activate the tendencies, characteristics, and traits of primitive mankind.

Many of people's negative tendencies, characteristics, and patterns of behavior have their origins in this ancient rhythm that primitive mankind set up in the center of humanity. As a result, all primitive instinctual and emotional atoms of self-consciousness must be liberated from the dark caverns of the unconscious and uplifted. This leads to the rapid transformation of the consciousness.

This aspect represents an opportunity for people to energize their lives with the energies of ray one in a positive, constructive way that frees the atoms of self-consciousness from the influences of the more primitive, pre-cognitive fragments of consciousness. This results in significant regeneration, vitality, and renewal physically and emotionally. In this way, people are freed from the ancient past and its rhythm to experience the present moment in a way that generates a more beautiful tomorrow, impelled by the Soul's evolutionary intent (which expresses via the Ascendant).

People can use the interplay of the energies of the Moon and Pluto to clear away the debris of the past—old, obsolete patterns of emotions and instincts that date back to a time when mankind feared for its life each and every day. For many, danger lurked everywhere. Regardless of people's level of evolvement, Pluto destroys the old and obsolete, so a new life structure can be built. It represents the powers of transformation and rejuvenation. However, its energies can never be used selfishly. When someone appropriates the forces of will to dominate, control, or manipulate others, they are misusing its energies. Appropriating ray one (divine will) for personal gain can have disastrous consequences.

For Jesus, the interplay of these two types of energy provided Him with the stamina and vitality necessary to withstand the many burning ghats of transformation that His mind and consciousness were subjected to, while strengthening Him to endure the rigors of His mission.

Since most of the negative astral-emotional and instinctual patterns of behavior had been eliminated prior to His incarnation, Jesus utilized the interplay of these two energies to transform His will into the will of the Soul. This resulted in the transformation and then sacrifice of His will to the will of the Soul. Toward the end of His life, this combination of energies was used to sacrifice the will of the Soul to the will of the Monad (the will of God). Transformation always involves preliminary phases of transmutation, death, and endings prior to transformation and rebirth. Through periodic psychic transformations, the consciousness of Jesus shifted from one level to successively higher levels.

This combination of energies deepened His understanding of mankind and carried Him through the inner planes of life from revelation to revelation. As a result, Jesus not only became aware of His mission, He was able to anchor a portion of the divine light in the three planes of matter.

Once Jesus attained the third initiation, the interplay of the energies of the Moon and Pluto enhanced His occult powers and command over the forces of the three matter planes. Also, with the complete elimination of His responsiveness to the influences of the Moon and to the past, the Moon became a portal for a new sub-quality of the ray six energies of Neptune. This, in effect, created a second Neptune sextile Pluto aspect in His chart. This particular sextile helped unify the integrated personality and Soul and later, contributed to the interplay and exchange of the ray one energies of Vulcan that were conditioned by Neptune as the Soul-centered ruler of Cancer. This awakened the builder aspect of ray one.

During His ministry, Jesus used the interplay of these energies to pierce the obsolete emotional patterns and its various forms of glamour found within society. These patterns relate to the veiling astral forces that envelop the consciousness of mankind and imprison it in the astral-emotional world.

Moon trine Mercury (6 degrees 32 minutes)

Since both the Moon and Mercury are vehicles for the energies magnetized by ray four, this trine greatly intensified the effects that the energies magnetized by ray four have upon the consciousness. Ray four energies resonate with the buddhic plane and with harmony brought about through the resolution of duality. This is accomplished by relating different types of energies to each other in a way that initially generates a point of tension. Resolution of this tension shifts the consciousness into a higher, more harmonious state. All conflicts that exist within the human consciousness represent a temporary condition of differences in vibration, quality, note, and color.

In a purely energetic sense, ray seven is a lower expression of ray one, ray six is a lower expression of ray two. Ray five is a lower expression of ray three. This is true in terms of energy as it moves through the ethers. Ray four in particular is the medium by which the lower expression of energy is related to its higher expression, resulting in a new balance and harmony.

When the Moon is trine Mercury, the concrete mind and intellect work well with the emotional feeling nature, resulting in a sense of peace and harmony in people's lives. So many people are caught up in a conflict between their past life and early childhood behavioral patterns and desires and their thoughts, beliefs, ideas, and goals as an adult. The clash between people's emotions and feelings versus the concrete mind and intellect is often pronounced. The astral-emotional forces active in the sub-conscious often plague people throughout their lives and often derail their efforts to successfully accomplish personal goals and objectives. Their feelings take them in one direction and their thoughts and ideas take them in another.

In general, this trine relates the emotional aspect of the personal consciousness to the mental aspect in a way that harmonizes them in relation to each other, thereby resolving much of the dissonance within the consciousness.

The interplay of the energies of this trine was one of the first influences that Jesus would have consciously responded to when He was young. The harmonious effects of this trine resulted in a childhood that was different from most children. Even though Jesus was extremely sensitive to the feelings and emotions of people around Him, the Moon trine Mercury aspect conferred an ability to objectively observe the feelings of others through the application of the light of His mind. This allowed Him to have a greater understanding of the feelings of others.

Since Jesus had resolved the clash between the mental and emotional aspects of the consciousness prior to incarnating, the harmony that existed between His feelings and thoughts prepared Him for taking the second initiation at a relatively young age. He used the energies of this trine to balance and then harmonize the love and intelligence aspects of consciousness at each level as He progressed.

Since the emotional aspect of consciousness is involved in the ability to recall events, experiences, knowledge, etc., this trine is often associated with people who have a good memory, common sense, good reasoning abilities, and communication skills. When the Moon is trine Mercury, the emotions and elements of the past do not overwhelm the mind and disrupt the thinking processes and communications.

Again, once Jesus attained the second initiation and approached the third initiation, the energies of Neptune started to express via the Moon's placement in Cancer. Since Mercury was trine Neptune in the chart of Jesus, this new center of Neptunian influence would have further intensified the spiritualization of the mind and consciousness of Jesus and heightened His devotion to the God of love.

With the Cancer Moon placed in the sixth house of work and service in Jesus's chart, the effects of this new interplay of energies between Mercury and the Moon would have streamed through the ajna center and prompted a conscious awareness of His need to engage in spiritual work and service to God and mankind.

This is very different from the interactions of Mercury and the Moon during the early years of Jesus's life, which was an interplay and exchange of the ray four energies of Mercury with the ray four energies of the Moon in relation to the basic center. Such influence brings about a basic understanding of the nature of life on earth that young people need.

The harmony between the emotional and mental aspects of consciousness ensured that any dissonance that arose within the consciousness of Jesus between the emotional patterns of the past and the new thoughts and ideas of the Piscean Age were quickly balanced and harmonized with each other.

Ray four Mercury has a special relationship to the buddhic plane and pure reasoning once many of the dualities of the personal consciousness are resolved and the ajna center became receptive to ray four. The ray four energies streaming through the ajna ultimately lead to a sense of the universality of life. At-one-ment consciousness unfolds as the pure love-wisdom of the buddhic plane impacts the life, mind, and consciousness of the initiate.

When Jesus was in His late twenties and early thirties, the higher pure love-wisdom and the essential love of the Soul blended together harmoniously (as a result of this trine), resulting in a time when there was no difference between them in vibration, note, color, or quality. Blending the love aspects of the Soul with the love-wisdom aspect emanating from the heart center of the Spiritual Triad brings forth a much higher level of peace and harmony, wisdom and truth. The Neptunian energies (via the location where the Moon was placed in Cancer) generated a clear channel from the upper buddhic center onto the heart center in the greater crown center.

Although ray six was the dominant ray influence in Jesus's life, it is the ray two, ray four, ray six line of energies that advance the disciple and initiate along the path of the heart. Here, ray four Mercury conditioned with Pisces (ray two and ray six) harmoniously blended with the ray four Moon and later with the higher ray six energies of Neptune which the Moon had previously veiled.

Once Jesus attained the third initiation, the astral-emotional matter forces that the Moon represents (which tend to block the light in relation to the personal consciousness) were completely dissolved, dissipated, or transmuted. This activity cleared away all the egocentric astral-emotional patterns and lower forces. Jesus no longer responded to people's feelings and emotions personally; rather, He demonstrated unconditional love and compassion for others.

Once cleared, there were no obstructions or distorting influences that could interfere with the pure love-wisdom of the Triad streaming directly from the buddhic plane into His consciousness via the heart center in the greater crown center. This eventually resulted in the embodiment of the love-wisdom of the Divine and the attainment of Christ consciousness.

Moon trine Mid-heaven (5 degrees 39 minutes)

This trine is one of several aspects that indicate Jesus had a relatively stable and nurturing home life and a very good relationship with his mother. The trine of the Moon to the Mid-heaven conferred the energies and qualities necessary for Jesus to relate harmoniously to people as a spiritual leader and the messenger of the Age of Pisces.

Usually, the Moon trine Mid-heaven is a favorable influence for dealing with people in positions of authority, but due to the opposition of Uranus to Pluto and the conjunctions of Uranus to the Sun, Venus, and Mercury, Jesus's ability to deal favorably with authority figures was disrupted, especially once transiting Uranus squared His natal Uranus. This clash was intensified when Jesus started to express His new Piscean understanding and realizations, which pitted Him against the established authority figures of Judea and Rome.

Moon trine North Node (3 degrees 7 minutes)

In general, the aspects to the nodes in a chart relate to people's ability to resonate with the social trends and prevailing attitudes of society. In Jesus's chart, the nodes strongly tied into His life in relation to His mission, but not Him personally.

Many of the aspects formed to the Nodes in Jesus's chart convey an impression that Jesus was harmoniously aligned with the Judean society and life. Since the South Node was conjunct Pluto and the North Node was conjunct Uranus, however, Jesus was integrally tied into the social-political-religious upheaval that was occurring on earth due to the transition from the Age of Aries to the Age of Pisces. He was not aligned with the past (represented by the lunar South Node), which the societal authorities tend to uphold.

The tension between the past and the future as represented by the opposition of Uranus to Pluto and the South Node, along with the aspects Uranus and Pluto formed to His personal planets, sensitized Jesus to the disruptions taking place two thousand years ago. Such social disruption was necessary in order to clear the path for the future to unfold.

Aspects to the Moon discussed in earlier chapters:

Sun trine Moon

Chapter 12

Mercury, the Messenger

Mercury, the smallest of the nine planets of our solar system, plays a significant role in the evolution of human consciousness. From ancient times, Mercury has been the messenger of the Divine. Though much of the understanding given to mankind has been lost or rejected, Mercury remains the great messenger of God both literally and figuratively.

Esotericism recognizes Mercury's role as the divine messenger who brings forth some aspect of the divine plan from the upper mental-plane world of the Soul, which is the world of ideas and causality. All that is manifest originates as a seed idea. In this role, Mercury is the intermediary between the fifth kingdom of the Soul and the human kingdom and the agent who links or relates the concrete mind to the abstract mind.

The energies of Mercury relate, link, bridge, and connect two things to each other. By connecting two ideas, people derive a new thought or idea. By connecting two centers of light and being (e.g., the personal self to the Soul), a higher state of mind is attained. Thus, Mercury is the messenger who relates, links, and connects this to that.

Mercury activates the mental processes that help people attain successively higher states of mind. This activity culminates with the realization and subsequent embodiment of the cosmic ray two quality of love-wisdom. This realization is the underlying purpose for which all life (animate and inanimate) exists in all planes across our solar system. By understanding Mercury astrologically, people can understand how love is awakened within the hearts and minds of mankind at successively higher levels.

Mercury, as the messenger, represents the vehicle through which the factor of consciousness (which originates with the Soul) is anchored in the physical body. This factor of consciousness enables mankind to be self-conscious and consciously aware of its physical, astral-emotional, and mental aspects of personal consciousness, and later aware of itself as a Soul and then as the spiritual self of the Triad. This conscious awareness collectively constitutes the personal mind, the mind of the Soul, and the mind of the Triad. People must bring forth the factor of mind before they can begin to unfold the subtle senses and intellectual capacities that ultimately reveal the second aspect of the Divine.

The energies of Mercury bring forth the faculties of the personal mind that receive and interpret the impulses and impressions of the mind of the Soul. This occurs once a relationship or alignment has been established within the consciousness between the personal mind and Soul.

The ability to be self-conscious distinguishes human beings from the animal kingdom. This factor of the mind is not something that is innate to the physical form, like cellular intelligence. The self-conscious mind started to unfold once the rod of mind was anchored in the etheric body of primitive mankind. The rod of mind is the Divine Flame anchored within the etheric bodies of Homo sapiens before their physical bodies took on the dense physical substances of earth.

Connecting the principle of the mind to the physical forms of primitive mankind set the processes into motion whereby the self-conscious mind could unfold within the physical body. The self-conscious mind of mankind has been slowly but progressively unfolding for millions of years. Mercury is always involved in the development of the self-conscious mind.

Today, the energies of Mercury bring forth the mental aspect of the threefold personal consciousness. Mercury symbolically represents the dynamic of the psyche referred to as intelligence. People use the energies of Mercury to develop the concrete mind, rational logical thought, and the ability to communicate with one another.

Astrologically, the development of human intelligence and the ability to communicate are what Mercury is associated with most frequently. Human intelligence corresponds to the phase of the evolution of consciousness that takes place as the planetary forces of Mercury impact the brain consciousness, which, in turn, is then imprinted upon the mental field of the mind.

At the stage of development of threefold personal consciousness, Mercury expresses primarily in relation to the lower mental plane. During this initial stage, the evolutionary impetus is for mankind to acquire knowledge and understanding in the school of life. As knowledge is obtained via the physical senses and subsequently imprinted upon the mind (located in the mid-mental plane area), the ability to give meaning to that which has been learned on earth unfolds. Meaning enables people to conceptualize life in larger, more integrated, and inclusive terms.

During the long period of this development, the meaning that mankind assigns to what has been learned tends to be skewed by the cultural preferences and personal biases, beliefs, and prejudices of the little self. For this reason, the meaning people assign to that which they have learned is often faulty from the perspective of the Soul.

Mercury is always involved in the development of the self-conscious mind. Specifically, the energies of Mercury are used to create a relationship between two things or two dynamics of the psyche in such a way that knowledge is gained and intelligence is brought forth. This occurs as two elements of the psyche are associated or related to each other. This process gives rise to an awareness of the apparent conflicts within the psyche.

People spend much of their lives resolving the apparent conflicts between the various elements and patterns of consciousness within each of the three aspects of the personal consciousness and between one aspect of consciousness and another aspect. Astrologically, these conflicts are represented by the hard aspects. These clashes within the threefold personal consciousness are merely apparent, however, since only the human consciousness perceives such conflicts.

Conflicts within the psyche are a product of the factor of separatism and personal desire. Together, these two result in the unfoldment of personal preferences, biases, prejudices, etc. During the early stages of development, people do not realize the degree to which the conflicts they experience in their outer lives reflect conflicts within their own psyches.

People experience periods of harmony from time to time as they resolve a conflict between two seemingly opposite emotions, feelings, thoughts, or beliefs. But such periods of harmony are temporary during the stage of human development, for soon a new conflict within the psyche arises that disrupts one's peace.

Once people complete the development of the three aspects of personal consciousness and integrate the three aspects into a state of personal wholeness, they step upon the path as a spiritual probationer and begin to relate elements of the integrated threefold personal consciousness to the corresponding elements of the mind of the Soul. This activity to relate the personal consciousness to the Soul also involves Mercury.

When a relationship is established between the integrated personality and Soul, the energies of the Soul begin to stream onto the individual. This activity slowly brings forth the threefold higher mind. As the higher mind unfolds within the consciousness, the energies emanating from Mercury help people relate the nature, qualities, values, and objectives of the Soul with those of the integrated personality.

Historically, people are oblivious to the differences between themselves and the Soul. They are unaware that they are the dweller-on-the-threshold. This ignorance continues until the battle begins between the personality and the Soul. This battle is memorialized in the Bhagavad-Gita. Here, the personality is represented by Arjuna who must fight his kinsmen. The kinsmen represent all that the personality is tied to emotionally and mentally. Both what people love and what they hate. This battle takes place within the psyche and continues until the Soul (Krishna) is able to take command of one's life (at the third initiation).

The difference between the integrated personality and the Soul is the foremost duality people are confronted with upon the path. The energies of Mercury and Gemini (which Mercury rules at the personality level) impact the consciousness in a way that relates the integrated personality to the Soul. Venus, the Soul-centered ruler of Gemini, reveals how different the nature of the personality is from the Soul.

Once the energies of the Soul begin to stream through the awakened upper centers of the etheric body, people begin their quest for greater understanding. Prior to this time, people accept the thoughts, ideas, and opinions of others as their own, but there is no original thought. On the path, people seek greater knowledge and understanding and begin to think for themselves. This requires a higher frequency and quality of energy to impact the brain than the quality of energy that is needed to retain the thoughts and ideas of others and associate these thoughts in a way that brings forth a new concept or idea.

It is only by seeking a greater understanding that people generate the attractive forces needed to electromagnetically draw the higher energies of the Soul into the mind and onto the consciousness via the upper centers.

Once the stage of the integrated personality is achieved, people can use the higher qualities of Mercury to unfold a more systematic and comprehensive approach to understanding the nature of the physical plane and how it works. The desire for greater understanding electromagnetically attracts the energies of the three petals of the outer knowledge tier of the lotus. The influx of energies from the knowledge petals awakens people's understanding of the laws of nature and helps people gain a broader understanding of the concrete sciences. The consciousness must be impacted by this higher-frequency mental energy of the knowledge petals in order to conceptualize how things work on earth with any degree of accuracy.

The concrete sciences and their respective bodies of knowledge are the product of mankind's scientific research and investigation. Such activity relates primarily to ray five (knowledge, the concrete sciences) and to the path of the mind, not the path of the heart. This higher level of mental development, which takes place as energy streams from the knowledge tier of petals into the etheric body (the throat center in particular), is prerequisite to awakening the essential love of the Soul within these forms of earth. The outer knowledge petals must unfold before the middle love tier of petals can unfold.

The influx of the three sub-qualities of the intelligence aspect of the Soul impact the consciousness once the petals of the knowledge tier are electromagnetically pulled away from the jewel of the lotus. For this to happen, however, the electromagnetic forces people generate as they seek greater knowledge and understanding must exceed the attractive force that holds the knowledge petals tightly to the jewel.

As the energies emanating from the knowledge petals stream through the upper centers, a greater understanding of the nature of the physical-etheric world and the laws that govern it unfolds. In this way, the intelligence aspect of the higher self is unfolded and developed during incarnation on earth. It was the rod of mind anchored in the etheric energy field of primitive mankind in ancient times that manifests on earth as, first the personal mind and then the three aspects of the consciousness of the higher mind (which are the three manifest aspects of the mind of the Soul). Intelligence is innate to all animals, but only human beings can unfold the mind and self-consciousness at successively higher levels.

A well-developed concrete mind with advanced mental faculties (including the faculty of discrimination which distinguishes the Soul from the personality) is a prerequisite to stepping onto the path of the Soul. This means that the personal mind must be able to interpret the impressions and impulses of the Soul into words before the original thought and ideas of the Soul can be registered and comprehended within the (brain) consciousness.

The energies of Mercury are involved in the development of the mental faculties and capacities of mankind, but it is the Soul who is the Thinker. The concrete mind is the mirror that reflects the original ideas developed by the Soul and imprints them onto the (brain) consciousness. The mind, however, can reflect the ideas of the Soul only when it has been sufficiently cleansed of the egocentric dross that covers the surface of the mind and blocks the reflected light and impressions of the Soul.

Once the personality light and the light of the Soul become one, and the elements of self-consciousness are no longer attached to anything in the three planes of earth; the egocentric personal self is sacrificed to the higher self. This is when the Soul takes command of the personality vehicle. This cannot occur as long as people identify their selfhood with the appetites and drives of the physical and subtle vehicles, rather than with the indwelling life of the Soul.

The abstract mind, on the other hand, is unfolded and developed once people generate a mental stream of light that links the knowledge petals to the manasic center. The manasic center retains the principle of mind that mankind is slowly unfolding. It is this principle that is brought forth, first at the personal level as the concrete mind, then at the level of the Soul as the higher mind, and finally at the level of the Spiritual Triad as the creative active intelligence of the Triad.

Mercury is the agent that transmits the factor of illumination in relation to the principle of manas (mind). Ultimately, it is the agent that illumes the consciousness to the existence of the three aspects of the Monad—the integrated personality, the Soul, and the Triad. This illuminating principle of mind is the substance that enables people to interpret the formless symbolic imagery of the abstract mind into words, while it is the abstract mind that interprets the impulses of the higher intuitional mind into universal symbols.

At the higher buddhic level, the emanation of the ray four energies that Mercury transmits brings forth pure illumination. Specifically, it brings forth an illumined awareness of the meaning behind the outer world. This is brought forth via the abstract mind as the Soul peers into the manasic world of meaning and causation. This world maintains the meaning behind all that exists in Creation and conveys that meaning to the consciousness once the concrete mind, the higher mind, and the abstract mind are linked and working together. The world of ideas of the Soul and the world of meaning of the manasic center both underlie the three planes of earth and the concrete mind.

Mercury is a sacred planet that expresses most clearly in the fourth plane of the evolutionary system of earth, the buddhic plane. In relation to the buddhic plane, the energies of Mercury are used to bring forth the intuitional mind and its faculty of pure reasoning. The faculty of pure reasoning enables truth to spontaneously arise within the spiritual mind without mental deliberation. At this much higher level, Mercury works to relate the mind of the Spiritual Triad to the divine order and celestial harmony of the universe.

At the buddhic level, celestial harmony arises within the mind as a natural expression of the balance and harmony of the world of the Real. This state of harmony is attained only when the self-consciousness is no longer attached to or identified with anything that differentiates the integrated personality from the Soul. Duality has been resolved.

Mercury represents the energy that relates the brain to the personal mind, the personal mind to the mind of the Soul, the mind of the Soul to the active intelligence of the Triad, and relates the intelligence to the buddhic intuitional mind. Truly, Mercury is the vehicle that relates and enlightens.

Mercury in Pisces

The sign Mercury is placed in provides important clues as to people's communication skills, how the mind and intellect work, and the kinds of things that people are likely to think and talk about. Both the information that people notice and that which they ignore is greatly influenced by Mercury's sign.

The placement of Mercury in Pisces poses significant problems for people whose consciousness is still polarized at the astral-emotional level, especially when the lower quality of forces is present in the astral body. When this is the case, the placement of Mercury in Pisces often activates a selfish emotional nature that can easily distort people's perception of reality, resulting in fantasies, imagined slights, and illusions that have no basis in reality.

Under Piscean influence, the personal mind does not operate in the same way it does for most people. Often the sensitivity that the energies of Pisces confer results in people being overwhelmed by the feelings and thoughts of others. When this occurs, people's ability to understand the rational world is disrupted. This is due to the ray two and ray six energies Pisces transmits which stimulate the forces of the astral body.

During the early phases of personal development before the heart center is awakened, the energies of both ray two and ray six are drawn into the solar plexus. When this occurs, the influences of Pisces often lead to confusion, drama, and emotionalism. This placement of Mercury is especially troublesome for people whose consciousness is polarized in the lower astral-emotional realm. Here, the potent emotions can disrupt people's thinking and decision-making abilities, and adversely affect their ability to communicate rationally.

On the other hand, this placement of Mercury in Pisces is ideal for those who are spiritually advanced. Here, the ability to visualize one's thoughts and memories contribute to a mental capacity that is quite unusual and often inspired. Pisces contributes an inclusive, unifying factor to the personal mind that orients people toward the spiritual world. It often brings forth a concern for the well-being of others. This includes a concern for the well-being of friends and loved ones, as well as a concern for humanity in general.

Since the unifying factor of ray two Pisces has the opposite effect upon the intellect compared to the separating factor that usually conditions it, this placement of Mercury in Pisces does not promote intellectualism. Nor does it confer an interest in studying the knowledge of the world. Instead, the mind tends to be more oriented toward the nonphysical world. This includes the astral-emotional world and the higher spiritual worlds. People with Mercury in Pisces are often more interested in spirituality and in developing their psychic abilities, visualization, and the higher creative imagination than they are with the concrete mind and logical, rational thinking abilities.

For most people, the development of the personal intellect is emphasized between the ages of fourteen and twenty-eight. This was not the case in Jesus's life due to the strong influence of Pisces. Jesus did not focus on advancing the personal mind and intellect. Nor did He focus His thoughts on the material things of earth. Since Pisces is antithetical to the three matter planes of earth, as well as antithetical to the factor of separatism, the mind of Jesus was relatively free of many of the divisive mental influences most people experience.

This placement of Mercury in Pisces oriented Jesus in a positive and constructive way to the spirituality of Judea at a young age. This was possible since He did not have patterns of consciousness that connected Him to the troubling astral forces that activate egocentric emotionalism. These had been eliminated prior to incarnation.

Mercury in Pisces naturally aligned and attuned the mind of Jesus to the mind of the Soul and its quality of essential love, and later (once He had brought forth the higher mind) attuned Him in heart and mind to the world of the intuitional mind, pure reasoning, love, and wisdom.

Once the third initiation has been attained, Mercury is no longer involved in the development of the personal mind or the unfoldment of the threefold mind of the Soul. At this higher stage, the placement of Mercury in Pisces is the astrological signature of the initiate who can serve as a messenger of the Divine. Here, the mind of the Soul supplants the concrete mind as the initiating, driving factor in life. The concrete mind remains a valuable tool only in terms of the Soul's service work on earth. Here, Mercury is no longer engaged in developing the mental aspect of personal consciousness. The personal light of the mind has been absorbed into the causal light of the world of the Soul.

Before the mind of the Soul is able to supplant the concrete mind, the vision of the Soul must be unfolded within the consciousness. This occurs as the ajna is increasingly magnetized receptive toward ray four energies. People begin to perceive the visions of the Soul as the energies (magnetized by pure ray four) stream through the ajna and impact the consciousness.

Only when the ajna is magnetized to ray four energies can the third eye be developed. The threefold kundalini is also involved in this activity, along with the uplifted energies of the centers along the spine. Together, these uplifted energies draw down the higher ray four sub-qualities, first from the Soul and then from the buddhic center. These, in turn, blend and unify with the uplifted purified energies streaming into the ajna from the upper centers.

The spiritualization of the personal consciousness, along with the awakening of the ajna, involves a rather lengthy process whereby the self-consciousness that expresses via the basic, sacral, and solar plexus centers are transformed in nature and quality, and then uplifted into the upper etheric centers. Again, this activity occurs as people naturally abide by the basic laws that govern humanity and establish right relations one with another.

When this is the case, people exhibit personal responsibility, kindness, considerateness, integrity, honesty, forgiveness, and human decency. Later, as people continue to progress, the self-consciousness that expresses via the solar plexus, heart, and throat centers are transformed and uplifted into the ajna. This occurs as people respond to the Laws of the Soul, even when they are unaware of them. Mercury in Pisces contributes the quality of love people must respond to in feeling and thought in order to transfer the elements of self-consciousness from the heart and throat centers into the ajna center.

The transference of the refined astral forces into the ajna center brings forth and advances the faculty of the higher creative imagination, clairvoyance, and the inner mind's eye—the vision of the Soul within the form. Prior to this development, the Monad sees only into the world of the Soul, while people operating at the level of the Soul-infused personality see into or sense the world of the Soul but nothing higher.

The inner mind's eye is a faculty of vision that is needed in order for the initiate to see that which exists in the world of the Soul and in the higher formless planes of light. The energies of Mercury are integrally involved in the processes that help generate this faculty of sight—the inner mind's eye. Through this eye, the interrelated and interconnected reality that exists in the higher planes is slowly revealed.

Jesus used the energies of Mercury to unfold the third eye and to link to and eventually bring forth the intuitional mind. He also used the energies of Mercury to relate the abstract mind to the higher intuitional mind. Because of the close relationship He established between these two aspects of the mind, Jesus became receptive of the impressions of the intuitional mind at a relatively young age. Once interpreted into words, the impressions He perceived were relayed to the concrete mind and brain without significant distortion. By way of the inner mind's eye, Jesus perceived successively higher revelations and realizations.

Mercury in Pisces also activates the potential for telepathic communications. Telepathy enables an initiate to hear that which is being communicated from the spirit side of life by the initiates and masters. This ability leads to the unfoldment of the skill and ability to telepathically receive the communications of the enlightened ones of the higher planes. It was exceedingly important for Jesus to develop this higher form of telepathy in order to fulfill His mission.

Mercury in Pisces is one of the many astrological factors that oriented Jesus to the spiritual world and focused His thoughts and feelings upon the Father and the heavenly realm. This placement also unfolded and enhanced His higher creative imagination. Eventually, the energies of Mercury in Pisces helped Jesus to relate His consciousness to the heart of the world of the Soul and later relate His consciousness to the pure love-wisdom aspect of the Spiritual Self.

Both in relation to the Soul and to the higher buddhic center, Mercury serves as the factor that relates the mind to the second aspect of the Divine (love-wisdom) at each level. Jesus became so consciously responsive to the essential love of the Soul and the pure love-wisdom of the Triad that He became the embodiment of love itself. Love flowed freely through Him. This was possible once the lower concrete mind was free of the personal elements of consciousness that obstruct the influx of the unifying, blending, magnetic qualities of love-wisdom.

Mercury in Pisces also intensified Jesus's sensitivity to the pain and suffering of others especially when He was young. Since the power of divine will initially expresses via the mental nature, Jesus's mental awareness of and sensitivity to the plight of mankind brought forth a strong desire and determination to relieve the pain of others. This resulted in His development of phenomenal healing abilities.

Jesus was unusually compassionate, caring, and empathetically responsive to the feelings and thoughts of others because of the strong influence of Pisces and Neptune. Sensitive people often feel the emotional pain of others, but they often fail to realize that the emotional pain they are feeling originates with someone or something in their environment, not with them. They accept it as their own. Jesus was able to feel the pain and suffering of others, but He did not personally identify with their pain or claim it as His own.

Mercury and Duality

Although Venus is said to be the alter ego of the earth, Mercury resonates with the human race itself. The close relationship of human beings to Mercury is due to the fact that the human race is on the ray four just like Mercury. (Each of the four kingdoms in nature is on a different ray.)

Both Mercury and the human race are associated with duality and with the knowledge that is gained when people resolve duality. The multitude of dualities that people need to address during the stage of development of the threefold personal consciousness is daunting. Humanity is confronted with duality at every stage up to the fifth initiation.

According to esoteric thought, duality is not limited to the cosmic physical plane. Nor was it expected to appear on earth except in a relatively minor way in relation to the physical body. Duality originated and continues to exist in the cosmic astral plane and involves two competing cosmic intentions.

There are no words that adequately describe the nature of this cosmic astral duality. It isn't really a conflict between cosmic good and cosmic evil except in the sense that cosmic good corresponds to the purpose which the Solar Logos serves. The purpose behind Creation that both the Planetary Logos and the Solar Logos serve relates to the evolution of life and consciousness out of matter. Thus, the evil that exists in the cosmic astral plane refers to a cosmic intention that rejects this activity of the Logos to blend and unify the three aspects of the universal mind and works against the efforts to awaken the heart center of the ONE. Its focus is involutionary and involves encasing life in the dense substances of the cosmic physical plane.

This quality of evil of the cosmic astral plane has a corresponding outpost in the lower astral plane of earth. Primitive mankind is said to have generated emotional-desire forces that attracted these involutionary forces of cosmic evil. It is they who created a center of darkness in the lower astral plane, and it is they who generate and illicit resistance to the evolutionary efforts of the Planetary Logos. A large number of people respond to their influence and resist all evolutionary efforts to fulfill the purpose the Logos serves.

Cosmic duality is a temporary situation necessary in order for the cosmic initiates of the star system of Sirius to develop certain cosmic skills, capacities, powers (siddhis) and abilities. Once the Masters of Sirius develop them, the forces of darkness that oppose the unification of the three aspects of the universal mind at the cosmic astral level will be absorbed back into the All.

Without the sustaining energies from the cosmic astral plane, the field of darkness on earth will begin to dissipate. As long as mankind generates intense emotions, selfish ill will, hatred, and violence, however, this astral center of darkness will remain vital. On earth, mankind opened the door to evil and is responsible for shutting the door.

The other significant factor that ties Mercury and humanity together is the fact that both relate to the factual mind—the center known as active intelligence. Humanity is responsible for the full development and perfection of the third aspect of the Divine, active intelligence. This includes the concrete mind, the higher mind, and the abstract mind.

Collectively, the human race is responsible for manifesting or objectifying the third aspect of the human Monad on earth. The collective minds of humanity constitutes the conscious life of the third center of the Planetary Logos—the planetary throat center. The Masters of the Spiritual Hierarchy, on the other hand, comprise the conscious life of the planetary heart center.

Once people complete their development of these three aspects of personal consciousness according to their own unique patterning, they are able to shift their consciousness into the light of the world of the Soul and begin to unfold and develop love-wisdom. As they do, they begin to resonate with the Masters of the Spiritual Hierarchy.

Once initiates have developed both the active intelligence and love-wisdom, they are offered the occult training needed to become the co-creative agents of the Divine. As co-creators, the initiate works to bring forth the perfected world envisioned within the mind of the Logos. This involves transforming the three planes of earth (the mind-created worlds) into a state of manifest perfection.

Before mankind is able to fully manifest active intelligence on earth, the preferences and interests (dualities) of the little self must be eliminated from the collective minds of humanity. Thus, humanity must attain a significantly higher state of mind before the divine purpose is realized in terms of the Third Aspect of the Monad, active intelligence.

For this reason, it is exceedingly important to understand the steps and stages of the path of the Soul that lead to the attainment of successively higher levels of initiation.

Chapter 13

Transformations of the Mind

Mercury opposite Pluto (18 minutes)

Mercury was eighteen minutes away from an exact opposition with Pluto when Jesus was born. To understand the significance of this, it is helpful to think of an aspect in the birth chart in terms of the effects that planetary transits have when they form an aspect to a planet.

As Saturn and the outer planets come within five degrees of forming an exact aspect to a planet of the natal chart, subtle changes start to take place in the psyche. When the two planets are within twenty-five minutes of forming an exact aspect, the point of tension generated by the transiting planet usually precipitates an event in people's lives.

With the opposition of Mercury to Pluto being so close in the chart of Jesus, Pluto repeatedly precipitated powerful experiences and events in the life of Jesus that simultaneously impacted the two dynamics of the psyche that Mercury and Pluto represent. When a transiting planet formed a major aspect to Mercury, it also formed a major aspect to Pluto. This greatly intensified the periodic changes taking place in the mind of Jesus, resulting in significant transformations of His life, mind, and consciousness.

Both dynamics of the psyche represented by Mercury and Pluto were impacted simultaneously, since the opposition was within the orb of event precipitation. If the orb was wider, major events precipitated by the slow transits of the outer planets would be experienced in relation to one psychic dynamic at a time. For Jesus, a transiting planet to this opposition would also have activated the power of the opposition itself, forcing Him to establish a relationship between the two psychic dynamics that Mercury and Pluto represent. Thus, the effect that this potent opposition had on Jesus was intense and significant. Also, this opposition of Mercury and Pluto represented one of the two arms of the mutable cross, the importance of which was revealed toward the end of His life on earth.

Aspects of ease formed by transiting planets to this opposition helped to relate the will (Pluto) to the personal mind (Mercury). Hard aspects formed by transiting planets to this Mercury-Pluto opposition generated significant tension that could be resolved only by moving to the midpoint of the opposition. This involved removing all sense of identification with the Mercurial psychic dynamic (intelligence, concrete mind, etc.) and with the plutonian psychic dynamic (personal will). At the mid-point, ray four Mercury and ray one Pluto along with ray two Virgo and ray two and ray six Pisces were blended and unified, resulting in a higher quality of faculties, skills, capacities, and so forth.

Again, Mercury represents the concrete mind and the functional capacity of the intellect at the personal level. Its placement and aspects provide information as to how the concrete mind works and what topics concern and interest the individual. The astrological factors associated with Mercury affect the quality of the personal mind that people develop and their ability to communicate their thoughts and ideas to others.

The concrete mind is comprised of certain mental faculties and capacities. This includes such things as the faculty of discrimination, memory, and rational, logical thought. This ability to think rationally and logically at the personal level, however, relates only to the three planes of earth. Over the years, the personal mind and intellect of mankind have produced the concrete sciences and knowledge. This is the factual, scientifically verifiable world of mankind.

The intellect that the energies of Mercury bring forth at the personal level is used to gather, categorize, and organize thoughts that already exist. It does not conceptualize original ideas or thought. However, it enables people to associate different facts to arrive at a new conclusion or understanding. The ray one energies of Pluto, on the other hand, relate to the impersonal will of the Divine.

In Jesus's life, the role Pluto played far exceeded the purpose it usually serves in relation to the evolution of consciousness. This is because Pluto served as the powerful focusing lens for the energies of the epic grand trine. Once the personal mind was sufficiently developed and Pluto (the will) was related to Mercury (the dynamic of the intellect), Pluto focused all seven rays that the planets of the epic grand trine transmitted into the mind of Jesus. In this way, the three aspects and the four attributes of God were relatively unified in the mind and consciousness of Jesus almost simultaneously.

Ray one pierces the subtle bodies (the mental, astral, and etheric force fields) and directly stimulates the brain consciousness. It is not impeded by the mental or astral force fields like the other ray energies. As ray one energies move through the subtle bodies, they stimulate the forces present in all three force fields. For this reason, the effect Pluto has on people depends on the quality of forces present in the respective subtle bodies.

Ray one forces are especially potent in terms of stimulating the physical-instinctual and lower astral-emotional patterns of behavior and characteristics, as they stream through the deepest levels of the psyche.

Plutonian energies often activate the character, tendencies, and traits of the instinctual, lower emotional nature, such as fear (especially fear that relates to survival), anger, hostility, aggression, vindictiveness, manipulation, and unbridled selfishness and greed.

Pluto transmits the ray one power that people experience most often in its aspect as the destroyer. Since the energies of Pluto stimulate the emotional and instinctual patterns of behavior present in the subtle bodies, less evolved people with this aspect can be somewhat ruthless, even malevolent. It is common for their speech to be accusatory, emotionally charged, abrupt, harsh, demanding, and willful.

People with this aspect who are still at the early stages of personal development often victimize others directly or indirectly through passive-aggressive behavior or emotional manipulation and domination. Those who are more advanced, on the other hand, tend to be victimized by people around them. In either case, the perpetrator is expressing the lower astral-instinctual forces that Pluto has activated.

Few people understand the impersonal will aspect of the Divine. Nor do they understand its purpose or understand what it stimulates in relation to human consciousness. In general, the instinctual mind and the lower astral-emotional nature operate below the light of conscious awareness. This makes it hard to understand how the destructive forces that Pluto activates are usually forces within one's own causal field. Instead, people with this aspect often feel as if they are being unfairly victimized.

When Mercury and Pluto form a close opposition to each other, people are sensitive to the dark, destructive forces of the outer world. The opposition of these two energies suggests that Jesus from a young age was aware of mankind's harshness and malevolence. As He grew up, He was particularly sensitive to the dark underbelly of the Roman-Judean society. However, the great influx of love-wisdom that poured onto Jesus precluded Him from responding to people's harshness in a negative way.

Ray one in its aspect as the destroyer precipitates events and experiences that can result in the transmutation of forces and the elimination of the forms and structures in people's lives that are obsolete, including such things as, a job, home, faith, or belief system. During the evolution of consciousness, the various mental structures in people's lives are subject to ongoing dissolution and destruction.

The destruction of the old structures, beliefs, and ideas is needed before more appropriate forms and structures can be created. For this reason, when Pluto forms a hard aspect to Mercury, it triggers significant transformation of the mind and forces the elimination of obsolete emotional and mental patterns, forms, and structures of the psyche. When eliminated, new structures must to be created through which the consciousness can continue its development, but at a higher level. People use the forces of the second sub-aspect of ray one—the builder sub-aspect—to create more appropriate structures and forms to replace those that were destroyed.

Throughout life, the consciousness is repeatedly transformed. With each major transformation, the consciousness shifts to a higher level. During this evolutionary journey, the consciousness shifts higher in terms of quality, inclusiveness, expansiveness, sensitivity, note, color, and vibration within a particular plane of development (there are seven sub-planes), as well as shift from one plane to a higher plane, e.g., from the astral plane to the mental plane.

This Pluto opposition to Mercury along with Pluto's opposition to the Sun sensitized Jesus to the malevolence in the world and substantiated His belief in evil and Satan. On a more positive note, the interplay of the energies of this opposition helped clear His mind and transform His thinking, resulting in greater one-pointed focus and concentration.

Pluto does not represent hell or the actions of Satan, although it can sure seem like it. Generally, the problem lies with the character of the person who expresses its intense force. Even today, much of humanity continues to be responsive to and expressive of the lower instinctual, feeling nature of primitive mankind.

The lowest, most destructive forces of hatred that people have generated over the years are still active in the collective unconscious, but so are the highest most beautiful expressions of love and light. The innermost point of every atom is divine light.

People's ability to control the way they react to the events in their lives is a developed capacity. Control over the forces of three matter planes is not innate to human beings; rather, it is a skill that people must develop and constantly exercise once they have attained a mental polarization of the consciousness. It is the light of their own personal mind strengthened by the light of the Soul that people must apply to their physical-instinctual and astral-emotional natures to control them.

Mental control and then mastery of the lower forces that express in people's lives represent the beginning of true human evolution. Until control is gained, people's development involves the unfoldment of the intelligences of the physical and subtle bodies (the vehicles of the Soul), not to the evolvement of consciousness. Thus, the development of the faculties, capacities, skills, etc., of the threefold personal consciousness relates to the development of a form vehicle (the personality). The evolutionary objective is to refine and purify the subtle bodies and personality so that the Soul can use them to express its nature and qualities on earth.

On the path, people develop the ability to respond to the higher, more refined types and qualities of forces and refuse to react to the lower, coarse types and qualities of forces. Only by aligning and attuning to the Soul and its values and qualities can the consciousness stop expressing a nature that is characteristic of the involutionary elemental lives of the respective physical and subtle bodies. On the path, people slowly eliminate their conscious response to the lower forces of the physical and subtle bodies as they align and attune first to the Soul, and then to the Real Self.

All energies seek to express physically regardless of their nature and quality or the effect they might have on the personal consciousness. When people do not utilize the forces of Pluto to transmute the obsolete forms and structures in their lives, someone in their environment is likely to express these forces for them. People can be victimized by the destructive forces of Pluto when they refuse to make the changes in their life that Pluto is activating. Often, people's own psychic resistance to this process of transformation is what victimizes them.

Because of the quality of the low-vibratory forces Pluto activates and the way people react and respond to them, people with this aspect are either the perpetrators of violence, harsh speech, and interrogations, or they are victimized by others. Frequently people with this aspect are rather opinionated. This trait also triggers resistance and opposition, especially to the individual's ideas, thoughts, and views.

Although Jesus did not express the kind of behavior that less evolved people with this aspect often do, He was not immune from the ruthless acts and behavior of others that this combination of energies precipitates.

When considering the effects this opposition had on Jesus, it is important to look at the purpose that this opposition served in relation to Jesus and His mission. Pluto in its aspect as the destroyer is always the agent behind the transformation of the consciousness. By eliminating obsolete emotional and mental patterns of consciousness, people are able to bring forth new, better equipped, and more expansive forms and structures of the mind that enable them to experience a greater truth and understanding.

There comes a point when old habits and obsolete ways of life block further growth. When these are eliminated, the consciousness is transformed and rejuvenated. The capacities of the new forms that replace them should allow for a greater understanding, resulting in an expansion of the consciousness. Obsolete forms and structures can include people's beliefs and thoughts, their superstitions, and personal emotional and mental patterns. Often the death of the physical body relates to the need of the Soul to appropriate a better, more capable physical body.

When Mercury is in aspect to Pluto in the natal chart, people's thoughts are deepened, strengthened, and intensified. The combination of these two energies is often used to develop concentration and one-pointed focus. This relates to the ability to focus the mind without being distracted by other considerations. One-pointed focus and concentration represent the most important skill people can develop upon the path. Without it, people are unable to maintain their focus long enough in meditation to shift their consciousness away from the impulses of the body and emotions, and still the chatter of the mind. This is necessary in order to sense the world of the Soul and the higher planes of light.

It was His one-pointed focus and great powers of concentration that enabled Jesus to progress quickly. The power of Jesus's thoughts, ideas, and words were greatly intensified by this aspect. Undoubtedly Jesus was exceptionally persuasive.

Many people with this opposition have fanatical, intensely-held ideas, beliefs, and opinions, especially when they are focused on the development of the mental aspect of personal consciousness. Since Jesus had attained a higher level of spiritual development prior to incarnating, it wasn't His nature to force His ideas onto others or overpower them, yet His words and ideas had a power that few people have ever seen.

Once the second initiation had been attained and the ajna center was magnetized receptive toward ray four and the energies of Mercury, the energies that Pluto transmitted helped Jesus to perceive the motives behind the words and actions of others. Jesus could see through the masks people wear and perceive their inner character. Undoubtedly, many people found this unsettling, especially those who had something to hide.

By way of His ajna center, Jesus could pierce the shields that people hide behind. He could even peer through the walls that conceal the unconscious. Nothing obstructed His vision. This penetrating vision that the opposition of Pluto to Mercury helped unfold was not clairvoyance, although Jesus was very clairvoyant. Nor was it the intuition, though He was very intuitive. Due to the involvement of the will, the form of vision He developed as He approached the fourth initiation is comparable to the concept of the all-seeing Eye of God.

Pluto is always associated with a heightened interest in the occult. When functioning at the personal level, this interest includes a fascination with occult powers, sexuality, and the taboos of society. Often people have an anti-establishment disposition that leads to conflicts with authority figures. The energies generated by this opposition encourage people to challenge authority figures and their right to govern. This is appropriate when the individual is on the path of initiation. But when people are functioning at the level of the instinctual, astral-emotional aspect of personal consciousness, their challenges are usually unconstructive, frequently disruptive, and even destructive.

Mercury opposite Pluto and Mars conjunct Saturn are the two tightest aspects in the chart of Jesus. Pluto's opposition to Mercury and Uranus, and its inconjunction to Mars and Saturn clearly tied Jesus into the struggle between the waning Age of Aries and the dawning

Piscean Age. A clash between the ideas and principles of these two Ages first arose within the mind of Jesus. During His ministry, however, this clash generated a number of conflicts between Him and the society. By necessity, this transition from the Age of Aries into the Age of Pisces called elements of Judaism into question.

The energies that stream onto the earth during a particular Age are also magnetized by the rays transmitted by the sign of that Age. The ray of an Age serves as the deep, underlying magnetic currents that span the two thousand years of the Age. Also, there is an additional ray of manifestation that greatly affects the development of the mind and consciousness during a particular Age.

During the Age of Pisces, the dominant ray of manifestation was ray six. This is in addition to the ray two and ray six energies that Pisces transmits into our solar system. With this dual emphasis upon ray six, the unfoldment of devotion and dedication to an ideal has been the most important influence affecting people and their personal and spiritual growth for the past two thousand years. During the Age of Aquarius, the dominant ray of manifestation on earth will be ray seven. However, ray five, which Aquarius transmits, will also be an important magnetic quality impacting the growth of consciousness during the Age of Aquarius.

It is the rays, not the planetary forces that condition the unfolding spiritual consciousness during a particular Age. Each Age pertains specifically to the development of a way to approach the Divine. Since Judaism was developed during the Age of Aries, it is an approach along the ray one, ray three, ray five, and ray seven line of manifestation. This approach to the Divine corresponds to the path of power and mind. Since Mercury rules Aries at the level of the Soul, the spirituality of the Age of Aries emphasized law and religious authority.

At the personality level, the Arian approach involved cultivating obedience to the will of God (as conceived by mankind). With Mercury as the Soul-centered ruler of Aries, the spirituality of the Age of Aries involved the unfoldment of knowledge in terms of universal law. The spirituality that was being impressed upon humanity during the Arian Age focused primarily on the establishment of the universal laws of humanity. The intent of such laws is to shift human consciousness away from the characteristics and tendencies that arise due to the nature of the physical body and its instinctual nature. Growth during the Age of Aries related to people's obedience to such things as the Ten Commandments: do not kill, do not steal, do not bear false witness, do not covet, honor your father and mother, and so forth.

The Age of Pisces, on the other hand, is a ray six approach to the Divine, not a ray one, ray three, or ray seven approach. This ray six approach involves cultivating devotion to God in the aspect of love. It represents a movement away from a wrathful, willful God that was worshipped and feared during the Age of Aries. Here, Mars as the ruler of Aries at the personality level is exceedingly active. The spirituality of the Age of Aries, however, involved Mercury as the Soul-centered ruler of Aries. By way of the influence of Mercury, Moses intuited spiritual law for the Hebrews during the early centuries of the Age of Aries.

Unfortunately, the lower ray six influences of Mars were carried from the Age of Aries into the Age of Pisces, due to the fact that ray six was the dominant ray of manifestation during the Age of Pisces. The non-sacred planet, Mars, represents the lower personality expression of ray six.

Esoterically, Mars at the personality level represents the "desire-in-action" dynamic of the psyche. This is the most common expression of the energies of Mars when people are at the stage of personal development. Since the consciousness of mankind has been polarized at the astral-emotional level throughout the Age of Pisces, this lower, personal expression of ray six Mars has permeated the two ray six World Religions of the Piscean Age—Christianity and Islam.

At the higher Soul level, this shift from the Age of Aries to the Age of Pisces involved a rather dramatic shift—from ray four (Harmony through Conflict), which Mercury[41] transmits, to ray one Pluto, divine will. At the level of the Soul, this shift activated a higher spiritual expression of divine will and a dedication to the will of God.

At the Soul Level, ray one Pluto compels the unfoldment and development of the love aspect of the Divine. This ray one Soul approach to the Divine during the Age of Pisces is very different from the way people approach the Divine when they are functioning at the personality level. The approach to the Divine at the Soul level can be defined as the will-to-love.

Since ray six Mars rules Aries at the level of the personality and the sacred ray six planet, Neptune, rules Pisces, the shift from the Age of Aries to the Age of Pisces represents a major change in emphasis. In the Age of Aries the emphasis was on obedience to an authoritarian God of law. In the Age of Pisces the emphasis is on devotion to a forgiving, merciful, loving God. Very different aspects of the Divine are emphasized with respect to these two Ages, both at the personality level and at the Soul level.

Esoteric analysis of the chart of Jesus reveals that the Soul's intent and objective for Jesus was to align with, attune to, and then sacrifice His personal will to the will of the Soul. This sacrifice of the personal will to the will of the Soul corresponds perfectly with

---

[41] Esoterically, Mercury represents the first impulse of an idea that is projected into the upper mental plane as a seed idea. The seed idea moves from the world of ideas once they are clothed in mental substance into the astral plane, where it is clothed in desire. Once clothed with desire, the idea streams onto the brain consciousness, where it brings forth new thoughts and ideas. In the Age of Aries, Mercury, as the Soul-centered ruler of Aries, brought forth many of the religious rules, laws, regulations, and commandments that dominated the Age.

the shift from the personality ruler of Pisces (Neptune and to an extent Jupiter) to the Soul-centered ruler of Pisces, Pluto.

Pluto, as the Soul-centered ruler of Pisces, opposite the stellium planets in Pisces indicates the initial conflict that Jesus faced was a conflict between the Soul and the integrated personality in terms of the will. Jesus's path called for Him to shift away from obedience to a rather stern Father of the covenant and move toward cultivating devotion to a loving Father. This He accomplished by embodying the fullness of the will-to-love, which Pluto in combination with Neptune and Pisces bring forth.

This opposition of Pluto to Mercury in the chart of Jesus was central to bringing about the understanding Jesus needed in order to make this transition in mind and consciousness from the Age of Aries into the Age of Pisces. This involved a complete transformation from His Arian mind-set to the new Piscean mind-set. This transformation called for eliminating or transforming His beliefs, thoughts, opinions, and ideas (Mercury) that aligned with the Age of Aries, while unfolding those that were of a Piscean quality and nature, i.e., the will-to-love. This transformation of His consciousness occurred in Jesus's life as people challenged His thoughts, beliefs, and ideas. Undoubtedly, many of His ideas drew ridicule and scorn.

Again, the clash between the principles of these two Ages initially played out within His own psyche as Jesus worked out His truth during the early days of the Piscean Age. The persistent conflicts within His own psyche between the ideas of these two Ages led Him to the burning ghat again and again, where the fires of spirit burned away His obsolete Arian views, beliefs, and ideas. Each time He experienced the burning ghat of transformation, His consciousness shifted upward.

All of His thoughts and beliefs that were strictly Arian in nature needed to be burned away. This freed up His mind to receive and comprehend the new Piscean concepts, principles, and ideas, especially in terms of this new Piscean approach to the Divine. Many of the new Piscean ideas and beliefs, however, only represented a higher level of spirituality than what the Soul of Jesus had demonstrated in past lives during the Age of Aries. The level of spirituality Jesus attained in His previous lifetimes prepared Him well for attaining Christ consciousness during the early days of the Age of Pisces.

The moment Jesus's public ministry started, this clash between these two Ages arose in the outer world of His day-to-day life. The clashes He experienced involved people who aligned themselves with the Judean establishment (especially the scribes and Pharisees). These clashes were emblematic of the clash between these two Ages that was occurring two thousand years ago within the consciousness of mankind.

This conflict between the past and the future centered on the two different approaches to the Divine that these two Ages represent. Those who strictly adhered to the rules, regulations, and laws of Judaism embodied the forces of resistance and strongly opposed the new Piscean teachings that Jesus was presenting.

It was this opposition of Pluto to Mercury along with Pluto's opposition to Uranus that generated much of the energy that fueled the conflicts between these two very different mind-sets. In this way, the new Piscean principles, beliefs, ideas, and concepts were worked out and formulated in the mind of Jesus and subsequently anchored in the center called humanity as the path of the heart.

Throughout the Piscean Age, the heart centers of mankind have been slowly opening, first at the personal level and then in relation to the Soul and its essential love. The opening of the heart center is a long process of cultivating a loving, caring, and considerate personal disposition. By way of loving one another, sharing one's bounty with others, and helping others improve the quality of their lives, the petals of the heart center unfold.

Since most of the planets in Jesus's chart formed an aspect to this opposition of Mercury and Uranus to Pluto, Jesus's teachings added to the tension in Judea during the latter days of this transition between the two Ages. Judaism was not the only Arian religion in the world, but it was the religion that gave birth to the two ray-six World Religions of the Piscean Age: Christianity and Islam. Over time, these two religions supplanted most of the other Arian religions on earth.

Destruction and endings as well as reconstruction and new beginnings (resulting in transformation and growth) fall under the dominion of Pluto. Pluto's great impact upon the life of Jesus and on Judea, itself, cannot be denied. The energies and influences of Pluto definitely transformed the mind and consciousness of Jesus. This was necessary in order for Him to become the messenger of the Piscean Age.

Eventually, Jesus sacrificed His personal will to the will of the Soul. This occurred as He approached the third initiation and transcended the threefold personal consciousness. This process of plutonian endings and new beginnings then continued as Jesus approached the fourth initiation.

Once the initiate attains the fourth initiation, all that binds the consciousness to the three planes of earth is severed. The buddhic state of mind (which is the pure love-wisdom aspect of the Spiritual Triad) is attained. This state of mind is known as Christ consciousness. Christ consciousness is attained when the mind of the higher self is completely transformed by the pure reasoning and love-wisdom of the planes of light.

Mercury conjunct Uranus (1 degree 56 minutes)

While Mercury represents the concrete mind and intelligence at the personal level of development initially, Uranus corresponds to the abstract mind and the intelligence aspect of the Spiritual Self. Again, the abstract mind is the faculty that interprets the seed ideas of the intuitive mind and interprets the refined light patterns of wisdom and truth into deeply symbolic, archetypal images, and prototypes. The personal mind, in turn, interprets these symbolic images into words. The intuited realizations imaged by the abstract mind must be translated into words before the consciousness can comprehend that which has been intuited.

The Masters of the Spiritual Hierarchy (who are responsive to the emanations of love from the planetary heart) deposit seed ideas into the upper mental-plane world in an effort to awaken mankind to a new understanding, invention, or discovery. These seed ideas have a specific purpose, intent, and objective in relation to the growth of human consciousness and the advancement of life on earth.

Unfortunately, the seed ideas deposited in the upper mental plane often do not have the effect upon the knowledge and understanding of mankind that the Masters intended. Distortion can enter each step of the process. The abstract mind can fail to generate the best symbol or image to represent the essential message of the seed idea. The Soul can fail to accurately conceptualize that which it perceives as it focuses on the world of meaning and causation. Most significant, the concrete mind with its personal biases and preferences, established beliefs and opinions, frequently uses inappropriate words to describe the ideas that the Soul has formulated. Even when there is a relatively accurate understanding of the seed idea, people often fail to use the best words to define or describe that which they have intuited.

Any of these situations results in a failure to bring forth the understanding that the Masters had intended. There are always forces of resistance on earth that interfere with establishing new beliefs, thoughts, ideas, and understanding. In many instances, the words chosen to interpret that which is intuited are purposefully biased by the personally oriented brain consciousness. This results in a failure of the words to accurately communicate the intent and meaning of the seed ideas. For these reasons, the mental plane is looked at by the Masters as a realm of illusion. (Illusion relates only to intuited revelations, not to the factual reality of earth. Facts are facts. The sun rises in the morning and sets in the evening.)

From the perspective of the Masters who reside in the world of the Real, the thoughts that dominate mankind in all areas of life on earth often violate the nature and character of the world of the Real. Since the thoughts and ideas that correspond to the spirit side of life are often faulty, people's understanding of the nature of the human constitution and the purpose of life is often distorted. This includes mankind's theologies even when they are based on the words of a master who incarnated to present a new, greater understanding of truth.

For disciples, when Mercury and Uranus are conjunct, a greater understanding of truth can be perceived without the usual degree of personal distortion. Still, the moment truth is stepped down from the world of experience and formulated into words, truth is circumscribed. By definition, words contribute an element of distortion and misunderstanding of the truth that is experienced in the planes of light and the world of the Real. Truth can only be experienced in the formless planes of light, where words do not veil or conceal the experience.

Although Jesus was free of many of the personal biases and preferences that plague most people, some religious and cultural distortion still entered His mind. Regardless of the purity of His own realizations, He needed to use words that people were familiar with in order to communicate His understanding.

According to traditional astrology, this conjunction of Mercury and Uranus brings about a harmonious relationship between the lower octave mental energy and the higher octave mental energy of Uranus. In other words, this close conjunction of Mercury and Uranus in Jesus's chart indicates that His concrete mind worked well with the higher expressions of the mind (the mind of the Soul, and later the mind of the Real Self) as soon as Jesus had unfolded the higher expression of the mind.

A unity of the lower concrete mind with the higher abstract mind usually requires tremendous work to achieve, since they represent two distinctively different centers of conscious life with very different values, qualities, nature, and perspectives. The concrete mind is the mind of the personal self, which is operative in the three planes of matter, while the abstract mind is the mind of the Spiritual Triad, which is accessed via the mind of the Soul.

To bring about a union of the lower and higher aspects of the mind, people need to accept the processes whereby the energies of Uranus break up the crystallized, obsolete personal thoughts, ideas, views, and opinions. This includes allowing the social and cultural patterns of thought, which have crystallized in the concrete mind, to be removed, transmuted, or destroyed. Clearing the mind of its egocentric mental patterns is necessary in order to prepare the faculties of the personal mind to perceive a higher level of understanding. Even those who are capable of perceiving the original thoughts of the Soul are often unwilling to let go of their personal beliefs and ideas that are contrary to the original ideas they have intuited.

The concrete mind must be cleansed of its self-referencing influences before the consciousness can shift upward into the world of the Soul and later shift into the planes of light of the Spiritual Triad. Neither the factor of concretization nor separatism has any effect upon the mind of the Soul or the intuitional mind.

During the early stages of development, the concretization of an idea is necessary in order to envelop an idea with lower mental, astral, and physical-etheric substances. Ideas must be objectified in order for the brain consciousness to perceive them. At some point, however, all crystallized thought patterns become an obstruction to further growth and must be eliminated. It is the energies of Uranus that disrupts of the magnetic forces that hold all crystallized patterns together.

This conjunction indicates that from an early age, Jesus had a relatively clear channel between His burgeoning personal mind and the abstract mind. In fact, the combination of Mercury, the Sun, and Uranus indicates that the span of the rainbow bridge that links the personal mind to the manasic center of active intelligence had been constructed prior to incarnation. In that earlier life, both the abstract mind and the thinking capacity had been reasonably well developed.

Because of this prior life development, Jesus only needed to bring forth the prerequisite development of the concrete mind and intellect before He could reestablish the link between the concrete mind and the manasic center. This occurred relatively early in His life. This functional unity of the concrete mind, the Soul intelligence, and the manasic abstract mind, combined with His exceptionally strong astral-buddhic sensitivity, enabled Jesus to experience prophetic, intuitive impressions emanating from the manasic center, and later from the buddhic center. This is quite unusual.

Jesus had a lightning-quick mind and was a probably a genius compared to those around Him. Due to His strong Piscean conditioning, however, He was not a genius in terms of the concrete sciences. Rather, His brilliance was exhibited in relation to His understanding of how things worked on earth and in the spirit side of life. Without a doubt, He was mentally astute, quick-minded, and had great insight and ingenuity.

With an interplay and exchange of the energies of Uranus and Mercury, the mind typically works so rapidly that people with Uranus conjunct Mercury often become impatient with the slow plodding pace of other people's minds and with their inability to understand what seems logical and obvious to them.

This fast-paced mental activity definitely isolated Jesus during the years leading up to His ministry. Few people (if any) could truly understand the realizations and revelations Jesus had experienced. The energies of Uranus contribute a high degree of independent thought, which can isolate people from others due the abstract nature of the thoughts.

In reaction to people's challenges to His thoughts and ideas, along with His extreme sensitivity to the feelings of others, Jesus probably withdrew from society and spent many years in prayer, contemplation, and meditation. Perhaps He spent this time contemplating how He could best serve God and mankind. Perhaps He left Galilee in search of understanding.

Jesus's extreme independence is emphasized in a number of ways in His chart. Though He had learned to compensate for it, during His ministry, Jesus became impatient with the pious Pharisees who knew the letter of the law but failed to grasp the spirit of the law—the universal significances behind the law. His statement that *"The Sabbath was made for man, not man for the Sabbath"*[42] is a perfect example. This statement is indicative of Jesus's ability to perceive the meaning behind the words, and suggests that He was quite willing to let go of many of the beliefs of Judaism.

To the learned Judean, on the other hand, Jesus was probably looked at as an opinionated know-it-all. To them, Jesus did not have the credentials to back up His words. Most likely Jesus was so broadminded that He made those seeped in the Judean culture, beliefs, taboos, and traditions, feel uncomfortable. Many were incensed by His statements. Others recognized them as truth.

The mental traits and characteristics that this combination of energies confers most likely affected Jesus's relationships with His peers adversely, especially when He was a teenager. But Jesus was in a class all His own that only the passage of time would reveal. Fortunately, the strong Neptunian and Piscean unifying qualities that brought forth His compassion and love for others offset His strong independent nature. This prevented Him from appearing arrogant. In spite of the otherworldly influences that pulled Jesus ever higher, He had a sense of shared commonality with the people in His community, which He honored in His life even though He was much further along the path.

The close conjunction of Mercury, the Sun, and Uranus in Pisces brought together ray two (pure love-wisdom), ray four (harmonious ideation via the resolution of duality), and ray six (devotion and dedication to an ideal). This further emphasized the influence of the ray two, ray four, and ray six line and the path of the heart. Ray seven, on the other hand, entered His life via Uranus. Ray seven links matter to spirit and, in so doing, sets up a new order and rhythm in people's lives.

Jesus experienced frequent flashes of insight as a result of this conjunction. The interplay and exchange of these two energies led Jesus from one realization to another and from revelation to a greater revelation, as the waves of light from the planes of light poured into His mind, especially during intense prayer, contemplation, and meditation.

Alone and somewhat isolated, Jesus spent much of His adult life in prayer and intense contemplation. This allowed Him to attain successively higher states of mind quite rapidly. Eventually, He achieved spiritual enlightenment as the light from the centers of the Triad flooded His mind.

---

[42] Mark 2:27. (RSV) (italics added)

Because of this close relationship between the personal mind, the higher abstract mind, and His (brain) consciousness (represented by the conjunction of Mercury, Uranus, and the Sun), Jesus became attuned to the universal mind. This allowed Him to have great insights into the world of the Real that ultimately led Him to the attainment of Christ consciousness.

As Jesus had unfolded the higher mental capacities and senses, His inner spiritual life became more prominent than His outer life. By way of these higher senses, Jesus perceived the deeper significances and meanings that underlie the manifest world. Eventually, He became attuned to the divine plan and discovered what He was to teach others.

Jesus probably had a photographic memory, but more importantly, Jesus could recall the wisdom of His former lives as a Son of God. The ability to recall the wisdom of a past life is a common experience of initiates. Although Jesus was unique throughout His life, once He became attuned to both the world of meaning and causation and the world that He referred to as the kingdom of heaven, Jesus exceeded the point of evolvement that any Soul originating in the evolutionary system of earth had previously attained. (The Buddha's development did not begin on earth.)

During His life, Jesus blended and subsequently unified active intelligence and love-wisdom. This achievement enabled Him to perceive and conceptualize the world of the Real and communicate the nature of the kingdom of heaven in a way that allowed people to begin to conceptualize life on the other side of the matter plane of earth. This was necessary in order for Jesus to anchor the new Piscean principles, ideas, and understanding within the minds of humanity.

Of course that which Jesus communicated was miniscule compared to that which He could have communicated, if only the people He encountered were at a higher point of development. Still, He was able to link the hearts and minds of mankind to a new idea—that God Is love. This concept has transformed humanity over the course of the last two thousand years, especially in the West.

Mercury trine Neptune (4 degrees 12 minutes)

Throughout Jesus's life, the trine of Neptune to Mercury spiritually transformed His mind and consciousness in a way very different from how the conjunction of Uranus to Mercury affected Him. In general, Uranus relates to the intelligence aspect of the Divine in its aspect of the higher mind, while Neptune relates to the love aspect of the Divine.

Although Uranus corresponds to freedom and independence of the individual, Neptune corresponds to freedom from limitations, especially those that the three planes of matter impose upon the consciousness. Although the principle of Uranus corresponds to personal liberation, the energies of Neptune correspond to spiritual liberation—the liberation of the consciousness from personal thoughts, feelings, emotions, and all self-centered elements of the consciousness.

Since the energies of Neptune have an effect upon the consciousness that is antithetical to the ego-centered personal self, the personal mind often distorts the understanding that Neptunian energies offer. This distortion, in turn, creates glamour, delusion, and confusion. Distortion can occur up until the time when the third initiation is attained. The lowest level that Neptune can express without significant distortion is the level of the Soul.

Although Neptune is a transmitter of ray six, Neptune has a close affinity to the second aspect of God at the ray four buddhic-plane level of the Spiritual Triad. This transcendent realm of oneness and unifying love is not something that can be intellectually comprehended. During incarnation, it must be experienced in the deeper states of meditation and contemplation.

The qualities of Neptune help people realize that all life in the seven planes of the evolutionary system of earth is interrelated and interconnected. By way of the influences of Neptune, initiates are able to experience the pure love-wisdom aspect of the formless world of the Real, which is transcendent of the unified personality-Soul reality. More than any other planetary influence, Neptune resonates with the life of the heart of the Planetary Logos.

When Jesus attained the third initiation (probably when He was in His late twenties), the personality no longer distorted His perception of this world of love-wisdom. In consciousness, He attuned to the heart of God and to the Masters of the Spiritual Hierarchy. This level of sensitivity and responsiveness enabled Jesus to perceive the wisdom of the higher realms.

Mercury trine Neptune represents the interplay of energies that bring forth the mystical experience of oneness with God,

I and the Father are one.[43]

I am in the Father and the Father is in me.[44]

A large number of the verses found in the book of John are best understood from the perspective of the mystic who, during a moment transcendent of the personality, is able to experience oneness with the Divine. It is this great unified reality that lies on the other side

---

[43] John 10:30. (RSV) (italics added)
[44] John 14:10. (RSV) (italics added)

of the veils of maya and illusion. This is the realm that Jesus referred to as the kingdom of heaven.

In a mundane sense, Mercury is involved in the unfoldment and development of the concrete mind and intellect, but at a higher level, its ray four energies are used to unfold and develop the faculty of pure reasoning, which is a faculty of the intuitional mind that functions in relation to the sublime truth of the Real Self.

Jesus was clairvoyant, clairaudient, clairsentient, and a spiritual idealist. He was a true intuitive, a prognosticator, and a prophet as a result of unfolding and developing the higher faculties of sensitive response. By unfolding successively higher senses and faculties, He perceived and expressed the qualities of the upper sub-plane regions of all five planes of human and super-human experience—the physical-etheric, astral, mental, buddhic, and atmic planes. Metaphysically speaking, Jesus was born a son of man and died a Son of God in its richest symbolic sense.

This trine with Neptune so sensitized the mind of Jesus that He was innately attuned to the feelings and thoughts of others. Instead of misusing this ability or accepting the feelings of others as His own, Jesus responded with great empathy, compassion, and love for others. This type of sensitivity allowed Him to connect heart to heart with others, rather than relate to them via the solar plexus, which is how most people relate to one another.

When Jesus spoke to a crowd, He was able to unify the crowd into one spiritual group of living love. People heard Him with their hearts as well as with their ears. Due to Jesus's attunement, love streamed in from the heart of God through His heart into the hearts of the spiritual seekers who gathered to hear Him. Still, due to His acute sensitivities, Jesus needed to regularly withdraw from the crowds and enter the silence of prayer and contemplation in order to maintain His spiritual attunement and balance. At this higher level of sensitivity, it was imperative for Him to maintain His attunement to the Soul and to the Monad. This is not easy to do in a crowd.

Neptune corresponds best to the love aspect of the Triad which the intellect is unable to perceive directly. This aspect of pure love-wisdom is transcendent of the concrete mind. When the manasic active intelligence aspect of the Triad is developed at the same time that the mind is linked to the buddhic center (via the love petals of the lotus), the impressions emanating from the Masters of love-wisdom of the Spiritual Hierarchy can be clearly perceived and understood, free of distortion.

The impulses and impressions Jesus perceived as a result of extending His mind from the Soul to both the manasic intelligence center and the buddhic intuitional center enabled Him to perceive the impulses and impressions of the Divine and, in turn, express them in words, thoughts, ideas, and concepts that others could understand.

It is for this reason that both the feeling, love aspect and the mental, intelligence aspect must be simultaneously developed, first at the level of the personality and then at the level of the Soul. Only then can people perceive the universal truth that spontaneously arises within the intuitional mind of the Spiritual Triad.

When the pathway is created that extends people's sensitivity into the buddhic-intuitional world, a mystical union with God is no longer a lofty experience that touches the initiate from time to time. Instead, union or oneness with God is the reality of the initiate. When the higher senses and intelligence capacities are perfected, impressions from the higher planes, as well as the impulses emanating from the universe, can be conceptualized without the initiate's attention needing to drop down to the mental plane level in order to clothe the perceived revelations into words that the brain is able to register. This is important.

This trine combines all three ray influences of the path of the heart: Ray two (Mercury in Pisces), ray four (Mercury), and ray six (Neptune, plus Mercury in Pisces). It therefore relates to the mystical experience of oneness with God and to the path of the heart. At its deepest level, this trine corresponds to the urge to unfold, develop, and demonstrate Christ consciousness on earth.

Mercury trine Mid-heaven (53 minutes)

As discussed earlier, the conjunction of Neptune with the Mid-heaven served as the capstone of the epic grand trine in the chart of Jesus. Four planets plus the North Node formed trine aspects to the Mid-heaven, while Pluto formed a sextile. The only hard aspect to this cusp of the tenth house was a quincunx from Mars.

At the personal level, the Mid-heaven corresponds to the social-professional goals people establish in their lives and work to attain. For disciples and initiates, the Mid-heaven corresponds to the evolutionary goals the Soul establishes. In both instances, the Mid-heaven represents the summit of achievement after years of development and growth. The Mid-heaven represents the mount of initiation once people step upon the path.

An initiation is the recognition by the Masters that an individual has unfolded, developed, and mastered one of the seven principles of the mind in relation to a particular plane. This development includes the development of the seven sub-ray aspects of a principle to one degree or another. Each principle of consciousness and each of its seven sub-principles relate to one or other of the seven rays.

When people are on the path of human development, professional success and social status are the rewards granted for doing the developmental work necessary to succeed. This climb to the summit of life—the Mid-heaven—pertains to the development of the threefold personal consciousness and includes the acquisition of certain skills, capacities, and abilities that are needed to succeed socially and professionally.

For disciples, the climb to the summit of the Mid-heaven symbolizes a long, arduous climb during which time the disciple attains a mastery over one of the principles of consciousness that the forces of a particular plane unfold and advance. Neptune conjunct the Mid-heaven in the chart of Jesus speaks to the reward that was before Jesus as He worked to reach the summit of the mount of initiation, not once or twice, but four different times.

Both the Mid-heaven and Neptune were in Scorpio (the sign of the spiritual tests and trials). Mars, as the personality and Soul-centered ruler of Scorpio, indicates that the attainment of the third initiation was not as easy for Jesus as people might think. As with all disciples, Jesus's path involved spiritual tests and trials that He had to pass before He could proceed forward. In Jesus's case, however, He had been on the path of initiation long before His current incarnation and had passed many of the tests that disciples today are facing for the first time.

The ultimate evolutionary goal for mankind is to attain oneness with the Monad or Father Spirit. This involves the development of the three aspects of Divine, first in relation to the integrated personality (active intelligence), then in relation to the Soul (love-wisdom), and finally in relation to the Spiritual Self (will-purpose).

The Soul intent and goal before Jesus was to fully embody the pure love-wisdom of the buddhic center. This called for a number of mental adjustments. Due to the interplay of the ray-magnetized planetary forces of the kite configuration, Jesus was substantially transformed and renewed by successively higher-plane energies each time He climbed to the summit of the mount of initiation. Practically every aspect of His consciousness was subjected to the evolutionary processes of transmutation and transformation, endings, and new beginnings—cyclic death and rebirth at successively higher levels.

In the view of others, Jesus submitted to the arduous spiritual work required to reach the mount's summit on four separate occasions. Once He had attained the third initiation and was beginning His ascent to the summit for a fourth time, His mind was fixed upon the truth of the planes of light that He was beginning to perceive.

His ability to freely communicate His deep spiritual understanding to others was ensured by this trine and strengthened by His Capricorn Ascendant. The large number of aspects formed to the fourth- and tenth-house cusps of His chart also indicates that Jesus received a significant amount of spiritual training and education in the home during his early years. He also received significant training telepathically in His early years from His own spirit guides. Later, Jesus received a significant amount of spiritual training from the Masters.

Then, just prior to His ministry, Jesus came under the instruction and guidance of the Great Chohan who oversees the Chohans[45] of the Seven Ashrams of the Spiritual Hierarchy. This Great Chohan was originally referred to as the Maha Bodhisattva. In the West, this Great Chohan who is the head of the Teaching Department of Shamballa is referred to as the Planetary Teacher, the Christ.

In a mundane sense, favorable aspects to the Mid-heaven usually indicate favorable relations and communications with authority figures and in the home, and excellent communication skills professionally. Though a cursory delineation of the aspects to the Mid-heaven suggests that Jesus had a good relationship with authority figures in His early years, this wasn't the case throughout His life. The very nature of His teachings and His mission as the messenger of the Piscean Age disrupted His relationships with authority figures, since the teachings He presented were foreign to the religious, social, and political norms of His day.

Aspects to Mercury discussed in earlier chapters:

Sun conjunct Mercury
Moon trine Mercury

---

[45] A Chohan is a sixth-degree ascended master who oversees the activity of one of the seven ray Ashrams, e.g., the Chohan of the Ray Six Ashram or Chohan of the Ray Seven Ashram, etc.

Chapter 14

Venus, the Revealing Light

The energies of Venus carry the universal law of attraction into people's lives. For this reason, Venus is associated with affections, intimate relationships, and partnerships. Venus's association with affections, however, is valid only at the personal level. In a larger sense, Venus corresponds to what people find attractive—what they value. Venus is not the planet of love as many people think, since it is a transmitter of ray five conditioned energies. Venus is the revealer of love. Love is the essential underlying quality of our cosmic ray two solar system.

Venus represents the aspect of the mind that reveals love. By way of the light of Venus, people sense the attractive, unifying forces, and atomic affinities between themselves and others and between them and the material things of earth. Venus is the great Logos of Gnosis. It is the Lord of Knowledge at the personal level and the Lord of Wisdom at the higher levels. In relation to the principles of consciousness, Venus is more Sophia (the goddess of wisdom) than she is Aphrodite (the goddess of love). Esoterically, Venus represents the Logos who reveals the cosmic principle of love through the factor of the mind.

Historically, people have confused this revealing light of the mind with that which this light reveals. When people are caught up in the ancient glamour of desire for the things of earth, the mind is beguiled. This leads to the pursuit of what is pleasing to the eyes and pleasurable to the form.

People seek a partner who loves them and is personally desirable. Few people seek a partner who will help unfold the love that is within them, yet this is the true objective behind differentiating the physical forms into the two sexes. The division of the physical life forms by sex was chosen as the methodology that could best awaken love within these forms of earth.

Historically, the first aspect of love (the electromagnetic forces of attraction) that unfolded within these physical forms was linked to the physical-instinctual nature that draws two people together to procreate. Thus, the initial quality of love that mankind unfolded within these forms corresponds to the elemental life of the physical body, not to the human spirit or consciousness.

During this Second Solar System, the quality of divine love-wisdom that most people express in life relates to the astral-emotional personal nature and to the astral forces that express via the solar plexus, not to the etheric heart center. Love stimulated by the lower and mid-levels of astral forces relates primarily to the personal desire nature and lust, rather than the love of the Soul or the pure love-wisdom of the Triad.

In consciousness, people connect to one another via their emotion-based atoms of self-consciousness, which are brought forth as a result of the influx of the lower astral forces. In other words, most relationships involve an exchange of forces between solar plexus centers of two people. Sexual relationships, on the other hand, are an exchange of forces between two people's sacral centers, as well as their solar plexus centers.

According to traditional astrology, Venus represents feminine sexuality and beauty, and all that is esthetically pleasing. Here, the astrological factors associated with Venus provide important information pertaining to what people are attracted to and value in a personal sense. This includes money, possessions, the material comforts of life, and other people. These factors also provide information about the way people express personal love and affections in their relationships. Much of what people love and find desirous depends on how they see themselves and how they identify their selfhood. During the stage of personal development, people define their selfhood in terms of their feelings, thoughts, and beliefs, along with their physical bodies.

It is by way of the Venusian energies that the principle of love emerges into human awareness. It might seem unusual for a ray five planet (the factor of mind) to be associated with love, but it is. Again, Venus represents the component of the mind that reveals love. It represents the light that reveals the attractive complementary forces of someone or something in relation to oneself. Ultimately, Venus reveals the cosmic quality of love-wisdom in relation to the ONE.

Ray five represents the bridging light that connects the psychic dynamics conditioned by the ray two, ray four, and ray six line to the psychic dynamics conditioned by the ray one, ray three, ray five, and ray seven line. Ray five serves as the bridge between these two. By way of the mind, the line of love and the line of mind and power are linked to each other.

Since Venus reveals what people resonate with and therefore value, Venus reveals what is needed to satisfy basic instinctual-emotional survival needs and desires. This means that love is rather limited in potency within the personal mind and highly distorted by the personal self.

Through the agency of Venus, however, people become aware of successively higher and more inclusive expressions of love. By way of Venus, successively higher expressions of the second aspect of the Divine are anchored within these forms of earth and brought forth in people's lives. People's evolutionary need to unfold, express, and eventually embody love-wisdom at the personality, Soul, and then at the Triad exemplifies the primary directive that underlies the life of our solar system during this Second Solar System.

Venus plays an exceedingly important role in relation to the evolution of human consciousness on earth and the evolution of life across the entire solar system in the seven planes of the cosmic physical plane. It resonates best with the seven planes of the cosmic astral plane. All evolutions and planes of life are caught up in the evolutionary processes that reveal love, since all expressions of life in our solar system are involved in unfolding, awakening, and perfecting the cosmic principle of love-wisdom. In this sense, the heart center of the ONE is slowly awakened.

Relative to the evolution of consciousness on earth, this process to manifest and perfect love during this Second Solar System begins with the unfoldment of love within these human forms. The divine intent behind this effort to condition all units of life and consciousness with love is the directive that compels life forward to achieve the manifest perfection envisioned within the mind of God.

Love first unfolds within the consciousness as a result of the attractive affinities people experience in relation to a spouse, family members, friends, and associates. As people progress, they expand their love for others, e.g., for fellow parishioners, the community, their ethnic group, country, their pets, the environment, and, eventually, mankind as a whole.

Initially, the essential quality of love emanating from the Soul is squeezed through the small portal of the personal heart onto others. As people express love toward those outside their immediate circle, the atoms of self-consciousness begin to shift from the solar plexus into the heart center. This intensifies the magnetization of the heart center. Eventually, the magnetization of the heart center is strong enough to draw the essential love of the Soul into and through the astral body into and through the etheric heart center. In this way, the etheric heart center is slowly awakened to the essential love of the Soul. When this occurs, the energies of the love petals of the lotus begin to stream into the etheric heart center in the back of the spine and out the petals of etheric heart center in the front of the body, streaming into the aura. By way of this energy people are able to sense love around them.

That which people sense in their environment via the heart center is very different from what they sense via the solar plexus. The quality of love people experience and express via the heart center is relatively free of personal egocentric taints, biases, and preferences compared to what people sense via the solar plexus. The activity of the heart center awakens a more inclusive, encompassing love, and a desire to help others live a better, more pleasant life.

When people are engaged in heart-felt activities, they electromagnetically attract the inclusive and free-flowing essential love of the Soul into the heart center. As a result, people become more loving, forgiving, and compassionate, and work to improve the lot of humanity without a need to be recognized for their work. As greater light and love of the Soul pours through the upper centers, a greater, more inclusive expression of love is unfolded in these forms of earth. Slowly, love is progressively revealed at successively higher levels.

The capacity to embrace mankind with love as well as embrace the life of the other three kingdoms of nature relates to the greater purpose of the universe, which is to awaken the heart center of the ONE who embodies the seven solar systems. Our solar system is but one of the seven major chakras of life, the heart chakra. Ever so slowly, the life of our solar system awakens to that loving-intelligent Being who is the inner essence of all that is.

At the level of the Soul, Venus rules Gemini, while at the personality level, Mercury rules Gemini. The energies of Mercury relate one thing to another. Once related, the actions of Venus blend their energies together. The resulting harmonization of the two energies brings forth knowledge. By blending the energies of Mercury and Venus, the consciousness is uplifted. Slowly, all knowledge is transformed into wisdom and the logical thinking capacity is transformed into pure reasoning.

Both Mercury and Venus are related to that factor of the consciousness that is the product of the union of the principles of the Father spirit and Mother matter. Initially, Mercury advances consciousness through the generation of an awareness of conflicts in the psyche. By relating apparent opposites, greater knowledge and understanding are brought forth.

The opportunity to relate and then advance two dynamics of the psyche is especially evident in a chart whenever two planets (two centers of energy) form an opposition to each other. Initially, people personally identify with the psychic dynamic represented by one side of the opposition and project the other. By projecting the other dynamic onto the people in their lives, they objectify the dynamic in the outer world, so they can begin to relate to it, i.e., relate to each other the two conflicting psychic dynamics in the psyche that the planets represent. By way of Venus, they can then be harmonized in relation to each other.

So many personal relationships serve as a vehicle for bringing forth a mercurial awareness of certain pairs of opposites within the burgeoning human mind and consciousness. Ultimately, there are no pairs of opposites, since all life and form in the seven planes of the evolutionary system of earth are members of the one body of the Logos.

Once the apparent oppositions in the personal mind are resolved, greater understanding is brought forth. Both the ray four Moon and ray four Mercury are involved in this activity to relate two things to each other within the mind and consciousness. The Moon is involved in relating the conflicts (duality) within the astral-emotional nature. It also relates the present moment to the past. Mercury, on the other hand, is initially involved in relating the conflicts with the mental aspect of consciousness. Duality exists for the purpose of Venusian blending and harmonization. When harmonized, some aspect of love is revealed.

Once two dynamics of the psyche are connected or linked to each other, the actions of Venus blend and unify their ray-magnetized energies. This blending takes place at the centermost point between them—the midpoint. Several systems of spirituality stress the importance of walking the middle path. On the middle path, people do not align themselves with one side of the duality or the other. This speaks to the purpose that the three crosses of the heavens—the mutable, fixed, and cardinal crosses—serve in relation to the evolution of consciousness.

The manifest world was brought forth by separating the One into the multitude. This act created a temporary state of duality wherein the multitude becomes manifest, consciously related, harmonized, and then unified once the duality has served its purpose in terms of awakening and bringing forth knowledge, love, and wisdom, along with the unfoldment of successively higher senses, skills, capacities and faculties necessary to actualize the higher expresses of wisdom, truth, beauty, and love.

In terms of the signs and the three crosses, people gain a greater understanding by developing a relationship between two signs that are in opposition to each other, and then blending the rays that the two signs transmit. This is true regardless of which of the three crosses is involved. On the mutable cross, Pisces offers greater understanding as a result of relating to and then blending with the rays, energies, and qualities of Virgo.

When people step on the path of discipleship, they move from the outer periphery of the chart (which relates to planetary forces) to the center where the rays of the signs in opposition to each other are blended at the midpoint between the signs. In consciousness, people must move to that point that is midway between the opposition. This is where Venus works best to harmonize and blend the different aspects of the mind. This middle point or portal opens onto the inner realm of the Soul and its essential love. There, the principles of the signs and their rays do not exist in a state of opposition to each other.

On the spiritual path, Mercury brings forth the initial awareness of the differences between the integrated personality and the Soul in terms of values, nature, virtues, characteristics, and qualities, while the energies of Venus harmonize these values, qualities, etc., in relation to each other. This lengthy process of relating and then harmonizing the dynamics of the psyche leads to the union of the integrated personality and Soul and later a union with the Monad.

Regardless of the level at which the consciousness is polarized, the intent of Venusian energies is to blend and harmonize two different energies or qualities. In this sense, Venusian energies help establish right relationships between all forms of life. Slowly, mankind is establishing right relations one toward another and will one day establish right relations with the sub-human kingdoms as well.

The processes whereby the integrated personality and Soul are harmonized with each other through the actions of Venus culminate with the revelation of the individual as a Son or Daughter of God, the perfected human being. At this stage, active intelligence is perfected and infused with the essential love of the Soul. At an even higher level, the revealing light of Venus harmonizes the perfected human being with divine purpose, but this is far in the future for most Souls.

As the initiation processes proceed, Venusian energy not only reveals a more expansive and inclusive quality of love-wisdom, but transforms mankind's purified knowledge and creative intelligence into loving intelligence.

Esoterically speaking, in ancient primordial days, it was the influences of Venus that initially attracted and linked primitive mankind to the Soul; thereby creating the Homo genus (Homo sapiens). This speaks to the close relationship and ancient bond between the Logos of Earth and the Logos of the sacred planet Venus. This close bond continues today, even though human beings are no longer progressing through the three planes of matter on Venus as they once did.

In the Aquarian Age, a large number of human beings will achieve complete identification with the Soul and its nature, and successfully transcend the integrated personality. They will become the co-creative agents helping the Returning One establish a new kingdom of nature on earth—the kingdom of the divine human.

On the path, conditional, affectionate personal love is transcended—supplanted by selfless, harmonious relationships between equals in which love is expressed consciously via the heart center. When this is the case, love will no longer be constrained as it currently is in most relationships. Thus, Venus represents the component of the mind that reveals the interrelation and interconnectedness of all forms of life. As people become aware of the interconnectedness of life and are able to experience life's interrelatedness, people will embody omnipresent love.

At the level of the Soul, people begin to experience oneness with others and start to realize that there is only the one life that moves through everything. This one life breathes life into all that exists. An awareness of the oneness of all life is progressively revealed as the commonality of the parts of the Totality is realized. Slowly, human consciousness awakens to this reality as the patterns of self-centered emotions, thoughts, and beliefs that cloud the consciousness are either eliminated or harmonized with the atoms of the higher mind. Thus, the role that Venus plays is exceedingly important in terms of the spiritualization of human consciousness.

Venus in Pisces

When Jesus was born, Venus appeared to be in the sign Pisces, the Soul-centered exaltation of Venus. This means that Pisces and Venus align well with each other in terms of their principles. The power through which Venus reveals the principle of love and stimulates the unfoldment and expression of love in people's lives is significantly enhanced by the ray two and ray six energies Pisces transmit.

At the personal level, Venus in Pisces typically manifests as a very sensitive, romantic person who is in great need of human affections and is often quite demonstrative of love and affections. Those with Venus in Pisces who are still functioning at the personal level often feel as if the world revolves around their personal feelings, desires, and needs, especially in relation to their affections. When their affectional needs are not met, people with Venus in Pisces often feel extreme loneliness and sorrow. If unchecked, such feelings can lead to acts of martyrdom.

Due to the extreme sensitivity of Pisceans to the collective emotions of mankind, people with this placement often gravitate to professional fields that allow them to express their sensitive feelings, e.g., the arts, healing, or social service professions. Some are drawn to religious faiths, especially those faiths that emphasize the Crucifixion of Jesus and the sinfulness of the flesh.

People with Venus in Pisces whose consciousness is polarized at the mental-plane level (rather than at the astral-emotional level) often express the depths of their feelings through moving literary works, musical compositions, and great works of art.

This placement of Venus enhanced the deep love, empathy, mercy, and compassion Jesus felt and expressed. Unlike anyone before Him, Jesus used the energies of Venus to fully reveal the second aspect of the Divine. This was possible in large part due to the grand trine that Venus formed involving the Moon and Neptune. More than any other factor, the interplay and exchange of energies of this grand trine, in combination with the strong influence of Pisces in His chart, revealed the loving nature of God, resulting in Jesus's formulation of this new approach to the Divine, the path of the heart.

Once Jesus attained the third initiation and started to function as a Soul, the energies of the Soul-centered ruler of Pisces, ray one Pluto (divine will), started to impact His life. But due to the overwhelming emphasis in His life upon this love-wisdom aspect, Pluto did not express itself as the destroyer. Rather, the second sub-aspect of ray one, the builder aspect, started to condition the psychic dynamics that the planets in Pisces represented. By way of the influx of divine will-purpose in its building sub-aspect, Jesus brought forth this new path of the heart for others to tread.

As a third-degree initiate, Jesus had resolved the apparent conflicts between the principle of intelligence (which the integrated personality is responsible for unfolding and mastering) and the principle of love (which the Soul is responsible for developing in these human forms of earth).

The power of Pluto as the Soul-centered ruler of Pisces provided Jesus with the energy needed to perform miracles and to firmly anchor the concept of the kingdom of heaven on earth. Over the past two thousand years, mankind has strengthened this concept and infused it with the motivating power of desire.

One day, heaven will be objectified enough to precipitate on earth. This will occur when enough people function on earth at the level of the Soul. Too many people distort this concept of the kingdom of heaven, preventing it from precipitating at this time. People's mean-spirited insistence upon a judgment day as prerequisite to the establishment of the kingdom of heaven hampers the manifestation of this new day. When more people incarnate with a consciousness polarized at the level of the Soul, the sixth root race will appear—the Homo divinus—the divine human. It is the sixth root race of mankind that will create a new heaven and a new earth.

Venus in Pisces enabled Jesus to embody and express a truly inclusive love of others, as well as express an unbounded love for God. Later, its energies helped to open His inner mind's eye with a quality of light that revealed the kingdom of heaven.

Aspects to Venus in Pisces

Venus was conjunct the Sun, Uranus, and North Node and was trine the Moon and Neptune in the chart of Jesus. Again, Venus formed its own grand trine configuration within the epic grand trine. Since Venus did not form an aspect to Mercury, Mars, Saturn, or Pluto, it appears that the psychic dynamic that Venus represents was not as active in terms of the development of the integrated personality and the higher self as some of the other dynamics.

Most likely, the Venusian activity to harmonize and blend the apparent opposites within the psyche had already been accomplished prior to Jesus's incarnation. Also, Venus's placement in Pisces indicates that this factor of the mind that reveals love had reached its culminating point of fruition in a recent past life. When Jesus incarnated, the doorway was already open to receive the fullness of Venus's revealing power.

Venus trine Neptune (4 degrees 21 minutes)

During the stage of Jesus's personal development, He wasn't caught up in the confusing material and relational issues of romance that the psychic dynamic of Venus often is involved. This means that the deeper significances and meaning behind the symbolism of this trine of Venus to Neptune is important.

The interplay and exchange of the ray energies of this trine brought forth a comforting gentleness and a forgiving spirit, kindness and empathy, and a heightened sensitivity and love for others. Jesus truly loved mankind. His devotion to a loving God and His great love and compassion for others are repeatedly emphasized in His chart.

Jesus's love for others is represented by a number of threads within the fabric of His being. His great love served as the impetus behind His desire to heal. Such a heart-felt desire to heal did not arise out of a desire for name and fame; rather, it was in response to the impressions of His Soul, which this trine revealed. Nor did His ability to heal arise spontaneously. It was developed. However, it appears that His desire to heal others and to relieve them of their pain and suffering had been cultivated for lifetimes. The desire to heal others naturally arises when the consciousness of the disciple starts to register the essential love of the Soul.

Jesus's ability to cast out evil spirits and to calm the winds and rough seas did not arise from the same astrological influences as this desire to heal. Granted, both His ability to control the forces of the three matter planes and to heal others unfolded due to His great love for humanity. But His ability to command the planetary forces of nature and free someone of discarnate spirits requires a higher level of spiritual training, one that involves the line of mind and power: rays one, three, five, and seven.

As a rule, learning how to control the types of matter forces present in the three planes of matter only begins once the initiate approaches the fourth initiation. This training further intensifies as the initiate approaches the fifth initiation, when human perfection is attained.

Throughout much of history, the ability to heal was a developed capacity and skill that involved creating a channel linking the mind to a reservoir of healing energies in the world of the Soul. By way of this channel, healing energies stream onto and through the healer onto the person in need of healing. This type of healing unfolds as a result of people's love for one another and their desire to help others.

The capacity to heal is usually developed as a result of the strong influence of the ray two, ray four, and ray six line. Today, there are a number of healing techniques that involve the transmission of energies along the ray one, ray three, ray five, and ray seven line of rays. This is in accordance with the rays that are being activated as the planet approaches the Age of Aquarius. In the Aquarian Age, healing will be a group activity.

Jesus demonstrated command over the forces of the three planes of earth and exhibited great healing abilities as a result of mastering both ray lines. This resulted in His ability to heal and to perform miracles of a unique quality and caliber.

Advanced Souls with Venus trine Neptune have the potential to heal as a result of combining the powers of both ray lines as Jesus did. This is possible because the energies of ray five Venus bridge these two ray lines. Here, the love and intelligence of the Soul are empowered by the will of the Soul.

People with Venus trine Neptune frequently idealize their mothers, so much so that men find it nearly impossible to find a romantic partner who measures up to their ideal romantic partner. The inclusive love that Venus reveals via this trine is universal and less personal.

The otherworldly influences of Neptune make it difficult, if not impossible, to love just one person. People with Venus trine Neptune are known to impersonalize and idealize love. They tend to be so inclusive in their expression of love that they often have difficulty with the usual monogamous relationship. No person seems to fit their ideal. This is especially true for men with Venus in Pisces.

This Venus trine Neptune aspect in the chart of Jesus conferred a powerful mystical influence and quality, and guaranteed He would receive significant spiritual inspiration and guidance throughout His life. By way of the interplay and exchange of the energies of this trine, Jesus was able to experience a union with the Soul at an early age. Once He achieved a union of the integrated personality and Soul, this Venus-Neptune trine sensitized Him to the impressions of the Masters of the Spiritual Hierarchy.

As a result, Jesus was able to demonstrate the higher wisdom and will that was needed to successfully fulfill His mission. Jesus fulfilled His mission because of His willingness to engage in the spiritual work necessary to prepare Himself for His mission. Foremost of which was His willingness to sacrifice His personal will and love to the universal, all-inclusive will-to-love which the Masters of Love-Wisdom embody.

Venus conjunct Uranus (6 degrees 36 minutes)

The conjunction of Venus and Uranus is wide, but since the Sun and Uranus are closely conjunct and Venus is trine the Moon and Neptune (two of the three points of the epic grand trine), Venus conjunct Uranus had a greater effect upon Jesus than might be expected. The revealing light of Venus awakened the revealing light of the higher mind. This is important, since it is the higher mind that ultimately reveals the planes of light and the world of the Real.

People with Venus conjunct Uranus often have a sparkling, effervescent personality. This influence helped to offset the serious and resolute qualities that Jesus's Capricorn Ascendant conferred. Although this conjunction is usually thought of in relation to people's social and romantic interests and concerns, it had a very different effect upon Jesus. This combination of energies first revealed the mind of the Soul, and then the abstract mind. A Venus-Uranus conjunction reveals a different sub-quality of love than that which Venus trine Neptune reveals.

When people are on the path, the Venus conjunct Uranus aspect represents an ability to easily transfer the consciousness from the personal life to the impersonal, self-less life of the Soul. Here, the initiate readily perceives the impressions of the Masters, especially the impressions of the Masters of the Ashram that the Soul has been accepted into. Once the third initiation has been attained, the planetary mission that the new master begins to serve is part of the mission of His or Her Soul Group. In this sense, Jesus's mission was a mission of the entire Ray Six Ashram of the Masters who, collectively, worked through Him to implement the divine plan for the Piscean Age.

This Venus-Uranus conjunction, and to a lesser degree Venus trine Neptune, confer the ability to unify people into a Soul group on earth. When an initiate heads up the group, the individual skills, talents, and capacities of the group collectively constitute a group consciousness that is capable of registering and implementing a particular aspect of the divine plan on earth. Jesus used the law of attraction (via Venus) at the level of the Soul to gather His disciples during the early days of His ministry, and through its unified group light and energy, He distributed His teachings.

Venus conjunct Uranus can free the consciousness from that which people love at the personal level (via the solar plexus), so they can love freely via the heart center. Venus trine Uranus in Pisces aligns well with the overall evolutionary objective of the Age of Pisces. Its influence encourages people to engage in the type of spiritual activities that reveal and advance the second aspect of the divine mind, love-wisdom. This includes selflessly serving one another. The missions of both the Buddha and Jesus centered on freeing human consciousness from the control and influence of the forces of the three planes of earth, so they are free to experience their divine nature.

Venus conjunct North Node (5 degrees 7 minutes)

Since the consciousness of the average person is polarized at the astral-emotional level, the traditional astrological meaning behind most astrological factors relates to what someone functioning at the personal level of consciousness is likely to experience.

For this reason, the delineation of this aspect of Venus typically refers to having good timing in relation to second-house factors (e.g., money, earning ability, material possessions) and seventh-house factors (e.g., relationships, partnerships, and relations with the public).

Just as the areas of life that the twelve houses represent do not have the same meaning once the third initiation is attained, the meaning assigned to the aspects between the planets and the lunar nodes must also be modified. For people on the path, the Nodes relate to the evolutionary journey of the Soul, not to the personality and its growth.

The conjunction of Venus and North Node suggests that the generosity and love expressed in recent past lives was to be carried into His current life. More importantly, this conjunction indicates that the goal of the Soul of Jesus was to reveal the kingdom of heaven (the world of the Real) to others. This aspect also speaks to the opportunity Jesus had to reveal this new path of the heart. On this path people are freed from their excessive preoccupation with the three planes of earth.

Only when people are fully liberated from the influences of matter can they begin to express the spirit of pure love. This calls for the transformation of all aspects of personal consciousness. Such transformation is accomplished by uplifting the energies and forces of the threefold personal consciousness in vibration, note, and qualities as a result of the processes that purify them of their self-serving characteristics.

This work to transform and renew the earth by cleansing the consciousness of separatism and selfishness is that which purifies the three planes of earth. Only then can the kingdom of heaven be firmly established on earth.

Aspects to Venus discussed in earlier chapters:

Moon trine Venus
Sun conjunct Venus

Chapter 15

Mars, Desire in Action

With this discussion of Mars, the analysis of the inner personal planets and luminaries in Jesus's chart is complete. Although most people use the energies of the personal planets to unfold and develop the psychic dynamics of the threefold personal consciousness, the ray energies of the Sun and all of the planets can be used to advance not only the personal consciousness, but also the higher mind. Only the rays of the signs are involved in unfolding the Real Self of the planes of light.

As a rule, the planetary forces of Mars represent the forces of desire which, when expressed physically, lead to action, initiative, and the manifest expression of something on earth. For this reason, Mars is esoterically referred to as desire-in-action.

Mars rules the personal desire nature, but it also rules the desire of the Soul to incarnate on earth. Desire-in-action is an apt description of the effects that the energies of Mars have on people functioning at the personal level, since Mars is associated with the solar plexus center. Desire-in action arises as the result of blending ray-six magnetized energies with a small amount of ray one.

Esoterically, the physical actions and activities that Mars activates represent the way people use the fires of life emanating from the divine plane. Mankind expresses these fires primarily in relation to the astral-emotional aspect of the personal consciousness. Though personal thoughts also stimulate physical activity, actions, and initiative, the planetary forces of Mars align best with the astral-emotional desire nature.

Prior to the time when people step upon the path, Mars is associated with the physical body and its drives and appetites. It is affiliated with sexuality (propagation of the species) and other instinctual aspects of consciousness. Mars is especially linked to physical vitality and prana.

Most often, Mars is associated with people's personal will, ambitions, and initiative, usually of a very strong personal nature. In general, the Mars dynamic of the psyche is associated with personal desires and the drive to satisfy those desires. This is the situation up until the consciousness is mentally polarized and people begin to apply the Soul-infused light of mind upon the emotional nature.

During the early stages of development of the personal consciousness, the energies of Mars initially express in relation to the instinctual fight-or-flight dynamic and the lower instinctual, emotional nature. Mars specifically corresponds to the masculine dynamic and identity. This involves the masculine polarity of the physical body and its sexuality. Mars represents the positive polarity of the physical body that repels and compels. For this reason, it is associated with physical aggression. Venus, on the other hand, represents the attractive, receptive, feminine dynamic of the mind and the negative, receptive polarity of the physical body.

The astrological factors associated with Mars provide clues as to the nature, quality, and actions people initiate. They also indicate whether the self-initiated, self-referencing, and often aggressive actions that the psychic dynamic Mars represents are likely to be expressed physically, emotionally, or mentally.

The chart of Jesus indicates that the focus of His development and growth centered overwhelmingly on the ray two, ray four, and ray six line of manifestation, the love-wisdom line of development. His need to develop the concrete mind was marginal at best. Two thousand years ago, the developmental focus of mankind wasn't on the mental aspect of personal consciousness. The lack of emphasis upon the development of the concrete mind meant that Jesus acquired little knowledge prior to when He started to sense and respond to life in the planes of light that would have distorted His perception of the Real.

With His mind relatively free of the thoughts and ideas of others, it was easier for Jesus to shift His consciousness from the astral heart center to the heart of the Soul, and later to shift His consciousness from the Soul to the buddhic center of pure love-wisdom.

For much of the past two thousand years, mankind's development has centered primarily on the unfoldment of devotion and dedication, especially in relation to the love aspect of the Divine. In general, the development of the personal mental faculties and capacities was minimal. Today, the consciousness of the average person on earth is still polarized at the astral-emotional level. However, thanks to mankind's emphasis upon universal secular education during the past few centuries, this situation is quickly changing.

The development of the rational, concrete mind and its mental faculties and capacities is a relatively new evolutionary impulse that humanity has been experiencing ever since the energies of the Age of Aquarius started to impact mankind once the earth moved into the five-hundred-year transition period between the Age of Pisces and the Age of Aquarius in the eighteen century.

Two thousand years ago, there was little need to develop the faculty of discrimination or discernment to determine what was appropriate. Nor was there a need for individuals to discern between appropriate and inappropriate behavior and conduct. The different societies and cultures of the world established such things for its people.

Today, the planetary evolutionary impulses compel humanity to unfold and develop the mind and its faculties. Only then can people begin to develop the higher senses and faculties needed to accurately interpret the light patterns and imagery of the intuition and abstract mind and begin to comprehend the wisdom of the higher planes.

To the extent possible at the time, Jesus had developed the intellect. He then went on to master the mental faculties and capacities necessary to attain the higher states of mind. The parables and analogies that Jesus used during His ministry indicate that the higher abstract mind was as important if not more important to Him than the concrete mind.

During His ministry, Jesus relied heavily upon the abstract mind to convey His understanding of the spirit side of life. Having developed both the abstract and intuitional aspects of the mind, the truth of the higher planes of light spontaneously arose within His mind irrespective of the development of His concrete mind.

Mars in Aries

Understanding Aries is the key to understanding the mission of Jesus and the concepts of redemption and resurrection. In terms of the evolution of consciousness, everything begins with this first sign of the zodiac. By way of Aries, a new impulse of essential life emanates from the Divine. As the transmitter of ray one, Aries is the purveyor of the fire of will-purpose, which is projected into our solar system in an effort to awaken the heart center of the ONE. All cycles begin with Aries.

By way of Aries, the impulses of essential life are received in the divine plane—the plane of fiery life. The Masters of Shamballa (where the will of God is known) register these impulses and, through the agency of that which Mercury transmits, develop primal seed ideas that express divine purpose. Each of the seven Ray Ashrams of the Spiritual Hierarchy intuits these seed ideas and transforms this purpose into a plan for the advancement of mankind, depending on the ray that the Ashram is on.

As the highest of the seven planes of the cosmic physical plane, the divine plane is the source of all life in the seven planes of earth. From a differentiation of the divine plane into a plane of one or other of the seven rays, the six planes below the divine plane came into existence.

The human Monad is the recipient of this divine life-force and transmits a portion of it onto the Soul, which, in turn, transmits a portion of the divine life-force onto the individual via the silver cord. There is a constant, ongoing cycle of anchoring divine life, which is the very presence of God, on earth. Essential life brings forth divine ideas, first at the level of the Monad and Shamballa, and then at the level of the Soul and the Spiritual Hierarchy. All life forms that exist originate as a divine idea, and all divine ideas originate with the impulses of the universal mind. The impulses of the universal mind are the impulses of the life that emanate from the ONE.

By way of the energies of Mars, people express these impulses of essential life as a devotional drive. At the personal level, this devotional drive is expressed mainly in terms of ensuring safety, survival, security, and satisfying one's desires. At the higher Soul-centered level, people use the impulses of essential life via Mercury (the Soul-centered ruler of Aries) to generate divine ideas.

Aries disseminates the creative fires of life. Only through an understanding of Aries can people understand that *"God is a consuming fire."*[46] Aries represents the initiating impulses of the will-to-be and the light-of-life that redeem essential life from its imprisonment in matter. The work of resurrecting or redeeming essential life out of physical and subtle matter is ongoing. Historically, few people have attained the higher state of mind that is capable of resurrecting essential life in terms of their own lives, let alone in relation to the three planes of earth. All planetary servers and saviors are involved in the work to redeem essential life from the magnetism of the forces of matter.

Aries relates to the three types of liberating fires that burn through the forces imprisoning conscious life. Mankind is the agent who utilizes the fiery impulses of life (in the form of mental fire) to free life and consciousness from its captivity by the magnetic forces of the physical atom. This liberation takes place at the first initiation. The Soul is the agent that frees essential life from its captivity by the involutionary forces of the atoms of subtle matter (the lower mental, astral, and etheric planes). Resurrection of essential life from the magnetism of mental matter takes place at the third initiation.

The liberation of essential life from physical and subtle matter is what Easter represents esoterically—the resurrection of essential life from the tomb of matter. It also represents a turning of the elemental lives of matter from their involutionary path to an evolutionary path. This liberation is possible since the ray one energy of Aries pierces all form and burns up the atomic electromagnetic forces, but touches not the inner life.

When Mars is in Aries, there is usually a large amount of relatively unbridled and

---

[46] Hebrews 12:29. (RSV)

uncontained astral energy seeking to express through the physical body. Since the dynamic of Mars within the psyche compels people to express astral desire forces physically, Mars is esoterically thought of as the energy-of-action.

When the consciousness is polarized at the astral-emotional level (especially from the age of seven to twenty one), the energy of Mars is frequently used to satisfy personal desires. Often there is an intense drive to succeed and to win at all costs when Mars is in Aries. The ray six energies that Mars transmits are associated with war and aggression. Historically, Mars has been referred to as the god of war.

Unless modified by other astrological factors, Mars in Aries confers a rather headstrong, independent disposition—one that is intolerant of anything that stands in the way of desired action and activity. When people's efforts to satisfy their desires are blocked, anger and aggression can arise.

People with this placement of Mars often demonstrate great courage and initiative, but also great impulsiveness. A strong competitive streak that pits them against others is common, even when they are engaging in noncompetitive activity. The lower ray six forces of Mars contain a willful quality that people frequently express as a strong urge to act. There is often a need to triumph over others, to win at all costs, and to be a leader. People with Mars in Aries can be egotistical, egoistic, aggressive, and self-serving. Of course, this is the lowest expression of this divine life-force.

Aries transmits ray one and ray seven onto the earth. Again, ray one represents the will of the Divine, while ray seven represents the physical-plane expression of ray one. Ray seven imposes a new rhythm in people's lives through ritual, order, and organization. The objective of ray seven energies in relation to Aries is to bring organization and direction to one's daily life as a result of the using the essential life force appropriately. Ray seven relates spirit to matter.

Personal desire first arose on earth during the ancient Atlantean period when the feeling nature was just beginning to unfold within the bodies of primitive mankind. As the astral-sentient, feeling nature was unfolding, a group of primitive human beings started to appropriate this fiery life-force for their own personal use. Primitive mankind combined the astral-emotional sentient forces (ray six Mars) and the fiery life-force (ray one Aries). This combination brought forth personal desire within human consciousness. It was this combined force that primitive man used to acquire and possess the things of earth. Personal desire, in turn, created divisions and separatism within the burgeoning feeling nature of this group of Atlanteans.

Mars represents the motivating forces of desire that help bring something into manifestation on earth. However, when this desire force started to be directed by the self-serving feelings of primitive mankind, the evolution of human consciousness was disrupted. Self-serving activity violates the basic nature of the all-inclusive Logos, as well as violates the purpose of the Logos for which all things exist. This was the beginning of mankind's mis-creations on earth. For this reason, human consciousness is now thought of in relation to the consciousness of the little self and the consciousness of the higher self. The little self is permeated with separatism. This factor of separatism within ray three energies of the First Solar System brought forth differentiated life forms, but it was not to affect consciousness. Misuse of the forces of essential life by the little self continues today.

Esoterically, separatism is the greatest sin of mankind. It is a great obstacle within the consciousness that interferes with people's ability to attain spiritual realization. Separatism is the precipitating cause behind the arising of illusion, glamour, and maya. For millennia, people have generated selfish forces that have distorted human consciousness and obstructed the progressive unfoldment of divine ideas on earth.

The many pairs of opposites (duality) within human consciousness are a product of the divisions within the consciousness that this factor of separatism has created. Duality afflicts both the astral-emotional aspect and the mental aspect of consciousness. This human condition is a product of the misuse of essential life forces.

People are burdened more today by the potent phantoms of duality than they were two thousand years ago. As a result, people are more strongly identified with the form vehicles (the physical body and the threefold personal consciousness) and their natures, rather than identified with the incarnating human spirit and its qualities and values. On the path, the goal is to liberate oneself from illusion, glamour, and maya.

Mankind's struggle with duality is especially intense during the stage of discipleship (from the first initiation up through the third initiation). The duality disciples are confronted with relates to the great differences that exist between the nature of the integrated personality and the nature of the Soul. The very nature of the integrated personality is due to the effects that this factor of separatism has had upon the threefold personal consciousness for millennia.

Everyone on the path experiences this war of dualities as they progress, and in all cases, it is the psychic dynamic of Mars that urges the person into battle. Through Mars, the disciple becomes the spiritual warrior. This pertains to Mars as the Soul-centered ruler of Scorpio, not to Mars as the personality-ruler of Aries.

For those on the path of the heart, this battle centers on the differences between the personal astral-emotional desire nature and the essential love of the Soul. Here, Mars, as the Soul-centered ruler of Scorpio, drives the disciple into battle against mankind's self-serving devotions and desires. Ray six Scorpio always represents the battlefield, the Kurukshetra of the Bhagavad Gita, where the struggle between the disciple (Arjuna) and the Soul (Krishna) play out.

The first externalization of this struggle with duality took place in ancient times when mankind became aware of the duality within human consciousness referred to as good and evil. Granted, there is cosmic evil involving competing cosmic intentions; however, the bulk of what mankind views as evil pertains to what people have deemed personally, religiously, socially, and culturally unacceptable. More often than not, good and evil reflect the divisions within people's own psyches, not true evil.

During the stage of discipleship, the distinct differences between the nature and values of the Soul and those of the threefold personal consciousness are reflected upon the screen of the mind for people to choose between. This occurs once people experience the magnetic attractive power of the Soul and become aware of the higher, selfless thoughts, ideas, values, and virtues of the Soul.

The two major World Religions that mankind developed during the Piscean Age (Christianity and Islam) defined this struggle as a battle between good and evil. Both World Religions are closely associated with the lower personal expression of ray six and Mars. This results in a devotion and dedication to a religious ideal that is divisive and separating in nature.

Since Christianity and Islam are often an expression of ray six Mars and Scorpio at the personal level, both Christians and Muslims are called on to move away from an egoistic, selfish expression of the ray six energies of Mars to a higher ray six expression of Pisces and Neptune. This cannot be achieved, however, until Mars and Scorpio complete their work in relation to the tests and trials of discipleship.

Both ray six World Religions have historically expressed many of the martial qualities associated with the forces of Mars and ray six that people express at the personal level. Both World Religions involve intense personal dedication, courage, and religious idealism. When examining Christianity throughout its history, a certain degree of militarism, fanaticism, and a preoccupation with the blood of Christ and the Crucifixion are evident. People are naturally responsive to fanaticism, militarism, and to blood-letting of some kind when the consciousness responds to the planetary forces of Mars at the lower personal level.

Christianity and Islam are both permeated with the taints of conflict and competition. Both were spread and gained acceptance through military battles. Although the militarism within Christianity is not as obvious today as it was a few centuries back, it is still present. The war of opposites stimulated by the influences of Mars also applies to the war declared by orthodox Christianity and Islam on women throughout their history, for the negative polarity of women is opposite the polarity of the male physical body and the symbolism of Mars as expressed at the personal level.

Both religions have consistently warred against human sexuality and the efforts to balance the two physical polarities. They have also warred against the scientific factual world. Science is a product of the stimulation of the mind and does not involve the lower, astral emotional feeling realm where Mars is exceedingly active. Though mental development has made great strides during the past century, the urges of Mars expressing through the lower astral-emotional field still dominate the personality aspect of humanity. Thus, the two World Religions of the Piscean Age are representative of the lower expression of ray six and the forces of Mars, due primarily to the polarization of people's consciousness at the lower astral-emotional level.

Mental control and then mastery of one's own divisive personality is prerequisite to people's ability to demonstrate the nature, values, virtues, and qualities of the Soul. Only then can the divine ideas be perceived. Once the Soul, itself, is focused upward, these ideas arise within the mind of the Soul as essential life pours in. (During the early stages of personal development, the Soul is focused downward into the illusion-filled world of the personal self.)

The driving forces of personal desire, along with such things as racism, bigotry, and misogyny arise due to the way mankind has express the forces of Mars. They are a product of people's self-centered, personal emotional nature, and its urge to battle. This urge to battle, however, should be focused on resolving the duality within one's own consciousness, not focused on people of a different ethnic group, nation, or faith.

As long as people believe that their own denomination or sect is the only way to heaven and that they must criticize and attack other approaches to the Divine, there will be people who are Mars-driven and oriented toward separatism and ego-centered devotion. Such a lower ray six approach to the Divine is incapable of advancing spirituality in the three planes of earth.

The teachings that Jesus brought forth were an expression of the higher ray two and ray six qualities of Neptune and Pisces. However, the followers of Jesus almost immediately institutionalized a religion that was permeated with the lower expression of Mars and ray six. Early Christianity was plagued by conflicts within and between the early Christian churches for several centuries. In the fourth century, the Roman Empire finally stepped in to resolve some of the theological differences between the churches.

In spite of conflict, the early Christian Church was filled with a great spiritual fervor and power. Countless people reached new heights of spirituality, especially during the first few centuries of Christianity. As people worked out their understanding of the message and mission of Jesus, they started to think for themselves for the first time. Many of the early church fathers attained significant spiritual progress as they worked through the meanings and significances of Jesus's life and teachings.

Throughout the Age of Pisces, there have been great souls who lived truly spiritual lives, having resolved the warring dualities within their own consciousness. Many of them embodied and expressed the higher octave of ray six. Some even transcended the foremost duality and unified the integrated personality and the Soul.

This war of the dualities plays out in all aspects of life. It plays out in people's struggles with others. It plays out in the clash between people's emotions and desires versus their mentally-derived goals and objectives. Today, it plays out in the secular world as a struggle between ideologies and political partisanships. Many people use the energies of Mars in a way that creates further division and fans the flames of conflict between people, cultures, ethnic groups, nations, religions, and different forms of government.

The higher ray two and ray six qualities of Pisces and Neptune slowly uplift people out of the world of the separate self into the world of the Soul, and later uplift the unified Soul-personality self into the planes of light and the world of the Real. This is in sharp contrast to the effects that the ray six forces of the non-sacred planet Mars have, which stimulate self-centered drives, actions, and aggression among those still functioning at the lower stages of evolvement.

The evolution of consciousness calls for people to understand the purpose and the complexities of these personal battles, both the internal and external ones. The conflicts people experience repeatedly reflect inner psychic conflicts. Resolution of these conflicts helps shift the consciousness upward from the lower astral to the upper astral, and from the astral-emotional aspect of consciousness to the lower mental aspect, and from the lower mental into the upper mental.

At the mental level, this battling involves conflicting thoughts, ideas, beliefs, partisanship, and ideologies. Such mental conflicts are also triggered by Mars. For those on the path, however, the central struggle pertains to resolving the differences between the nature, characteristics, and traits of the integrated personality and the nature, values, and qualities of the Soul.

The important role Mars plays in the evolution of consciousness (as the agent of action and compelling urges) should not be underestimated. Mars is definitely the expression of desire-in-action; however, the type of actions it stimulates is dependent on the level of development and the quality of people's minds that directs their urges. It is said that the Solar Logos desired to create and that the various Planetary Logoi who embody the planets (due to cosmic desire and necessity) offered to assist the Solar Logos. They each set the processes of Creation into motion that brought forth life in their respective spheres of influence.

Desire is not wrong in and of itself. In fact, it is a necessity. Without desire, potential cannot be actualized. Desire is a necessary factor for the unfoldment, development, and mastery of successively higher states of mind and consciousness.[47] The intent behind the desire is what must be considered. The intent behind the compelling forces of desire either advances divine purpose or works against that purpose.

At the personal stage of development, all desire calls for sacrifice. Something must be given up to acquire that which is desired. There is only so much time in the day and so much energy the body is able to express. Mars is not the agent of sacrifice that Saturn and Pluto are, but it is the driving force that urges a person to sacrifice once the decision has been made to do so. Neptune as the higher expression of ray six, on the other hand, represents the urge to sacrifice all that is of a lower nature, quality, and capacity in order to realize one's true nature.

As a disciple, the opposition of Venus-ruled Taurus to Mars-ruled Scorpio represents the duality that, when resolved, specifically leads people onto the path of initiation. Though Taurus initially relates to the desires of the personal self (the not-self), Scorpio relates to sacrificing the not-self in order to bring forth the higher self. Through sacrifice, people can start to comprehend the relationship that exists between Mars, Pluto, and Scorpio, and begin to understand the meaning behind the tests and trials that people on the path experience.

Initially, Mars appears to be of minor importance in the life of Jesus. This is understandable since most of the conflicts between the pairs of opposites within the personal consciousness, along with His identification with the physical masculine nature and emotional nature, had been mastered long before His incarnation. Regardless, Mars was still important in Jesus's life.

Jesus is often referred to as the great sacrifice. This term refers to a planetary server who sacrifices everything for the purpose of redeeming life and liberating the consciousness of mankind from its imprisonment within the forms of the involutionary life of the three planes of matter. Spiritual liberation is liberation from the not-self. This liberation is necessary before people can identify their selfhood with the creative human spirit, rather than with the form lives of the physical and subtle bodies.

On the path, the sacrifices people are called to make are cumulative and progressive. They involve relinquishing successively greater and more comprehensive aspects of the not-self: All aspects of the little self must be sacrificed in order to realize a union of the self and Soul. All aspects of the personal concrete mind and intelligence must be transformed into the aspects of the threefold mind of the Soul. All individualized and separate forms of personal love must be released from the self and offered to the inclusive, unconditioned essential love of the Soul. And all expressions of the personal will must be sacrificed to the inclusive, empowering will of the Soul.

---

[47] When desire relates to the development of the higher self, it is referred to as aspiration.

Sacrifice of the not-self advances the higher self and leads to the eventual union of the integrated personality with the Soul. At-one-ment consciousness takes place at the third initiation once the threefold personal consciousness is fully sacrificed to the threefold Soul.

Jesus didn't unfold a self-focused or self-serving personality in His early years like most people do, since the Soul had already transformed the personality vehicle into an instrument of the Soul prior to His incarnation. Using Christian terminology, Jesus was free of sin and the desires of the flesh.

Esoterically, there were few patterns within the psyche of Jesus that would have distracted Him from transcending the personality and achieving a union with the Soul. In His early years, He merely needed to demonstrate the level of spirituality indicative of a second-degree initiate. This He accomplished by cultivating love, forgiveness, humility, and thanksgiving. Nor did Jesus experience the warring dualities within His threefold personal consciousness that most people experience, since the psychic dualities that plague mankind had also been resolved prior to incarnation. With this personal battle out of the way and the threefold personal consciousness integrated and working harmoniously, Jesus was ready to achieve a union of the integrated personality and Soul at a young age. Once attained, Jesus stepped forward to serve God and mankind.

Once He had been attained the third initiation, however, Jesus experienced planetary duality. Two thousand years ago, planetary duality was expressed as a struggle between good and evil. But it also manifested in Jesus's life as a struggle between the ideas and beliefs of the waning Age of Aries and the new principles, ideas, and values of the Age of Pisces. The clash between these two Ages is quite obvious throughout the synoptic Gospels.

Jesus demonstrated how to resolve duality in a way that is applicable to the resolution of all pairs of opposites at all levels. This involves forgiveness, never harboring grudges, and applying love to all conditions and situations. Most of all, it is an acceptance that some situations and conditions cannot be changed. This results in the ability to submit to the will of God (the will of the Soul) regardless of the consequences. This relates to the working out of universal law.

> *Father, if thou art willing, remove this cup from me; nevertheless not my will, but thine, be done.*[48]

---

[48] Luke 22:42. (RSV) (italics added)

Chapter 16

Mars, Saturn, and Pluto—the Antagonists

Mars Conjunct Saturn (13 minutes)

Mars is so closely conjunct Saturn in the chart of Jesus that it is impossible to discuss Mars as an independent dynamic within the consciousness of Jesus. Only thirteen minutes separated the placement of Mars from Saturn when Jesus was born. This indicates that the energies of Mars and Saturn were unified in terms of the mind of Jesus. Being so closely conjoined, they represent a psychic dynamic very different from what Mars and Saturn represent individually.

Mars, Saturn, and Pluto represent the antagonists in the life story of Jesus. The planetary forces of these three planets were the precipitating causal factors behind many of the disturbing and disruptive events and situations Jesus experienced. For example, since the energy of the conjunction of Mars and Saturn and their inconjunction to Pluto expressed in the third house, the forces of these three planets were activated in relation to Judas's betrayal, and in relation to the other disciples denying that they were followers of Jesus. Although the third house is the area of life that represents one's brothers and sisters, at the initiate level Jesus was at, the third-house represented His spiritual brothers and sisters. This included the twelve disciples.

Given the epic grand trine, this close conjunction between Mars and Saturn suggests that during a recent past life, the integrated personality had walked up to the doorway on the mount of Capricorn that opens onto the path of initiation, but did not walk through.

On the third climb to the summit of the mount, Saturn, as the Lord of Karma, stands blocking the way onto the path of initiation until all three types of tests and trials of the third initiation have been passed. These three tests require disciples to demonstrate their mastery of the ray three, ray two, and finally the ray one sub-qualities that are operative at the mental-plane level. In terms of Jesus's life, the ray one sub-quality of the third initiation had yet to be passed when He incarnated. Only when Jesus demonstrated His mastery of all three sub-qualities of the third initiation did He step onto the path of initiation. The three temptations represent the time when Jesus mastered the mental plane and attained the third initiation.

Neither Mars nor Saturn was part of the epic grand trine in Jesus's chart. However, they tied into the kite configuration since they formed an inconjunction to Pluto (150 degrees of separation plus or minus three degrees). This suggests that the development of the Mars dynamic within the psyche of Jesus was peripheral to the overall spiritualization of His consciousness. However, the conjunction of Mars and Saturn in the third house was exceedingly important in relation to His mission and to His ability to formulate the path of the heart.

In the chart of Jesus, it appears as if the psychological dynamic Mars represents was initially thwarted and wasn't important to Jesus's personal development and growth, as it is for most people, especially males. Though the Mars and Saturn dynamics of the psyche were minimally integrated with the other psychic dynamics, they were very involved in the development and formulation of the Piscean teachings that Jesus delivered. They were also active at the time of His Crucifixion.

In the early years of Jesus's life, the conjunction of Mars to Saturn served as an obstructive force within His psyche that prevented Him from developing a strong identity with the physical body and its masculine polarity. The preponderance of the feminine polarity in His chart suggests that this obstruction imposed upon the Mars dynamic of the psyche had been in place for several lifetimes. The blocking forces of Saturn also prevented Jesus from unfolding a strong desire nature. In effect, Jesus was blocked from using the energies of Mars to desire the things of earth. This block wasn't something that was imposed upon Him. Rather, it was something that was self-generated in recent past lives.

Over time, this tight conjunction of Mars and Saturn built up points of tension that precipitated a series of crises in Jesus's life. The resolution of these crises resulted in His attainment of successively higher states of mind.

For most people, Mars is the vehicle for the lower, more personal expression of ray six—devotion and dedication of oneself to someone or something. People's personal devotion to Jesus or their devotion to Krishna, to Shiva, and so forth, even people's dedication to communism—all are representative of the way people use the planetary forces of Mars.

Mars is the agent of desire in the sense that the forces of Mars compel action, especially in relation to acquiring what is personally desired. Although the term desire is used in this analysis primarily in relation to people's selfish desires, desire is the force and motivating factor or urge behind all manifestation. It was the great desire of the Solar Logos that set the entire evolution of life and mind into motion across the entire solar system, resulting in the manifest worlds of Creation found throughout the seven planes of the cosmic physical plane.

In Jesus's life, Saturn blocked the unfoldment of the psychic dynamic of Mars that expresses as a desire for the material things of earth. Here, the energies of Saturn were used to build in the structures of the mind that contained and controlled the personal emotional desire nature. This containment of the urges of personal desire was further strengthened by the placement of the Saturn in Aries, which Mars rules at the personality level.

The influences of the tight conjunction of Mars and Saturn also safeguarded Jesus from developing a strong egocentric perspective. Though a strong sense of self must be developed upon the path and ultimately transcended, the self-centered urges that Mars typically evokes make it exceedingly difficult to transcend the threefold personality.

The third-house placement of this Mars-Saturn conjunction provided Jesus with the energies needed to structure His concrete mind. Saturn mitigated the influence that the lower emotional-desire nature would have had on His thoughts and diminished His interest in learning the secular knowledge of the world.

Esoterically, the concrete mind is the slayer of the real. This is an accurate description as long as the consciousness is polarized at the astral-emotional or lower mental level. Here, the mind is preoccupied with physical-plane life and caught up in the swirling forces of illusion and maya. As the energies of the Soul stream through the upper etheric centers and impact the consciousness, however, the concrete mind is slowly transformed into the revealer of the Real through the actions of Venus. Only then can the initiate begin to comprehend the nature of the world of the Real while incarnate.

Traditional astrology considers Mars the lesser malefic and Saturn the greater malefic. It is quite unusual to have the lesser and greater malefic forming such a tight conjunction. However, it is not the planetary forces of these two planets that are malefic. Rather, it is the way the average person emotionally reacts and mentally responds to these planetary forces that makes them malefic, especially when the two planets are linked by a hard aspect (the square, opposition, and often the conjunction).

Mars and Saturn are thought of as malefic for very different reasons. Saturn is often thought of as malefic because of the difficult experiences it precipitates, especially on the self-indulgent person. Saturn has a maturing, isolating influence that can disrupt and even block the flow of people's emotions and feelings. Whereas the energies of Saturn express via the mental body and impact the concrete mind and intellect, the energies of Mars usually stimulate people's feelings and desires and impact the consciousness via the astral body.

The energies of Saturn are directly involved in the processes that unfold and develop the mental aspect of personal consciousness. This includes the unfoldment of the concrete mind and its faculties and capacities, such as logical, rational thought and discrimination. Saturn, as the enforcer of the universal laws of humanity and the lord of karma, demands personal integrity, honesty, and human decency, performance of duty, self-discipline, fairness, and justice. It encourages people to shoulder personal and social responsibility.

Saturn is a hard taskmaster that binds people to the millstone of life until their consciousness is polarized at the mental level and their violations of universal law have been resolved. When people resist shouldering personal responsibility and are not inclined to impose self-discipline (especially in relation to the emotional, self-indulgent elements of one's nature), the effects that Saturn has can be rather burdensome. By way of Saturn and the effects that its energies have on the personal consciousness, people become responsible human beings, capable of fulfilling their personal, familial, and social obligations and duties.

Mars, on the other hand, is commonly thought of as malefic due to the difficult experiences people have when hard aspects prevent them from satisfying personal desire and indulgencies or interfere with them becoming the leaders they so want to be. When this is the case, Mars is often associated with egotism, selfishness, anger, self-centered activity, and aggression. For many people, the planetary forces of Mars stimulate the more primitive instinctual and lower astral-emotional aspects of personal consciousness.

When this energy of action is activated by the instinctual mind, people act in ways that are more expressive of the evolutionary directives that govern animal behavior than the directives that govern mankind—the universal laws of humanity. Throughout history, mankind has responded to the evolutionary directives that motivate animal behavior. People often fail to respond to the evolutionary directives that govern human behavior. This is understandable, given people's identification of their selfhood with the physical body which is an animal form.

For the average person, the forces of Mars that prompt the physical body to take action originate at the midrange levels of the astral–emotional desire body. It is this level of emotionalism (me-ism) that the energies of Saturn tend to obstruct. People usually express the energies of Mars as personal desire, since emotion-based desire is the primary force that prompts most people to act.

What few people realize is that the physical body is an automaton. Its actions are typically compelled by self-centered emotions, desires, and other elements of the threefold consciousness. In general, the astral-emotional forces are the most common motivating forces behind people's actions. This is due to the level of development the average person has attained.

What Mars actually represents, however, is the motive power to manifest and express on earth. Once people begin to respond to the Soul, the forces of Mars serve as the driving force behind people's spiritual aspirations. Here, Mars represents the driving, motivating force people use to realize higher ideals and to manifest the higher seed ideas here on earth. In this sense, the desire forces of ray six Mars are used to give life to new thoughts, understanding, and discoveries.

When ray three Saturn conjuncts ray six Mars, it tends to dampen or thwart people's ability to freely express their emotions and feelings, and interferes with their ability to initiate actions—at least in relation to the self-focused emotional nature and personal indulgences. Also, Mars is associated with men's identification of their selfhood with the masculinity of the physical body. When Saturn conjuncts Mars, Saturn has a significant inhibiting effect upon men's ability to express their sexuality and physical prowess in a healthy, constructive way.

As a result of Saturn's influence, the mind is filled with all kinds of groupings, structures, and limitations. Initially, these structures act as a crucible within which new elements of consciousness are unfolded and developed. Such structures allow people to apply the light of mind to the free-flowing astral-emotional nature to contain the emotions. However, these structures of the mind tend to become obsolete as people progress.

With the forces of Saturn oriented toward developing the mental aspect of the personal consciousness, they frequently block, limit, and deny the free flow of feelings and emotions. By nature, Saturn acts as a blocking force not only in terms of the emotions, but in relation to people's self-serving physical activities and initiative. Saturn demands responsible actions and initiatives that are well thought out. This is especially true when Saturn conjuncts Mars.

When people's efforts to obtain that which they desire are blocked, frustration and anger often arise. People either externalize their frustration and anger through aggressive behavior and actions, or they internalize these potent forces. Physical devitalization and depression are frequent manifestations of internalized anger. Then, when pent-up anger is suddenly released (often as a result of the actions of Uranus), people with this conjunction often lash out in ways that are more destructive than if they would have expressed their anger when it first arose.

During the early stages of personal development, people frequently react to the obstructions Saturn throws up in a negative, self-centered way. They blame others for their difficulties and frequently engage in vengeful, retaliatory acts to punish others for causing them pain and despair. Incidents of anger, rage, and spiteful retaliation are common when Saturn forms a hard aspect to Mars.

As the ray three qualities of Saturn stimulate the development of the concrete mind and intellect, they confer stability, an enduring strength, a single-minded focus, and a capacity for hard work. In general, Saturn is associated with self-discipline and with Spartan-like traits and characteristics.

Once the consciousness is polarized at the mental level, the Saturn-Mars conjunction offers people great strength, courage, equanimity, and prudence, especially when faced with a dangerous situation. The Mars-Saturn conjunction conferred the strength, courage, and stability Jesus needed in order to present the teachings of the Piscean Age in the midst of great resistance. The empowerment this conjunction in the third house conferred kept Him from second-guessing Himself and His mission in the face of significant challenges.

People who are still at the stage of personal development, however, tend to express this Mars-Saturn dynamic in a way that advances their selfish ambitions. When Mars and Saturn are linked by a hard aspect, people (especially males) tend to express this dynamic as a strong drive for power and control, and frequently exhibit a might-makes-right attitude without any consideration of how others might feel. The more selfish and egocentric people are, the greater the danger that this conjunction poses to the individual and to society.

Others who have a close conjunction of Mars and Saturn react to the challenges they experience in an inordinately passive way. They often have difficulty expressing their own personal will. Though they may become frustrated and angry at their inability to stand up for themselves, they find it extremely difficult to stand up for their own basic rights, due to the inhibiting forces of Saturn.

Being free of the personal desire nature, Jesus didn't generate the frustration and anger that many people with this conjunction often do. However, this conjunction still created points of tension in His life that could have enhanced His penchant toward rebellion, especially against authority figures and the established institutions of society. Major conflicts with authority figures are common when Mars and Saturn are conjunct. This is due to the fact that Capricorn (which Saturn rules) establishes the issues of the tenth house of profession and government.

The self-centered characteristics and behavior that the energies of Mars often activate were not something that Jesus felt a need to express. If anything, this conjunction reflected causal patterns generated in recent past lives in which harsh religious disciplines were imposed upon the free flowing astral-emotional desire nature. For this reason, it is unlikely that Jesus felt personally frustrated as a result of the suppressive forces of Saturn. Due to His Capricorn Ascendant, the energies of Saturn and the repressive effects they had on His astral-emotional nature and desires probably seemed quite natural, reflecting both His early religious training and home environment.

According to traditional astrology, the Mars-Saturn combination of forces is common in the charts of people whose fathers (Saturn) are authoritarian. Frequently their fathers have rigid religious beliefs and ideas that they impose on their children. This domineering authoritarianism is frequently imprinted upon their children in a way that diminishes their ability to express themselves in a healthy, constructive way. This is especially true for young men. Children who experience strict authoritarianism in the home frequently feel rejected and have a fear of failure and domination by others. Authoritarianism experienced in the home is often representative of causal patterns of the psyche that repress or suppress normal human behavior.

Whether this was the experience of Jesus in His childhood isn't known. Due to the extreme sensitivity that the epic grand trine conferred, however, it is unlikely that Jesus related to this authoritarianism very well. Since this conjunction was in the third house in Jesus's chart, this authoritarianism expressed in relation to His own mind, even though He probably was sensitive to the authoritarianism within the society, which Joseph may or may not have reflected.

Undoubtedly, this Mars-Saturn dynamic made Jesus supersensitive to people's anger and tension. This super-sensitivity, in turn, forewarned Him when a situation was getting out of hand. Jesus frequently needed to quickly remove Himself from certain situations before conflicts arose. Jesus was definitely supersensitive to any type of authoritarian behavior.

The astrological symbolism of this Mars-Saturn authority dynamic of His psyche aligns well with the God of the covenant who imposed stringent rules, laws, and commandments upon the Judean people and retaliated when the people wavered from His commandments and decrees. In many ways, the God of Judaism is a projection of the authoritarian father figure onto society.

How people react to the obstructive forces that Saturn imposes upon the action dynamic of Mars when Mars and Saturn are conjunct depends on the house and sign placement of the conjunction and the point of evolvement that the individual has achieved.

People with a potent Mars-Saturn psychic dynamic are more likely to react in a violent, cruel way when their consciousness is still polarized at the mid-astral level. Such people tend to exhibit dictatorial, authoritarian tendencies. Dictatorial tendencies, however, are more common when Saturn squares Mars than they are when Mars and Saturn are conjunct. When conjunct, people are more likely to become the victim of cruelty and violence than the perpetrator.

Incidents in which people are victimized by others when the Mars-Saturn conjunction is transited suggest that one's own personal frustrations and repressed anger may be the originating cause for the victimization. All energy must express. It can be blocked, repressed, or contained for a while, but it will eventually express. Since the hard aspects of Mars to Saturn in the natal chart are so often associated with cruelty, ruthlessness, harsh and insensitive behavior, there could be some past-life pattern that is the precipitating factor behind such behavior.

Jesus experienced a number of clashes during His ministry and He definitely became a victim of harsh cruelty and violence. The question is, why? Was Jesus being victimized by something within His own psyche or something within His causal body that this Mars-Saturn conjunction represented? Was His Crucifixion the result of His own repressed anger that was suddenly released by a transit? The inconjunction of Pluto to Saturn and Mars in His chart, along with Pluto's opposition to the Sun, Mercury, and Uranus, indicate that Jesus was very likely to experience conflict and victimization. Does this mean that there was something within the psyche of Jesus that was a causal factor to His own Crucifixion?

The reason why Jesus had a tight Mars-Saturn conjunction in His chart most likely reflected some pattern in His causal body.[49] However, this Mars-Saturn dynamic was more reflective of the spiritual disciplines that recent past lives of Jesus had imposed on themselves to suppress or repress their so-called sinful nature, i.e., their own instinctual-emotional nature. Many spiritual seekers two thousand years ago ardently denied the flesh and the pleasures of the body. Many of the different spiritual paths required the seeker to deny the natural urges of the physical body.

Throughout history, the religious fight against sin and temptation was often accomplished by way of denying and repressing the appetites of the physical body. This was especially true in the early Judeo-Christian world, when many of the natural expressions of the instinctual-emotional nature of mankind were looked at as Satan tempting them.

However, spiritual disciplines and techniques that are physically punitive and repressive do not transmute the lower instinctual-emotional patterns of behavior. Nor do they eliminate people's conscious responsiveness to the lower intelligences of the form vehicles. Rather, they only create and strengthen the repressive structures of the mind that contain and control the instinctual-emotional nature. Although Saturn contributes self-discipline and structure to the mind and consciousness, people frequently use the energies of Saturn to contain and even suppress the instinctual, astral-emotional nature.

When this is the case, the repressed forces slowly build up; creating a point of tension that can shatter the mental force fields containing them, often disastrously. Uranus is the agent that shatters the saturnine containment fields and releases the imprisoned forces into the light of people's conscious awareness. The shattering of the saturnine structures that contain the repressed physical and emotional nature often results in a sudden explosive release of the repressed forces. The release of such pent-up forces triggers the very type of

---

[49] The more evolved people are, the greater the likelihood that their own natal chart represents the Soul's intent.

actions and behavior that the individual was trying to deny or repress. Pluto also releases pent-up instinctual and astral-emotional forces, but in a different way.

Most likely, one or more of Jesus's past lives had created harsh patterns of self-discipline, repression, and denial which were imposed upon the instinctual-emotional aspects of the personal consciousness. Such harsh patterns act as a powerful authority figure within the psyche that enforces the religious laws, rules, beliefs, and dogma. Here, the religious authority dynamic within the psyche becomes the harsh and even cruel oppressor of the flesh—the traits, tendencies, nature, and characteristics of the physical instinctual mind and the lower astral-emotional nature. When this is the case, the instinctual appetites and drives along with the personal emotional-desire nature may be controlled and restrained by the repressive authoritarian dynamic of the psyche, but they are not transcended.

For millennia, such self-denying spiritual disciplines (including acts of self-immolation) were the accepted methodology that spiritual seekers used to break the influence that the physical body and its appetites had upon the consciousness. For seven years, the Buddha denied Himself the basic comforts of life, including food. During this period, the Buddha would only eat a few grains of rice per day.

The early Christian mystics frequently engaged in acts of self-denial, self-flagellation, self-mortification, and even self-immolation. Many denied themselves food and water while standing on a pole-stand, where they baked in the scorching sun day after day. Self-denial, sacrifice, self-imposed physical austerities, and martyrdom were acceptable techniques to approach the Divine two thousand years ago.

By adopting these physically repressive techniques, the ancient spiritual seekers often freed their consciousness from the control that the physical-etheric and lower astral forces exerted over the consciousness, but at a high price. Although these harsh repressive techniques can help strengthen one-pointed focus and mental control, such techniques can adversely affect people in a number of ways.

It is quite likely that this Mars-Saturn conjunction in Jesus's chart represented a harsh religious authority dynamic within the causal patterns of Jesus. These patterns were probably created in past lives as a result of the harsh disciplines, spiritual austerities, and self-denial the personality of recent lifetimes had imposed upon their lives.

Such a harsh religious authority figure within the mind can successfully repress the temptations of the flesh (to use a Christian term), but it constitutes a great obstacle to the attainment of the third initiation and completely blocks the attainment of the fourth initiation. Using such psychologically repressive techniques initially strengthens the personal mind and willpower. They are contrary to the nature of the Soul and, therefore, block someone from transcending the integrated personality.

A better way to empower the mind and gain control and mastery of the physical body is by becoming a vegetarian, as long as people do not repress their desire for meat. Mastery of threefold personal consciousness is most easily gained when the energies radiating from the opened petals of the intelligence, love, and sacrifice tier of petals are able to stream through the upper etheric centers. It is by way of the will of the Soul emanating from the petals of the sacrifice tier that the entire threefold personality is eventually mastered and transcended. This method of empowerment, however, was not an option prior to the influx of love-wisdom two thousand years ago.

The mental faculties of mankind were so underdeveloped that there was little light of mind that could align with the Soul and attract the high-frequency energies of the Soul. In order to activate the flow of energies from the petals of the lotus, the concrete mind and intellect must be unfolded and developed first. Only then can the Soul energies infuse the personal mind with sufficient light to achieve a mastery of the physical body and the emotional desire nature. Without the light and will of the Soul pouring into the mind, spiritual seekers in the past had to use harsh tactics to control the drives and appetites of the body and the physical-instinctual and emotional aspects in order to attain the first and second initiations.

These two threshold initiations are prerequisite to stepping upon the spiritual path. However, they are not prerequisite to the religious path. Since it was mankind who left the path during Atlantean days and chose to learn through trial and error and the exercise of free will, mankind has been basically on its own to find its way back to the path.

Today, controlling the physical and lower emotional nature by creating a repressive authority-figure dynamic within the psyche is not the best way to master the instinctual and astral-emotional desire mind, now that people have adequately developed the mind and mental faculties.

The will of the Soul is the power that is needed to master the instinctual mind and desire mind without denying or repressing the normal expressions of the body and its nature. As the energies of the Soul pour into the mind over time, the mind becomes infused with the light and power needed to attain the first two initiations. This infusion of Soul light via the petals of the lotus enables people to progressively shift their identity away from the form and its nature to the values and qualities of the Soul.

The accepted methodology for those on the path today is to engage in spiritual studies, meditation, prayer, and service to others. This activity helps to align and attune the consciousness to the Soul. By holding the attention higher and by meditating and engaging in spiritual studies of an uplifting, spiritual quality, the atoms of self-consciousness attached to the instinctual and emotional aspects of personal consciousness are freed from the influences of the form natures.

In this way, the consciousness is liberated from the drama of personal life in a positive, uplifting way, rather than through repression and denial. When the noisy voices of the outer world are stilled, the original thoughts and inspiration of one's own Soul can be heard. But when people create a repressive or oppressive authority dynamic within the psyche (even when it seems to be needed in order to get control of the physical appetites and drives), they are strengthening something within the consciousness that is contrary in nature to the essential love of the Soul.

Any form of repression becomes a problem at the third initiation, since such an authoritarian dynamic runs counter to the values and nature of the Soul and must be eliminated before the personal consciousness can be transcended. Building up an authority dynamic in the psyche only adds more work to the third initiation. Mental and spiritual disciplines are most definitely needed on the path, but not suppression of the normal urges and tendencies of the form vehicles. Such things fall away as people focus more of their attention upward, e.g., on the Soul and what they need to do in order for them to express the values, virtues, and qualities of the Soul. As long as repressive tendencies are present in the psyche, the Soul is unable to transfigure over the physical body.

From a psychological perspective, a better approach to mastering the threefold personal consciousness is to engage in service work on behalf of others, while holding oneself in the light of the Soul. Invocations of divine light and love into the three planes of earth and prayers for the health and well-being of mankind are always helpful. Practicing mindfulness and harmlessness in thought, word, and deed are especially helpful.

These activities shift the consciousness higher naturally. There is no denial or repression of that which is religiously thought of as improper. Instead, people's characteristics and tendencies of a lower, negative quality fall away, due to a lack of attention, for people's conscious response to them is what gives them life. In this way the consciousness is liberated from the lower instinctual and emotional-desire forces without adopting harsh repressive techniques.

In relation to Jesus, His chart indicates that it was not in His nature to be the perpetrator of violence and cruelty, but He was likely to experience conflict and cruelty, even violence. The combination of the forces of Mars and Saturn is an irritating vibration or note that often aggravates other people, especially when a transiting planet forms a hard aspect to it. The synoptic Gospels record a number of incidents of the hostility and rancor of the people who had gathered around Jesus. The Judean Pharisees and scribes (who were the most ardent defenders of Judaism) repeatedly challenged and ridiculed Jesus. To them, many of Jesus's statements violated the teachings of the Torah. Discord arose so often that Jesus taught primarily in the nation of Galilee, not in Judea. Major conflicts with authority figures are common when Mars and Saturn are conjunct.

Undoubtedly, this conjunction was the contributing factor behind many of the clashes Jesus experienced in relation to His teachings, but such clashes were not in response to a tendency toward violence and cruelty within Him—yet violence and cruelty were very much a part of His life experience. Why?

Due to the lofty state of mind Jesus had attained and the fact that this Mars-Saturn conjunction was in the third house of communications and learning, the harsh effects this conjunction had on Jesus played out in relation to a clash between the knowledge of the outgoing Age of Aries and the knowledge and understanding of the incoming Age of Pisces. Jesus's mission involved presenting the steps and stages of this new Piscean approach to the Divine—the path of the heart—which clashed with the teachings of the Age of Aries.

Interestingly, transiting Uranus breached the mental force field of this Mars-Saturn conjunction at the time of Jesus's arrest and Crucifixion. Transiting Uranus was just one of the precipitating factors behind the Crucifixion[50] of Jesus. This release of the forces of the Mars-Saturn conjunction prompted great fear among the people. The Sanhedrin in particular feared what Rome would do as a result of the uprising His teachings caused in Jerusalem just before Passover in 33 CE. Their fear was so great that their hearts and minds were filled with violence and cruelty against Jesus. He was arrested and brought before the Sanhedrin and then before Pontius Pilate on charges of insurrection. Jesus was crucified on Friday, April 3, 33 CE.

The harshness and cruelty that is common when Mars and Saturn are linked by a hard aspect was definitely expressed at His Crucifixion, but not by Jesus. Theologians often say that the Crucifixion was necessary to complete the story of Jesus. Without this event, there would be no Resurrection. Does this mean that the Crucifixion was part of the fabric of the life story of Jesus and, therefore, part of the karma of His Soul in terms of His mission?

By the time Jesus was crucified, He had attained the fourth initiation and was, therefore, a Planetary Server free of all personal karma. It is quite likely that His Crucifixion was a necessary part of His mission. As a planetary server, Jesus met the collective patterns of violence and cruelty that mankind had generated throughout history. Rather than responding with hatred and anger, Jesus responded with love and forgiveness. He forgave those who wanted to kill Him.

The astral body of the planet contains an immense amount of hatred and cruelty that mankind has generated over the years. Mankind's inhumanity toward others has dominated life on earth throughout history. Such forces of hate move through the lowest regions of the astral bodies of mankind as they circumnavigate the globe. Negative emotional forces may

---

[50] The sequel to *Path of the Soul* discusses this event in great detail.

flow through a person's astral body, but unless an individual holds onto hatred and violence, they usually have little effect.

Once initiates resolve their personal karma and the limiting causal patterns of the Soul, they are often called to transmute a portion of the planetary karma. The Crucifixion of Jesus neutralized a portion of the karma of mankind. A vast amount of planetary karma is mercifully withheld from mankind and released from time to time when humanity is better equipped to meet it. All planetary servers, however, must meet some portion of mankind's collective karma. By experiencing the effects of the negative forces mankind has set into motion, karma is neutralized (often through suffering).

Since the Crucifixion took place after Jesus had transcended the personality and was functioning as the Soul, the cruelty He experienced represented an opportunity to demonstrate the ultimate sacrifice—the sacrifice of one's life to benefit others. Here, it is imperative to sacrifice without regret or anger. Masters instantly forgive those who seek to harm them. If they do not, the life paths of the victim and the perpetrator are bound to each other until some future moment when the energies can be rebalanced and harmonized in relation to each other. This is the universal law of karma.

Thus, this tight conjunction of Saturn to Mars served a number of purposes in Jesus's life. First, Saturn prevented Jesus from becoming preoccupied with the personal instinctual-desire mind and succumbing to the instinctual-emotional drive to satisfy personal desire. Second, the Mars-Saturn conjunction kept Him from emotionally identifying His selfhood with the physical body and from thinking of Himself in relation to the masculine polarity of the physical body.

Third, the effects this Saturn-Mars conjunction had on Jesus pertained to the major life lesson He needed to address, given the point of evolvement His Soul had attained. This involved sacrificing His personal will to the will of the Soul (the will of God). Saturn's actions definitely disrupted Jesus's ability to express His personal will. (This struggle between the personal will and the will of the Soul had started prior to Jesus's incarnation.) His inability to express His personal will in a powerful way was the most important life lesson Jesus had to face before He could attain a state of mind transcendent of the integrated personality.

Once Jesus attained the third initiation and functioned as a Soul, He not only came under the influence of a higher quality of the ray energies, but He also came under the influence of different rays and principles. At the Soul level, nine of the twelve signs are ruled by different planetary rulers than they are at the personal level (see addendum: Table One).

Again, Pluto, as the agent and transmitter of the potent ray one energies of divine will, rules Pisces at the Soul level. This shift in the planetary ruler of Pisces from Neptune to

Pluto eventually led Jesus from the path of the heart onto the path of power. This represents a movement off the mystical path onto the path of power. On the path of power, initiates learn how to master, wield, and command the forces of the three planes of matter in response to divine will and purpose.

According to esoteric thought, people should first embody and identify with the essential love of the Soul before they begin to wield the ray one energies of divine will, especially in its aspect as the destroyer. Otherwise the individual is likely to wield this power selfishly to advance his or her own personal interests. Such action would further bury the consciousness into matter and bind the person to the involutionary path of matter.

By the time Jesus attained the third initiation, Neptune (as the personality ruler of Pisces) had sufficiently conditioned His consciousness with ray two and ray six, and had completed its synthesizing work to blend and harmonize many of the dynamics of the threefold personal consciousness with the Soul. This initial Neptune-Piscean activity brought forth a deep love and devotion to the God of love and helped Jesus to unify the integrated personality and Soul into one field of light.

Once He attained the third initiation, the will energies poured onto Him via Pluto. In Jesus's life, this resulted in His ability to wield a power that is referred to as the will-to-love. The influx of this will-to-love brought the mind and consciousness of Jesus under the impulses and impressions of the divine plan and attuned Him to His mission. In the end, the Saturn-Mars conjunction in the third house helped Jesus to comprehend and then formulate the new teachings of the Piscean Age.

By way of this Mars-Saturn conjunction in Aries in the third house, the principles and seed ideas of the Piscean Age were compelled with the forces of desire (Mars) and provided with the appropriate mental form and structure (Saturn) that were needed to give material form and structure to the new Piscean ideas and concepts. The form and structure Saturn provided here relates to translating the new Piscean seed ideas and revelations into words.

This Mars-Saturn dynamic helped Jesus transform the formless truth of the buddhic plane into words, ideas, sentences, beliefs, analogies, and parables, so others could comprehend the new teachings of the Piscean Age. Specifically, the new principles and seed ideas of the Piscean Age offered mankind a new understanding of the nature of God—that God is love—and a new understanding of mankind's relationship to God. This represents the crux of Jesus's mission: to inform people that the nature of God is love and that through their loving devotion and spiritual dedication, they too can have a personal relationship with the God of love.

Esoterically, the sign Aries represents the initiating impulses that the Masters use to project new seed ideas into the world of the Soul for mankind to intuit, while Saturn and the third house relate to the form that is needed to clothe these formless ideas into knowledge. The third-house thought impulses of Mercury (as the Soul-centered ruler of Aries), the motivating power of Mars, and the concretizing factor of Saturn were all needed to bring forth the teachings of the Piscean Age.

Although the sign Pisces is a vehicle for the transmission of ray two and ray six, during the Piscean Age, ray six was the dominant building quality that poured onto the earth. Thus, the new ideas and principles unfolding within the consciousness of humanity during the Age of Pisces stream onto people via the underlying magnetism of ray six—devotion and dedication to an ideal.

Ray two was not in manifestation during much of the Piscean Age, but ray six was present throughout the Age. Ray two came back into manifestation in 1525 CE, after being inactive for centuries. It will attain its full power of manifestation in 2025 CE. Ray two is one of several rays of manifestation that will be pouring onto the earth for centuries to come.

Today, the love of Jesus is emphasized in Christianity because of the intense manifestation of ray two, love, which He awakened within the collective minds of humanity. Today, more people are able to love one another than ever before. In fact, it is much easier to live by this commandment today than it was when Jesus first voiced the commandment.

At Wesak in 2025, the Masters of love-wisdom will gather for the centennial enclave of the Spiritual Hierarchy. At each centennial enclave, the Masters decide what advancements mankind is ready to bring forth over the course of the next century. Frequently, a large number of people are ready for a higher stage of development; however, the forces of resistance on earth are too strong for the Masters to transmit the new understanding.

The decisions that the Spiritual Hierarchy will make in 2025 will greatly affect the rate at which people progress between 2025 and 2125. One of the most important factors that the Spiritual Hierarchy will take into account at this enclave is the extent to which mankind is responding to ray two energies in a positive, constructive way.

Should the energies of Aquarius intensify further before an adequate number of people are responding to ray two energies—ray two Jupiter is the soul-centered ruler of Aquarius—the evolution of human consciousness could be set back substantially for centuries. The lack of adequate response to ray two would result in an Aquarian Age governed by the personal intellect and mental principles void of love, compassion, forgiveness, and mercy. Heartless despots could dominate the nations of earth. Unless a sufficient number of people are responding to ray two, love-wisdom, the advancement of human consciousness in terms of the Age of Aquarius and ray seven will be delayed.

Mars inconjunct Pluto (1 degree 46 minutes)

For years, traditional astrology ignored the inconjunction (150 degrees, plus or minus three degrees), since it is not an angular relationship that precipitates events or difficult experiences like a square or opposition. Nor does it demand immediate action. The tension that an inconjunction generates slowly builds up over time.

The energies of Pluto precipitate crises, endings, and new beginnings that result in transformation, renewal, and regeneration. The endings Pluto brings about can involve any aspect of life and are always followed by regeneration once people create new structures and levels of understanding, new thoughts and ideas.

Generally, inconjunctions create minor irritations and frustrations in people's daily life. These annoyances, irritations, and frustrations build up and eventually generate a point of tension that motivates people to make changes in their lives to overcome the dissonance that exists between the two dynamics of the psyche that the planets forming the inconjunction represent.

Again, growth in consciousness is dependent on the interplay of different types and qualities of energies and forces that impact the consciousness. The aspect that planets form to each other in the natal chart indicates the nature and quality of the relationship that exists between two dynamics of the psyche. This constant relating of one psychic dynamic to another and the subsequent blending of their rays, energies, and qualities advances the evolution of consciousness. New thoughts, ideas, and understanding arise within the consciousness.

When transiting planets form an aspect to two planets that are inconjunct, they condition the psychic dynamics that the planets represent with new types and qualities of energies. Inconjunctions prompt people to make needed adjustments and modifications within the psyche and can intensify any tension that exists between the two psychic dynamics. When this is the case, tension slowly builds up until the individual is forced to address the dissonance represented by the two inconjunct planets.

Inconjunctions are indicative of a condition within the mind and consciousness that needs to be adjusted in some way before people can take the next step forward in relation to the two psychic dynamics represented. This might involve a needed change in attitude or behavior, or possibly a change in the way people respond to different kinds of situations or conditions.

The kind and type of changes and modifications that are needed depend on whether the inconjunction is a waxing or waning inconjunction. A waxing inconjunction occurs when the faster planet is approaching its opposition to the slower planet. Here, the inconjunction aligns with the principle and symbolism of Virgo. With a waxing aspect, the two psychic dynamics represented by the planets forming the aspect have yet to be related to each other. This takes place at the opposition.

Virgo corresponds to the period of gestation just prior to the birth of some new awareness, understanding, or idea. This gestation period ends with the birth of something new in the consciousness, or possibly a new level of understanding. With the waxing inconjunction, there is a vague sense of something new, but the light of conscious awareness has yet to fully comprehend it. First, the two psychic dynamics need to be related to each other in terms of the principles and qualities, depending on the signs and houses where the two planets are placed. With a waxing aspect, a period of development and nurturing within the psychic womb needs to occur before it can manifest as an element of the consciousness.

The sign Virgo, in particular, corresponds to anchoring the seed of love-wisdom within the crucible of the heart, where it gestates prior to entering the light of people's conscious awareness. As a vehicle of ray two energies (love-wisdom), Virgo symbolically represents the Divine Mother who protects and nurtures love in the crucible of the heart until it is sufficiently mature to rise onto the ajna center and impact the consciousness. Allegorically, the Divine Mother receives the seed of the Father and, after due gestation within the human form, the infant Christ (love-wisdom) is brought forth within the consciousness. This is not a one-time event; rather, it occurs repeatedly and progressively.

A waning inconjunction, on the other hand, relates to Scorpio and its principles and symbolism. With a waning inconjunction of two planets, the two psychic dynamics represented have already been related to each other (at the opposition). During the phase of development represented by the waning inconjunction, a new element, or dynamic, of the psyche is subjected to the influences of Mars and Pluto as the rulers of Scorpio. This means that the new idea or understanding must be energized with astral-emotional desire (Mars) and willpower (Pluto). People can fail to adequately energize (i.e., fail to seek or desire) the new seed idea. This occurs when people fail to seek the growth in consciousness that a particular cycle of the two planets presents. The opportunity for growth that the cycle represents is then withheld until the next cycle of the two planets.

Since the growth in consciousness that inconjunctions offer is not veiled, an event in the outer world isn't needed to discover the meaning or significances that the inconjunct planets are offering. The adjustments needed within the consciousness tend to naturally take place over time, as long as people keep an open mind.

The Mars-Pluto inconjunction in Jesus's chart is a waning inconjunction which corresponds to the principles of Scorpio, Mars, and Pluto. The fact that Mars and Pluto are the planets forming the waning inconjunction greatly intensified the effect that the energies

Scorpio, Mars, and Pluto had in terms of the advancement of the concrete mind, knowledge, thoughts, and ideas of Jesus. This is due to the conjunction of Mars and Saturn in Aries in the third house and their inconjunction to Pluto in the eighth house of transmutation and transformation, endings and new beginnings.

Since Pluto is the personality-centered co-ruler of Scorpio and Mars is the personality co-ruler and the Soul-centered ruler of Scorpio, this waning inconjunction between Mars and Pluto in the chart of Jesus indicates that His concrete mind (beliefs, knowledge, thoughts) was in need of modifications before the personality and Soul could be unified. With Mercury as the ruler of Aries at the Soul level, these modifications and mental adjustments were especially important in relation to perceiving the principles of the incoming Age of Pisces.

A Mars-Pluto inconjunction represents dissonance within the consciousness that can interfere with people's ability to act, especially in relation to the personal emotional-desire nature. This aspect also reinforces the inhibiting effects that Saturn has on the Mars desire-in-action dynamic of the psyche. Because of this difficulty to act, people either become quite passive (even paralyzed when overwhelmed) or they overcompensate with aggressive, belligerent behavior.

When people are still developing the threefold personal consciousness, they often respond to the personal frustrations this Mars-Pluto inconjunction generates by becoming rather rigid and inflexible in their thinking and beliefs. This occurs when people are oriented toward the past and refuse to change their thinking or habits. Rigidly held beliefs, thoughts, and ideas, in turn, cause conflicts and power struggles, especially with those who are in positions of authority.

People with this aspect are frequently stubborn and resistant to change in some area of life. Since both Mars and Saturn formed an inconjunction to Pluto, the transformations Pluto called for impacted both the astral-emotional and mental aspect of consciousness. As a result of this inconjunction, many of the thoughts, ideas, and beliefs of the culture that Jesus held were challenged. The concrete mind needed to be cleared of its cultural biases and beliefs before the new Piscean thoughts and ideas could be formulated into a new approach to the Divine.

The inconjunction of Pluto to Mars interfered with Jesus's ability to take the initiative and act upon life from the level of the personality. This inconjunction further enhanced the suppressive effect that the conjunction of Saturn and Mars had in relation to the way the planetary forces of Mars usually express themselves. Mars confers such characteristics as courageous actions, initiative, and self-motivation. However, both Saturn conjunct Mars and Pluto inconjunct Mars interfere with people's ability to develop these attributes at the personal level.

Many people overcompensate for the difficulty they have initiating actions (due to this inconjunction) by exhibiting aggressive, belligerent behavior. Or, they repress their frustrations and anger and greatly fear violence and other people's aggressive actions. Either way, these energies can generate a vibration of irritation and anger, even hostility. People who refuse to express their anger constructively often find themselves in situations in which they become the victim of angry outbursts, even violence for seemingly no apparent reason.

The difficulties and annoying situations Jesus experienced as a result of this inconjunction represented a direct challenge to His ability to exercise His personal will. Most likely He discovered in His teenage years that He was unable to advance self-serving interests or fulfill His personal wishes. His response to this lesson was to seek to do the will of God. This eventually led Him to sacrifice His will to the will of God (the will of His Soul).

This does not mean that Jesus passively resigned Himself to the challenges that arose in His life. In fact, these challenges engendered a fighting spirit that helped Him to stand His ground in the face of opposition and to work hard to accomplish His mission. All pioneers and visionaries need such a trait in order to weather the forces of resistance and to ultimately break through their hardened thoughts and ideas of the past. Jesus definitely needed a fighting spirit in order to fulfill His mission in the midst of opposition.

The influences of this Mars inconjunct Pluto aspect impacted primarily the third-house area of Jesus's life: the concrete mind, education, knowledge, personally held thoughts, beliefs, ideas, and communications. It was this area of Jesus's life that was subjected to Pluto's cycles of transformation, endings and new beginnings, transmutation, renewal, and regeneration in relation to Mars and Saturn.

In particular, the religious authoritarian psychic dynamic represented by the Mars-Saturn conjunction needed to be eliminated. At the stage Jesus had attained, He no longer needed to rely on the techniques of repression and the so-called denial of the flesh as a way to control His physical-instinctual and astral-emotional nature.

The religious authority dynamic of the psyche is no longer needed once the energies of the love petals of the lotus stream through the upper etheric centers and unfold the love of the higher self. The influx of Soul energies results in not only the mastery of the physical-instinctual and astral-emotional aspects of the personal consciousness, but eventually results in a mastery of the mental aspect of consciousness and the subsequent transcendence of the threefold personality.

The transit of Saturn through the twelve signs and the aspects it formed to Mars slowly and systematically shifted the remaining atoms of self-consciousness operative at the astral-emotional level to the mental-plane level. In this way, the mental aspect of consciousness was strengthened, while the personal emotional nature was diminished.

The inconjunction of Pluto to the Mars-Saturn conjunction also indicates that Jesus incarnated with an exceedingly strong drive to succeed. Such a trait enabled Him to withstand the constant challenges and ridicule He experienced during His ministry as He delivered His teachings.

Although the inconjunctions that Pluto formed to Mars and Saturn were somewhat removed from the epic grand trine and, therefore, removed from the spiritualization of Jesus, they greatly intensified the dynamism that the kite configuration represented. They also provided Jesus with additional powers to transform Himself, especially in relation to His thoughts, knowledge, beliefs, and understanding.

The transformation of the mental aspect of consciousness that took place in Jesus's life as a result of Pluto's inconjunction to His third-house Mars in Aries released Him from the established thought of the Age of Aries. This was necessary before Jesus could develop the new Piscean approach to the Divine.

Chapter 17

Jupiter, the Great Beneficent

Jupiter, the ruler of Sagittarius at the personality level, is the great beneficent of the solar system with a socializing, expansive, and spiritualizing effect upon the consciousness of mankind. Jupiter does not represent a personal, ego-centric dynamic of the psyche like the Sun, Mercury, Venus, and Mars. Rather, it represents an impersonal psychic dynamic of the higher self. Because of Jupiter, mankind achieves goals and objectives and unfolds a higher, social standard of conduct and values.

On the mutable cross, three of four signs transmit ray two energies. The one exception is Sagittarius. The energies of Sagittarius are on ray four, ray five, or ray six. Jupiter, as the magnetically unifying ruler of Sagittarius, helps people achieve goals and objectives.

When people are at the early stages of development of the threefold personal consciousness, ray four tends to be the dominant magnetic influence emanating from Sagittarius. Here, the goals people establish in their lives tend to relate to physical accomplishments.[51] Initially, the Sagittarian energies magnetized by ray six relate to self-serving devotion and the ability to satisfy emotion-based desires. For the disciple, astral-emotional goals relate to the attainment of ideals and aspirations. The Sagittarian energies magnetized by ray five relate to mental achievements, goals, and objectives. Jupiter transmits the ray two, magnetically attractive, unifying forces that help people achieve their goals and objectives, regardless whether the goals relate to the physical, astral, or mental aspect of consciousness.

As the ruler of Sagittarius and co-ruler of Pisces, Jupiter's influences are strongly felt in relation to the ninth and twelfth house areas of life. Due to Jupiter's association with

---

[51] The basic center of the etheric body is initially magnetized receptive toward ray four, resulting in a physically competitive and sometimes combative disposition. Once the energies of the lotus pour through the upper centers, however, the ajna is magnetized receptive to ray four, which reveals the dualities present in the consciousness. People can begin to build the rainbow bridge to link the love petals of the Soul to the buddhic center at this time.

Sagittarius and the ninth house, ethics, religion, law, philosophy, long-distance travel, and all activities that result in an expansion of the consciousness (including higher education) are the major areas of concern in terms of the psychic dynamic that Jupiter represents.

The one word that best describes the effects that the energies of Jupiter have upon the consciousness is expansive. Jupiter represents the factor or quality that expands the consciousness beyond the individual's personal universe. This is accomplished by first awakening people to the needs of the family, then the needs of society, and finally the needs of mankind.

The energies of Jupiter are the only planetary energies on ray two that human consciousness is able to register to one degree or another. The other source of ray two energies is the heart center of the Solar Logos—the Spiritual Sun. This higher cosmic quality of ray two energies, however, cannot be registered within the consciousness of mankind prior to the third initiation. Until then, the Sun and its astrological sign relate to the personal self.

The placement of Jupiter by sign and house indicates the type of energy people are likely to experiment with and where they are likely to focus their attention in relation to personal and spiritual growth. The house Jupiter is located in the natal chart indicates the area of life that receives the ever-expanding, unifying ray two energies of Jupiter. The astrological sign conditioning Jupiter has a significant effect upon people's religious faith and belief in a higher power.

Jupiter represents the quality of energy that magnetically draws the consciousness higher. As the ray two energies radiating from Jupiter stream through the heart center in the upper astral body, they stimulate people's aspirations, idealism, and the higher creative imagination. The energies of Jupiter are also associated with spiritual vision—the vision of the Soul. Opening the inner mind's eye is a slow, progressive process. By way of the energies of Jupiter, the inner mind's eye is first opened in relation to the goals and objectives people perceive and subsequently work to achieve at the level of the personal self. As a disciple, the energies of Jupiter reveal the objectives of the Soul, especially in relation to the Soul's intent for a particular lifetime.

The light of Jupiter always shines upon the path and reveals the goals, objectives, and ideals to achieve that lie before people once the consciousness is polarized at the mental level. Slowly, people move forward upon the path from goal to goal.

In consciousness, people move from one state of mind to a higher state of mind, from one level of unity to a higher state of unity. Magnetized by the ray two aspect of the Divine, the energies of Jupiter awaken the mind to the essential love of the Soul and unify the aspects of the personal consciousness with those of the Soul. This cannot occur, however, until the light of mind has been intensified and expanded sufficiently to register the impressions of the Soul.

For those on the path, the goals and objectives Jupiter reveals relate to the progression of the Soul. This attracts both ray four and ray five energies into the ajna to help infuse the inner mind's eye with enough light to reveal true spiritual vision.

Goals and objectives are so important to Jupiter and Sagittarius that unless there is a goal to achieve, the vital life-forces of the physical body are diminished. This is also true of Pisces, which Jupiter co-rules, except that people are usually unable to perceive the lofty goals of Pisces prior to the second initiation. People with a strong influence of Sagittarius, Pisces, or Jupiter always must have a goal to work toward. Without one, life has little purpose.

By way of the energies and light of Jupiter, people perceive and consciously establish not only personal goals and objectives, but spiritual goals and objectives as well. With Jupiter, however, the goal is always something that is attainable on earth and perceived by the (brain) consciousness. This is very different from the goals people establish under the influence of Pisces.

Neither Pisces nor Neptune care about the three planes of earth. Nor do they care about the development of the threefold personal consciousness. Their focus is on the evolution of consciousness in relation to the Soul and the indwelling life within the form, not on the advancement of the form (the personality). For this reason, the goals people establish under the influences of Pisces and Neptune relate to cultivating higher values and virtues (compassion, empathy, mercy, and a caring, nurturing, peaceful spirit) and attaining such higher states of mind as, oneness with God, bliss, enlightenment, or Christ consciousness.

In relation to Sagittarius, the goals that Jupiter initially reveals represent the steps upon the evolutionary path that advance the development of the threefold personal consciousness. As people achieve one goal after another, however, they suddenly find themselves upon the path of the Soul. By way of the energies of Jupiter, the steps taken and the goals achieved upon the path of the Soul eventually lead to the unfoldment of wisdom and the faculty of pure reasoning. The goals Jupiter reveals as the co-ruler of Pisces, on the other hand, involve the steps upon the path that lead to the embodiment of love, first the essential love of the Soul and later the pure love of the Real Self.

The light of both Jupiter and Neptune help people see a distant goal or ideal. Once perceived, people must determine what they need to do in order to reach the goal. The ray two magnetic, attractive forces of Jupiter draw people toward the goals they set. Once the goal is reached, a new goal is envisioned. The far-off goals that Neptune reveals, on the other hand, are ultimately transcendent of life in the three planes of earth. Here, people move forward upon the path and attain higher states of mind and consciousness as a result of their efforts to attain the goals perceived via the inner mind's eye.[52] Once the goal or objective is achieved, they see another goal ahead.

The light of Jupiter not only shines upon the path and the goals ahead, but its energies help people reach the goal and incorporate the newly discovered ideal that the goal embodies into their everyday consciousness. This is due to the unifying magnetic forces of ray two energies, which blend and unite complementary aspects of the consciousness.

Initially, as people work to reach their goals, they are confronted with conflicting elements within their consciousness that make it difficult to attain their objectives. Again, most conflicts in the outer world represent conflicts within the psyche. The resolution of the warring dualities within the psyche and their subsequent blending and harmonization lead to the development of some new faculty, capacity, or ability. This enables people to see a far-off goal previously obscured by the dissonance within the psyche.

Cycles upon cycles of transformation and growth in consciousness lie before humanity. Initially, Jupiter is centrally involved in the progressive unification of the different aspects of personal consciousness, along with the ray two energies of the mutable cross, especially those emanating from Gemini, Virgo, and Pisces.

During the first stage of unification, people must liberate their consciousness from the world of form by resolving the dualities that dominate the personal consciousness. This includes eliminating the separatism that has created conflict and division within the mind and consciousness. The forces of separatism and division always veil the divine presence. Again, the factor of separatism is a directive imposed upon inert matter during the First Solar System. The more people identify their selfhood with the values, qualities, and nature of the Soul, the more people are freed from duality to experience the beauty of the world of the Soul.

In relation to Jupiter, the duality people face is of a higher order. Only when the dualities within the astral-emotional desire nature (the conflicting emotions and desires) are reasonably resolved, can people clearly perceive the dualities that Jupiter illumines. The oppositions or dualities revealed by Jupiter relate to the conflict in nature and quality between the heart center and the solar plexus center. This refers to the conflicts that exist between the patterns of consciousness that were unfolded as a result of the ray two energies of Jupiter and those brought forth as a result of the planetary forces of the solar plexus and ray six Mars.

As the energies of Jupiter impact the consciousness, they initially unfold the outer petals of the heart center of the etheric body. Then, as energy streams across the outer

---

[52] People are often unaware of how these goals come to mind. Often, it isn't until initiates step upon the path of initiation that they fully realize the important role that the intuition and the inner mind's eye play in revealing the path.

meridians of the petals of the heart center, it awakens people's love for family, close friends, and associates. Over time, people's sensitivity to the needs of others and their sense of responsibility for the family and the well-being of others unfolds within the consciousness.

The ray two energies streaming across the outer petals of the heart center also provide the unifying quality needed to integrate the threefold personal consciousness into a state of personal wholeness. Thus, the stage of the integrated personality is also attained as a result of the unifying ray two energies of Jupiter. This occurs once a reasonable number of the atoms of the emotional self-consciousness have been uplifted to the heart center, and a reasonable number of the atoms of the mental self-consciousness have built into the throat center, transferred from the sacral center.

Transference of the self-consciousness from the lower centers to the upper centers is a progressive activity that takes place over lifetimes as people become less consciously responsive to the forces of the lower centers and more consciously responsive to the energies of the upper centers.

Transferring a portion of the mental self-consciousness from the sacral center into the throat center is necessary before the throat center is magnetically potent enough to attract the relatively pure ray three energies of the Soul (via the intelligence petals) into the inner petals of the throat center. Similarly, transferring a portion of the emotional self-consciousness from the solar plexus to the heart center must take place before the heart center is magnetically potent enough to open the inner petals of the heart center and draw the energies of the love petals of the Soul into the etheric heart center. The energies of Jupiter stream into the heart center at the second sub-plane level of the subtle bodies. On the path, people retrace the energy back to the heart of the Soul as they awaken their sensitivity and responsiveness to the higher, more subtle qualities of essential love of the Soul.

Jupiter issues the clarion call to come up higher, away from emotion-based desires and people's preoccupation with materiality and self-indulgence. It gently calls on people to establish a higher ethical standard and code of behavior to live by, and impels the cultivation of a broad-minded perspective. Jupiter awakens people's concern for the well-being of others and encourages people to interact with one another with fairness, equanimity, human decency, consideration, and respect.

A sense of civic responsibility arises within the consciousness as ray two energies stream through the heart center out into people's environment. People on the path have a greater social responsibility than the average person, for they are called to work on behalf of humanity to improve people's lives and wellbeing.

Jupiter was the first teacher of primitive mankind. It was consequent to the influence of Jupiter that mankind started to perceive and then formulate the universal laws of humanity.

These laws govern people's behavior and moral conduct toward others as they unfold and develop the threefold personal consciousness. Obedience to the universal laws of humanity further distinguishes human beings from the animal kingdom.

The universal laws of humanity started to arise within human consciousness once people consciously responded to the energies of the outer petals of the etheric heart center and throat center. Due to universal secular education and individual study, more people are shifting the focus of their consciousness from the solar plexus to the heart center and from the sacral center to the throat center. This transference of the atoms of self-consciousness from the sacral center to the throat center takes place as people seek greater knowledge and understanding. In this way the consciousness becomes polarized in the mental aspect of personal consciousness, allowing rational, logical thought to unfold. The blending of the energies of the integrated personality and Soul can then begin.

The astral-emotional aspect of personal consciousness is systematically transferred from the solar plexus into the heart center whenever people love one another, i.e., their family, fellow parishioners, and close friends. As their love for others increases, a sense of social responsibility arises, as well as a higher code of behavior and conduct. Abiding by a higher code of conduct is indicative of people's ability to respond to the energies of ray two Jupiter.

The universal laws of humanity were established to regulate the physical-instinctual, astral-emotional, and lower mental aspects of personal consciousness and to regulate people's tendencies, proclivities, and behavioral characteristics. They govern human consciousness, even when people are still responsive to the cellular intelligences of the physical body and the subtle bodies (via the solar plexus, sacral, and basic centers).

Historically, each culture developed its own version of the universal laws of humanity by codifying different secular laws, philosophical principles, and religious tenets. In this way, different societies established ethical standards, values, principles, morality, human virtues, social regulations, rules, laws, and so forth. Becoming an honorable, ethical, and decent human being, however, only represents the first phase of Jupiter's work. People become socially and civically responsible as their consciousness expands beyond the little self.

Thus, the energies of Jupiter help transform people into ethical, moral, decent human beings of great integrity and honesty. And they transform the decent, honorable human being into the Soul. While the first phase of Jupiter's work is to encourage obedience to the laws of humanity, the second phase brings forth a sense of social and spiritual responsibility and cooperation with others. This represents an expansion of one's sphere of interest from the self, family, and friends to the greater society and culture. Initially, this involves joining together with others of like mind to accomplish goals and objectives that cannot be accomplished on one's own.

Jupiter is the energy that expands the consciousness through people's work, travel, higher education, and associations with service-oriented groups of people. At the mental level, the term group pertains to the groups that people join to accomplish mutually agreed-upon objectives. These objectives are oriented toward improving the society and the lives of its citizens. As a result of this group activity, the boundaries that demarcate people's personal universe expand outward. By way of their group activity, people become more tolerant of other people's ideas, opinions, and beliefs.

The group consciousness people develop by working with others to achieve an objective is the first step toward achieving the much more inclusive and extensive group consciousness of the Soul. The group consciousness of the Soul is an abstract concept that has yet to be sufficiently realized on earth. Again, the Soul functions in a state of group light, consciousness, and initiation, not in the much smaller field of personal light and consciousness. The unfoldment of the group consciousness of the Soul is a higher expression of the ray two energies of Jupiter, especially in relation to the energies of Aquarius.

Astrologically speaking, group consciousness is represented by the sign Aquarius, which Jupiter rules at the level of the Soul. During the Aquarian Age, group work, group consciousness, group light, and group initiation will supplant individual spiritual effort for large numbers of people. The directives Jesus gave His disciples at the Last Supper helped unify His disciples into an early form of the group consciousness of the Soul.

Surprisingly, Jupiter will prove to be more important to the spiritualization of human consciousness in the Aquarian Age than it was in the Piscean Age. The ray two quality of Jupiter resonates with the essential love of the Soul and with the Angels of the Presence. For this reason, the Masters of the Spiritual Hierarchy are referred to as the Masters of love-wisdom, regardless of their Ashram. Though the energies of Jupiter primarily condition the mental aspect of the personal consciousness, they are most effective at the level of the Soul and Triad.

With Jupiter, duality is resolved by creating a middle path between each pair of opposites. Through detachment and dispassion, people no longer choose one side of an emotional or mental duality over the other (e.g., the Venusian affectionate side versus the Mars aggressive side). When the middle path is trod, the energies of Jupiter can be used to unify the respective pairs of opposites within the psyche.

With Jupiter, people are able to unify the personal consciousness with successively higher aspects of the self. Being the magnetic, attractive, unifying force that blends and unifies complementary energies to create a greater whole, Jupiter is involved in all aspects of the processes that unify the consciousness at successively higher levels.

The temporary division of the psyche into a multitude of oppositional patterns of consciousness (duality) enables certain capacities, faculties, skills, and capabilities to unfold, but once a particular development has been achieved, the psychic division within the consciousness that helped to bring forth a particular faculty, capacity, or skill must be healed. This healing occurs as the ray energies of the two psychic dynamics blend with each other. This activity results in a higher quality, note, and color. The culmination of the blending of the energies of the dynamics of the psyche is unification.

Jupiter becomes an active spiritual dynamic of the psyche once the consciousness is responsive to the essential love of the Soul. This unifying psychic dynamic of Jupiter comes alive within the consciousness as people work to master their astral-emotional nature. Here, the qualities of essential love and will (the third petal of the love tier) blend with the light of mind to provide the quality of energies necessary to master the feeling, sentient aspect of personal consciousness.

Not until people consciously awaken their own etheric heart centers to the essential love of the Soul (as a result of their love for others) do they begin to express a quality of love that is free of personal preferences, biases, and prejudices. Only then can people express unconditional love. This occurs when the essential love of the Soul radiating from the love petals repeatedly streams into the mind and through the etheric heart center. People express this influx of love as compassion, mercy, forgiveness, and a love for humanity.

As people consciously respond to and demonstrate higher spiritual qualities, values, and virtues in their lives, the love of the higher self is unfolded. This higher quality of Jupiter transforms the personality into the essential nature, values, and qualities of the Soul. This takes place as the energies of the Soul stream through the upper centers of the etheric body.

Jupiter is also involved in attracting the purified energies of the etheric centers along the spine, and transferring these energies into the ajna center. Together with the higher ray four energies of Mercury that magnetize the ajna, Jupiter helps to awaken the brain consciousness to the nature, values, and qualities of the Soul. In this way, the personal self is transformed into the higher self.

The Jupiter dynamic of the psyche (which is developed as the energies of the etheric heart center are drawn into the ajna) is the factor that helps to resolve the dualities in the (brain) consciousness. Once the mental dualities are resolved, Jupiter helps blend and harmonize the heart and mind with respect to each other, and later harmonizes the refined threefold personal consciousness with the Soul.

Eventually, all of the oppositions within the personal consciousness that interfere with attaining a unity of the personality and Soul are resolved. Whether people use the unifying energies of Jupiter to inflate the ego or they use them to unify the personality with the Soul depends on the goals they individually establish.

The moment the consciousness is liberated from the three planes of matter, people shift from an egocentric personal consciousness to the group consciousness of the Soul. At this stage, people realize that the higher levels of achievement are never attained alone. They then turn back toward the earth, to help those still struggling along the way. Isolation and singularity are contrary to the all-inclusive nature of the Divine. The path that leads home is never trod alone.

Until people are interested in helping their brothers and sisters along the way, the world of the Real remains hidden. Isolation from others is a temporary but often necessary situation when people are trying to break free from certain kinds of bonds that imprison the consciousness in the three planes of earth. Once people have earned their freedom as a Soul, they realize they must turn back to help others, for the Soul's nature is to serve and to sacrifice. It is not to proceed forward alone.

Jupiter in Taurus

The interplay of so many different types and qualities of energies and rays impacting the consciousness can make it difficult to understand the different kinds of influences in people's lives. For example, in the astrological chart of humanity, which has a zero degree Aries Ascendant, Taurus rules the second house. Venus, as the ruler of Taurus at the personal level, helps establish the second-house issues. This means that ray five Venus and Taurus also had an influence upon Jesus in terms of His second-house stellium of planets in Pisces. Also, with ray two Jupiter in the sign of Taurus in Jesus's chart, its influence upon the planets in Pisces in the second house was strengthened, since Jupiter is the co-ruler of Pisces. This further intensified the influence of ray two in Jesus's life.

It is the ray five light of Venus that initially reveals what people instinctually need to survive on earth. During the early stage of personal development, the ajna center resonates to ray five, and therefore to Venus. For this reason, people with Jupiter in Taurus are often preoccupied with obtaining the wealth and possessions they feel they need to live the good life. Disciples with Jupiter in Taurus are often quite generous and philanthropic.

When the little self appropriates the expansive qualities of Jupiter purely for oneself, however, feelings of superiority are common, along with a preoccupation with money, material possessions, aesthetic beauty, and ostentatious surroundings. Such tendencies can lead to an inflated ego and an exaggerated sense of self-importance. There is a tendency to identify with the status quo in such fields as religion, higher education, law, and philosophy, since Taurus is a fixed earth sign. The conservative stance in religion and politics that people often exhibit when Jupiter is in Taurus helps to align people with the established order of society which, in turn, often elevates their social status and position.

At the personal level, people with Jupiter in Taurus often have an air of elitism and self-importance that, to them, justifies their disproportional need for the expensive finer things of life. Because of these tendencies, people with this placement of Jupiter gravitate to businesses that focus on profits and acquiring wealth. Driven by a strong desire for the things of earth, they often reach the upper strata of society and are frequently looked upon as the pillars of society. However, such characteristics and behavior represent people with Jupiter in Taurus only when they are at the developmental stage of the threefold personal consciousness.

Some people are able to complete this stage of personal development by age twenty-nine and begin their work to unfold the higher mind. Others fail to complete the development of the threefold personal consciousness during their lifetimes. Since there is little, if any, spiritual vision at the stage of personal development, professional success and obtaining great wealth are the main driving forces in people's lives. This is true even for those who are religiously devout.

Although the focus of disciples is still on material things, it is because of the quality of ray two energies that Jupiter transmits that they begin to shift away from serving themselves to serving the needs of the society and fulfilling social duties and responsibilities. During this higher social phase of personal development, people begin to think about the best use of their money and material resources in relation to their church, society, philanthropic activities, and higher education. The need to be a good steward of the world's resources is often their guiding principle. This translates into generous financial support for those causes they value.

This spirit of philanthropy unfolds as people begin to accept their social responsibilities. Here, the objective is to utilize one's material resources and goods in a more beneficial way socially and religiously. Even during this final phase of development of the personal consciousness, the philanthropist is still self-referencing, expecting others to acknowledge their generosity.

As people learn the life lessons associated with being a good steward of the material resources of earth, they begin to unfold higher values and standards more in line with the nature of the Soul than the egocentric personal self. This leads people onto the path of spiritual probation and then discipleship. At this point, they look for ways to share their material resources in an effort to help those less well-off. The objective behind their charity is to help improve the quality of life of others, not personal recognition. The emphasis is on that which will benefit the greater good.

Since Jesus had attained at least the second initiation prior to incarnating, He wouldn't have focused on materiality like so many who have Jupiter in Taurus. From an early age,

He was concerned about the well-being of others and was compassionate and generous toward the people in His life, even though He had few material resources to share. Jesus was definitely a generous Soul, but He was not interested in wealth and possessions. His lack of interest in the material things of earth was due to the level of evolvement achieved and the strong influence of Pisces in His chart.

Again, the second house corresponds to what people instinctively need to survive. More importantly, the second house represents the area of life that relates to what people value. With the strong influx of Piscean energies in the second house in Jesus's chart, what He felt He needed related to His spirituality. He valued the heavenly goods (spiritual capacities and faculties), not materiality. This resulted in the deep spiritualization of the mind of Jesus.

Free of being responsive to the matter forces that express through the lower etheric centers, Jesus's heart center was awakened to the quality of love emanating from the heart of the Soul, the sacred heart. By way of His etheric heart center, His unfolding consciousness was conditioned with the essential love of the Soul early in His life. Later, once He developed His mind and intellect, the energies of the heart and mind were blended and unified. This union of the heart and mind is the province of Jupiter.

Esoterically, Taurus stimulates the factor of consciousness known as desire, but this is much more than the selfish emotion-based desire for the things of earth. Again, desire is a motivating force that operates throughout the universe, not just at the lower astral level. Even the great cosmic Masters are said to be the sons of desire, for they desire to serve the purpose of the Solar Logos. In relation to Taurus, desire at its higher level relates to bringing forth the light that pierces the darkness and ultimately reveals truth.

According to esoteric astrology, Taurus at the Soul level is ruled by the etheric ray one planet Vulcan. Once Jesus became a third-degree initiate, Vulcan became the ruler and conditioning quality affecting the unification of His psyche with the higher aspects of the Triad. Becoming consciously responsive to the ray one energies of Vulcan was an exceedingly important development for both Jesus and the Buddha.

Vulcan is a sacred planet and the Soul-centered ruler of Taurus; it brings in the love-wisdom sub-quality of ray one. Also, the ray one energies of Vulcan are the vehicle for divine purpose, as well as the vehicle for the life aspect of the Logos that Vulcan transmits upon the waves of divine will.

Jesus's statement, *"The thief comes only to steal and kill and destroy; I came that they may have life, and have it abundantly,"*[53] relates specifically to this placement of Jupiter in

---

[53] John 10:10. (RSV) (italics added)

Taurus and to this aspect of life and light that Taurus transmits onto Vulcan. Esoterically, this biblical verse relates to the essential life (compelled by the desires of the Divine) that courses through the planet, the solar system, and the universe, giving life to all that exists. Only a minute portion of the divine life-force that exists in the universe is able to flow into the three planes of matter. This is due to the density of the matter of the three planes of earth and to people's lack of conscious response to the purpose that this divine life-force serves. After the incarnation of Jesus, however, a greater influx of life and light streamed onto the earth than had prior to His incarnation.

> *And Jesus uttered a loud cry, and breathed his last. And the curtain of the Temple was torn in two, from top to bottom.*[54]

Although the curtain referred to in this verse pertained to the curtain that concealed the inner shrine in the Temple, according to the ancient wisdom teachings, the Crucifixion of Jesus created a tear in all three matter veils that envelop the earth—its three subtle bodies. Through the tear in the mental-, astral-, and physical-etheric veils, greater life and light streamed onto the earth. (The Buddha is said to have torn the astral and etheric veils of matter when He attained enlightenment.) Through these tears, greater light poured onto the earth. Great was the darkness in terms of human consciousness prior to the incarnation of these two great Souls.

There has been a slow but steady increase in the divine life-force present in the three planes of matter since the incarnation of Jesus and the Buddha. A greater influx of light and of life now pours into the planes of earth, but it is still a minimal amount compared to what could stream into the three planes of earth. The problem is that much of the lower, dense vibratory forces of the three planes of matter need to be transmuted.

Once the Coming One returns to earth, people who are further along the path will begin to express ray one in this aspect of essential life and true abundance. The effect this will have on mankind is unfathomable. This ray one quality of life is known as the thunderbolt that pierces the veils of the mind. This results in flashes of the intuition and, over time, enlightenment. This is the province of Vulcan, the ruler of Taurus at the Soul level. When combined with the higher ray four qualities of the buddhic-intuitional plane, Ray one expresses as pure wisdom and purpose-driven light at the triadal level. Thus, Jesus not only anchored the principle of love, but He also anchored the principle of wisdom. This placement of Jupiter in Taurus brought forth wisdom's light in Jesus's life.

At last, people have sufficiently advanced the concrete mind and have unfolded enough of the mind of the Soul to become enlightened as a result of the influences of ray one Vulcan.

---

[54] Mark 15:38. (RSV) (italics added)

Now many people are able to forge the tools that blend and unify the heart and mind. As the three rays of aspect and the four rays of attribute that people have unfolded blend with each other, divine purpose and wisdom are starting to appear on earth.

During the advanced phases of blending the energies of the integrated personality and Soul, people can use the energies of Jupiter to unify the head and heart. This work culminates with first, the union of the integrated personality and Soul, and then a union with the Triad. Only then can the Soul-infused consciousness apply the light of wisdom and the pure love of the buddhic plane to the conditions and situations of earth and resolve many of the problems of mankind. This planetary work begins once the energies of the centers of Vulcan and Jupiter express through people's unified heart and mind.

As the consciousness is unified with the successively greater aspects of the Real Self, the consciousness ultimately becomes so expansive that it encompasses all of the expressions of life within the body of the Logos. No longer are there force fields in the cosmic physical plane of earth that block the master's awareness. At this lofty stage, the master breaches the boundary of the planetary life and transcends all consciousness associated with the seven planes of the cosmic physical plane. At this point, the master, as a free spirit, begins to respond to the life of the cosmic astral or cosmic mental plane.

Jupiter in the Fourth House

Ray two Jupiter in the fourth house of Jesus's chart guaranteed a loving, supportive home environment. Love was the quality that conditioned His inner emotional world and His early home life. In fact, He built His life upon a foundation of love. Without any major aspects to other planets, Jupiter transmitted a relatively pure, unconditional love into Jesus's life.

The houses of the natal chart concern the twelve areas of people's lives through which experiences are gained and experiments with the different types of energies are attempted. Initially, the twelve houses are representative of division and separatism, limitations and restrictions within the personal consciousness. This division within the chart is emblematic of the different and often unintegrated aspects of the personal mind. Although the houses limit the growth in consciousness to a particular area of life when people are at the stage of personal development, the houses are transfigured into the mansions of the Soul when the disciple approaches the third initiation. At this stage, the areas of life represented by the houses are primarily influenced by the rays the respective signs of the zodiac transmit, not the planetary forces the planets in the houses transmit. The cusps of the houses no longer represent distinctively separate areas of the psyche.

In Jesus's early years, when He was developing the basic structures of the personality and its faculties and capacities, Jupiter in the fourth house was important, even though it wasn't directly involved in the development of His threefold personal consciousness, since it didn't form an aspect to any other planet in the chart of Jesus.

The fourth house corresponds to Cancer in the chart of humanity and serves as the foundation that underlies people's conscious life. Cancer represents the gate into conscious life and the place where the atoms of self-consciousness originate in relation to the form. Here, the atoms of self-consciousness arise within the astral-emotional field of forces. This emotional, sentient field corresponds to the inner feeling nature and to both the personal mother and to the cosmic principle of the Mother. This nurturing, sustaining principle of the Mother guides, guards, and protects the unfolding principles of conscious life within the form.

This placement of Jupiter in the fourth house suggests that Jesus grew up in a loving nurturing environment in the home and to those experiences that correspond to the matrix of the nurturing divine Mother. The fourth house is the foundation and the starting point at which successively greater atoms of self-consciousness begin their journey upward to the mount, the tenth house cusp.

The mountain goat of Capricorn represents the personal self which climbs from the base of the mount (the Nadir) up to the Mid-heaven. For the average person, this climb represents a time when the skills, capacities, faculties, and abilities he or she needs in order to be successful on earth are developed. For the individual on the path, this climb up the mount represents the unfoldment and development of the virtues, values, skills, capacities, and qualities that are required to attain a particular initiation.

This placement of Jupiter in the fourth house suggests that Jesus's climb to the summit of the mount of initiation specifically involved unfolding and mastering the magnetic, attractive, unifying ray two energies emanating from Jupiter. In relation to His attainment of the first and second initiations, this process involved becoming aware of the aspect of divine love and its purpose, then demonstrating it in His life.

On the path, as people approach the second initiation, the more potent energies radiating from the unfolded love petals pour into the mind. The influx of the energies from the love tier of petals creates a dynamic situation, since the energies of the Soul rotate clockwise, while the energies of the personality rotate counterclockwise.

This difference in the direction that the energies of these two centers of life rotate creates vortices of swirling energies within the subtle bodies. As the Soul energies stream through the upper centers, their clockwise motion loosens the cohering bond that exists between the self-consciousness and the lower emotional and mental patterns of consciousness. This action often precipitates learning experiences and events in people's lives. Depending on the strength of the Soul energies, a centrifugal force is set up in the aura that spins the abandoned, lower personality forces out of the subtle bodies.

As people approach the second initiation, the clockwise motion of the Soul around the indwelling life within the form generates energy within the astral body that precipitate the tribulations commonly referred to as the tests and trials of the path. In effect, people must choose between two seemingly opposite qualities, values, and character. The one relates to the lower egocentric nature of the personality, while the other relates to the selfless nature of the Soul.

The energy exchange and interplay of the energies of the Soul and the integrated personality slowly detach the self-consciousness from the physical body and the patterns of the egocentric personal consciousness. Slowly, the atoms of self-conscious life are freed from the threefold world of form.

Only when the second initiation has been attained do people pursue the deeper spiritual studies, meditation, and service work necessary to transcend the integrated personality. At this point, the energies represented by the natal chart begin to turn upward, creating a sphere of rapidly moving energies as the will of the Soul begins to impact the consciousness directly.

The energies of the upper etheric centers begin to turn upon themselves, creating a sphere of fast-moving revolving energies rather than rotating vortices. Eventually, the unified centers of the personality and Soul become one sphere of light. Slowly, the conscious life and light of the integrated personality is transferred into the light of the Soul. When the light of the integrated personality and the light of the Soul become one field of light, the foremost duality that confronts all people on the path is finally resolved and unity is achieved.

By the time this stage is attained, there are few if any forces left in the subtle bodies that are lower than the third gradation. Lower-grade astral and mental forces may pass through the aura as they circumnavigate the globe, but the atoms of self-consciousness no longer magnetically attach themselves to these lower grade forces.

At this point, the consciousness is primarily responsive to the Soul energies moving through the heart, throat, ajna, and crown centers. This represents a time when the feelings are synthesized into a unified field of at-one-ment consciousness, while the personality is synthesized and blended into a unified field of the mind. This includes both the personal mind and the mind of the Soul.

As an adult, Jesus became the embodiment of love-wisdom. Once His mind and consciousness were impacted by the energies of the Soul that streamed onto Him from the reverse direction of the wheel, the energies of Neptune and Jupiter greatly expanded His world beyond the three planes of earth. When this occurred, He became less identified with His activities on earth, and more responsive to His spiritual home, which He referred to as the kingdom of heaven.

The attractive, unifying quality of Jupiter enabled Jesus to become more inclusive of the second aspect of the Divine, which, in turn, further expanded and shifted His consciousness ever higher. Essential love radiated through His life into the outer world. At this point, the foundation of love that Jesus generated and experienced in His early years was transformed into love-wisdom.

By the time of His ministry, Jesus had completed this unification process—the purified consciousness of the integrated personality and the Soul were unified. By then, He had established an alignment and attunement with the Masters of the Spiritual Hierarchy and with the head of the Teaching Department of the planet. At this point, the Soul-infused personality of Jesus became a vehicle that His Soul used on earth to serve mankind. The consciousness of Jesus was polarized in the world of the Soul throughout His ministry, not in the personality.

Eventually, His consciousness was so filled with pure love-wisdom that it breached the enveloping force field of the causal body that had contained His consciousness as a Soul. Once the boundaries of the causal body were breached, the world of the Real poured in. At this stage, a master approaching the Divine through love begins his or her service as a World Savior.

Aspects to Jupiter

Initially, challenging aspects to Jupiter highlight issues that need to be resolved before the threefold personal consciousness can be integrated into a unified whole. This primarily relates to reaching successively higher goals and objectives in relation to Sagittarius. Ultimately, this activity leads to the unification of the integrated personality and Soul. Once the conflicting elements of consciousness between the integrated personality and the Soul are balanced in relation to each other and harmonized, the Jupiter dynamic serves as a generator of the unifying light that blends and unifies the integrated personality and Soul into one center of light.

Planets that form a hard aspect to Jupiter represent a psychic dynamic that is still operating from an isolated, egocentric perspective. The type of aspect formed to Jupiter indicates the quality of the relationship that exists between the two psychic dynamics represented by the planets. The way people express the challenging aspects to Jupiter often indicates the level of evolvement they have attained.

Left unresolved, the energies of challenging aspects to Jupiter tend to manifest as an air of self-importance, egotism, mental and spiritual superiority, and an uncompromising self-righteousness. There is frequently an exaggerated sense of self-importance in some area of life, depending on the signs, houses, and other planets involved.

Such characteristics and traits represent the ego's selfish appropriation of the expansive qualities of Jupiter, which is common when ray two energies impact the consciousness prior to the time when people are sufficiently aligned and attuned to the Soul. When the little self appropriates the expansive quality of ray two, people exhibit an inflated ego and air of superiority. Such tendencies make it substantially harder to become an initiate.

In the chart of Jesus, Jupiter does not form a major aspect to any planet or luminary. As the co-ruler of Pisces, however, Jupiter played a very important role in His life. The ray two influence of Jupiter on the Sun, Mercury, and Venus in the chart of Jesus conferred a stabilizing, positive optimism. This influence helped Jesus to realize that the nature of God is love.

The one major aspect that Jupiter formed in the chart of Jesus was a trine to the Ascendant. This trine of Jupiter to His Capricorn Ascendant mitigated the somber seriousness that His Capricorn Ascendant is known to confer. In effect, the somber influence of Saturn was balanced and uplifted by the expansive enthusiasm of Jupiter, resulting in an ability to convey His teachings in a warm, loving, yet practical way. Jupiter conferred a loving, magnetically attractive quality that conditioned Jesus's mind and speech throughout His life.

Since Jupiter did not form an aspect to any planet in the chart of Jesus, Jupiter did not represent an unfolding social dynamic within the psyche. The lack of integration of Jupiter in the chart of Jesus is ironic, since Jupiter rules institutionalized religion, philosophy, and other codified systems of thought. However, Jupiter's lack of integration prevented the ray two quality and the psychic dynamic of Jupiter (the love aspect of the higher mind) from being tainted by the personal consciousness during the stage of personal development. The ray two Jupiter dynamic remained pure.

Since Jupiter did not form a major aspect to other planets, the ray two Jupiter dynamic of the psyche functioned free of all developmental issues, needs, and concerns in relation to the threefold personal consciousness. In effect, the ray two quality of love-wisdom was not impacted or modified by the influences of other planetary energies during His life. Nor were the ray two energies of Jupiter impacted by the elements of self-consciousness of the personality. This suggests that Jesus had perfected and fully embodied this quality of love-wisdom prior to incarnating. The social dynamic that Jupiter usually represents wasn't in need of further development in order for Jesus to fulfill His mission.

The pure ray two energies of Jupiter had a great effect upon Jesus and helped offset the more circumspect, cautious ray three Capricorn influence of His Ascendant. Free of all planetary relationships, the gregarious, socially integrating and spiritually uplifting principle of Jupiter promoted a deep spiritual idealism that wasn't affected by personal issues. The purity of the ray two energies remained consistently free of all personal and social conditioning throughout His life.

The fact that Jupiter was free of the modifying influences that other planets contribute when they aspect Jupiter also ensured that the ray one energies of the sacred planet Vulcan (which impacted Jesus's life after the third initiation as a result of Jupiter's placement in Taurus) remained pure as well. Once the third initiation was attained, the energies of Vulcan initiated the blending of ray two with ray one, divine love with divine will-purpose. Together, these two conferred enlightenment and the revelations of the Divine (via the faculty of pure reasoning).

Jupiter trine Ascendant (2 degrees 39 minutes)

The planetary forces of Jupiter are beneficial at all levels including the level of development of the threefold personal consciousness, but they are relatively unimportant in terms of personal growth during the early stages of development, since people tend to focus its magnetically attractive forces on satisfying their personal desires. Once the consciousness is polarized at the mental level, however, the magnetically unifying ray two energies that Jupiter transmits are used to help people reach the goals and objectives they establish for themselves.

The factor of expansion that accompanies the energies of Jupiter begins to impact the consciousness significantly once it is mentally polarized. For this reason, Jupiter relates to higher education, philosophy, religion, codified law, and higher education. Its real importance, however, is not perceived until people approach the difficult second initiation. The work required to master the astral-emotional desire aspect of personal consciousness opens the gateways of the mind to the ray two energies of Jupiter. This intensifies the effect that the energies of the love tier of petals have upon the consciousness.

In addition, once the second initiation has been attained, the Ascendant begins to express the intent of the Soul in relation to the spiritual path. When Jesus attained the second initiation, His selfhood shifted away from the integrated personality to the Soul and its selfless qualities, virtues, nature, and values. As this was occurring, the trine of Jupiter to the Ascendant allowed Jesus to freely express the essential love of the Soul in His life.

Then, as Jesus approached the third initiation, He awakened in mind and consciousness to the love of God. Since Jupiter was the co-ruler of His Piscean Sun, the aspect of Jupiter trine the Ascendant suggests that the second initiation had been attained in a recent past life and that there was a strong bond between the personality and the Soul.

It is fortuitous that Jupiter did not form a major aspect to any planet in Jesus's chart. If it had, the other planet would have conditioned the relatively pure ray two energies streaming into His life, possibly creating a situation that needed to be worked out before Jesus could fully attune to the Soul.

The astrological connection of the physical body to the Ascendant continues throughout life. In terms of the evolution of consciousness, however the Ascendant represents the Soul and its intent, especially once the disciple approaches the third initiation.

The beneficial influence of this trine of Jupiter to the Ascendant in Jesus's chart conferred good health and a somewhat jovial spirit. It also protected Him from physical harm—at least up until His Crucifixion. Jesus definitely needed this added protection due to the oppositions that Pluto formed to His Sun and Uranus and the inconjunction of Pluto to Mars and Saturn.

As the energies of the Soul poured through His upper centers, Jesus became better attuned to the Soul's intent and purpose as it expressed in His life via the Ascendant. This enabled Him to share His newfound spiritual realizations with others. The Capricorn influence of authority, stability, practicality, and strength that the Ascendant contributed combined well with the uplifting qualities that ray two Jupiter contributed. This resulted in great enthusiasm, faith, hope, generosity, love, and confidence.

Undoubtedly, Jupiter played an important role in Jesus's life as the agent of ray-two magnetized energy, anchoring and sustaining a rhythm of essential love in His life. This trine of Jupiter to His Ascendant created a way for Jesus to express love free of other conditioning qualities.

In terms of Jesus's ministry and teachings, the trine of Jupiter to the Ascendant in Jesus's chart conferred the quality of energies needed to be a great spiritual teacher and the voice for the teachings of the Piscean Age in the western world. Truly, love streamed through Him on the waves of His voice as He spoke.

Jupiter quintile Sun (2 degrees 7 minutes)

The quintile is an obscure aspect that has little effect upon people's lives initially. It is the most esoteric of all aspects and is minimally active in people's lives in terms of the interplay and exchange of energies prior to the attainment of the second initiation.

Quintiles are indicative of a developed area of deep spirituality and suggestive of past-life connections, faculties, skills, and capacities that can be easily unfolded in the current life. The quintile is considered a favorable aspect, not a hard aspect. Its symbolism aligns with the five-pointed star and the goal of attaining human perfection. (Perfection involves mastering the five principles of human and supra-human consciousness.)

Esoterically, quintiles relate to developed spiritual capacities of past lives that connected the disciple to the World Teacher, the Christ, who oversees the Spiritual Hierarchy. The World Teacher heads up the second (love-wisdom) department of Shamballa and serves as the hierophant of the initiation ceremonies at the first and second initiations. Often, there is also a connection to the Ancient of Days, Sanat Kumara, who serves as the voice and initiating agent of the Logos. Sanat Kumara officiates at the third, fourth, and fifth initiations. Both the World Teacher and Sanat Kumara are active in esoteric groups, but rarely in terms of the individual.

The Sun-Jupiter quintile in Jesus's chart suggests that He incarnated as an initiate on the ray two, ray six path, even though the path of the heart had yet to be developed on earth. A quintile between the ray two, ray six Piscean Sun and ray two Jupiter in Jesus's chart indicates that love–wisdom was the fundamental quality that naturally unfolded in Jesus's life, especially as He approached the third initiation. It also suggests that the second initiation had been attained prior to His incarnation.

Due to this Sun quintile Jupiter aspect, love freely poured onto Jesus from the buddhic-intuitional center of the Triad, heightening His spiritual idealism and fervor and enhancing His spiritual leadership skills. He had an innate, natural resonance to the ray two qualities of Jupiter, enabling Him to receive and more fully respond to the second aspect of the Divine. It also sensitized Jesus to the higher principles of universal law, even though the spiritualizing activity that took place as a result of this quintile was hidden from view until Jesus attained the third initiation.

Once Jesus had sacrificed His personal will to the will of the Soul at the third initiation, the energies of Vulcan, as the Soul ruler of Taurus, started to stream onto Him. The sacred energies of Vulcan conditioning Jupiter intensified the second sub-ray aspect of ray one, which is the creator aspect of God.

Simultaneously with the activation of this quintile, ray one Pluto, as the Soul-centered ruler of Pisces, started to impact the dynamics of the psyche represented by the planets in Pisces. With the activation of the quintiles of ray two Jupiter in Taurus to the Sun, Mercury, and Vulcan, Jesus was able to transition from the path of the heart onto the path of power. The interplay of these energies generated the light of enlightenment, conveyed a sense of divine will and purpose, and deepened Jesus's awareness and understanding that the God of love was within Him and within one another.

Jupiter quintile Mercury (48 minutes)

The quintile relationship of Mercury to Jupiter helped Jesus comprehend the nature, qualities, and principles of the Divine at a much deeper level, and conferred an ability to discuss these principles in a way that people could begin to understand the nature of God.

Jupiter quintile Mercury also suggests that the concrete mind and the intuitional mind (Mercury's resonance with the buddhic plane) were naturally linked via the abstract mind. The bridging of these three aspects of the mind enabled Jesus to use parables, symbols, and analogies to communicate His deep understanding and realizations. As a result of the bridging of these aspects of the mind, He was able to express both the wisdom and understanding of the higher mind and the intuitional mind.

Jupiter quintile Vulcan

This represents another link or connection to the higher planes that was generated during past-life spiritual activities. This relationship between ray two Jupiter in the sign of Taurus to Vulcan (the Soul-centered ruler of Taurus) accelerated the blending of ray two and ray one within the mind of Jesus, resulting in the unfoldment of the builder sub-aspect of ray one. The ramifications of this are immense.

By way of Vulcan, initiates and masters are able to use the tools of creation to forge the structures and forms on earth that objectify divine purpose. This involves the unfoldment of the faculties and skills that the Triads use to create life forms in the seven planes of the cosmic physical plane. All forms are a means whereby a mind can be unfolded with the potential to manifest on earth what the Logos envisions. By way of the creative, evocative Word, the Solar Logos set the processes into motion that are progressively unfolding more complex manifestations of life, mind, and being.

Chapter 18

Saturn, Lord of Karma

Saturn is a far cry from benevolent Jupiter. Jupiter broadens and expands the consciousness, while Saturn restricts, blocks, denies, and limits the consciousness to a narrow range of possibilities. Historically, Saturn has had many names: the Grim Reaper, Lord of Karma, Satan, the Old Devil, the Cold Clammy Hand of Fate, and Father Time. None of them are very flattering.

Saturn frowns on ostentatious displays of wealth and lavish indulgences and often seems to take the fun out of life. Its influence can be so devitalizing, both physically and emotionally, that its gloomy reputation is well deserved.

Although the effects that Saturn has on people have been thought of as the work of Satan by some people and as fate by others, esoteric astrology does not accept either of these views. It is not that Jupiter is good and Saturn is bad (although people often react to the influences of these two planets as if this were true).

The ray two energies of Jupiter represent the attractive, unifying, magnetic quality intricately linked to the consciousness and to the second aspect of the divine mind—love-wisdom. Jupiter expands the consciousness from one state to a higher, more inclusive state of mind, sensitivity, realization, and revelation. The ray three energies of Saturn, on the other hand, contain a concretizing factor that constricts, separates, divides, and differentiates. Saturn is intricately linked to the material world and to the life forms of matter, as well as to the laws of karma, which tie it into the evolutionary development of the threefold personality, especially in relation to the unfoldment of the mental aspect of personal consciousness.

During the early phases of human development, the aspects of consciousness Jupiter and Saturn bring forth stand in sharp contrast to each other. In terms of the evolution of consciousness, both Jupiter and Saturn are thought of as social planets that express via the mental body and help advance the concrete mind and mental aspect of consciousness. This does not mean that the principles represented by Jupiter and Saturn (love and intelligence) oppose each other; rather, Jupiter and Saturn simply have different objectives and goals.

Saturn requires people to abide by the universal laws of humanity and to uphold the basic universal laws, principles, rules of conduct, and behavior that govern the human being. It calls for the polarization of the consciousness at the mental-plane level of the concrete mind and intellect. Saturn is central to the development of the mental aspect of consciousness, but it is not involved in the development of the emotional, feeling, sentient aspect of personal consciousness, even though its energies often have an unpleasant effect upon the feelings and emotions.

The ray three energies of Saturn are important in relation to the development of the concrete mind, the intelligence, rational, logical thought, and the various mental faculties, such as discrimination and discernment. Saturn's objective is to make people think, which, in turn, helps polarize the consciousness at the mental level.

Saturn is also the agent that applies corrective measures to rectify a situation or condition caused by people's violations of universal law. This task relates to the universe's need to maintain a balanced, harmonious state of divine order—one that is ever so slowly shifting to a higher state. Saturn is the hard taskmaster responsible for impartially enforcing universal law. This does not mean that there is a God who punishes people for their transgressions of His law. Rather, people's transgressions create a dissonance within the energies of the solar system that interfere with the working out of divine purpose.

Everything that occurs on earth and in the heavens relates to the working out of universal law. The purpose of universal law is to bring the perfection envisioned in the mind of God (the Solar Logos) into a state of manifest existence in this solar system. Allegorically, this envisioned perfection corresponds to the awakened and active life of the heart center of the ONE. The progressive unfoldment of this perfection takes place as a result of the working out of the impersonal principles and laws that govern all life from the atomic level to the highest, most sublime, level. All life evolves and expresses itself in the manifest worlds of the seven planes of the cosmic physical plane.

Saturn is the enforcing agent of the law of karma and its subsidiary law of cause and effect. If you spit into a strong wind, you will probably get wet. When energy is set into motion, a force pattern is generated within the aura that can interfere with people's ability to progress. By experiencing the difficulties caused by violating universal law, people learn how things work.

Primitive human beings demanded free will and sought to learn from their own mistakes through trial and error. Free will was granted, even though primitive man had yet to develop spiritual vision and was unable to discern right from wrong in terms of universal law. The god-men of the Spiritual Hierarchy, in turn, stopped their training of the primitive human beings and withdrew from the surface of the earth.

Undoubtedly, Saturn presents the difficult life lessons and growth experiences mankind needs in order to learn how things work in the cosmic physical plane of earth. Universal law defines and codifies how things work. It is not the arbitrary preferences of some deity. By way of the limiting, difficult, and often painful events and experiences that Saturn precipitates as a result of such violations, knowledge is gained. The objective is for people to learn and to grow in mind and consciousness as human beings, gods-in-the-making.

As a rule, people are unable to perceive the linkage between cause and effect until they are responsive to the impressions of the Soul and the causal realm. Causation originates in the upper mental plane beyond the range of the concrete mind. This means that people often have a blind spot when it comes to perceiving the connection between their thoughts, words, and actions, and the type of events they experience.

The law of cause and effect governs the exchange and interplay of forces in the three planes of earth. Until mankind is able to perceive the cause-effect relationship behind all that takes place on earth, people will continue to make the type of mistakes they have made throughout history.

Violations of universal law frequently occur when people are attached to the things of earth and identify their selfhood and being with the physical body and its nature. When this is the case, people set negative forces into motion (via their thoughts, words, and actions) that have unpleasant repercussions.

The type of experiences Saturn precipitates suggests that Saturn serves as the debt collector who forces people to pay off their karma, but this is misleading. The energies of Saturn merely precipitate the type of events and experiences that are an expression of the quality of energy that people have set into motion. It is not an exact tit for tat; rather, is an expression of energy that has been set into motion.

In general, the unpleasant effects Saturn can have on people are due to the factor of concretization that conditions the energies of Saturn and brings all things into the manifest, objective side of life. This factor crystallizes energy, i.e., transforms energy into matter, both physical and subtle matter. This includes people's thoughts, beliefs, and feelings, as well as the objects of the outer physical world. Without the concretizing factor of ray three Saturn, there would be no manifest world.

By way of this concretizing factor, Saturn also gives structure to the mind and consciousness, differentiating the mind into various psychic dynamics, patterns of behavior, feelings, and thoughts. Without these structural parameters within the psyche, there would be chaos. During the early phases of the evolution of consciousness, the burgeoning consciousness needs structure to restrict and limit the conscious awareness to a limited field of possibilities. The mental structures of the psyche provide the framework within which the threefold personal consciousness can unfold. Within these structures, all personal development takes place. This field of saturnine forces shields and protects the burgeoning ego during the early phases of development.

The saturnine structuring of the consciousness provides a safe environment for the unfoldment and development of the threefold consciousness. In this way, the burgeoning ego is protected against the vast array of both lower and higher types of forces and energies that stream through the ethers of earth.

Saturn establishes the boundaries of people's reality within which the threefold personal consciousness operates. It defines people's reality and establishes the truth that people can accept. Thus, this concretizing factor that travels upon the ray three energies of Saturn objectifies patterns of personal consciousness.

By way of the light of Saturn, people become conscious of the objective manifest world. Thus, Saturn bestows existence and reality to the temporal life found in the three planes of earth. The energies of Saturn, however, can just as easily objectify absolute truth as they objectify the illusions of mankind. Except in the lives of a relatively small number of people, the reality of the higher planes has yet to be objectified. Currently, planetary servers are working to bring the world of the Soul into objective, manifest existence on earth.

Saturn represents what people are cognizant of at any moment in time. By way of the saturnine structuring of the psyche, people derive a sense of who they are, often a faulty one. Saturn always corresponds to the structures within the consciousness that define and separate the self from others. In this sense, Saturn acts as the gatekeeper for the burgeoning personal self, allowing or blocking certain types of energies from impacting the consciousness. This activity is necessary until a higher stage of development has been achieved. Saturn, therefore, blocks the way forward until the necessary prerequisite development within the threefold personal consciousness has taken place.

During the early stages of development of the personal consciousness, people often think of the limitations and restrictions they experience in life (consequent to Saturn's activities) as obstacles that serve no apparent reason or purpose, yet they do. Nothing occurs in heaven or on earth that does not have an explainable cause and purpose.

The limitations, sorrow, emotional pain, debilitation, loneliness, loss, sadness, and isolation, etc., that people frequently experience as a result of Saturn's forces can stop them in their tracks. Ideally, this causes people to examine their lives closely. By uncovering the underlying cause, people can begin to see what emotional and mental patterns of consciousness and behavior need adjustment and determine what steps and measures they need to take to move forward. This is how people progress at the stage of personal development.

Saturn often precipitates difficult experiences that seem to limit and restrict people, thwart their desires, and isolate them from others. The purpose of such is to motivate people to remove some habits and patterns of the emotional-desire nature or lower mental nature that have become obsolete. This must occur in order for the consciousness to be polarized at the mental level, which is the evolutionary requirement for the human race to achieve at this time. This involves the development of the concrete mind, enhancement of the rational, logical, thinking capacity, a deepening of the intelligence, and the development of the faculties of discernment and discrimination.

There is no evolutionary directive for humanity to progress higher than this mental stage of development. As a result of this evolutionary directive, the influences of Saturn (as the enforcer of the evolutionary directives in relation to mankind) can cause people to feel discouraged, isolated, and sad for no apparent reason. People can suddenly feel unfulfilled in some way or have some inchoate sense of failure. The remedy is to concentrate on the development of the intellect and rational thought and to focus on the well-being of others through service work.

In relation to the evolution of consciousness, Saturn's planetary forces stimulate the mental field of forces. Saturn electromagnetically attracts a greater amount of the stream of life into the mental body, which can result in a reduction of the amount of divine life-force available to the astral-emotional and physical aspects of life. This can result in episodes of physical devitalization and emotional depletion.

Only when people are mentally polarized can they unfold the self-discipline and control necessary to participate in the evolution of their consciousness. Until this time, people are caught up in the fast-moving forces coursing through their subtle bodies into the three lower centers of the etheric body.

Rarely do people realize the extent to which these lower forces control them. They think that their selfish and negative actions and emotional reactions are representative of them when, in fact, they are the consequences of a lower quality of forces that has stimulated the consciousness. As such forces stream through their subtle bodies into their etheric centers, they stimulate certain behavior, actions, feelings, thoughts, and ideas. Personal control of these lower forces is not possible before the consciousness is polarized at the mental level and the mind is infused with a degree of the will of the Soul.

Saturn calls on people to develop the faculty of discrimination and one-pointed focus, and encourages people to become fair-minded, just, and decent human beings. Its efforts compel people to obey the laws of humanity. Only then do people fully exhibit the behavior that distinguishes the human kingdom from the animal kingdom.

When functioning at the astral-emotional level, it is difficult to see how the sorrow and loneliness that people experience as a result of a strong Saturn influence represents an opportunity to grow and advance, but they do. Through physical and emotional pain, people are presented with choices.

As people choose a more rational way to deal with something, greater freedom is gained. Slowly, the atoms of self-consciousness are freed from the little self and its nature and behavior as people eliminate the emotional and mental patterns of consciousness that relegate them to a lower state of mind.

Eliminating obsolete life structures (e.g., jobs, relationships, habits, old patterns of thought and feelings) is not easy, since these reflect dynamics that are psychologically entrenched. People often prefer what is familiar, even when it is personally and spiritually limiting and restrictive. Many people prefer to live with someone who is physically, emotionally, or mentally abusive, rather than be alone.

Through the type of experiences Saturn precipitates, old patterns that seem to provide safety and security are activated and must be dealt with in relation to people's current point of evolvement. These life structures provide the framework within which the consciousness functions; however, this framework must be flexible enough for the consciousness to expand and grow.

Due to this concretizing factor that accompanies the ray three energies of Saturn, the scaffolding of the personal self becomes rigid over time, creating all sorts of difficulties. Even when the structures in people's lives are no longer valid or appropriate, people often prefer them rather than venturing into new, unfamiliar fields of experimentation and experience.

In relation to the evolution of consciousness, problems always arise when the structures of the psyche become rigid and obsolete. Obsolete structures block growth and development. When the crystallized structures of the psyche (needed during earlier phases of development) become obsolete, they interfere with the progressive advancement of the consciousness.

Saturn's sign, house placement, and aspects can indicate the kinds of structures that people need to create in their lives, as well as the forms of rigid patterns of feelings, emotions, thoughts, and beliefs that need to be eliminated. Thus, the astrological factors associated with Saturn in the chart provide clues as to the work required to progress. They also provide clues as to the tribulations people are likely to experience as a result of Saturn's influence.

In general, the difficulties that Saturn precipitates in people's lives are the tests and trials of maturation. Saturn always has a maturing effect upon people. The effect is so powerful that the boundaries of the different stages of people's life are demarcated by the waxing and waning squares, the opposition, and the conjunction of transiting Saturn to the location of Saturn in the natal chart. For example, the first square of transiting Saturn to natal Saturn marks the end of the first phase of a child's life and the beginning of the unfoldment of the atoms of self-consciousness in relation to the feelings and emotions.

This second phase of development of the threefold personal consciousness spans from the square of transiting Saturn to natal Saturn up to the opposition of transiting Saturn to natal Saturn, roughly from the ages of seven to fourteen. During this phase, the astral body is tied into the physical-etheric body via the solar plexus center. This allows the astral forces to express in people's lives via the physical body, resulting in the expression of astral-emotional patterns of consciousness (desires, feelings, and emotions) on earth. The psychic patterns that underlie people's political allegiance and religious orientation are typically established at this time. Through their desires and sentient feeling nature, people learn how to connect and relate to one another.

Prior to fourteen years of age, there isn't a saturnine authority dynamic of the psyche. Here, parents serve as the authority figure. The psychic dynamic of Saturn is brought forth as people unfold and develop the mental aspect of personal consciousness during the third phase of personal development. Generally, this phase spans the ages of fourteen to twenty-nine. The task before people during this stage is to develop the faculties and capacities of the mental aspect of personal consciousness.[55]

During this third phase of development, a significant portion of the stream of consciousness and the streams of life and consciousness (via the silver cord) magnetize the mental body. In this way, the energies necessary to unfold the concrete mind, rational, logical thinking, the personal intelligence, and the various faculties of the mind pour into the physical-etheric body from the mental body and impact the consciousness.

Saturn aligns best with this third phase of personal development when the mental aspect of the personal consciousness is unfolded and developed. During this phase, people realize the importance of personal integrity, honesty, honor, fair-mindedness, self-discipline, and the fulfillment of duty and responsibility. Again, the energies of Saturn are important to the development of the faculties of the mind and intelligence. Over time, they help polarize the consciousness at the mental level. These energies have little effect upon the development of the emotional aspect of consciousness, but they can be used to contain and restrain the unruly emotions.

---

[55] There are exceptions to this developmental time line. Some advanced Souls are capable of unfolding logical, rational thought between the ages of seven and fourteen, while others do not unfold the capacity for logical, rational thought at any point in their lives. Since 1974, a large number of people have started to transition into the fourth phase at twenty-one years of age, instead of twenty-nine.

The hard aspects of Saturn generate points of tension in people's lives, the purpose of which is to compel people to learn and grow in understanding and knowledge. Once people have unfolded and developed the basic faculties, capabilities, and capacities of the threefold personal consciousness, however, a point is reached in which further growth and development of the mental aspect of personal consciousness is dependent on an ability to collaborate with others.

By way of the limitations people experience, they realize that they are unable to accomplish something by themselves that they would like to accomplish. Saturn compels people to work with others to accomplish social goals and objectives and exposes them to the world of social responsibility and duty.

The intent of Saturn is to help people combine their own individual identities, authority, and purposes with those of the society. At this stage, one's own authority and purpose are superseded to a degree by the needs of society. People learn and grow as they come together and work with others to accomplish things that they cannot achieve on their own. This is strictly group work at the personal level. Saturn, as the enforcer of universal law, calls for people to engage in group activity in an effort to awaken people to their social responsibility and obligations. This activity is prerequisite to unfolding and advancing the higher self.

Only by working in concert with others can people begin to shoulder their personal, familial, and social responsibilities and duties, and begin to identify their selfhood with the true values and character of the human being. During this phase when the mental aspect of personal consciousness is unfolding, young people need to leave behind (transcend) the tendencies, characteristics, behavior, and traits of primitive mankind, i.e., the creature tendencies, drives, and appetites that are innate to the physical body.

During this developmental stage of the mental aspect of personal consciousness, the difficulties people experience in relation to Saturn's influence center on the struggle between the little self and its self-serving interests and concerns versus the mentally-polarized self that is more responsible, decent, ethical, and considerate of others. According to universal law, the further people progress, the greater the responsibility they have for others.

Saturn requires people to move away from a total preoccupation with their personal desires and interests. This is accomplished by focusing on what they can do to satisfy the needs of others in the community, state, nation, and world. Saturn insists on the development of a quality of consciousness that can be achieved only when people join together with others. In this way, Saturn pushes the boundaries of the personal self out, but ever so slightly.

Within the world of one's immediate family and neighborhood, only a relatively small portion of mental development that is possible can be achieved. The mental development that takes place in the family and community of close friends is almost always emotionally charged and, therefore, somewhat distorted.

Working with others to accomplish mutual goals and objectives helps people advance their communication skills, mental reasoning, and rational thinking capacity. For this reason, Saturn is thought of as an impersonal, social planet, while the Sun, the Moon, Mercury, Venus, and Mars are thought of as having a significant personal dimension. However, the inner planets transmit rays that are just as important to the development of the higher mind as the rays the outer planets transmit.

People must act responsibly and be integrated into the society-at-large long before they are ready to step upon the spiritual path. This is due to the selfless, expansive, and inclusive nature of the advanced Soul. The eye of the Soul is never on oneself; rather, it is fixed on the needs of others.

The evolution of consciousness is always a struggle between the past and future, i.e., between yesterday and tomorrow in terms of the threefold personal consciousness and it development. Saturn corresponds to the past, since its energies were used to give it form and structure, both personally and societally. Saturn therefore represents the societal establishment, since its institutions are associated with the crystallization of the past.

This concept of the past, however, is found only in relation to human consciousness and the three planes of earth. This sense of the past is due the way brain consciousness records events. An illusionary sense of time arises by attaching the atoms of self-consciousness to events. This is the case even though the energies of Saturn (like all energies) operate in the eternal moment of the now. In this eternal moment, the higher energies of Saturn anchor seed ideas in the upper mental plane for mankind to intuit and bring forth in the objective, manifest side of life. Thus, Saturn also relates to the future.

By way of Saturn, mental-plane forces become manifest on earth as words, concepts, philosophies, and systems of thought. Thoughts are material things that the mind transmits. Therefore, everyone on the path must be exceedingly careful of their thoughts. Historically, the thought forms mankind has set into motion have created a reality that is more illusion than real from the perspective of the Soul. When people are focused on the development of the threefold personal consciousness, there is a great difference between the mind-created, manifest side of life and the world of potentiality and purpose.

Although the Soul is the creator of all original thought, many of the thought forms and desire forms found in the three planes of earth have been created by the unenlightened minds of humanity. Historically, mankind has used the energies of Saturn to validate a reality of desire forms and thought forms that limit and restrict people's lives and interfere with people's ability to perceive the impressions of the Soul. For millennia, people have slowly advanced the threefold personality vehicle in a world of illusion that humanity has created via the crystallizing forces of Saturn.

The development of the threefold personality, therefore, takes place in the man-made world of the unreal. This is the human condition until people are able to respond to the impressions of the Soul and begin to perceive a world of the nature, values, and qualities of the Soul.

Saturn is often blamed for many of the limitations and restrictions in people's lives; however, these limitations exist in people's own psyche, not with Saturn. Saturn's energies were used to objectify these limitations, but it is the personality that has given life to the limitation within the psyche that relate to the past. On the path, the objective is to eliminate the obsolete patterns of beliefs, thoughts, and feelings and to build the flexible mental scaffolding needed in order to gain experience in new areas of life.

Over the millennia, the burgeoning minds of mankind have created and transmitted feelings and thoughts that violate the laws governing the evolution of consciousness. Mankind has created the dense vibratory worlds of illusion, glamour, and maya that imprison the consciousness within the unreal and block the impulses and impressions radiating from the Soul and the planes of light.

This pollution of the substances of the three planes of matter occurs when the stream of consciousness emanating from the Soul are combined with the forces of the three planes of matter. The consequence of this combination of forces was and is the unfoldment of a type of self-consciousness that is highly conditioned by the nature of the physical body and the lower astral- and mental-plane forces. For this reason, the incarnating human soul is esoterically referred to as part animal and part human.[56]

This condition of illusion in the three planes of earth (which mankind's thoughts and desires have created) has nothing to do with the physical-etheric, astral, or lower mental-plane substances themselves. Rather, it is human consciousness that has organized the atomic substances of the three planes of earth in a way that generates illusion, glamour, and beguiling maya. This condition, however, exists only in relation to human consciousness.

Illusion is an even greater problem today than it was two thousand years ago. Today, people are developing their mental aspect of personal consciousness at a time when their consciousness is still polarized at the astral-emotional level. This means that the faculties of the mind (the intellect) are being strongly influenced and controlled by the lower astral

---

[56] The human soul that incarnates directly through the physical-etheric, astral, and lower mental bodies should not be confused with the Soul in the upper mental plane. The unfoldment and development of the human soul is referred to as the personality. The human potentiality that the Soul unfolds is referred to as the threefold higher self, the higher mind.

forces. When this is the case, great deception, falsehoods, and lies can appear perfectly accurate and truthful to the individual. As a result, glamour and illusion continue to beguile the minds of humanity.

Fortunately, illusion is limited to the threefold personal consciousness. By aligning and attuning with the Soul and awakening the values, qualities, and character of the Soul within the consciousness, people are able to free themselves from illusion.

Since people have given life to their negative, distorted emotions and thoughts, they must liberate themselves from them. This factor of concretization that has objectified hatred, anger, greed, vengeance, etc., was never intended to be used by mankind to crystallize such selfish emotional and mental patterns of consciousness. Mankind was (and is) expected to develop the higher senses, faculties, and capacities that enable people to perceive the seed ideas of the divine mind and then precipitate these ideas in the manifest objective world of earth, not generate greater illusion and glamour.

This is still the objective of the Logos, but first mankind must develop spiritual vision and eventually unfold the capacity to precipitate the radiant imagery of perfection envisioned within the mind of God. Mankind was and is intended to become the co-creative agent of that perfection on earth. This calls for the development and mastery of the third aspect of God, active intelligence, first—but this isn't possible when the consciousness is imprisoned in a mental world of illusion or an astral-emotional world of glamour and deception.

The Logos was well aware that eons of time would pass before the personality vehicles of mankind would be prepared to serve as divine co-creators. Human beings needed to develop various skills, capacities, faculties, senses, and abilities before they could begin to create that perfection on earth via active intelligence. In relation to human consciousness today, this factor of saturnine crystallization of negative and self-referencing emotional and mental patterns of consciousness represents burdensome restrictions that limit freedom of thought and confine it to a narrow range of investigation. Such concretized patterns of emotions, feelings, thoughts, and ideas interfere with people's progression.

Only when people are oriented upward (rather than preoccupied with the material world) do the ideas of the Soul begin to stream into the inner mind. The greater the clarity of mind people achieve (a mind relatively free of egocentric preferences, beliefs, and ideas), the greater people's ability to accurately register and express divine seed ideas. People must work to cleanse the mind of its selfish nature before they can more accurately perceive the nature and intent of new seed ideas.

Although mankind uses the concretizing factor present in the energies of Saturn to generate this mental-plane veil of illusion, Saturn is not the cause of illusion. The concretizing factor of Saturn does not discriminate between appropriate thought (in relation to the Divine) and inappropriate thought. Nor does Saturn bring forth distorted thoughts and ideas, since these are the creations of the unevolved mind. Once people eliminate the selfish traits and characteristics that distort the higher ideas and values, and achieve clarity of mind, they can use the energies of Saturn to bring forth truth on earth.

On the path, people must systematically break up all of the concretized patterns of thought, feelings, behavior, and actions that serve no purpose and have a negative, obstructing effect upon their consciousness. Otherwise, the quality of energy that people are able to register and respond to will remain limited and distorted.

Saturn forces people to observe the structures in their minds and lives periodically, and to build new, more appropriate structures. This is not easy for people to do until they place their feet upon the path and regularly observe the self from the perspective of first the Soul-infused mind, and later from the perspective of the mind of the Soul.

Only when the creature nature of the body no longer dominates the threefold personal consciousness can people become the honorable, considerate, responsible, and decent human beings they are intended to be. Such characteristics are indicative of someone who has reached the final phase of development of the personal consciousness. When people exhibit such characteristics consistently, they are ready to step upon the spiritual probationary path and begin to unfold the three aspects of the higher mind.

In relation to the evolution of consciousness, Saturn's most important responsibility relates to the development of the lower mental aspect of the threefold personal consciousness. However, Saturn is also responsible for the structures of the higher mind through which the Soul expresses itself on earth. Thus, Saturn is involved in the development of the mind at the personality level and at the level of the higher self. (Saturn is both the personality ruler and Soul-centered ruler of Capricorn.)

Building in the structures of the higher mind allows the intelligence aspect of the Soul to unfold during incarnation. In this way, the faculty of loving, creative intelligence is brought forth and clarity of mind is achieved. These structures of the higher mind are also important in relation to the ability to control and later master the physical instinctual appetites and drives and the emotional desire nature.

People on the path can use the energies of Saturn to give form (interpret into words) to the seed ideas they intuit.. As the Soul-centered ruler of Capricorn, Saturn has an especially strong link to the impersonal world of ideas.

Chapter 19

Third House Saturn in Aries

Initially, Saturn in Jesus's chart appears to be of marginal significance, since it doesn't aspect any of the planets of the epic grand trine. Upon closer examination, however, Saturn played an instrumental role in terms of Jesus's ability to fulfill His mission. Specifically, Saturn in Aries in the third house gives form to new ideas and thoughts, as well as to new initiatives. This activity is especially important in relation to mankind's ability conceptualize the new seed ideas that the Masters of love-wisdom transmit.

By way of the energies of Saturn, Jesus was able to formulate what He intuited into new ideas, concepts, and commandments in relation to the dawning Age of Pisces. Giving form and structure to people's thoughts and ideas is an important function of Saturn. Additionally, Jesus's Capricorn Ascendant (which Saturn rules) enabled Him to articulate His spiritual understanding in a practical earthy way, making it easier for others to understand His teachings.

Generally, the astrological factors associated with Saturn in the natal chart provide clues as to a person's life path or dharma, in the sense of duties and responsibilities. Saturn's placement in Aries in Jesus's chart, however, does not reflect His personal dharma as much as it relates to His mission.

Saturn's placement in Aries suggests that Jesus was starting a completely new cycle of development of the personality. In other words, the threefold personal consciousness He unfolded was a completely new evolutionary impulse or intention of the Soul. It was not a continuation of the path of development that the personalities of recent past lives had walked. The previous cycle of development of the personality had been completed. Much of the scaffolding upholding the threefold personality had been destroyed prior to His incarnation. The inconjunction of Pluto to Saturn and Mars in the third house, however, indicates that there were still some modifications of the mental aspect of personal consciousness that were needed.

Although each new life is an opportunity to attain the highest level of progression achieved in a former lifetime and then advance beyond this point, the astrological factors of Jesus's chart indicate that the development of the integrated personality had been completed prior to incarnation. The focus was now on completing the transformation of the integrated personality into an instrument of the Soul. This was necessary before the Soul could reveal the new Piscean approach to the Divine.[57]

Saturn's placement in Aries and its conjunction with Mars frequently suggests that a stern, repressive personality trait was present in the psychological makeup. Again, the psychic dynamic that Saturn represented related to the presence of a strong authoritative dynamic within the psyche of Jesus that sternly rejected the drives and appetites of the physical body and the personal desires. According to Christianity, Jesus ardently rejected the flesh and its penchant toward indulgence and pleasure-seeking.

If Jesus had not transcended the influences of the personal instinctual and emotional aspects of the personal consciousness at a relatively young age, the negative and more aggressive expressions of this dynamic might have appeared in His life. Although Jesus didn't express the malevolence that is common when Saturn forms a tight conjunction to Mars in Aries, this potent psychic dynamic was an area of the psyche through which danger and violence could enter His life.

People who have Saturn in Aries are frequently unable to assert themselves in a positive, constructive way during the stage of personal development. (This is also true when Saturn forms a hard aspect to Mars.) The average person reacts to this situation with anger, and often acts as if he or she has the right to control others. In some cases, the individual is immobilized in some area of life and unable to act. This inability to act is usually concealed behind shyness and social awkwardness, even among those who demonstrate a very controlled and polished formality. This is common when people are able to repress their proclivity to act in an aggressive, retaliatory way. Here, the desire to retaliate or to act aggressively is merely restrained.

It would be easy to assume that Jesus's refusal to defend Himself at His trial before the Sanhedrin, along with His exhortations to react passively when confronted (e.g., to turn the other cheek) were due to His inability to assert Himself, which is common with this placement of Saturn—but that would be missing the point.

You have heard that it was said, 'An eye for an eye, and a tooth for a tooth.'
But I say to you, do not resist one who is evil. But if anyone strikes you on

---

[57] The advanced Soul aligns and attunes to the divine plan and works to implement the divine plan on earth via the refined integrated personality.

the right cheek, turn to him the other also; and if any would sue you and take your coat, let him have your cloak as well; and if any one forces you to go one mile, go with him two miles. Give to him who begs from you, and do not refuse him who would borrow from you. You have heard that it was said, 'You shall love your neighbor and hate your enemy. But I say to you, love your enemies and pray for those who persecute you, so that you may be sons of your Father who is in heaven; for he makes his sun rise on the evil and on the good, and sends rain on the just and on the unjust.[58]

From an early age, Jesus did not have the basic characteristics and traits of the little self that cause people to react angrily when confronted or when they are unable to satisfy their desires.

Jesus expressed the forces of this conjunction in a very different way than how many people express them. Similar to the way the personalities of His past lives used the energies of Saturn, Jesus used these saturnine forces to strengthen His resistance to sin and temptation. Using the energies of Saturn as a psychic authority figure, Jesus is likely to have denied, repressed, and suppressed the physical appetites and personal desire nature. The likelihood that there was a strong, authority figure dynamic within the psyche of Jesus is also suggested by the Mars-Saturn conjunction in Aries, especially since His Ascendant was in Capricorn.

For the average person, arbitrary control and repression of the feeling nature can be dangerous during the early phases of personal development. When the forces of desire are repeatedly blocked, people often strike out. Here, people's containment field isn't strong enough to repress the anger for long. Cruelty is often linked to the long-term inability to satisfy one's desires.

Since Saturn in Aries reinforces the symbolism that the Saturn conjunct Mars aspect represents, it helps to recall the effects that this aspect can have on a person. The negative consequences frequently seen when Saturn is placed in Aries and is conjunct Mars are usually quite prominent during the early stages of development of the threefold personal consciousness.

Saturn typically blocks, obstructs, or in some other way prevents people from expressing the personal desire dynamic. In general, this aspect disrupts people's ability to satisfy personal desires and interferes with the ability to express personal courage, self-confidence, leadership skills, ego assuredness, and the sexual prowess of men's masculinity.

---

[58] Matt. 5:38–45. (RSV) (italics added)

What was being denied by the exceptionally tight conjunction of Mars and Saturn in Aries represented an obstructive force within the psyche of Jesus that repressed the instinctual drives and His personal desires. This repressive force prevented Jesus from focusing on satisfying self-serving desires or expressing the usual masculine sexual urges.

The rather egocentric way that the forces of Mars express is beneficial in the early phases of development of personal consciousness, since they help people unfold a strong sense of self. Jesus, on the other hand, had developed a strong identity and selfhood long before His current incarnation.

If Jesus would have unfolded the typical masculine behavior, tendencies, and characteristics that Mars stimulates in males, He would have needed to confront and eliminate them before He could have attained the second initiation. In other words, if He would have unfolded the typical masculine traits and characteristics in His early years, He would have had to painstakingly eliminate many of the atoms of self-consciousness that linked His selfhood to His male body and its nature. This would have slowed His progression and possibly deterred Him from fulfilling His mission.

The average male with this Saturn-Mars conjunction has an inner struggle between wanting to respond to perceived slights and thinking he should restrain himself. If he doesn't respond, he fears others will take advantage of him. Many people initially restrain themselves and then lash out at others later. It is the nature of the Mars dynamic to challenge others and demonstrate personal courage and prowess. When Saturn conjuncts Mars, however, such behavior is inhibited.

For Jesus, Saturn didn't have an unwelcomed blocking, inhibiting effect upon Him, since His consciousness was no longer polarized at the lower astral or mental level. Nor did He have a need to demonstrate personal courage or prowess. Rather, the effect this dynamic had on Jesus merely reinforced a past-life tendency to impose harsh spiritual practices and disciplinary actions upon Himself, especially in His early years. If Jesus would have unfolded a tendency to strike back at others, He would have needed to work through this tendency and eliminate it before He could attain the second initiation.

Again, stringent denial of all human needs and desires was a common technique used by spiritual seekers in many parts of the world two thousand years ago. Feats of great personal sacrifice and martyrdom were common among the early Christians. Even the Buddha denied himself all that His princely life had to offer and withdrew to a cave to discover why people suffered. There, the Buddha practiced the most stringent forms of self-denial and extreme austerity for many years, only to discover that such extreme practices were counterproductive.

Mars and Saturn usually represent distinctively different and often incompatible dynamics of the psyche, but with Mars at 17 degrees Aries 53 minutes and Saturn at 18 degrees Aries 6 minutes, the two distinct psychic dynamics that Mars and Saturn usually represent were uniquely unified in Jesus's life. This suggests that the Mars-Saturn conjunction served a greater purpose than is readily observable.

It is unlikely that Jesus looked at this Saturn-fueled denial of His physical-instinctual and astral-emotional nature as being something that was imposed upon Him by society or His religion. Rather, Saturn's limiting and suppressive nature was basically indicative of Jesus's own underlying disposition. Also, due to the strong influences of Pisces and Neptune, it wasn't Jesus's nature to flaunt the usual male machismo. Nor was it His nature to assert Himself in a selfish manner. He did not desire name, fame, or wealth. Thus, the effect that Saturn in Aries conjunct Mars had on Jesus aligned well with His own predisposition.

Using the planetary forces of Saturn to limit and deny the basic urges and tendencies of the physical body was a technique that His past lives had adopted for religious reasons. It wasn't as if there was something preventing Jesus from doing the things He wanted to do. He didn't feel as if someone else was preventing Him from having what He desired. In fact, His personality and identity aligned much better with the nature of Saturn than with Mars.

From an early age, much of Jesus's focus was on developing the higher mind and its psychic structures. The upper mental-plane structures of the mind that people develop (the higher senses, capacities, and mental faculties) are comprised of refined mental light, not lower mental-plane matter. Through such structures of the higher mind, the Soul expresses itself on earth.

This placement of Mars and Saturn in Aries makes the most sense when the Soul-centered ruler of Aries, ray four Mercury, is considered. In relation to the evolution of human consciousness, all manifestation begins with an original idea that moves from the level of the Soul into the lower mental body, and then onto the astral body, where it is infused with the motivating forces of desire before it impacts the consciousness. This relates to the involutionary arc of energy. The evolution of consciousness, on the other hand, retraces this path of involutionary energy back to its source.

At the personal level, Mercury is always associated with communications, personal ideas, basic knowledge, and thought. Its ray four magnetic qualities help people become aware of the tension-generating dualities that exist within the threefold personal consciousness. As the Soul-centered ruler of Aries, however, Mercury relates to people's awareness of the differences between the nature and values of the integrated personality and those of the Soul. Mercury awakens people to the differences between the integrated personality and Soul, and works to relate them to each other. Through the progressive resolution of this personality-Soul duality, the link between the concrete mind and the unfolding higher mind is strengthened. The ray four quality of Mercury prompts people to work through this major duality.

Slowly, the consciousness begins to shift from the concrete mind and self to the mind of the higher self. It is only by way of the higher mind (brought forth as a result of the influx of energies of the Soul via the petals of the lotus) that people can clearly perceive their Soul's intent and later perceive their Soul's mission in relation to the divine plan. Such awareness and understanding are strengthened as people unfold the pure reasoning, harmony, beauty, wisdom, and truth of the higher intuitional mind.

Although the planetary head center (Shamballa) is the birthplace of divine life and purpose in relation to the seven planes of earth, the Masters of the Spiritual Hierarchy are responsible for intuiting that purpose and creating the primal seed ideas (the Plan) to help implement the will and purpose of the Logos on earth. It is the energies of Mercury that are used to construct the light patterns behind these seed ideas. It is also the messenger of these seed ideas to mankind as the soul-centered ruler of Aries. When implemented on earth, seed ideas advance humanity as a group.

As Jesus perceived the new seed ideas of the Age of Pisces and formulated them into a body of teachings, He, in effect, became the Light of Life.

Saturn in the Third House

Initially, the placement of Saturn in the third house can adversely impede the development of the intellect, while the Saturn conjunct Mars in Aries can have an adverse effect upon people's ability to express the astral-emotional desire aspect of personal consciousness.

The effect Saturn in the third house had on Jesus prevented Him from unfolding the self-serving emotional and mental patterns of consciousness. Since such emotional and mental patterning represents the scaffolding of the personality, this placement of Saturn in Aries and its conjunction with Mars is another indication that much of the scaffolding of the self-serving personality had been destroyed in a recent past life.

Saturn's placement in the third house created situations in Jesus's life in which any poorly formed ideas, thoughts, and beliefs He held were challenged by others. This forced Him to reevaluate many of His beliefs and opinions, causing Him to seek spiritual validation of His ideas. The consequence of these challenges sharpened His mind and intellect into a tool of heightened precision.

Although Saturn is behind the generation of all thought forms, Saturn in the third house confers a higher degree of crystallization of people's thoughts, ideas, and communications.

For most people, Saturn's placement in the third house crystallizes their distorted thoughts and beliefs, resulting in a mental rigidity, a strengthening of the veiling forces of illusion, and a type of mental frustration that adversely impacts people's ability to communicate clearly. People with Saturn in the third house frequently have difficulty communicating with others. Typically, their thoughts and ideas are persistently challenged by themselves, as well by others. This is especially true when people express rigid ideas and thoughts that they believe to be accurate even when they are not.

People who respond constructively to the life lessons that Saturn in the third house offers usually need to examine their thoughts, beliefs, and ideas closely, and work hard to eliminate those that are rigidly held and obsolete in terms of their current point of evolvement. This effort results in clarity of mind.

Saturn serves as the evolutionary agent that forces people to examine their thoughts, words, beliefs, and behaviors. Disciples, in particular, tend to withdraw from others in order to focus on freeing themselves from the behaviors and communications that seem to cause others to challenge them. For the average person, these challenges are often triggered by their self-referencing nature and patterns of self-centered emotions, thoughts, and actions. Rigid thoughts and ideas are especially troublesome when people believe their truth to be the truth of God, and they attempt to convince others that their truth is the only truth.

Jesus most likely experienced a degree of frustration over His communications skills when He was young. The degree of frustration He experienced at that time was enhanced by His Capricorn Ascendant. As a result, Jesus became reticent about speaking in certain situations, especially in His teenage years.

This situation caused Jesus to withdraw from others. In relative isolation, He closely examined His thoughts, words, and beliefs. In order for people to observe the mental aspect of their consciousness, they must shift their attention into the light of the Soul. Only from the perspective of the Soul can people objectively observe their thoughts and beliefs. Similarly, people must observe their emotions and feelings from the perspective of the light of the concrete mind. Neither aspect of personal consciousness is capable of observing itself. Such self-examination helps people become aware of their old patterns of feelings, thoughts, and beliefs, and determine which ones need to be modified or removed.

Since Jesus had completed much of this examination in a recent past life, during His early years the mental catharsis and self-examination Jesus experienced was relatively minor. As He matured, however, His self-examination focused on eliminating some of the social and religious beliefs and ideas that violated His new-found sensibilities. Unbeknownst to Him, they were of the nature of the Age of Aries. This called for eliminating ideas and beliefs that had become obsolete in terms of the dawning Age of Pisces.

The problem wasn't that Jesus held rigid ideas, opinions, and beliefs that were outside of the tenets of Jewish law, rules, and regulations. Rather, Jesus needed to eliminate His allegiance to certain social-religious beliefs and ideas He held dearly that clashed with the principles and qualities of the dawning Age of Pisces. This initially created tension in His life between the institutionalized beliefs of Judaism that originated in the Age of Aries and the new thoughts, principles, and ideas of the Piscean Age that Jesus was intuiting. This resulted in a struggle between His mind and heart, especially when Jesus was a young man.

Attaining liberation from the threefold personal consciousness was emphasized in the birth chart of Jesus by the conjunction of Uranus, Mercury, and the Sun in the second house, in combination with Pluto's opposition to these planets from the eighth house of transformation. The conjunction of Uranus to Mercury ensured that all obsolete mental patterns—thoughts, ideas, and beliefs—were periodically challenged and released, allowing for new ideas and thoughts to arise. Eventually, the way was cleared for Jesus to develop new thoughts, ideas, and beliefs that aligned with the principles of the Age of Pisces.

This resulted in the development of new structures within the higher mind that were built around the thoughts, ideas, and principles of the Piscean Age, which Jesus perceived and intuited. These, in turn, were challenged by the people around Him. These challenges were not the usual type of challenges Saturn precipitates, which force people to fine-tune their thoughts and ideas. Rather, the challenges Jesus experienced related to a conflict between the principles, beliefs, and ideas of these two Ages.

The energies of Uranus represent the magnetic quality needed to shatter the electromagnetic forces that hold the old emotional and mental patterns together. Since Jesus was acting in the capacity of a planetary server during His ministry, this Uranian disruption of the integrity of old patterns was forceful enough to disrupt some of the emotional and mental patterns of others.

On the personal level, the conjunction of Uranus to Mercury offset many of the tendencies that Saturn in the third house confers. Saturn is intensely protective of the three aspects of personal consciousness and often generates an especially ardent resistance to changing one's mind, thoughts, beliefs, and opinions.

If it wasn't for the shattering effect that Uranus had on the scaffolding of the personal mind and intellect of Jesus (His thoughts, beliefs, opinions) and the transformative effects that Pluto contributed, Jesus would probably have been rather doctrinaire and rigid in His thinking. This type of behavior would have precluded Him from serving as the Piscean messenger.

Instead, Jesus welcomed the changes taking place within His mind and consciousness once transiting Uranus formed a square to Venus, then to the Nodes, Uranus, the Sun, the earth, Vulcan, Mercury, and finally Pluto. Uranus squared all of these when Jesus was between the ages of eighteen and twenty-two. Due to the intense, unsettling, and disruptive types of experiences that Jesus experienced during this time, the remaining scaffolding of His personality collapsed, liberating His consciousness from its identification with the threefold personal self. Jesus's personality characteristics and His beliefs prior to His eighteenth birthday were profoundly different from His characteristics and what He believed after His twenty-second birthday. Having experienced a complete metamorphosis, Jesus became a totally different person.

At this time, Jesus started to reject some of Judaic dietary and behavioral regulations, but continued to adhere to the Mosaic Law and commandments. Due to His attunement to His Soul, Jesus was able to understand the deeper meaning behind the statements of the Torah. It was this difference between His level of understanding and the level of understanding of the average Judeans that caused Him tremendous angst during His ministry.

Many of the frustrations Jesus experienced in relation to the clash between His truth and the truth of others were created by people's inability to comprehend His new-found truth. Throughout His adult years, Jesus perceived the spirit behind the laws, commandments, rules, and regulations of the Torah. Jesus wasn't beholden to the literal word of the Torah. This caused Him significant problems with other Judeans, especially those who interpreted the Torah literally. When questioned about why His disciples were gathering grain on the Sabbath, Jesus replied, *The Sabbath was made for man, not man for the Sabbath.*[59]

On a more positive note, this third-house placement of Saturn enabled Jesus to use the words people were familiar with in order to communicate His lofty understanding of the nature of God and the nature of the spirit side of life (heaven). Jesus became proficient at using parables and analogies to communicate His understanding. His prolific usage of parables and analogies indicates that His consciousness was polarized at the level of the abstract mind. At this level, Saturn shares its influence with mentally liberating Uranus.

Only when people have developed the abstract mind are they able to perceive the meaning and causation that underlies life on earth. The abstract mind enables people to perceive the cause behind such things as people's behavior and actions, as well as comprehend how everything in the three planes of matter is a symbol.

Saturn's placement in the third house heightened Jesus's ability to give concrete form to His lofty intuitions, realizations, and revelations. In this sense, the crystallizing factor found in the energies of Saturn was used to interpret the formless seed ideas of the higher planes. Thus, Saturn also plays an important role in terms of the material objectification of seed ideas on earth. This means that the ray three energies Saturn transmits can be used to objectify and implement the divine plan and purpose of the Logos on earth.

---

[59] Mark 2:27. (RSV) (italics added)

It is unlikely that Jesus exhibited the characteristics and tendencies that people with this placement of Saturn frequently exhibit. It wasn't in His nature to react selfishly, due to the otherworldly pull of Pisces and Neptune. The characteristics that people often exhibit when Saturn is located in the third house include a hyper-rationality, an impersonal coldness, and a critical nature. The only one of these characteristics that Jesus seems to have exhibited in His life was occasional criticism, especially in relation to the Judean Pharisees and scribes who repeatedly questioned the accuracy of His teachings. But Jesus's criticism of the pious and devout Pharisees was not self-serving. Nor was it due to a personal dislike of these two groups of people.

The scribes and Pharisees adhered to every word of the Torah and strictly adhered to its laws, regulations, and prohibitions. They were the protective vanguards of Judaism who ardently defended the laws, rules, and regulations of Jewish society. They were the protectors of institutionalized Judaism.

The nature of Jesus's mission and the teachings of the Piscean Age resulted in an unavoidable clash with the authority figures of Judaism. A conflict between the religious tenets and the secular beliefs of the Age of Aries and the new teachings of the Piscean Age was inevitable.

The psychic dynamics that Saturn and Mars represented were not integrated into the mind of Jesus in the same way as the psychic dynamics represented by planets of the epic grand trine were, yet they were extremely important in terms of His ability to fulfill His mission as the messenger of the Piscean Age. Once Jesus attained the third initiation, the blending of the higher ray six qualities of Mars and the ray three energies of Saturn in the third house enabled Him to anchor and express pure love-wisdom.

Saturn in the third house offered the material substance that stabilized and integrated love-wisdom with the other dynamics of the psyche of Jesus. In this way, formless truth, along with the wisdom emanating from the buddhic plane, became manifest in the three matter planes of earth via the mind and consciousness of Jesus.

This speaks to the evolutionary processes whereby greater and more inclusive elements of truth are slowly revealed. The slow pace with which this is taking place on earth is due to the strong resistance within the collective minds of humanity to new, more inclusive expressions of truth.

The Esoteric Significances of Saturn in Aries and the Third House

According to esoteric astrology, Aries transmits ray one and ray seven. As these two rays are related to each other, a new, higher rhythm and order can be established in people's lives. Rays one and seven correspond to the occult path of power.

On the path of power, people achieve control over the forces of the three planes of matter. This is the power to create good on earth, i.e., the power to manifest the purpose of the Logos. This is the path initiates take once they have completed the path of the heart or the path of the mind.

The Ray One Ashram of the Spiritual Hierarchy remains relatively empty and unorganized compared to the ashrams on the other six rays. This is due to mankind's tendencies to misappropriate the power of the will to satisfy personal desires and self-serving interests, but more importantly, ray one Monads will not incarnate on earth through the world of Soul until the Third Solar System, which lies far in the future.

Ideally, initiates complete the path of the heart or the path of the love-infused mind before they step onto the path of power. When people gain an understanding of how to control the forces of matter before they have attained the third initiation, they tend to misuse their understanding to obtain what they desire without any consideration of how their actions might affect the lives of others. Using the power of divine will selfishly is, by definition, black magic.

The placement of Saturn and Mars in Aries is not the only astrological factor on this ray one, ray seven line in Jesus's chart. The opposition of ray seven Uranus to ray one Pluto represents a potent expression of this line of power that Jesus had to deal with throughout His life.

Once the energies of the sacrifice tier of petals (the will of the Soul) stream through the crown center for an extended period of time, an interest in sacrificing one's allegiance to, and identification with, the form nature in its three aspects arises. When this is the case, the kundalini energy streams upward from the base of the spine to the crown center via the central sushumna channel of the etheric spine. As it rises up the etheric spine, it opens the innermost petals of the five centers along the spine, which conceal the jewels of divine life-force. Once the petals of the centers of the etheric body (which are naught but forces) have been consumed by this fiery life-force, the inner jewels of the etheric centers along the spine are revealed.

This flow of the kundalini up the sushumna awakens the consciousness to the will of the Soul. Once the sushumna is active from the basic center to the crown center, and all of the inner petals of the centers along the spine have opened, the impulses of life penetrate the physical-etheric form in a profound way, intensifying the light at the center of each atom of the physical-etheric body.

The influx of divine will enlivens each center with life-force. Slowly the matter forces that comprise the etheric petals of the centers are transmuted into light. This activity begins once people have attained the third initiation.

Eventually, ray one, in its three sub-types, express in people's lives as the will-to-be, the will-to-love, and the will-to-create. Prior to the third initiation only a small amount of divine will expresses in people's lives. Once the third initiation is attained, however, the will that expresses via the centers starts to intensify. This more potent expression of the will streaming through the jewels of the etheric centers is the power that is used to manifest divine purpose. This is the power that divine co-creators can use to create on earth the perfection envisioned within the mind of God.

In Jesus's chart, Saturn's placement in Aries inhibited any effort to use the ray one, ray seven energies personally. Should Jesus have sought to do so, He would have encountered significant frustrations, adversity, and tribulation. The message behind such difficulties is: there is more to life than the personal self and its interests.

To understand this potent expression of the will of the Divine at its most basic level, people need to understand the truly life-giving factor of the life-forces which originate with the Monad. This ray one life-force gives life to the instinctual, sentient, and mental aspects of human consciousness, and gives life to the forms through which the mind and consciousness are being advanced.

In relation to mankind, the human Monad is the originating source of divine life-forces transmitted onto the Soul. The Soul, in turn, transmits a portion of this divine life-force through the subtle bodies onto the physical-etheric body (and brain consciousness) via the silver cord. To the Divine, conferring life to all that exists is a means, not an end. Its purpose is to bring forth the vehicles through which the divine mind can express itself in the objective manifest world of earth. Humanity will not be the vehicle of the divine mind until far in the future.

Esoterically, the initiating impulses of life begin with the living light of Aries. This living light stimulates the mind of the Logos. The living light of the crown center of planetary life, Shamballa, dimensionally underlies all manifest life. All that exists on earth is the outermost expression of the mind of the Logos brought forth through the activities of the three exoteric Buddhas of Activity and the Monads.

Before Jesus could serve as the Piscean messenger, He needed to attain the third initiation and come under the direct influence of the ray four energies of Mercury as the Soul-ruler of Aries. This influence stimulated the development of His intuitional mind and pure reasoning. Mercury became the primary magnetic influence that conditioned Saturn at the Soul level. Only then—by way of the magnetic forces of Mercury—could the ray one and ray seven energies of Aries pour directly into the higher mind of Jesus.

Since the buddhic intuitional plane is the source of all truly inspired thought and ideas,

Saturn in Aries in the third house is an ideal placement for bringing forth a higher, more inclusive system of thought and belief, e.g., the teachings of the Piscean Age.

Receptivity of the pure wisdom and love of the buddhic plane begins once Saturn completes its work at the personal level. This includes the development of an exceptionally disciplined mind and one-pointed focus. An ability to focus the mind for extended periods of time without being distracted is necessary before people are able to intuit and subsequently interpret the seed ideas of the formless planes of light without distortion.

By way of Mercury's resonance with the buddhic-intuitional realm, Jesus could perceive the hidden characteristics, nature, and tendencies of people. This capacity was greatly advanced during His ministry, once His consciousness shifted from the upper mental-causal level into the buddhic plane. From this higher perspective, Jesus could see through the auric field enveloping people and intuitively perceive the light within them. He wasn't deceived by people's feigned propriety. Jesus truly knew who came *"in sheep's clothing but inwardly are ravenous wolves."*[60]

Once Jesus stepped onto the path of power, this placement of Saturn in Aries enabled Him to demonstrate such occult powers as the casting out of spirits, transforming water into wine, awakening the dead, giving sight to the blind, and so forth. Jesus needed to exhibit such miracles before people would listen to Him and accept His teachings.

---

[60] Matt. 7:15. (RSV) (italics added)

Chapter 20

Dweller-on-the-Threshold

As people approach the third initiation, they find themselves in the midst of a great struggle between two major centers of life and light. Each center represents a nature, values, qualities, and character so different from the other center that they are each given a unique title. The one is referred to as the dweller-on-the-threshold and the other is the Angel of the Presence.

This discussion of Saturn would not be complete without relating the personality to the dweller-on-the-threshold. The dweller is composed of the structures of the mind and patterns of behavior, thoughts, and beliefs of countless personalities that were crystallized by the concretizing forces of Saturn. The dweller is the integrated personality.

For countless lifetimes, the burgeoning personal self was not aware of the dweller. Nor was it aware of the Angel of the Presence. Neither the dweller nor the Angel makes its appearance known until people have sufficiently brought forth the intelligence and love aspects of the higher self and have made significant progress in unfolding the will aspect.

The unfoldment and development of the three aspects of the Soul results in an awareness of the single most important duality people face upon the path: the duality between the integrated personality center and the Soul with its selfless values and qualities.

Only when people have achieved a mastery of the physical instinctual and astral-emotional nature and are approaching the third initiation is the dweller revealed by the light of the Angel. Everyone must observe themselves objectively as the dweller and resolve the remaining forms of duality that exist between the disciple and the Soul before union or at-one-ment with the Soul is achieved. This is the law.

This requires people to still the physical and astral emotional aspects of personal consciousness, and shift the consciousness into the light of the Soul-infused mind during meditation. From the perspective of the Soul-infused mind, both the dweller and the Angel of the Presence are revealed by the inner mind's eye. From this inner perspective, the form and character of the dweller is clearly seen in the radiant light and beauty of the Angel.

There is more than a passing resemblance between the dweller, Saturn, and Satan. In fact, much of the symbolism of the dweller and Satan are interchangeable. Both are intimately associated with the effects Saturn has on the personal consciousness.

In a number of ways, Saturn builds the form that the dweller-on-the-threshold assumes within the psyche. This involves both the outer form of the dweller and the egocentric nature of the personal self. Both are a product of people's experiences in the three matter planes and their personal reactions to the energies of Saturn, lifetime after lifetime.

Slowly, light is brought forth in these forms as the light of the Angel of the Presence is reflected upon the mirror of the Soul-infused mind. Initially, people do not realize that the higher self is the manifest objectification of the Soul during incarnation. Why would they? Up to this stage, people have only known the reflected self in the three planes of earth and have accepted the distorted reflections of the Real as being the real.

The form of the dweller has been created over the course of countless lifetimes. It is composed of all of the structures and patterns of thought, feelings, and behavior of the little self. Its selfhood is the self of countless personalities composed of the elements of the physical-instinctual, astral-emotional, and lower mental natures of these lifetimes.

Since all facets of the egocentric personality and all expressions and interests of the personal self (the not-self) are sacrificed at the third initiation, the last remnants of the self-consciousness attached to the material forces and elements of the threefold personal consciousness must be uplifted and transformed into the mind of the Soul. This is the evolutionary journey.

The dweller is comprised of the many elements of self-consciousness that are linked to the patterns of the separate personal self (feelings, thoughts, actions, etc.), both those of the current lifetime and those of past lifetimes. One by one the atoms of self-consciousness must be redeemed from the matter world.

The dweller gives life to people's likes and dislikes. It is the personal self that desires, feels, thinks, and acts within a reality that is limited and circumscribed. The dweller is the product of the personalities of countless lives, comprised of the atoms of self-consciousness that have a vibration and a nature of the three matter planes.

For millennia, the Angel of the Presence has stood before the gate that opens onto paradise (the world of the Real), blocking the personal self from entering. Initially, it does not dawn upon the individual that he or she is the dweller. Only when the disciple approaches the third initiation and stands in the light of the Angel is the personal self clearly seen as the dweller.

For millennia, the Angel has blocked the way to paradise. Because of the vibrations, characteristics, qualities, and nature of the dweller, the Angel cannot let it pass, for the dweller is composed of the vestments of the unreal, the subtle bodies, and comprised of egocentric patterns of consciousness which must not soil the pristine light, harmony, and sublime beauty of the kingdom.

The Soul-infused mind eventually shifts its attention and orientation away from the dweller to the radiant Angel. At some point, the advanced disciple throws all of his or her weight behind the efforts of the Angel. Before disciples can enter paradise, they must completely transform everything they identify as their selfhood into the selfless nature, values, and qualities of the Soul. This accelerates the attunement of the personal mind with the mind of the Soul. Suddenly, the realization dawns, I am that. I am the Angel. I am the Soul. That is my true self. (Much later, comes the realization, I am that I am. I am the Monad, the Father Spirit.)

The dweller represents all of the forms and structures in people's lives that Saturn crystallized and objectified over the course of many lifetimes as the threefold personal consciousness was being developed. Only when the Soul-infused mind throws its weight behind the efforts of the Angel and identifies its selfhood with the Soul can the Soul take command of the refined integrated personality and fully express itself through people's lives on earth.

At this higher stage, Saturn becomes the agent of the Angel. In its higher Soul-centered role, Saturn requires people to fully sacrifice the not-self before passage onto the divine presence is granted. Only by sacrificing all vestiges of the not-self can people finalize the transfer of all of the atoms of self-consciousness from the attributes of consciousness of the dweller into the three aspects of the Divine operative at the level of the Soul. Unless the personal unreal is sacrificed, it will continue to veil the Real.

The inner life and light of the dweller, however, is essentially the same life and light as that of the Soul. The apparent division is a temporal illusion caused by the fallen elements of the consciousness mistakenly identified with and attached to the not-self.

With the realization that the essence of the dweller and essence of the Angel are one and the same, the blazing light of the Soul burns up the outer form of the dweller. The form of the dweller is consumed by the radiance of the fiery life of the Angel. The light of the personal self and the light of the higher self are unified into one field of light.

When people have successfully accomplished the spiritual work necessary to attain the third initiation, and the outer garments of the separate self (the dweller) have been transmuted by the fiery life of the Angel, what remains is the purified personality instrument capable of expressing the creative loving intelligence of the Soul on earth. The dweller exists no more.

All atoms of self-consciousness vacate the personality form and merge into the world of the Soul beyond the sin of separatism. All lower vibratory forces (egocentric emotions, thoughts) that once differentiated the dweller from the Angel have been transmuted, and the personal self is transformed into the higher self—the manifest Soul.

Henceforth, the Soul is able to express its nature, capacities, and qualities through the instrumentality of the higher mind to perform its service work on behalf of mankind. This is the objective behind all path work regardless of one's religion, race, nationality, sex, etc.

The union of the purified integrated personality and the Soul represents a great step forward upon the path, but this step is just one of the many steps. The work of the higher self that is required once a union of the integrated personality and Soul has been attained involves the unfoldment and development of the threefold Triad. Only then can the hierarchal training on the path of power begin. By way of this training, the initiate becomes a divine co-creator.

Saturn inconjunct Pluto (1 degree 59 minutes)

Saturn's conjunction to Mars and its inconjunction to Pluto epitomize the dweller. Both aspects are hard, challenging aspects. Hard aspects to a third-house Saturn in Aries indicate that the mental aspect of Jesus needed to go through a series of transformations before He could become the messenger of the Piscean Age.

Saturn and Pluto precipitated the difficult events and experiences in Jesus's life involving certain individuals who represented the antagonists in the story of Jesus, while the planets of the epic grand trine triggered the kinds of events and experiences that resulted in the attainment of Christ consciousness.

The events and experiences that the planetary antagonists precipitated in the story of Jesus challenged, maligned, and rejected Jesus. This group included the scribes and Pharisees, the Sanhedrin Court, Pontius Pilate, and Judas Iscariot. Prior to His ministry, Jesus most likely considered His experiences that the planetary antagonists precipitated in His life as the temptations of Satan, the devil, or evil spirits.

Planetary antagonists always generate points of tension that people must work through to succeed. Hard aspects between Saturn and Pluto generate tension in people's lives. Both planets are astrologically associated with darkness and destruction, and both are associated with the figure of Lucifer, the Dark Prince of the underworld. The underworld symbolizes the immediate depths of the unconscious, where the atoms of the emotional self-consciousness are trapped in the patterns of ancient glamour of the lower astral-emotional world. The early Christians referred to this realm as purgatory.

In Greek mythology, the evolution of consciousness was portrayed as a struggle of the warrior to conquer darkness. The myths of the world graphically describe the conquests of the warrior who defeats the hideous forms of darkness and becomes the victorious hero.

The story of Hercules is just one of many examples of this struggle between darkness and light. Such conflicts often take place in the outer world, but they always represent the duality within the mind and consciousness. Each victory of the spiritual warrior over some form of darkness increases the light and consciousness of the spiritual warrior. This is the story of humanity, for the human race moves through life on ray four (harmony through conflict).

There is only light—a light that human consciousness cannot perceive until the darkness of the form world is defeated by the spirit. Slowly, light conquers the darkness of the world of form. This has been a struggle mankind has engaged in since ancient times when the rod of mind was first implanted in these human forms. As people journey to their spiritual home, the antagonists in their lives frequently represent some element of this darkness in relation to the light of their burgeoning consciousness.

For those on the path, the symbolism of this struggle relates to the struggle between the Soul and the integrated personality for command of one's life on earth. The Soul must defeat the enveloping darkness of the little self that imprisons the consciousness and obstructs the fullness of divine life and light from expressing through the personality form. Darkness relates specifically to the matter forces and to the elements of the personal consciousness that block the light and hold the indwelling life captive in the dark unreal of the underworld of the three planes of earth. Darkness's greatest tool is its beguiling illusion that the unreal is the Real.

The Soul's objective is to awaken and then uplift the burgeoning personal consciousness into the light and control of first the rational mind and then the mind of the Soul. For lifetimes, the Soul struggles against the matter nature of the involutionary physical-etheric, astral-emotional, and lower-mental forces. Eventually, people integrate and unify the threefold personal consciousness and function as an integrated personality. This takes place as a result of the increasing light and power of the personal mind.

As the planetary forces impact the consciousness, the light of knowledge unfolds within these forms of earth. Slowly, knowledge is transformed by the seven rays into the light of wisdom. As the light of the lotus streams through the upper centers, it centrifugally expels many of the dark forces that imprison the atoms of self-consciousness in the lower sub-plane levels. During the stage of human development, the planetary forces of Saturn are associated with these veiling forms of matter. This includes the integrated personality, as well as the physical and subtle bodies.

The destroyer sub-aspect of ray one brings about the death of the matter forms that people have mistakenly identified their selfhood with for lifetimes. Here, death pertains to the death of the little self—the self of hatred, the self of greed, the self of vengeance, and so forth.

The potent ray one forces of Pluto transport people into the darkness and reveal the hideous forms that the atoms of self-consciousness have taken on. It is the hideous forms of the little self (the self of hatred, of vengeance, of cruelty, etc.) that the spiritual warrior must slay. The freedom Pluto offers is gained through the struggle, pain, and losses that spiritual heroes experience in their quest for light and spiritual realizations.

When the plutonian transformative processes are activated by an inconjunction of Pluto to Saturn, tremendous growth is possible, but for a price: the death of the little self—the death of old beliefs, old habits and ways of life, old thoughts and ideas, separatism, selfishness, and egotism. This includes the death of the old astral-emotional desire nature steeped in the magnetism of ancient astral glamour. Saturn inconjunct Pluto offers people an opportunity to sever the cords that attach their atoms of self-consciousness to the things of earth. The death of the personal self as the dweller results in the rebirth of the self as the Soul.

Pluto's ray one energies in its third sub-aspect as the destroyer are always involved in the evolutionary processes that strip away the obsolete saturnine forms and structures of the not-self. When a person is still attached to the things of earth and personally identified with them, rather than with the spirit, the plutonian destruction of the scaffolding that upholds the little self can be painful.

Pluto often carries people into the lower astral realm of ancient glamour and darkness to meet the hideous emotional patterns and desire forms of the little self. There, the disciple must battle the forms of darkness and slay the monsters that reside in the dark recesses of the mind. Such a battle can be emotionally gut-wrenching and exasperating, yet all people must engage in this battle before the spirit is victorious. In consciousness, people must be liberated from the dark and dank depths of the lower astral-emotional realm, as well as liberated from the illusions of the reflected lower mental realm, before they can rise up into the supernal light of the Divine.

Disciples who are ready to shift their identification upward, away from the little self, often welcome the transformative processes Pluto precipitates. They welcome the loss of the not-self and its desire-fueled, chaotic life. But even when people are willing participants in their transformation, it isn't easy; for transcendence of the little self requires them to relinquish all of the ways of life they have known in hopes of attaining some lofty spiritual objective. Up until the vision of the higher self is fully developed, such sacrifices must be accepted on faith alone. The death of people's identification of their selfhood with the not-self comes about once people stop identifying their selfhood with the little self and its reflected light and set out to conquer the darkness that veils the light.

The plutonian death of the not-self takes place slowly, usually after years of demonstrating dispassion toward, detachment from, and renunciation of the things of earth. This involves detaching oneself from the material world and from the physical body and the ego-centered personal consciousness, while identifying oneself with the Soul and its values and qualities. This calls for unwavering dedication to the journey, self-discipline, study, prayer, service work, and meditation. It calls for aligning and attuning to the Soul each day.

The consequence of the transforming experiences of Pluto is abundant life. This has nothing to do with material bounty. A greater abundance of life is possible only when the involutionary forces of the threefold personal consciousness no longer control people's lives and drain them of vital life-forces. Through the struggle and the pain of loss and despair, people are repeatedly compelled to examine themselves and their lives. Eventually, this self-examination leads them from the Hall of Knowledge into the Hall of Wisdom.

Modern astrology associates Pluto with the rebirth experience that immediately follows the destruction, painful losses, and endings that Pluto precipitates in its role as the destroyer. With each incident of plutonian loss, some part of the scaffolding of the little self is destroyed and cannot be replaced as it once was. Instead, a new centering of the self takes place. This new center demands a more expanded psychic structure through which a higher level of the mind and consciousness are able to operate and grow.

The builder sub-aspect of ray one is the agent of rebirth. Before people experience rebirth, however, they must first experience plutonian death and destruction. Through the pain of losing something that was once valued, the self is reborn, born anew. The theme of plutonian-triggered rebirth always relates to greater life, light, and being, as well as to the destruction of the veiling forces within the mind and consciousness.

Allegorically, the light of the mind is victorious over darkness once the consciousness is sufficiently freed from the instinctual drives and selfish emotional desire patterns, but this victory is short lived. At this stage, the struggle between the mental aspect of the personal consciousness and the Soul begins. This struggle causes the changes within the consciousness that help shift the personality center into that great center of the Soul. Once achieved, the work of the disciple is finished and the work of the initiate begins.

From the moment when people first step upon the path of probation up through the second initiation, they are caught in a struggle between light and darkness. Again and again, the spiritual warrior battles the hideous forms of darkness that capture the life and light of the personal self. From darkness to light, from the unreal to the real, the spiritual seeker moves from a lower state to a higher state.

Eventually the psychic structure through which the personal self was developed is destroyed. But this destruction should not occur before the threefold mind of the higher self is sufficiently developed. Only then can the scaffolding of the personal self safely fall away.

The interplay and exchange of energies that take place when Saturn is inconjunct Pluto precipitate the frustrating types of experiences that can shake the very foundation of the personality structure, but usually does not destroy it. Once the disciple approaches the third initiation and is psychologically ready to transcend the egocentric self, the interplay of the energies of this Saturn-Pluto inconjunction can precipitate an event so devastating that the scaffolding that upholds the egocentric personality collapses. This frees the consciousness, allowing it to shift upward into the world of the Soul.

Though portions of the psychic scaffolding that uphold the world of the little self periodically fall away, when Saturn is inconjunct Pluto, there is usually one exceedingly traumatic event that takes place. This event represents a profound turning point. Accepted disciples with this inconjunction are more likely to experience the type of traumatic event that destroys the entire scaffolding of the little self.

This event frees the consciousness from its evolutionary imprisonment within the life forms of matter. The emotional self-consciousness is transformed into the essential love of the higher self, the mental self-consciousness is transformed into the creative intelligence of the higher mind, and the personal will is transformed into the will of the Soul.

Though the development and subsequent transformation of the personal consciousness takes place over a lengthy period of time (lifetimes), there is usually one critical moment when the egocentric personal self is no more, transformed into the higher self. The inconjunction of Saturn to Pluto is often the precipitating cause that shatters the form and entire psychic structure of the integrated personality. Henceforth, the disciple is the Soul. Symbolically, this event represents the time when the spiritual warrior rises up triumphantly as the hero god and enters the light. This final culminating point when people are liberated from the form world occurs after lifetimes of trials and tribulations that both Saturn and Pluto precipitate.

Leading up to this culminating moment, the inconjunction of Saturn to Pluto often confers an intolerance of one's own shortcomings and the shortcomings of others. At some point as a young man, Jesus became so acutely aware of His shortcomings that He turned all of His attention toward eliminating them. This is the work of all disciples. *"You must therefore be perfect, as your heavenly Father is perfect."*[61] It was Jesus's drive to perfect

---

[61] Matt. 5:48. (RSV) (italics added)

Himself that led Him to that climaxing moment, when the entire scaffolding of the integrated personality fell away and He was reborn as the Soul.

In summary, people first experience the tests and trials of maturation that Saturn precipitates. Saturn's tests relate specifically to the unfoldment and development of the threefold personal consciousness. In particular, they pertain to the work involved in polarizing the consciousness at the mental level. They also relate to the struggle to resolve duality within the threefold personal consciousness.

Once the consciousness is mentally polarized and the threefold personality is sufficiently integrated, Pluto presents the tests and trials of Scorpio that people must pass in order to attain one of the first three initiations. These tests involve the resolution of the duality that exists between the threefold higher self, which the disciple is currently unfolding, and the threefold personal consciousness.

Rebirth is experienced as the result of successfully passing the tests of Scorpio. Each death-rebirth experience is a minor death of some aspect of the personality. With each death and rebirth, people are one step closer to the climaxing moment of the third initiation, when the scaffolding of the entire personal self is destroyed. Only then is the Ego of the Soul (which has no egoistic factors like the personal self) is free to express through the purified and refined vehicles of the mind and subtle bodies. This represents the true rebirth, when people are born anew.

> *Truly, truly, I say to you, unless one is born anew, he cannot see the kingdom of God.*[62]

> *Truly, truly, I say to you, unless one is born of water and the spirit, he cannot enter the kingdom of God.*[63]

Since water is the universal symbol for emotions and the astral-fluid realm of consciousness, people are allegorically born of water at the second initiation. The second initiation can only occur once the energies of the love tier of petals have successfully brought forth the love aspect of the higher self. People are born of spirit at the third initiation, once the energies of the sacrifice tier of petals have completed their work. Only then can people enter the kingdom of God.

Pluto-Saturn aspects represent the compelling forces that stimulate the evolutionary processes of transformation, of death and rebirth, up through the third initiation. Once

---

[62] John 3:3. (RSV) (italics added)
[63] John 3:5. (RSV) (italics added)

the third initiation is attained, there are no saturnine forms and structures within the consciousness that need to be eliminated.

In Jesus's life, the inconjunction of Pluto to Saturn and Mars deepened His understanding of both the three planes of earth and the transpersonal world of the spirit, but it also intensified His aversion to materiality and many of the simple pleasures of life. Most important, this inconjunction precipitated the challenging events in His life that led Jesus to that moment when the entire scaffolding of personality collapsed, revealing His divinity. Once the scaffolding fell away, Jesus was born of spirit. He was reborn as the Soul.

In the wilderness, just after His baptism, Jesus faced the dweller-on-the-threshold—the tempter. There He passed the tests of the third initiation and became the initiate. He was then ready for His mission of service to God and mankind.

Aspects to Saturn discussed in earlier chapters:

Mars conjunct Saturn

PART THREE

The Mission

Chapter 21

Uranus, the Liberator

Though the outer planets of Uranus, Neptune, and Pluto were unknown at the time of Jesus's birth, the placement of the outer planets and the aspects they formed to each other and to the personal planets in His chart fashioned the most remarkable natal chart. When the deeper meanings and significances of the outer planets are considered, the aspects formed between the outer planets and the inner planets reveal Jesus's mission as the voice of the Piscean Age.

If astrologers consider only the sign and house placements of the inner planets and luminaries (Sun out to Saturn) and the aspects formed between them, it is impossible to see the uniqueness of Jesus or understand how He attained Christ consciousness. We would need to rely solely upon theology and its view that Jesus was born perfect as the Son of God. This means that the life, teachings, and mission of Jesus were due to His unique relationship to God from birth. This view robs mankind of its potential to attain Christ consciousness, and fails to explain how mankind can realize the perfection of the Father.

Uranus is the liberator that frees the consciousness from the crystallized personality world of separatism. The energies of Uranus break up the structures that confine and restrict the consciousness to the three planes of matter. These structures represent the boundaries within which the emotional and mental atoms of self-consciousness unfold. During the early stages of development of the personal consciousness, these psychic structures are needed.

By way of the structures of the mind, people unfold and develop the elements of personal consciousness within a rather limited matrix. The restrictions and limitations such structures impose limit people's considerations to a narrow focus. Initially, people's consciousness is limited to what the physical senses relay to the brain consciousness. This includes people's conscious response to the forces streaming through the lower centers of the etheric body.[64]

---

[64] The health of the physical body and its systems is dependent upon the different types of energy that freely flow through each of the centers of the etheric body. People's ability to consciously respond to the different

Lifestyles, relationships, jobs, cherished beliefs, ideas, feelings, emotions, and desires reflect the limiting structures of the mind. As people progress, these structures become obsolete. For this reason, as people grow in consciousness, many of their relationships, jobs, beliefs, etc., often change as well.

The mental patterns that Saturn crystalizes in relation to the threefold personal consciousness create the constricted and limited personal mind. However, this structuring of the mind is necessary, especially during the stage of development of the threefold personal self. It provides stability and security, and establishes order as the threefold personal consciousness is unfolded in the physical body. Within this structured world of the mind, people unfold personal characteristics, tendencies, skills, values, and belief systems.

Uranus is the agent that demagnetizes the subtle atomic valences that maintain the emotional and mental patterns of feelings and thoughts, thereby disrupting the electromagnetic forces that bind the atoms of self-consciousness to the patterns of the astral-emotional and mental aspects of personal consciousness.

People often run into difficulties when they try to expand their consciousness. Many find change difficult and unwelcome due to the saturnine crystallizing forces that objectify and maintain the personal consciousness. People's resistance to change originates with the repelling atomic forces that protect the integrity of the psyche as currently constituted.

The energies of Saturn are used to create the mental-plane foundation upon which first the concrete mind, then the mind of the Soul, and much later the intuitional mind are brought forth in these forms of earth. This progressive development of the mind takes place as the consciousness is linked to the successively higher centers of life, especially the three centers in the planes of light. Once the consciousness is aligned with these higher centers, higher qualities and types of forces pour into the mind and onto the consciousness. Over time, more refined vehicles with greater capacities, senses, and skills are brought forth. Slowly, mankind is transforming the manifest world of the three planes of matter into the manifest worlds of the essential love of the Soul.

Since people unfold the threefold personal consciousness within the structured matrix of the human psyche, there must be some mechanism whereby the consciousness is freed from their emotional and mental patterns of feelings, thoughts, and beliefs once these have served their developmental purpose. When the principle of consciousness of a particular plane is reasonably well developed, the structural boundaries that were needed to unfold

---

types and qualities of energy streaming through the seven major centers of the etheric body, however, is something that is developed during the course of people's lives.

and develop a particular principle must be eliminated, so a higher principle of consciousness can unfold within a more expansive psychic matrix.

The mechanism that helps liberate the self-consciousness from the obsolete mental patterns of the psyche is Uranus. Uranus shatters the structures that maintain and uphold certain patterns of behavior, biases, prejudices, beliefs, etc. that interfere with the processes that broaden and expand the consciousness. Slowly, the consciousness is freed from its identification with and attachment to the not-self.

Generally, Uranus is the first transpersonal energy that the human mind can use constructively. As the energies stream from the three petals of the intelligence tier and the first (the intelligence) petal of the love tier, people gain a greater understanding of the nature of the physical-etheric world. The first petal of the love tier relates to people's intelligent understanding of the astral world and corresponds to the love aspect the higher self. The first petal of the sacrifice tier relates to people's intelligent understanding of the mental plane and the will of the Soul.

People's ability to demonstrate mental creativity is due to the influx of the energies of the intelligence petals of the lotus streaming through the upper etheric centers. This activity represents the first stage of development of the threefold mind of the higher self. Uranus is not cognizant of the wishes and desires of the personal self. Nor is it interested in such, for the little self is steeped in maya, glamour, and illusion, and is an expression of the nature and characteristics of the form world, not the indwelling life.

Little of the planetary forces of Uranus can be used to advance the personal consciousness; however, they can be used to clear away the structures of personal consciousness that prevent people from further growth. Eliminating obsolete elements and patterns of consciousness is accomplished as a result of Uranus's demagnetization of the subtle molecular structures that maintain a particular behavior, emotional pattern, or mental pattern.

Many people are unable to respond to the exceedingly refined, high-frequency energies of Uranus in a positive, constructive way. They often experience the changes Uranus precipitates only as a result of the changes it precipitates in society. For them, Uranus tends to operate outside of the light of their conscious awareness. Once the consciousness is polarized at the mental level, however, Uranus begins to have a positive, mentally stimulating effect upon them.

People demonstrate an ability to respond consciously to the energies of Uranus once they are able to think for themselves and formulate new ideas and thoughts. When a new, original idea arises within the consciousness, as a result of a transit or progression of Uranus, it does not enter into the conscious awareness as a word—at least not until people have developed the capacity to simultaneously perceive and translate the subtle light impulses and symbolic imagery of the Soul into words.

The energies of Uranus stimulate the mind in a way that activates the manasic center at the first sub-plane level of the mental body. As energies stream from the manasic center and are registered by the mind, the abstract mind is unfolded. Before this can occur, however, people need to generate streams of mental light that connect each of the three petals of the intelligence tier to the manasic center. By way of the manasic center, the intelligence aspect of the Triad is brought forth.

The energy that emanates from the manasic center does not stimulate the consciousness via the etheric throat center; rather, the energies of the manasic center impact the consciousness via the throat center in the greater crown center. This energy stimulates the activity of the frontal lobe and pre-frontal cortex, which enhances people's ability to think, discern, evaluate, and choose appropriately. In other words, the executive function of the psyche is dependent upon the energy streaming from the manasic center through the opened throat center of the greater crown center (via the intelligence petals).

The two-way connecting streams of light between the personal mind and the manasic center are part of the rainbow bridge—the antahkarana. Since the streams of light that disciples generate to link the petals of the lotus to the three centers of the Triad have a different hue, the rainbow bridge is a fitting description. In addition, the ray of the Soul can be on any one of the seven rays.

The linking and subsequent alignment and attunement of the mind to the higher manasic center of the Triad develops the executive decision-making function and the abstract mind. The faculty of the abstract mind enables people to perceive and translate the impulses and impressions of the higher intuitional mind into symbolic imagery.

By way of the energies of Uranus, people first unfold and develop the mental faculties of the higher mind. By way of the higher mind, the disciple can perceive the meanings that underlie the universal symbols and images that the abstract mind creates (as it interprets the light patterns of the intuitional mind).

The abstract mind relates specifically to the manasic center and therefore to the world of meaning and causation that underlies the world of ideas. As the Soul meditates upon the manasic center, universal symbols and images impact the mind of the Soul. The Soul, in turn, develops original thought and ideas that express the messages that the universal symbols of the manasic center represent.

The ability to perceive the meaning behind the original thoughts of the Soul represents an advanced point of development. For most people, the Soul is focused downward and is caught up in the illusions of the personality for lifetimes. The Soul initially accepts the illusions of the burgeoning personal mind, but there is a point when the Soul is liberated from personal illusion and turns its focus upward, first to the manasic center and then to the buddhic center. Thus, the actions of Uranus free the Soul from its imprisonment in the three planes of earth.

Everything on earth is a mind-created life form of either human or nonhuman Monads. Since divine life-force is not innate to the life forms of earth, the Monads must sustain them. For mankind, this sustaining life-force streams through the subtle and physical-etheric bodies by way of the Silver cord.

All life forms found in the three planes of earth are the outer representations of an underlying idea of the universal mind. Thought begins at the highest level as an impulse motivated by purpose. Purpose ushers forth and manifests as meaning. Meaning manifests as an idea, and an idea manifests on earth as a form. This might be a thought form, a desire form, or a physical form.

Due to the rod of mind that was implanted in the etheric body of ancient Homo sapiens, the potential to become a mind-creating agent of the Divine was anchored within the energy field of mankind. The implantation of the rod of mind is what introduced the potential that, when fully actualized, transforms human beings into divine co-creators.

Millions of years since the rod of mind was first anchored in the etheric body of primitive mankind, people are still unaware of their potential to create, yet for millennia, they have mis-created by giving life and direction to a multitude of emotion-based desire forms and mental-based thought forms of a nature that violates universal law.

A consequence of mankind's mis-creations is a mental plane permeated with illusion, an astral plane saturated with the fog of deceiving glamour, and a personal consciousness caught up in the world of maya. People continue to set energy into motion that generates illusion, glamour, and maya because of their ignorance of universal laws and their identification with that which they are not. When this is the case, people fall short of actualizing their inner potential.

In relation to human consciousness, Uranus is the antidote for the crystallized mis-creations of mankind. Uranian forces break up crystallized thought forms, desire forms, and life structures, thereby freeing the atoms of self-consciousness from the crystallized emotional and mental patterns and structures of the personal consciousness.

For those on the path, Uranus's placement by sign and house represents the area of life where the self-consciousness is being liberated. For those a little farther along the path, the sign and house placement of Uranus represents the area of life where they are open to the original thoughts of the Soul. The planetary aspects that Uranus forms to other planets in a chart indicate the ease or difficulty people are likely to experience when bringing about significant changes in their lives, especially in relation to new thoughts, ideas, and beliefs pertaining to the area of life where Uranus is placed. For initiates, the aspects formed to Uranus indicate the ease or difficulty they are likely to have perceiving the original thoughts of the Soul and the symbols of the abstract mind, as well as communicating their higher understanding and realizations to others.

Mankind must be developmentally ready to perceive and understand what the impulses of a new seed idea can awaken within the consciousness. This may be a new discovery, a new invention, or a new approach to some aspect of life. If people cannot see the value of the seed idea, they will resist it before it can be properly formulated. Or, they will distort the idea and direct it into an area of life that is different from its original intent and purpose. This distortion often takes place before the idea is firmly established in people's minds.

The energies of Uranus plant the seed ideas in the soil of the fertile mind that bloom into new systems of thoughts and archetypes. The messenger of these ideas trigger shifts in the paradigms that have dominated the collective minds of humanity and governed a particular area of thought for an extended period of time. The greater the effect a new idea has on people, the greater the resistance that religious, social, ethnic, and political groups may have to the idea.

Today, many people are intuiting seed ideas so rapidly that it has created an even greater division within mankind between people whose consciousness is polarized at the astral-emotional level and those whose consciousness is polarized at the mental level. As a rule, people whose consciousness is polarized at the astral-emotional level do not see the same world or accept the same facts as truth as those whose consciousness is polarized at the mental level. They see very different worlds.

When the consciousness is polarized at the astral-emotional level, people are unable to sense these new ideas, let alone comprehend their divine purpose and intent. Emotion-based people, in particular, are likely to distort new ideas and attempt to destroy them or fit them into their feeling-based belief system of a bygone day. People who are mentally polarized are significantly more likely to accept new ideas and to recognize the paradigm shifts taking place within the society. This group of people stands in stark contrast to those whose consciousness is still polarized in the world of feelings and stuck in the past.

Uranus is a transpersonal energy that stimulates the higher mind and enables people to perceive new seed ideas. It often gives rise to liberating thoughts and new ideas, providing that the consciousness is polarized at the mental level. For many people, however, Uranus merely represents a disruptive influence. This is especially true when people are unaware of the evolutionary objective of Uranus to free the consciousness from what is no longer needed in people's lives. Uranus often removes people and possessions from people's lives that are no longer necessary to the evolutionary journey, even when people desire such to be in their lives. When this is the case, the events Uranus triggers are thought of as unpleasant and unwelcome shocks.

Many nations of the world are still unresponsive to Uranus and do not think of change in a positive light. Often such nations interfere with people's right to think independently of others. People need to have the right to freely express themselves before they can innovate, discover, and grow. Without this freedom, Uranus represents a dull note in the chart. The freedom to think and choose for oneself is sacrosanct. It is by choosing inappropriately that people learn, and it is by choosing appropriately (as defined by the values, qualities, and character of the Soul) that they progress.

The past of mankind further imprisons the consciousness when people are not free to think for themselves. Freedom does not mean that people have the right to harm the environment or harm one another. Nor does it mean they have a right to manipulate and dominate others for selfish gain. Regulations upon people's personal freedom are necessary in order to keep the unbridled greed, selfishness, vengeance, possessiveness, etc., of the unevolved person from adversely impacting the lives of others.

The struggle within the consciousness that Uranus triggers is a struggle between the psychic dynamic that upholds the stabilizing structures of the past and the dynamic that works to free oneself from what imprisons the consciousness (old beliefs, ideas, feelings, and thoughts). This struggle appears once the higher mind is reasonably well developed. The unfoldment of the higher mind sets up a struggle in which the nature, values, and characteristics of the higher self clash with those of the personal self.

More than anything, the effects that the energies of Uranus have upon the consciousness relate to the long-term process of liberating the consciousness from its preoccupation with a selfish existence, so people can attain their freedom from matter as a Soul and a Spirit.

People need to achieve freedom from the constraints that the involutionary, cellular intelligences impose upon the mind and consciousness before they can access the world of ideas. The personal ego always resists people's efforts to transition away from the three planes of matter life, since it is a matter form that is to be transcended.

Thus, the energies of Saturn are initially used to protect the burgeoning ego and the personality from higher-frequency forces of the world of spirit. The energies of Uranus, on the other hand, shatter the fortified walls protecting the ego. Saturn's inhibiting effect to people's progression arises from the psychic structures that mankind has created and needs during the early phases of personal development.

The breaking up of these structures that shield, protect, and maintain the self-of-old needs to take place periodically in order for mankind to progress. Obsolete feelings, ideas, thoughts, and beliefs must be superseded by more inclusive and expansive ones. In this way, the consciousness shifts upward from one sub-plane level to a higher sub-plane level and from one plane to a higher plane. This shift upward in consciousness requires people to align and attune to the Soul and the higher expressions of life on a daily basis. Otherwise people's attention will be repeatedly drawn into the world of personal drama that veils the world of the Soul and its light.

Uranus in Pisces

Uranus in Pisces represents a powerfully disruptive but liberating influence that impacts thoughts, beliefs, and spirituality of the society, and to a lesser degree the individual. This is true today, but it was also true two thousand years ago. When the faculties and capacities of the concrete mind (the logical, rational thinking capacity, and the faculty of discrimination) are minimally developed, the energies of Uranus primarily cause surprise, shock, dismay, and disruption.

As with all outer planets, Uranus's placement by sign has a similar effect upon a generation of people, since it takes Uranus seven years to transit a sign. Everyone born three or so years before and four years after Jesus's birth also had Uranus in Pisces.

When Uranus is in Pisces, it creates cracks in the psychic structures that protect the ego, especially in the area of people's religious faith. Pisces relates specifically to processes of synthesis—the unification of what has been learned in the school of life during countless lifetimes as a planet transits through the signs from Aries to Pisces. All of the new thoughts, beliefs, and ideas that have arisen within the minds of people as a result of Uranus's transit through the preceding eleven signs of the zodiac are synthesized into a new way of life when it is placed in Pisces. These changes relate to the changes in thought that have taken place during one's life as well as over the course of a number of lifetimes, especially in relation to people's faith.

Uranus in Pisces represents a period of synthesis in which the essence of all thought that liberates the consciousness from the influence of the subtle matter forces of the three planes of earth is extracted from the thread of the personality. This thread of the personality connects the various personalities to the Soul. The sign Pisces relates to the processes that synthesize the growth in consciousness that has taken place over the course of lifetimes in terms of a particular dynamic of the psyche. Symbolically, this Piscean synthesis is an alchemical process whereby the good of the personality is transformed into the gold of the real self.

At the time of Jesus, the synthesizing processes impacting mankind related specifically to changes in people's thoughts and beliefs caused by a diminishing of the Age of Aries ascendancy of the Age of Pisces.

Uranus's placement in Pisces two thousand years ago created a spiritual restlessness and nagging sense of divine discontent. People felt this restlessness even though they were unable to respond consciously or constructively to the energies of Uranus. In Judea, Uranus in Pisces intensified the desire for a Messiah. After centuries of foreign occupation and oppression, many of Jesus's peers ardently sought someone to liberate them. Exactly what people sought freedom from, however, depended on their point of evolvement and their ray makeup.

Those on the path use the liberating power that Uranus expresses to free themselves from the forces of the three matter planes. They seek spiritual liberation. Uranus represents a force that stimulates the mind in ways that liberate the consciousness from mental illusion and astral glamour. This occurs as people unfold the three aspects of the higher mind.

Two thousand years ago as Uranus transited Pisces, the discontent it aroused caused some people to rebel against the Roman authority. In others, it stimulated a vague yearning for a personal relationship with the Father. This was a new development in the West and in Judea in particular, since Yahweh moved through the Tribe Israel, not through the individual.

The individualization of the self that Uranus offers represents an important step forward in terms of the evolution of consciousness. Uranus is the agent that helps individualize the personal self and consciousness as people unfold and demonstrate an ability to think for themselves. People are individuated as they register and consciously respond to the Uranian principle of freedom.

A thread that runs through the teachings of Jesus is this all-important thread of individuality. (Unfortunately, it took another seventeen centuries before mankind collectively started to respond to this principle.) As a result of this liberating influence of Uranus, the thoughts, ideas, and beliefs of people started to separate out from those of the masses.

Two thousand years ago, the principle of Pisces was just starting to impact mankind. The new Piscean archetype beginning to dawn upon mankind represented a spiritual freedom from the past. The good of the past continues on from Age to Age, but the obsolete must be eliminated in order for that which is new to have the opportunity to unfold and be advanced.

The Piscean Archetype established at that time involved transitioning from the collective consciousness of the group (tribe, ethnic group, etc.) to that of the individual. Tribal consciousness is a group consciousness of the personality that has operated at the astral-emotional level since the middle period of Atlantean Civilization. Prior to the Age of Pisces, the consciousness of the Judean people was tribal in nature.

There are many unique magnetic qualities and principles that affect human consciousness throughout the approximately 2,160 years of an Age. Over the course of an Age, people bring forth new aspirations, ideals, and systems of thought as a result the electromagnetic influences of a new Age.

The magnetic influence of the Piscean Age started to impact the collective unconscious of mankind several centuries prior to the birth of Jesus. By the time the book of Matthew was written (around 85 CE), the magnetic influence of Aries had completely dissipated.

In summary, the seed ideas of the Age of Pisces that were deposited in the upper mental plane over the course of the Age relate to the unfoldment of the principle of Pisces. New types of spiritual aspirations and devotion, ideas, thoughts, and beliefs arose as people have slowly unfolded this principle. The changes in mind and consciousness that the energies of the new Piscean Age has brought forth involves the unfoldment of the loving heart, compassion, mercy, forgiveness, joy, and selflessness. Specifically, the Age of Pisces related to the creation of different spiritual disciplines, techniques, and methodologies for approaching the Divine than were present in the Age of Aries. Over the 2,160 years of the Age of Pisces, the collective minds of humanity have brought forth a multitude of ways to express ray six (dedication and devotion to an ideal).

By the time of His ministry, Jesus was personally responding to His intuition more than He was responding to the concrete mind. As a result, thoughts and ideas that related to this new Piscean Archetype poured into His consciousness directly from His intuitional mind and the planes of light.

The truth of the buddhic-intuitional plane always conflicts with the personally sanctioned social and religious laws and rules mankind has developed and adopted. By definition, buddhic-plane truth embodies the seed ideas and ideals that move people forward along the path. As a result, they tend to clash with the established beliefs, ideas, and religious laws of the past.

Uranus in Pisces in Jesus's chart served two main purposes. First, the close conjunction of Uranus to both the Sun and Mercury enabled Jesus to intuit the principles and teachings of the Age of Pisces and serve as the voice for the Piscean Age. Second, this combination of energies helped Jesus formulate His ongoing spiritual realizations and revelations into a new Piscean system of thought and belief.

Eventually, Jesus became so identified with this new Piscean archetype that there wasn't any separation between Him and the archetype. Soon after His personality light was merged into His soul light, He came to embody the Piscean principle and archetype. The conjunctions that Uranus formed, along with Uranus's trine to Neptune, are strong indicators that Jesus was to serve as the messenger for the dawning Piscean Age.

Prior to Jesus, there wasn't a mystical, loving approach to the Divine in the West. Nor did people have the capacity to experience a mystical oneness with God. The new Piscean paradigm that Jesus anchored on earth centered around one of the most profound experiences any initiate can have: God is love. It's not that God is the ultimate loving being of the universe. God is love. Such a realization can only be experienced when the consciousness becomes attuned to the essential love of the Soul and responsive to the pure love-wisdom of the buddhic-intuitional plane. Prior to this time, people may believe a union with the Divine is attainable, but it isn't until they experience this sense of being mystically connected to the Divine.

Before Jesus's birth, the Lord of Israel was a deity of law and power. Though a few people personally loved their Lord, Yahweh was not someone with whom people could easily establish a relationship. In fact, the light of the personal consciousness of all but a few individuals was too minute to even sense the presence of the Divine, let alone experience at-one-ment with the Divine.

Having realized that the nature of God is love, Jesus was able to anchor the principle of love in the planetary throat center of earth—the collective minds of humanity. With this realization, Jesus became so personally devoted to and identified with the loving Father that He was transformed into the Son of God. This is a state of mind that people can achieve. It is not a state granted to one person and withheld from others.

Through the exceedingly close relationship He established with the Father, Jesus was able to share His vision of the kingdom of heaven with others, as well as display the works of the Father. By way of this new Piscean Archetype, Jesus presented mankind with a new approach to God—the way of the heart—and offered mankind a new understanding of life's purpose. This was very unsettling to the established order of Judea and Rome.

Due to Uranus's close conjunction to the Sun and Mercury in Jesus's chart, along with the prominent position it had in the epic grand trine and kite configuration, there is no doubt that the religious and secular authority figures saw Jesus as a rebel and agitator who, in their minds, threatened the safety and security of the state and the rule of law. Historically, people with a prominent Uranus have always been looked at as rebels and revolutionaries.

All revolutionaries disrupt and disturb the social order, some for good and others for ill. What made Jesus especially dangerous to the authorities of Judea was that He had a following. Many people accepted His teachings and followed Him from community to community. Many joined Him at Jerusalem for the Jewish Holy Days.

Insurrection was something the Jewish Court (the Sanhedrin) was always concerned about, especially when the population of the city swelled during the Jewish Holy Days. Even though Jesus didn't encourage people to take action against the Sanhedrin or against

Rome, He was looked at as an insurrectionist. The teachings of Jesus were controversial and disruptive in relation to the the traditions of Judea.

In Jesus's mind, the vibrant spirituality of Israel was lost and needed to be restored. But to the authorities of Judah, His teachings only disrupted the status quo and violated the rule of law. Although Jesus didn't realize it at the time, He represented a new day, a new way of life, a new vision, and a new approach to the Divine. This new approach called for preparing oneself for eternal life. This was far different from the focus of Mosaic Law and the rules that governed social behavior and actions of Judeans.

On the personal level, this placement of Uranus in the chart of Jesus and its planetary aspects helped free Jesus from all conditioning patterns (both personal and cultural), as well as free Him from the usual trappings of the ego. By way of the influx of energies represented by the astrological factors of His chart, Jesus was liberated from the constraints that personal feelings, thoughts, and structures impose upon people and their lives.

Without the influx of the energies of Uranus, Jesus would not have been free emotionally, intellectually, or spiritually in the way He needed to be in order to release the past and embrace the new Piscean archetype of loving devotion. Because of Jesus's attunement to His manasic center and its natural resonance with Uranian energies, Jesus was often stimulated by the spiritually transforming impressions of the higher worlds, even at a young age. Later, as He developed the abstract mind and gained an understanding of the universal language of symbolism, Jesus was able to comprehend that which He intuited, and was able to translate His intuitions into words.

Jesus's belief that people could be perfect was unique. So was His idea that people could individually develop a personal relationship with the Divine. In Judaism, obedience to the Mosaic Law, rules, and the dietary and behavioral regulations was rewarded on earth, not in some heavenly realm after death.

Uranus represents a specific form of personal illumination that begins when the energies of the intelligence tier of petals stream into the upper centers. This activity stimulates mental creativity. Uranian energies always correspond to the forces that break through the walls of Saturn—the boundaries and barriers that restrict the mind to the past. The many ideas that have enlightened mankind throughout history and the inventions and discoveries that have improved people's lives are the children of a Uranian-stimulated mind.

Uranus is forever trying to shatter, revolutionize, and liberate the consciousness from the influences of obsolete emotional and mental patterns. As this freeing of the self-consciousness takes place, people begin to experience significant changes in their lives (depending on the area of life that is impacted by Uranus). Eventually, Uranus leads people to a realization of their own divine nature, untainted by personal conditioning.

Within the consciousness of mankind, there are a lot of areas of thought so rigid and dense that people refuse to seek the greater knowledge and understanding that Uranus offers. When this is the case, the changes in thought and belief that Uranus offers can affect people only by way of the changes taking place in the society and culture.

Usually the younger generation is more open to the new ideas and understanding that Uranus brings forth. Young people have yet to solidify the dense saturnine patterns and structures within the psyche that interfere with people's ability to accept new ideas and concepts. Prior to transiting Saturn's first return to its natal position in the birth chart (around 29 years of age), the concretizing factor of Saturn has yet to fully ensconce the consciousness within the crystallized boundaries of the psyche. Allegorically, until people reach this age, the protective walls of the ego are porous. The older generation usually dies out before a major new archetype or system of thought and belief is widely accepted.

More than any other influence, Uranus in Pisces freed Jesus from His past, personally, socially, and religiously, and revealed the nature of life both in the world of ideas and in the buddhic realm[65] of pure love-wisdom. By way of this liberating Uranian light, Jesus was able to hold Himself in the kingdom.

Uranus in the Second House

The second house may seem like an unusual placement for Uranus given the nature of Jesus's mission, but the deeper meanings and significances of the second house reveal the significance of this placement.

Throughout history, people have used the ray-five magnetized energies of Venus (ruler of Taurus) in a way that attaches their unfolding atoms of self-consciousness to the things of earth. This provides us with a clue to the deeper meanings of the second house. The second house relates to that which people value (love).

At the stage of personal development, the type of aspects formed to second-house planets indicate the ease or difficulty people have satisfying their survival needs and personal desires. For those on the path, however, the astrological factors associated with the second house relate to people's ability to actualize their spiritual values and aspirations.

Since an analysis of a chart must take into account the point of evolvement a person has attained, what people value reflects their point of evolvement and how they identify their selfhood. People's identity changes as they progress; so do their values. Initially, people's

---

[65] The buddhic-intuitional plane is the province of Neptune, not Uranus, but Uranus helps opens the inner mind's eye that sees into the higher planes of light.

identity and what they value are intertwined with the physical body and their personal emotions, desires, and needs, especially in relation to their survival, propagation, and security.

For those on the path, the astrological factors in relationship to the second house still relate to the resources they think they need, but what disciples value has shifted from possessing the things of earth to possessing the faculties and capacities needed to actualize their spiritual ideals.

A review of the passages of the three synoptic Gospels indicates that Jesus was not interested in the material things of life; He valued the things of God. Even during His early years, Jesus didn't express an interest in material things. The otherworldly influences of Pisces (which are antithetical to the material world) pulled Him away from such considerations.

The mysterious etheric planet, Vulcan, the builder, establishes the issues of the second house at the level of Soul. Here, Vulcan transmits ray one in its aspect of life-force, and expresses the creative purpose of the Solar Logos.

By way of the energies of Vulcan, initiates are impacted with the light of wisdom, which leads the initiate into a state of enlightenment. Enlightenment is possible only when the living life of the atmic center enters the etheric body at the first sub-plane level via the crown center and flows unimpeded onto the reservoir of kundalini at the basic center.

With the Sun, Mercury, and Uranus conjunct Vulcan in Jesus's chart, the empowering light of Vulcan poured directly onto the mind of Jesus once He had attained the transfiguration initiation (the third initiation). This is one of several indicators that suggest the influence of the will-purpose of the Divine was prominent in Jesus's life.

Divine will via Pluto (as the ruler of Pisces) and Vulcan (as the ruler of Taurus at the Soul level) enabled Jesus to take the last step upon the path of the heart and then transition onto the path of power and divine purpose—the path of the magi or white magicians.

According to the ancient wisdom archives, the Christ will return on the second sub-ray aspect of ray one (the builder) which Vulcan transmits. This will enable Him to use the potent creator quality of ray one to build the kingdom of heaven on earth.

Jesus started to exercise this second sub-aspect of ray one once He embodied pure love-wisdom and attained Christ consciousness, but He did not express it until His Resurrection. On the path of power, the laws that govern and regulate the substances of the three planes of earth are known and used to control the matter forces in accordance with the divine will and purpose. Initiates can safely and appropriately use the power of life, will, and purpose only when they are governed by divine intelligence, love, and will.

Chapter 22

Aspects to Uranus

Uranus opposite Pluto (2 degrees 14 minutes)

Oppositions in a birth chart generate conflict and struggle, especially when the opposition is being transited. The objective behind an opposition is to relate the two psychic dynamics that the planets opposing each other represent. Only by establishing a relationship between the opposing planets can their ray-magnetized energies begin to blend with each other. With the resolution of each duality, the dynamics of the psyche represented by the planets are more integrated and unified.

By relating the two dynamics of the psyche and resolving the apparent conflict between them, a greater more inclusive understanding is brought forth, one that lends itself to the eventual union of the two dynamics at some level. This is not as easy as it sounds since people's ability to attain successively higher states of mind is always impeded by their established patterns of actions, feelings, and thoughts.

Most people have yet to unfold the psychic dynamics that the outer planets represent. To them, the forces of the outer planets are outside of their consciousness. They are often societal forces, yet people react to the changes taking place in the society (due to the influences of the outer planets) in a way that reflects how the outer planets are impacting them by sign and house placement and the aspects formed to their natal planets or angles.

Although Uranus opposite Pluto had a tremendous impact upon Jesus and His life, the outer planets usually impact people collectively as a group. In other words, people primarily react to the changes the outer planets precipitate in the society, the ethnic group, the nation, and culture.

People's inability to consciously register the high-frequency energies of the outer planets is due to the limited light of mind that exists at the personal level. Historically, only the collective light of mind of human beings registered the high-frequency energies of the outer planets. The purpose of the outer planetary energies is to accelerate growth and transformation of the collective consciousness of the planetary center called humanity. As people become more interested in the well-being of humanity, the effects the outer planets have on society begin to affect them and their individual progression.

Though people were unable to personally relate to the high-frequency energies of Uranus and Pluto two thousand years ago, many of them personally experienced the disruptive and unsettling effects this opposition generated. For all but a few people, the tension this opposition precipitated created situations and conditions in society that were not to their liking. For example, many of the Judeans blamed Rome and its occupation of Judea for their suffering, yet the forces generated by this opposition were the cause behind so many of the unsettling disruptions people felt in Judea two thousand years ago.

Ray seven Uranus and ray one Pluto came into an exact opposition fifteen times between 5 BCE and 2 CE. At no other time between 600 BCE and 2400 CE do these two planets form an exact opposition as many times. Due to the amount of time that Uranus and Pluto were in opposition to each other, a whole generation born around the time of Jesus was impacted by the energies of this opposition throughout their lives. Since this aspect was within the orb of an opposition for more than ten years, many of Jesus's peers were impacted by the tension this opposition generated.

The magnetism of this opposition in the aura of so many Judeans two thousand years ago heightened the fervor in Judea for a Messiah. Though most Judeans sought a Messiah to free them from foreign occupation, many responded to Jesus's teachings and considered Him to be the Messiah. The Sanhedrin chose to look elsewhere for the Messiah.

When the outer planets impact the personal planets of a birth chart, the individual is impacted by the changes and disruptions that the outer planetary transits are precipitating within mankind as a group. When sufficiently advanced, the individual can serve as the agent who lends his or her voice to the changes that the outer planets are precipitating within the collective minds of humanity.

How people reacted two thousand years ago to the tension this opposition generated depended on their point of evolvement and which personal planets formed an aspect to the opposition. For most people, the energy generated by this Uranus-Pluto opposition merely stimulated their lower instinctual patterns of behavior and intensified their fears and defensiveness. For others, it activated a drive for power as a result of the deep-seated feelings of powerlessness that this opposition often confers.

The combination of Uranus and Pluto is the most intense and disruptive combination of energies to impact the government and society. (Uranus square Pluto is even more disruptive than the opposition.) Aspects formed between Uranus and Pluto have an especially powerful effect on the way people view the society and its traditions and institutions. The authority figures of all governments and institutions express ray one power to one degree or another, but when Uranus and Pluto form a hard aspect to each other and to the personal planets in the chart of an authority figure, there is a tendency to be manipulative, controlling, and authoritarian. A hard aspect of Uranus to Pluto in the charts of non-authority figures, on the other hand, often expresses as a tendency to vilify, resist, and rebel against authority figures.

People with a hard aspect of Uranus to Pluto often repudiate authority figures and government. Frequently they reject the authority that their rulers exercise. This repudiation of authority figures is strongest when Uranus and Pluto form a square aspect to each other, but it is also strong when these two planets oppose each other. The combination of the energies of Uranus and Pluto often leads to sudden unsettling, even explosive, acts of rebellion.

This is not a short-term problem, since people unfold patterns of thought and behavior during a hard transit that can affect their lives long after a transit is over. This is especially a problem for the society and government when a hard aspect between Uranus and Pluto are involved, since a large number of people tend to create similar patterns of thought and behavior in relation to the government during a transit.

Due to the fifteen exact oppositions Uranus and Pluto formed to each other before and after the time of Jesus's birth, this particular Uranus-Pluto opposition was an exceedingly disruptive opposition. This uncharacteristically long series of oppositions only intensified the tension between the waning Age of Aries and the dawning Age of Pisces.

To understand the nature of this disruption, it helps to understand the effects that Pluto has on mankind. Pluto is associated with death, endings, transmutation, and transformation. It symbolically represents cataclysmic events that are triggered by a sudden, powerful release of energy that was once contained. For this reason, Pluto is symbolically associated with volcanic eruptions, earthquakes, and the atomic bomb, as well as with intense emotional outbursts and violence.

The destroyer sub-aspect of Pluto impacts the world of nature, society, and the individual in rather unpleasant ways. When Pluto removes something from people's lives, it usually means that it has outlived its purpose and usefulness as currently constituted. Pluto never ends life. It touches not the unfolding spirit; rather, the death and endings pertain to the destruction of a structure or form through which the indwelling life expresses. The destruction of old, obsolete forms is necessary so better, more expansive forms can be created through which new lessons can be learned. During the stage of personal development, these containment force fields that Uranus and Pluto disrupt constitute the structures of the not-self.

This concept of containment force fields includes the physical body as well as different structures of the threefold personal consciousness. Different types of structures and forms serve as the containment fields through which people express themselves and grow as a result of their life lessons. Once the faculty, capacity, or skill that the containment field helps bring forth has been developed and the evolutionary lessons learned, a particular containment field is no longer needed. When this is the case, the containment field (relationships, jobs, beliefs, desires, etc.) becomes too restrictive and needs to be eliminated so a better structure—one that offers people new lessons and greater understanding—can be developed.

Two thousand years ago, the unsettling disruptions in the society that the fifteen oppositions of Uranus to Pluto precipitated helped to fuel the simmering conflict that was building between the dawning Age of Pisces and the Age of Aries.

At the time Jesus was born, only a few decades remained before the ray one, ray seven magnetism of the Age of Aries had completely dissipated and the ray two, ray six magnetism of the Age of Pisces had reached its full power. Although rays one and seven were the two dominant rays of manifestation during the two thousand years of Aries, ray two and ray six were the dominant underlying magnetic influences impacting mankind when Jesus was born.

Whenever one Age and its rays of manifestation are waning and a new Age and its rays start to impact the minds of mankind, tremendous stress arises within the society. This transition generates conflicts within society between the old and new ways of life. Every transition period results in a clash between those who identify with the ways of the past and those who respond to the incoming rays and energies. This, in turn, places tremendous stress upon the social, political, and religious institutions of the society. The political environment during Jesus's life was particularly tense and stressful.

Most of the institutions of His day, as well as the prevailing mind-set of most of the Judeans, were reflective of the Age of Aries. However, the rays of manifestation that supported the Age of Aries and its institutions had almost completely withdrawn. Although the new rays of manifestation pouring onto the earth were supportive of the Piscean Age and the teachings of Jesus, the collective society and its institutions resisted this transition into the new Age. For this reason, many of the people who followed Jesus in Judea and Galilee were women, outcasts, slaves, and the downtrodden.[66]

The shift from one Age to the next Age is often slow and socially troublesome, since the religious, cultural, social, and governmental institutions and structures are representative of the outgoing Age even though the planetary magnetism no longer supports them.

The social institutions and structures of the old Age are a product of mankind's response to the rays and qualities that built the civilizations of the old Age, while the institutions of

---

[66] Not only will women be the first to respond to the incoming Age of Aquarius, they are likely to lead humanity into the Aquarian Age. The Aquarian Age is an Age of the love-filled path of the mind, which men more than women are likely to resist and fight against.

the new Age have yet to be established. As ideas and concepts come forth during the early days of a new Age, the authorities and adherents of the old ways usually reject and ardently resist the changes and new ideas, and insist upon maintaining the old approach. Religious and political authority figures often exhibit the greatest resistance to the evolutionary changes taking place.

As part of the Uranus-Pluto cycle that began in Gemini, this opposition of Uranus to Pluto found in Jesus's chart occurred at the same time that the new impulse of love-wisdom from the universal mind (via the Uranus-Neptune cycle) was beginning to impact people at a deep level.

As the ray two energies streaming through Pluto in Virgo and Uranus in Pisces intensified in Jesus's life, mankind approached the most important event to impact the human race since Atlantean days: mankind collectively mounted the mutable cross. The gateway that leads onto the path of spiritual probation was opened to all seekers of truth at that time. On the path of probation, the rays of the four signs of the mutable cross (Gemini, Virgo, Sagittarius, and Pisces) are the most influential rays in relation to spiritual growth.

With Uranus placed in the synthesizing ray two, ray six sign of Pisces and Pluto in the ray two sign of Virgo, this opposition of Uranus and Pluto in Jesus's chart represented the vertical bar of the mutable cross in terms of the planetary service Jesus was to engage in on behalf of mankind. Pluto's opposition to the Sun in Jesus's chart resulted in His demonstration of the crucifixion of the integrated personality. This is something that all people must experience in one form or another upon the mutable cross—the sacrifice of the not-self to the essential love of the Soul.

On the mutable cross, the Mother Principle (Virgo) and the Father Principle (Pisces) are related to each other. In Jesus's life, relating these two principles to each other occurred as a result of relating ray seven Uranus to ray one Pluto, so they could work together.

Over time, the principles of Uranus and Pluto were related to each other within the consciousness of Jesus and eventually unified as a result of the blending activities of ray two Virgo and ray two, ray six Pisces. The blending of the two rays and two principles of an opposition always takes place at the midpoint between the two signs once the higher self is brought forth.

Due to the aspects formed between the outer planets and personal planets in Jesus's chart, their rays blended in a way that awakened the principles of Uranus and Pluto within the mind and consciousness of Jesus. This awakening occurred as this opposition was transited during His life. Once related to each other, the psychic dynamics that Uranus and Pluto represent started to work well together to further develop the mind of the higher self. This activity resulted in a synthesis of their principles and rays within the mind and consciousness of Jesus.

Although the interplay and exchange of all planetary and stellar energies relate to the evolution of consciousness, the energies generated by this opposition of Uranus in Pisces to Pluto in Virgo two thousand years ago opened the door for mankind to mount the mutable cross. This opened a portal within the world of the Soul to both the Mother Principle and the Father Principle. Through this portal, a sense of the duality of the cosmic Mother and the cosmic Father started to impact the Souls of humanity.

At the level of the Soul, the Pisces-Virgo opposition represents the cosmic duality of the Mother Principle and the Father Principle. Until there is a greater attunement between the personal consciousness and the Soul, however, mankind will continue to struggle with these two principles and distort their significance at the personal level.

During the Age of Aries, the Father Principle was dominant, as mankind universally expressed the energies of the personality ruler of Aries, Mars, rather than Mercury, the Soul-centered ruler of Aries. This resulted in almost total domination of men in the societies of the world. This situation was fueled by the dominating desire-in-action dynamic of Mars.

Men's domination in the cultures of the world was further strengthened by the fact that ray one and ray seven were the underlying rays of manifestation that expressed during the Age of Aries. This resulted in the establishment of a world view where men and their personal will, personal control, and hegemony over others resulted in the degradation and oppression of women.

During the stage when the threefold personal consciousness is being developed, the Mother Principle is associated with matter and represented by the sign Virgo, whereas the Father Principle is associated with spirit and represented by Pisces. The difference in terms of these two principles is one of different modes of operation, not one of gender. However, people consider them in terms of gender due to an identification of their selfhood with the physical body.

Such gender differences do not exist in the formless planes of light. There, the masters are balanced in terms of their positive-negative polarities and in relation to the active-reflective dynamics of conscious life. All masters can demonstrate both polarities and genders, for the reflective, receptive, attractive, and unifying qualities of the negative mother polarity and the capacity to act, repulse, and initiate activity that the positive father polarity stimulates are needed in the planes of light.

The principle of the Mother and the principle of Father have yet to be anchored within the personal mind in a healthy, positive way, let alone be unified. Historically, the western world has used the lower ray six energies of Mars in both the Age of Aries and the Age of

Pisces to repudiate and denigrate the Mother Principle, while strengthening the desire nature of the personal self.

The evolution of human consciousness depends on the magnetic interaction between the forces of the negative polarity (Mother Principle) and those of the positive polarity (Father Principle). This is necessary during incarnation in order for the blending and unification of different types and qualities of energies to occur. There is no preference for one polarity over the other except at the level of personal consciousness. The factor of separatism has skewed people's understanding and nullified the fact that the positive and negative polarities are equal and interactive parts of a whole.

Mankind often identifies the Mother Principle with nature (and, therefore, with the physical body), but has difficulty relating to the underlying principle of the Mother. When the clash between the Mother and Father Principles is at its greatest point of degradation, the physical body and its nature are vilified and thought of as being sinful. On the spiritual path, the personality and the natural drives and appetites of the physical body and personal consciousness are transcended. They are not to be vilified or repressed.

The form of Christianity institutionalized over the centuries had great difficulty integrating the Mother Principle with the Father Principle. The elevation of Mary to the status of Mother of God was an attempt by the church to acknowledge the role that the Divine Mother plays in terms of the spiritualization of mankind. However, she wasn't given a position co-equal to the Father and the Son.

The child of the union of the Mother Principle and the Father Principle is the Son, the principle of the Christ, the second aspect of the Divine. In relation to the evolution of human consciousness, the union of the Mother Principle and the Father Principle must be consummated in the three planes of matter in order to bring forth the Christ spirit. This is the modus operandi during this Second Solar System.

The Divine Mother is allegorically impregnated by the Divine Father and brings forth the Son, the child of love. Both the symbol of Mother as matter and the fecund mother who nurtures the Christ child in the womb of matter are both represented by Virgo, while Pisces represents the impregnating Father Spirit. Each time these two principles are unified, a greater expression of the dynamic of the Son (love) is brought forth.

As the principle of the Christ unfolds within human consciousness, the second aspect of the Divine (love-wisdom) is brought forth. The act of unfolding, developing, and mastering the vibratory quality of pure love-wisdom is the universal objective and goal established for the entire Second Solar System, not just the earth.

The Christ child born out of the love of the Father (spirit) for the Mother (matter) grows and slowly matures as people tread the spiritual path. The maturing of the Christ takes place in the womb of the three matter planes as the apparent differences between the integrated personality and the higher self are resolved and the two become one. The mature Christ corresponds to the unfoldment and development of pure reasoning and love-wisdom in relation to the heart center of the Triad.

As with all six oppositions of the zodiac (Aries-Libra, Taurus-Scorpio, Gemini-Sagittarius, Cancer-Capricorn, Leo-Aquarius, Virgo-Pisces), the struggle between two signs that are opposite each other concludes only when people are able to shift the consciousness away from the planetary forces of the outer signs of the chart that oppose each other and walk the middle path between the pair of opposites. The door to the path of the Soul is the midpoint between the six oppositions of the signs of the zodiac—the intersecting point of the three crosses—that leads inward. In terms of the Virgo-Pisces opposition, the midpoint between them relates specifically to the unfoldment of the principle of the Christ at the level of the Soul, since both Pisces and Virgo are the vehicles of ray two energies.

Two thousand years ago, this opposition of Uranus in Pisces to Pluto in Virgo generated the dynamism that propelled Jesus forward in His life through a series of very important transformations. Such transformations occurred as Jesus responded constructively to the conflicts this opposition precipitated, first within Himself and then in terms of His relationships with others. Responding constructively to these conflicts means Jesus responded to them as a Soul, not as the personal self. (Usually people respond to such oppositions from the level of the personal self. When this is the case, people either act as the aggressor or are victimized by the conflicts and struggles that hard aspects precipitate.)

Initially, in the life of Jesus, this opposition of Uranus and Pluto expressed as a clash of wills. By way of its vibratory effect, this Uranus-Pluto dynamic precipitated conflicts in Jesus's life that represented a clash within His psyche between His personal will and the will of His Soul. This personal conflict continued until that moment when Jesus threw all of His weight behind the Angel of the Presence and aligned fully with the will of God (the will of the Soul).

A number of astrological factors indicate that when Jesus incarnated He was at the stage in which His personal will and the will of the Soul needed to be related to each other in one final way before His personal will could be fully sacrificed to the will of the Soul—the will of God. The will of the Soul is always the last aspect of the higher self to unfold. Before Jesus could serve as the messenger and teacher of the new Piscean Age, He needed to work through and resolve the differences between His personal will and the will of the Soul at the mental level. Only then could He work through the planetary dialectic between the Age of Aries and the Age of Pisces in terms of His own feelings, thoughts, beliefs, and ideas.

It wasn't as easy for Jesus to unify the personal will and the will of the Soul as you would think. Jesus could have rejected the ray one power of the will that Pluto transmitted, or thought of it as the influence of Satan. If He had, Jesus would have battled Satan throughout His life and failed to relate and subsequently merge His personal will into the will of the Soul. A willingness to accept the changes that Pluto brought forth in His life was necessary before Jesus could serve as the voice for the dawning Age of Pisces.

Astrologically, Jesus was overwhelmingly influenced by the energies magnetized by rays two and six throughout His life, not by ray one will. In addition, His Soul was on ray six, His Monad was on ray two, and His astral body was either on ray two or ray six (most likely ray two). In recent lifetimes, His spiritual work involved uplifting His consciousness in terms of the love aspect of personal consciousness.

Keep in mind that the social-religious conditioning of ancient Judaism never looked at this ray one aspect of will in relation to the individual, since Judeans were tribal in consciousness. The Lord God of Judaism expressed Himself through the people of Israel, not through the individual. As a society, the will aspect of the Divine related to God Transcendent who Judeans worshiped in the Temple. Thus, the will of the Father was outside of and transcendent to the consciousness of Jesus—at least initially.

This ray seven Uranus opposition to ray one Pluto transformed Jesus's life from one of relative ease (given the sixteen trines) into an exceptionally dynamic life. How Jesus chose to address the effects of this Uranus-Pluto opposition in His life determined whether or not He would serve as the voice for the changes taking place within the consciousness of mankind as cosmic ray two (love-wisdom) was starting to impact humanity during the early days of Pisces. First, He needed to experience these profound changes within His own consciousness.

During the early years of His life, Jesus successfully related and then transferred His consciousness from the lower centers (basic, sacral, and solar plexus centers) into the upper centers (heart, throat, and crown centers). This was possible due to the rays that the planets and signs transmit that were involved in the oppositions Pluto formed.

Pluto in Virgo opposite Uranus, the Sun, and Mercury in Pisces first related the consciousness in respect to lower etheric centers to the consciousness of their corresponding upper centers. The solar plexus center was related to the heart center. The sacral center was related to the throat center. The ajna was related to the centers along the spine, and eventually the basic center was related to the crown center. Jesus's chart indicates that all seven major etheric centers were related to each other because of Pluto's opposition to His stellium of planets in Pisces.

Transference of the atoms of self-consciousness from the lower to the upper centers is needed in order to magnetize the upper centers, unfold the inner petals of the upper centers, and magnetically draw the energies from the respective tiers of petals into the upper etheric centers. This activity of relating the lower centers to the upper centers and transferring the consciousness from the lower personal world into the world of the Soul (via the upper centers) was almost complete prior to His incarnation. The atoms of self-consciousness, however, had yet to be fully transferred from the basic center to the crown center.

This transference of the atoms of self-consciousness to the upper centers and sacrificing the personal will to the will of the Soul was preliminary to becoming the instrument of the will of God and serving as the Piscean messenger. This was no easy task since Jesus's nature and disposition was along the ray two, ray four, and ray six line, not the ray one, ray three, ray five, ray seven line. If ray one Pluto hadn't been conditioned with Virgo and acted as the focalizing lens for the energies of the epic grand trine, it would have been difficult for Jesus to personally relate to the will aspect of the Soul. It was Virgo's ray two conditioning of Pluto and the ray two and ray six conditioning of His Sun and planets in Pisces that enabled Jesus to align to the will of the Soul and yet be attuned to the nature of God in its second divine aspect.

Slowly, the will of the Soul was brought forth as the energies from the sacrifice (will) tier of petals poured through His crown center. When the will of the Soul unfolds, it strengthens people's resolve to sacrifice all attachments to the things of earth and move more fully in consciousness into the world of the Soul. As all three sub-qualities of the sacrifice tier of petals impacted His consciousness, the sacrificing will of the higher self was greatly strengthened.

Due to this opposition of Pluto, Jesus experienced a number of sudden transformations that resulted in the complete elimination of the not-self and His identification with the things of earth. The consequence of this activity was that the essential love of the Soul became even more pronounced.

The task of unifying the personal will with the will of the Soul was completed at the third initiation. The pathway Jesus walked to blend these two expressions of the will and attain the third initiation was this opposition of ray seven Uranus in Pisces to ray one Pluto in Virgo. This was not possible, however, until Jesus first realized that God is love—that love is the essential nature of God.

For Jesus, the third initiation was achieved as a result of the ray two and ray six energies of Neptune and Pisces (vis à vis the epic grand trine) and the opposition of Pluto to the stellium of planets conditioned by ray two and ray six Pisces. Until the third initiation, people are not capable of experiencing God deep within them. Instead, the Divine is perceived as being outside of oneself and transcendent.

By way of the energies and qualities this opposition generated, the will of the Soul was anchored in Jesus's life and expressed through His mind and consciousness. The dynamism generated by the opposition of ray seven Uranus in Pisces to ray one Pluto in Virgo precipitated the type of experiences necessary and the realizations needed in order for Jesus to blend the will of the personality with the will of the Soul and attain the third initiation. This took place once He was fully transformed by the Soul, as the energies radiating from the sacrifice tier of petals streamed into His crown center. In consciousness, He responded to this energy by unfolding the sacrificing willpower of the higher mind and transcending the threefold personality. This led to a complete metamorphosis that opened the doorway within His mind to the Age of Pisces.

The opposition of the sign Virgo to Pisces represents one of the two bars of the mutable cross, especially in relation to the spiritualization of mankind as a whole. The opposition of ray seven Uranus in Pisces to ray one Pluto in Virgo, on the other hand, represents the spine of the etheric body. Specifically, the Uranus-Pluto opposition represents the central channel of the kundalini—the sushumna. Unlike the other two channels, the kundalini of the sushumna channel rises directly from the ray seven basic center to the ray one crown center of advanced disciples.

Throughout people's lives, the ray one, ray two, and ray three energies move from the Monad through the three channels of the kundalini (via the Triad and Soul) onto the reservoir of kundalini fire at the base of the etheric spine. The kundalini fire is the fiery life of the divine presence anchored in the etheric form of mankind. During the evolution of consciousness, this threefold impulse of life rises up the three channels and awakens people in consciousness to successively higher states of mind and consciousness. The rising of the kundalini up the sushumna to the crown center where the physical permanent atom and principle resides is achieved at the third initiation. Only then is the basic center linked in consciousness with the crown center, and God is anchored in the consciousness that expresses through these forms of earth.

During the stage of development of the personal consciousness, Uranus is often placed at the crown center, since it stimulates the mind, while Pluto is often placed at the basic center, the dark underworld. This placement is understandable, since the energy of the intelligence tier of petals (which Uranus relates to) readily streams onto the mind of all thinking people. When the crown center is unopened to the energies of the sacrifice tier of petals, the energies of Pluto stimulate the lower instinctual-emotional patterns of behavior. No energy pierces the deep levels of the unconscious like the ray one energies of Pluto.

Earlier, during the stage of personal development, the basic center is magnetized receptive toward ray four, which results in physical conflict and altercations (but not harmony through conflict). It is due to the ray four energies expressing via the basic center that the individual enters into battle and unfolds a strong sense of self. This often involves physical-emotional battling with others.

The true battle, however, pertains to people's efforts to resolve the many forms of duality found within the threefold personal consciousness. Here, too, the clash of two psychic dynamics can result in a conflict with others due to people's tendency to project fragments of their consciousness they reject onto other people, especially when they are still developing the threefold personal consciousness.

This battling within the consciousness begins once the ajna center is magnetized receptive toward ray four energies and the basic center is magnetized receptive toward ray seven energies. At this higher stage, ray seven energies help anchor the impulses of essential life within the form. This stage relates to the blending of Soul energies with those of the integrated personality, culminating with the unification of the integrated personality and Soul. The effort to resolve the many forms of duality present in the threefold personal consciousness does not begin until the first initiation has been attained and the individual is functioning as a disciple. Thus, this placement of Uranus at the crown center and Pluto at the basic center is relatively accurate during the stage of personal development. However, such a placement is contrary to the way energies work in relation to the advanced disciple and initiate.

At the higher stages, the evolutionary impulses no longer involve resolution of the multitude of dualities found in the worlds of the threefold personal consciousness. Rather, the evolutionary directive is to anchor the impulses of life within these forms of earth via the will of the Soul. This is the opportunity that this Uranus-Pluto opposition in Jesus's chart offered Him. Uranus relates spirit to matter and matter to spirit, and in so doing, it stimulates the mind in a way that sets up a new rhythm—one that allows new ideas and thoughts to arise.

Initially, the kundalini rising up the sushumna channel of the etheric spine to the crown center opens and magnetizes the crown center receptive toward ray one. Once the kundalini fire has risen from the basic center to the crown center, the ray one energies of Pluto are able to stream directly into the crown center. Henceforth, ray one divine will, along with the ray one energies radiating from the unfolded petals of the sacrifice tier of the lotus, stream exclusively into the crown center. Then, a two-way path is created from the basic center to the crown center and from the crown center to the basic center via the sushumna. Only then is the Divine presence truly anchored in these forms. But first the energies of the sacrifice petals must stream onto the consciousness via the crown center. This is necessary for the will of the Soul to unfold within the brain consciousness. The influx of the energies emanating from the unfolded sacrifice petals of the lotus transmits the ray one qualities of the Soul in its three sub-ray qualities. This in turn brings forth the qualities of the will needed to master the personal intellect and concrete mind, and transcend the threefold personal consciousness.

When Uranus and Pluto are in a hard aspect to each other and they aspect the Sun, relating the personal will to the will of the Soul is a struggle until the crown center is magnetized receptive to ray one and the basic center is magnetized receptive to ray seven. This clears the path for people to relate and then unify these two aspects of the will.

Though Jesus had unified the integrated personality and Soul and merged them into one light at the third initiation, His refined personality was still vulnerable to the explosive release of the plutonian energies of the destroyer. This was the price Jesus paid for ensuring an exceptionally rapid pace for achieving successively higher states of mind.

Throughout Jesus's life, the points of tension this opposition generated triggered periods of intense transformation, renewal, and spiritual regeneration. However, Pluto's opposition to Uranus, the Sun, and Mercury also represented a dangerous fault line within the psyche of Jesus, where energy quickly built up and needed to be released.

This condition made Jesus vulnerable to the ruthless actions of those individuals who were willing to use the forces of the destroyer against Him. This was the situation Jesus found Himself in during His ministry even though the integrated personality was merely the instrument of His Soul and held little if any light of His selfhood. Although Pluto posed significant danger to Jesus at different points in His life, the trine of Jupiter to His Ascendant, along with the planets of the epic grand trine, protected Him up until the overpowering transits of 33 CE.

Once the third initiation was achieved, the aura of Jesus magnetically invoked the will via the Monad. Although the Monad is not involved directly with the manifest personality, once Jesus attained the third initiation, the influences of the Monad started to impact Him directly. This pulled in divine will directly from the Monad and set up the next step that was before Jesus: dedicating His life to serving the will of God. This opened a new doorway in His mind—a doorway to the Monad through which the Father spirit expressed in His life.

Although Jesus continued His progression after attaining the third initiation, as He unfolded the aspects of the Divine at the level of the Triad, the conflicts that this Uranus-Pluto opposition generated in relation to the duality between the personality and Soul were over. The opposition of Uranus and Pluto became active only in a planetary sense and to a degree in relation to the contrast between the higher self and the Monad.

The energy generated by this opposition not only provided Jesus with the willpower needed to relate and then unify the integrated personality and Soul, it also conferred an exceedingly active dynamism that expanded the inclusiveness of His love beyond the capacity of the causal body to contain it. As a result, the field of the causal body was destroyed. When this occurred, the integrity of the causal forces that had previously obstructed the influx of the will of the Monad was disrupted, resulting in the elimination of the causal body, which had enveloped the Soul for millennia. This occurred at the fourth initiation.

For Jesus, the focal point of the energies of the Monad was a point in Virgo directly opposite the Sun. As the spirit of the Monad started to impact His consciousness, God Immanent was integrated into the unified light and being of Jesus. Henceforth, God was truly within Him. God acted through His consciousness. As a result of this experience, Jesus perceived divine purpose. This eventually resulted in the complete dissipation of the Soul-infused personality. This occurred as the blazing fire of divine life and purpose poured into His mind and consciousness.

By way of Pluto's opposition to His Piscean planets, Jesus developed a successively deeper and more profound relationship with the all-powerful and potent will of the Monad. Due to the strong otherworldly influences of Pisces and Neptune, however, the relationship Jesus established with the will of the Father was not a relationship with the destroyer sub-aspect of the Divine. Rather, Jesus established a relationship with the will in its aspect of the Creator.

This builder sub-aspect of ray one relates to love-wisdom at the level of the Monad and is esoterically referred to as the will-to love and the will-to-create. A relationship with the builder sub-aspect of the Divine was possible because Jesus was able to blend ray one and ray two at the level of the Spiritual Triad.

At this stage, Jesus was no longer the personality, the son of man. Nor was He the Soul. The purified and refined personality was now the instrument through which the Son of God expressed on earth and served God and mankind. The life and conscious being of Jesus had shifted into the higher atmic plane of light at the fourth initiation, beyond the Soul.

As a fourth-degree initiate, Jesus had transmuted or transformed all vestiges of duality. The tectonic fault line within the psyche represented by Pluto's opposition to His Piscean planets now represented a pathway that directly linked the will of the Father spirit (the Monad as it expressed through a point in Virgo) directly with the Soul-infused personality instrument.

Once Jesus was able to demonstrate Christ consciousness and control all types of forces in the three planes of matter, the power of the manifest spirit of the Monad expressed through Him. Jesus was now ready to serve as the voice of the Piscean Age.

Uranus trine Neptune (2 degrees 16 minutes)

Uranus and Neptune are both transpersonal planets that have a significant effect upon the development of the higher self. This development takes place as the energies emanating from the intelligence and love petals of the lotus impact the consciousness (via the awakened heart and throat centers), greatly expanding the light of mind. Only then do the energies of Uranus and Neptune stimulate the consciousness in a way that brings forth and advances first, the third aspect of the Divine (active intelligence) and then, the second aspect of the Divine (love-wisdom) at the level of the Soul.

All types and qualities of energy seek to express via the physical plane. This transmission of essential life from the divine plane to the physical plane relates to the involutionary arc of energy, not the evolutionary arc of human consciousness.

During this Second Solar System, divine purpose is focused on the unfoldment and development of the seven sub-qualities of ray two (love-wisdom) within human consciousness. This activity is very different from the ancient First Solar System, in which inert matter was infused with the third aspect of the Divine, active intelligence. The development of active intelligence in the First Solar System brought forth the form vehicles through which love-wisdom is unfolding during this Second Solar System.

The unfoldment of the Divine within the consciousness of mankind takes place as the outer planets come into an angular relationship with each other (Uranus to Neptune, Uranus to Pluto, and Neptune to Pluto). The cycles of the outer planets from their first conjunction in Aries through their conjunctions in each of the twelve signs back to a new conjunction in Aries represent an ordered progression of the planets through the twelve signs of the zodiac.

The primary Uranus-Neptune cycle is more than 3,700 years long. It begins when Uranus and Neptune first conjunct each other in the sign Aries. Uranus and Neptune conjunct each other a total of twenty-two times through the twelve signs of the zodiac during one primary cycle of Uranus-Neptune. These twenty-two cycles of Uranus and Neptune represent one great impulse of love-wisdom in relation to the cosmic mind and heart of the Solar Logos.

By way of these outer planetary cycles, the three aspects and four attributes of the Divine are brought forth within human consciousness. People become aware of the aspects, attributes, and nature of God as divine ideas slowly arise within the human mind. When the impulses of a seed idea are registered within a mind, a sub-quality of the Divine begins to awaken within the consciousness.

At the beginning of the current 3,700-year cycle of Uranus and Neptune, a new impulse of the cosmic principle of love-wisdom arose within the cosmic mind of the Solar Logos and ushered forth as a syllable of the Word. It is this syllable that continues to generate primal thought-impulses, seed ideas. This occurred in the early years of the tenth century BCE. However, the impulses of cosmic love-wisdom did not assume a watery feeling quality and begin to impact the consciousness of mankind (via the astral body) until Uranus and Neptune formed a conjunction in Cancer. This occurred in 60 BCE.

Consciousness is not innate to the physical body like intelligence. It originates outside the three planes of earth and unfolds within the brain consciousness during this Second Solar System. The astrological sign of Cancer represents the doorway in. Through this doorway, all seed ideas must pass in order to impact the brain consciousness of mankind. Once a stepped-down potency of a seed idea impacts the brain consciousness of mankind, it gives rise to atoms of self-consciousness. In this way, new ideals, aspirations, thoughts, and beliefs arise within the brain consciousness. Thus, the sign Cancer is the portal through which seed ideas move into the astral plane and subsequently into people's astral-emotional bodies onto the human consciousness of the brain.

The evolution of consciousness has been an exceedingly slow process. Due to the slow rate of movement of the outer planets, the opportunities for major shifts in the consciousness are limited. Plus, many of the opportunities that present themselves to humanity often result in distortions of the seed ideas due the lack of development. In general, people have an opportunity to awaken a new sub-quality of love-wisdom within their consciousness when Uranus and Neptune form an angular relationship to each other.

Each of the twenty-two cycles of Uranus and Neptune through the twelve signs of the zodiac takes around 171 years to complete. The trine of Uranus to Neptune in Jesus's chart corresponds to the Uranus-Neptune cycle that started in 61 BCE, when Uranus and Neptune formed a conjunction at 4 degrees Cancer 12 minutes. This particular Uranus-Neptune cycle was the first cycle in which people started to react to the ray two and ray six magnetic qualities of love-wisdom that were to unfold during the Piscean Age.

By way of this particular 171-year cycle of Uranus and Neptune, new awareness and understanding as to the nature of God as love started to unfold within the consciousness of mankind. The spiritualization of human consciousness which the interplay of the energies of Uranus and Neptune initiated two thousand years ago related specifically to the dawning awareness of the path of the heart, which Jesus introduced to mankind during the early days of the Piscean Age.

Ever since this particular cycle of Uranus and Neptune, the conjunction of these two planets has represented a seeding of a new sub-quality of the second aspect of the Divine (love-wisdom) within the consciousness of mankind. At the same time, as these new impulses of love-wisdom emanating from the universal mind started to impact the astral-emotional aspect of human consciousness, the Age of Aries was coming to an end.

During each of the twenty-two cycles of Uranus and Neptune, a new sub-quality of the nature of love-wisdom is brought forth as these two planets come into angular relationship with each other. The seeding of love-wisdom is always planted in the field of the heart center of collective humanity. From there, it streams into the etheric heart centers of people once they have opened their etheric heart centers to the love tier of petals. When the etheric heart center is closed, some of the blended Uranus-Neptune energies stream into the solar plexus center. When this occurs, the opportunity to unfold the sub-quality of love-wisdom that a particular Uranus-Neptune cycle offers is lost.

During each cycle of Uranus and Neptune, this seeding of love-wisdom in the opened heart centers of disciples and initiates bears fruit as heightened spiritual aspirations, new ideals, and higher spiritual realizations. The specific quality of spiritualization that occurs depends on the signs involved and whether the planetary aspect formed between Uranus and Neptune is hard or soft.

From roughly 65 BCE to the year of 275 CE, the different impulses of devotion to the cosmic principle of love impacted the collective sentient-feeling nature of mankind. After two conjunctions in Cancer, the next Uranus-Neptune conjunction took place in Leo in 280 CE. It was at this time that the light of the burgeoning personal mind started to reveal love to the personal consciousness.

This period from 65 BCE to 280 CE was an exceptionally important time for the spiritualization of mankind. New spiritual aspirations, thoughts, and ideals relating to the nature of God and mankind's relationship to the Divine started to unfold as the impulses of the cosmic Principle of Love-wisdom streamed into the upper gradations of the astral plane and through the awakened heart centers of disciples.

Having awakened His heart center at an early age, Jesus was impacted by the new impulses of love-wisdom that this new Uranus-Neptune cycle transmitted. As the mind and consciousness of Jesus was impacted by these new impulses, He experienced a series of profound revelations that led Him to the realization that God is love. As this aspect of love-wisdom continued to impact Him, He also realized that the God of love was within Him and within one another. From this point forward, Jesus was governed by the Laws of the Soul, not the universal laws of humanity.

The specific teachings that Jesus offered mankind aligned well with the divine plan for the awakening of the second aspect of the Divine within the hearts and minds of humanity. During the little over two thousand years of the Age of Pisces, the methodology for awakening love-wisdom within human consciousness called for the cultivation of a loving devotion to the God of love and an unwavering dedication to serving God and mankind.

In terms of this 3,700 year Uranus-Neptune cycle through the zodiac, this waxing trine of Uranus to Neptune in Jesus's chart represented the most favorable time to introduce the teachings of the Piscean Age. Thus, Jesus was born at a watershed moment in history when a new, potent impulses of the second aspect of the Divine, love-wisdom, was beginning to stream into the upper astral body of the planet for the first time, and from there, into the etheric heart centers of advanced disciples.

Of great significance was that all three outer planetary cycles (Uranus to Neptune, Uranus to Pluto, and Neptune to Pluto) had each started completely new cycles through the twelve signs just prior to Jesus's birth. This means that new and different types and qualities of energies were simultaneously impacting mankind for the first time. Plus, the ray one and ray seven magnetism of the Age of Aries was greatly diminished, while the ray two, ray six magnetism of Pisces had significantly increased. These new energies and ray qualities prepared the energies and forces of earth for the introduction of the teachings of the Piscean Age.

In a number of ways, the influx of these new qualities, rays, and energies impacting humanity was disruptive to the ancient societies. They were especially disruptive to theologically-based Judea, which was strongly Arian.

Jesus was born at a time when the love-wisdom aspect of the divine mind (which had ushered forth as a primal seed idea from the universal mind around 918 BCE) was just beginning to impact the astral body of the planet and the upper region of the astral bodies of disciples. Without sufficient development of the concrete mind, however, people were unable to understand what was affecting them, especially since it impacted mankind via the precognitive astral-emotional, feeling nature. Helping people understand love as a major aspect of the Divine and offering spiritual instructions to help people unfold this new impulse of love-wisdom were important elements of the mission of Jesus.

This trine of Uranus to Neptune in Jesus's chart set up a vibratory field around Jesus that magnetically attracted these new impulses of the second aspect of the Divine. The effects this high-frequency energy had upon Jesus significantly intensified His conscious sensitivity to this new impulse of the essential life of God in its expression as love. Slowly, a new spiritual paradigm awakened in the minds of humanity as the new impulses of the second aspect of the Divine poured into the astral body of the planet.

Jesus's sensitivity to the changes that these impulses had upon the consciousness of mankind was intensified by the large number of favorable aspects that Uranus and Neptune formed to His personal planets. This means that the higher frequency energies of Uranus and Neptune impacted His consciousness directly, rather than through the society or His group affiliations. As His consciousness was impacted by the interplay of ray seven and ray six energies of Uranus and Neptune, new devotional feelings, aspirations, and spiritual ideals filled His heart and mind.

Jesus was not the only person to be impacted by this trine of Uranus to Neptune, but He was the most advanced Soul and, therefore, the most responsive to the higher qualities of this new cosmic impulse of love-wisdom streaming into the ether of earth.

While Uranus was transiting through the sign Pisces, and Neptune was transiting Scorpio, Uranus and Neptune formed an exact trine to each other nine times between 7 BCE and 3 BCE. This heightened the impact that this new impulse of love-wisdom had on the consciousness of mankind.

As previously indicated, a trine represents the most favorable magnetic quality that blends and unifies the energies and principles that the planets forming a trine represent. In addition, the placement of Uranus in Pisces meant that the new types of feelings and aspirations arising within the feeling, sentient aspect of mankind related specifically to the nature of the Divine in its aspect of love-wisdom.

Although the energies of Uranus are always on ray seven, when Uranus is placed in Pisces, they are conditioned with ray two and ray six. Ray seven relates spirit to matter, the Father Principle to the Mother Principle, and the abstract mind to the concrete mind. With Uranus in Pisces conjunct the Sun and Mercury and trine Neptune, the ray seven magnetized energies of Uranus helped Jesus intuitively perceive and translate these new impulses of love-wisdom into a new system of spiritual thought—one that He was able to anchor in the planetary center, humanity.

Throughout much of Jesus's life, the energies of Uranus stimulated His mind in a way that brought forth new thoughts, ideas, and beliefs of a spiritual nature. As the energies of Neptune and Uranus blended and harmonized with each other during His life, they activated a series of profound realizations and revelations in relation to this cosmic principle of love.

Due to the strong influence of Pisces and Neptune in the birth chart of Jesus and His high level of evolvement, Jesus became especially responsive to the ray two and ray six energies pouring onto the earth during these early days of the Piscean Age.

The stimulation of the higher ray six Neptunian quality of devotion and dedication to an ideal, along with the strong influences of ray two and ray six that conditioned His planets in Pisces, empowered Jesus to formulate and develop this new approach to the Divine—the path of the heart.

Again, Uranus corresponds to the higher mind and to the intelligence of the Triad, the abstract mind. Neptune, on the other hand, corresponds to the love aspect of the higher mind and the intuitional mind, where pure truth and wisdom spontaneously arise.

Uranus trine Neptune is an excellent combination of energies that have a profound spiritualizing effect upon people. For Jesus, this trine not only had a spiritualizing effect upon Him, it also helped to link His abstract mind to the intuitional mind. The abstract mind perceives the meaning and causation behind the outer objective world and translates the formless impulses of the intuitional mind into the language of universal symbols. Pure truth and wisdom is realized when the initiate is able to link the abstract and intuitional minds to the mind of the Soul and the refined concrete mind. On the path, people must link all four expressions of the mind together.

There is no doubt that Jesus was exceptionally intuitive. In fact, it was His intuition that allowed Him to perceive the nature and qualities of the people around Him. It was as if he saw through people and could perceive their intentions. As a Soul, Jesus saw everything from a much higher perspective.

The intuitional mind and its senses are very different from the astral psychic senses and capacities. Psychic abilities relate to a developed sensitivity and responsiveness to the subtle forces of the astral and lower mental planes. The intuitional mind, on the other hand, corresponds to the higher buddhic plane. One or more of the astral senses (clairaudience, clairsentience, the higher imagination, clairvoyance, or spiritual idealism) must be developed before its corresponding intuitional sense can unfold, since the higher senses are really an extension of the physical senses.

The evolutionary objective of Uranus is to stimulate change and growth in relation to the evolution of consciousness. This involves precipitating changes within the various groups and institutions of society. This objective is always purposeful. Uranus is the agent that initiates the development of new archetypes and paradigms within society. It is the vehicle for the light that releases a higher, more inclusive knowledge and understanding.

Eventually, the life and light that Uranus transmits will awaken people to true Aquarian group consciousness, resulting in a realization of the interconnectedness of life. This awareness of the interconnectedness of mankind is commonly referred to as the brotherhood of mankind. The term brotherhood has nothing to do with gender; rather, it represents a realization of the interconnectedness of all people and an understanding of mankind's responsibility to help advance all forms of life: mineral, plant, animal, and human.

Uranus stands in sharp contrast to Saturn. Although the influence of Saturn dominates the development of the threefold personal consciousness, once people step upon the path, the dynamics of the psyche that Saturn and Uranus represent are locked in a struggle. This includes the ongoing struggle between the past and the future. Once the self-consciousness is sufficiently freed from the forces of the three planes of earth, however, the struggle comes to an end. Then, the energies of Uranus reveal successively greater revelations, while Saturn helps formulate the revelations into a quality of understanding that the brain can conceptualize.

Life involves a progressive unfoldment, development, and mastery of successively higher principles of consciousness. Once a conscious responsiveness to a higher principle and quality of energy has unfolded, the principle becomes manifest. It unfolds within the consciousness. Rigid structures through which a certain level of understanding and awareness was once gained must be destroyed, so a more appropriate structure can be developed through which a higher expression of the principle can unfold.

This ongoing need for change and growth in consciousness reaches a point of crisis when the earth moves into a new Age. Such a significant change in the planet's magnetism results in new types of energies, qualities, and principles impacting the minds and consciousness of humanity. The degree to which these new types and qualities of energy are able to impact the personal mind depends on the level of evolvement that has been attained.

Due to the new impulses of love that emanated from the universal mind two thousand years ago, this Uranus trine Neptune in the chart of Jesus activated higher spiritual aspirations and ideals in His life, and helped to unfold the faculty of the higher creative imagination. Unfortunately, people could not follow Jesus to the Neptunian heights of His unwavering devotion to the Father, whose essential nature is love-wisdom. As a result, the early church fathers established a religion that was influenced more by the lower octave of ray six Mars transmits, not by the higher ray six influences that Neptune transmits.

The higher ray six energies of Neptune that were so active in Jesus's life were too refined and otherworldly for the early church fathers to respond to constructively. For this reason, a type of personal devotion and dedication to an anthropomorphic deity was established—one that separated people from one another, rather than unite them in their common experiences as a human being and a Soul in progression.

Jesus is said to have been the first Soul originating in the evolutionary system of earth to unfold, develop, and embody this second aspect of the Divine. He is therefore remembered as love incarnate—the Christ. Jesus knew He was not the only Son. He knew that the works He did, others could do and *"greater works than these will he do."*[67]

Only today are people beginning to realize the deeper significances of this statement. All human beings have the potential to heal, to transmute negativity (evil), to change water into wine, to forgive, and to love unconditionally. All human beings have the potential to unfold the psychic and intuitive capacities that Jesus exhibited, and all people have the potential to know the spirit that moved through Jesus and accomplished all things. All people have the potential to realize that they are in the Father and the Father is in them. All can attain enlightenment and all can attain Christ consciousness. But when people are unfamiliar with the steps and stages of the path that lead to such realizations and achievements, it is difficult

---

[67] John 14:12. (RSV) (italics added)

to attain them. Most people do not realize that they are expected to achieve progressively higher states of mind.

All people must unfold and develop the higher self regardless of which one of the seven rays the Soul is on. Slowly, the three sub-ray qualities of love of the higher self are brought forth, developed, and mastered. Neptune is intricately involved in the development of the sensitivity that is needed in order for people to consciously respond to the essential love of the Soul. But when people's heart centers remain closed to the love of the Soul, the energies of Neptune fall into the force field of the solar plexus. When this occurs, the energies of Neptune activate the personal feelings and emotions. For this reason, people need to love and to serve one another and to forgive.

When the heart center is opened to the energies streaming from the love petals (especially when the heart center in the greater crown center is open to the energies of the buddhic center), Neptune awakens people's sensitivity and responsiveness to the presence of God— God Immanent. It is at this time that the principle of the Christ begins to unfold as the selfless, unifying, and magnetic quality of the heart and mind—pure love-wisdom. When the ray two energies and qualities emanating first from the Soul and then from the Triad impact the consciousness, the indwelling life has the potential to express itself on earth as love incarnate, Christ consciousness.

The highly refined qualities and energies of Neptune not only bring forth a sensitive responsiveness to the essential life and love of the world of the Real (especially in terms of the second aspect of God), they uplift the consciousness into the formless planes of light, where the interconnectedness of all life is an experienced reality. The nature of the world of the Real stands in sharp contrast to the reality that the intellect conceptualizes.

More so than other astrological factors, the Uranus trine Neptune aspect helps people unfold the refined senses and faculties necessary to consciously experience the essential love of the Soul, and later the love-wisdom of the Monad.

Uranus trine Mid-heaven (1 degree 3 minutes)

Since all three outer planets formed close major aspects to a large number of personal planets in the chart of Jesus, and all three outer planets formed major aspects to the Mid-heaven (Neptune was conjunct, Pluto was sextile, and Uranus was trine the Mid-heaven). Jesus was destined to serve as the voice for the dawning Age of Pisces. As the messenger of the Piscean Age, however, Jesus was not the usual type of spiritual teacher or prophet that Judea was familiar with. In fact He was an exceptionally unusual teacher, with a great depth and breadth of spiritual realization, wisdom, and experience.

People with this trine usually gain notoriety and success in rather unique and unusual ways.

Uranus conjunct North Node opposite South Node (1 degree 29 minutes)

The conjunction of Uranus to the North Node in Jesus's chart symbolically opened the doorway of His mind to the impulses that brought forth the new principles, thoughts, and ideas of the Piscean Age. Saturn would have been more central to the development of His personality if Jesus was to strictly adhere to rules that governed the people of Judea, but He was not. Instead, the liberating and revolutionizing planetary influence of Uranus and the spiritualizing influence of Neptune were the dominant influences in His life, not Saturn.

The South Node represents a portal within the consciousness through which the personal behavior and characteristics of the past seep into the daily life. Esoterically, the South Node provides clues as to the underlying causes that precipitated the current life. The South Node corresponds to the disposition, proclivities, traits, and behavioral characteristics that naturally arise in people's lives due to the patterns of past-life behavior. The sign and house placement of the South Node provides clues as to people's karmic lessons and issues. The planetary aspects formed to the South Node indicate the ease or difficulty people have in terms of learning their karmic lessons, resolving their karmic issues, and liberating themselves from the past.

The North Node, on the other hand, represents a portal within the mind that opens onto the future, especially in terms of the personality. This portal opens as people free themselves from their past. The sign and house placement of the North Node provides clues as to the qualities, characteristics, and goals that people need to cultivate in order to move away from the past and actualize their future, especially in relation to the threefold personal consciousness and its development. The North Node stands as the placeholder where the Soul's intent in terms of the personality can be fulfilled.

Since the planetary aspects to the North Node in Jesus's chart were favorable, practically every aspect of His mind and consciousness helped Him successfully fulfill His Soul's intent. Again, the immediate evolutionary goal before Jesus was to accept the will of God as expressed by the Soul and attain the third initiation; thereby, achieving the status of an initiate.

The North Node in Pisces indicates that the various aspects of the personal consciousness that had been developed and cultivated over the course of a number of lifetimes were now being synthesized, blended, and unified. This resulted in a new, refined spiritual dynamic within the psyche of Jesus. This involved the transformation of the integrated personality into a perfected instrument through which the Soul and then the Triad could express on earth.

With Uranus conjunct the North Node and Neptune trine the North Node, both Uranus and Neptune were important influences that helped free Jesus from His past, so He could realize at-one-ment consciousness. It was the magnetic pull of His North Node in the sign of Pisces that also intensified His attunement to His Soul. This attunement along with the conjunction of the North Node to Uranus propelled Jesus along a path of rapid personal growth which culminated when the personality light and the light of the Soul became one. This opened the door to the unfoldment and development of the Spiritual Triad.

This conjunction of Uranus to the North Node accelerated the rate at which Jesus achieved liberation from His past. Once reasonably freed from obsolete emotional and mental patterns, Jesus responded more fully to the changes that were taking place within the society. In effect, Jesus responded to the imprinting of love-wisdom upon the earth and became the voice for the Piscean Disposition.

Aspects to Uranus discussed in earlier chapters:

Moon trine Uranus
Sun conjunct Uranus
Mercury conjunct Uranus
Venus conjunct Uranus

Chapter 23

Neptune, God of the Deep Blue Sea

Understanding the deeply profound qualities of Neptune is the key to understanding the life, the Spirit, and the mission of Jesus. Neptune is the vehicle that awakens love, first in relation to the essential love of the Soul and then as pure love-wisdom of the planes of light. Only when people have eliminated the egocentric emotional and mental patterns that distinguish the personal mind and consciousness from the Soul can they begin to comprehend the higher purpose Neptune serves.

As the apex of the epic grand trine in the chart of Jesus and the agent of love-wisdom, Neptune guided Jesus from one stage to another onto Christ consciousness. The profound, mystical impulses of the Cosmic Christ that Pisces transmits through Neptune started to impact Jesus's life at an early age. More than any other astrological factor, Neptune awakened Jesus to the essential nature of God—love-wisdom. This revelation was Jesus's greatest gift to mankind.

The Soul holds the principle of the Christ close to its heart until people have sufficiently prepared the soil of the personality for the implantation of the seed of love-wisdom. As the waters of Neptune pour onto the seed, the Tree of Life arises within the mind and bears the fruit of wisdom and love. The unfoldment of Christ consciousness occurs as a result of Neptune's nourishing waters.

Neptune (Poseidon) rules the deep blue sea. For the initiate, the deep blue sea refers to the world of the Real that underlies both the personality and the world of the Soul. Although the energies of Neptune are often caught up in the collective unconscious when the threefold personal consciousness is being developed, the ray energies and qualities of energy that Neptune transmits align best with the pure love, wisdom, and truth of the buddhic-intuitional plane. The buddhic plane is the realm of the unbounded deep blue sea of perfect love.

In relation to human consciousness, the attraction of the Father Principle for the Mother Principle (spirit for matter) originates in the mysterious depths of the deep blue sea. Symbolically, their love for each other brings forth the Christ Principle—the only begotten Son.

The Son is not a mind-generated form of Creation like the personality; rather, it is the child of the interplay and exchange of energies between the Mother Principle and the Father Principle. The Son enters manifestation when the fertilized seed of their union is planted in the womb of matter. This is the methodology chosen to awaken the second aspect of the Divine within these human forms. The gifts of the union of Mother matter and the Father spirit are consciousness, love, wisdom, and truth.

Within the womb of form life, the Christ principle is nurtured and sustained until that moment when it unfolds in human consciousness. There, it slowly progresses from step to step and stage to stage until Christ consciousness is attained. This occurs when the self becomes consciously aware and expressive of the pure love-wisdom of the deep blue sea. Slowly, Christ consciousness is realized and human perfection is achieved. This is the primary objective of the evolutionary system of earth during this Second Solar System: the anchoring of the cosmic principle of love-wisdom on earth through its unfoldment in the manifest life of human beings.

With Neptune, this analysis moves from Uranus, the god of air, to the god of the deep blue waters. The god of the waters is the first born of the union of the Father and the Mother, and the first to raise the trident high. The trident is a symbol of the trinity: the Divine Father to the right, the Divine Mother to the left, and the only begotten Son who blazes forth in the middle once Christ consciousness is attained.

Christ consciousness is a state of at-one-ment or unity. It is a realized state of the inclusive universality of the Divine. Here, the all-embracing love of the deep blue waters washes over the self once initiates anchor their consciousness in the buddhic realm of pure love-wisdom. As a state of mind, Christ consciousness represents the conscious achievement of an unbounded, formless, and divinely supported state of mind far beyond the struggles of the personal self and beyond the Soul. More so than other states of mind, Christ consciousness is a state of harmony and true oneness with the Divine.

At-one-ment with the Divine is experienced in three successively higher, more expansive and inclusive stages. The first stage of oneness with the Divine occurs at the third initiation when human consciousness transcends the threefold personal consciousness and moves into the world of the Soul. At this stage, the self of the Soul-Personality union continues its progression, unfolding life, light, and being, free of separatism and duality.

The second stage of at-one-ment is a higher form of unity that is attained when the consciousness shifts upward from the Soul-personality unity into a state of pure love-wisdom, pure reasoning, truth, and unbounded light. This is Christ consciousness.

The third stage of union with the Divine is reached when the master transcends the Spiritual Triad and the planes of light. At this higher state, the Spiritual Self of perfect love and perfect intelligence is unified with perfect will. The manifestation of the three sub aspects of the human Monad is complete. The union of the threefold spiritual self with the Monad is esoterically known as identification with the Monad. (The threefold spiritual self or Triad is the manifest representation of the Father Spirit in the cosmic physical plane of earth.)

The energies of Neptune are the motivating force behind achieving oneness with the Divine at each of these three stages. They act as the driving, uplifting forces that help people attain oneness with the Soul and later attain oneness with the Monad in its aspect of pure wisdom and reasoning. Unfoldment of the love-wisdom of the Triad is a profound experience of the spiritual heart.

In relation to the evolution of human consciousness, the energies of Neptune are magnetized by the higher qualities of ray six. This higher expression of ray six first imparts an urge to evolve and grow beyond the world of knowledge. By responding to its uplifting impulses, the initiate transitions from the Hall of Knowledge into the Hall of Wisdom.

In the Hall of Wisdom, the three sub-aspects of the Divine at the level of the Triad are cultivated, unfolded, and mastered. The pure love-wisdom of the buddhic center is brought forth as the ray two magnetic, unifying, and attractive qualities of love-wisdom pour into the heart center of the greater crown center. Neptune is not the planetary transmitter of ray two, but it is the driving urge, desire, and motivating force behind the unfoldment, development, and subsequent embodiment of the second aspect of the Divine.

Since the Cosmic Logos who embodies the stars of Pisces transmits both ray two and ray six into our solar system, the two thousand years of the Piscean Age represents an opportunity for people to devote themselves to the unfoldment of pure love and wisdom. This involves conditioning all elements of the consciousness with unconditional love.

The best technique to use during the Piscean Age to unfold love-wisdom is an ardent devotion and dedication to the Divine in one or more of its seven sub-ray expressions of love-wisdom. The loving dedication of the scientist, the artist, and the mystic is each an expression of love-wisdom at the level of the personality, the Soul, and the Triad.

Neptune serves as the impulse behind people's aspirations to live in a perfect, ideal world. It is also the influence behind people's desire to improve the lives of others, as well as the stimulating influence behind people's longing for the kingdom of heaven. This longing arises as a result of the profound spiritual thirst and divine discontent that Neptune confers.

By way of the compelling voice of Neptune, people awaken from their sleep they call life to the light, love, wisdom, and truth of the indwelling life. They respond to the clarion call Neptune resounds to return home.

The essence of the spiritual journey for all people is a quest for pure love, wisdom, and truth. As people journey higher, they are called to sacrifice the unreal and the impermanent. Sacrificing one's attachments to the familiar things of life allows the consciousness to shift into the planes of light that illumine the world of the Real. It is this shift in consciousness the ego resists.

As a result of people's resistance to the uplift of their consciousness beyond the planes of earth, they often react to Neptune's otherworldly pull in a distorted way, such as through drugs, alcohol, and the destabilizing fantasies of an overactive imagination. The effects of the extremely high-frequency energies and the magnetic qualities of Neptune are problematic for those who are identified with and attached to ego-centered existence on earth. Neptune is especially problematic in relation to the concrete mind, which is plagued by the differentiating quality of separatism.

Both the energies of Neptune and the solar plexus center are magnetized responsive to ray six. When the emotional desire world of the personal self is prominent, the energies of Neptune energize the forces present in the astral body that stream through the solar plexus center. It is this activity that gives rise to glamour and confusion.

It is not unusual for the energies of Neptune to result in physical addictions, unusual sexual expression and fantasies, food addictions and disorders, as well as illusions, delusions, and psychological disorders. All of these relate to an activation of the patterns of astral-emotional self-consciousness that mankind has created over the millennia. (The squares of transiting Neptune are especially problematic.)

People at the stage of personal development often find Neptune disturbing and disruptive, especially when they form hard aspects to their personal planets. Neptune is often associated with a seemingly inexplicable loss of physical energy and vitality, especially in relation to the area of life represented by the house where Neptune is placed. It is also associated with unusual medical problems and diseases that are difficult to diagnose. This is due to the strong otherworldly magnetic pull that the energies of Neptune have on the consciousness. The most common effect Neptune has on people at the personal level is a heightened sensitivity to the feelings and emotions of others, both those that are positive and those that are negative.

The stimulation of the astral-emotional content that occurs as Neptunian energies impact the solar plexus often clouds people's thinking in some area of life, and can lead to ego inflation or deflation, and physical debilitation. Often, people express Neptune's energies as an enthralling romantic state of ecstatic uplift, or debilitating confusion and a lack of initiative. For these reasons, traditional astrology often looks at Neptune in relation to confusion, delusion, and deceit.

For most people, the psychic dynamic that Neptune represents has yet to be unfolded within the consciousness. What arises in the consciousness when Neptune is active seems to originate outside of oneself. Until people unfold and develop the love aspect of the higher self, the influence of Neptune will remain foreign and unintelligible. Unfoldment of the love aspect of the higher self requires people to reorient and attune themselves to the Soul.

People often resist their inner promptings to reorient themselves toward the Soul and its values and qualities, since reorientation of the mind to the Soul requires sacrifice of some aspect of the not-self. Sacrifice of the not-self does not occur all at once; rather, it takes place over time as people achieve successfully higher levels of initiation. Few people are ready to sacrifice the personal self to the Soul, and even fewer are ready to sacrifice personal affections and love in order to embody and express unconditional love.

The transpersonal qualities of Neptune call for people to sacrifice that which they think they are (in terms of their personal feelings, emotions, and desires) by way of the transformative power of love. This is necessary in order for people to experience their divine nature. People are as much God today as they will ever be. The key to realizing this truth is to free yourself from what you are not.

For countless lifetimes, the voices of the physical body, the personal emotions, thoughts, and beliefs have drowned out the voice of the indwelling God and veiled what otherwise could be perceived. This is as it should be as long as people think they are the separate self and exhibit the characteristics and tendencies of the lower form nature of mankind. Believing you are righteous and holy when you are still developing the threefold personal consciousness often results in people thinking they are spiritually superior. The air of spiritual superiority is an astral glamour that permeates the consciousness of many religious people and must be eliminated upon the path.

Neptune is definitely antithetical to the world Saturn has built, especially in terms of the structures of the psyche. These structures define people's personal truth and reality. As people grow, these structures need to expand in order to allow a greater understanding and truth to unfold. When these structures are rigid, the internal evolutionary forces can build up within the structure to an explosive point and create a crisis in people's lives. The loss of certain boundaries of the psyche before people have developed a strong sense of self, however, can result in people's inability to accept the scientifically derived facts of the mental world. This is why the polarization of the consciousness at the mental level is important before people step upon the path.

When people express the energies of Neptune through the heart center, Neptune motivates people to move away from their egocentric nature and excessive preoccupation with life in the three planes of earth. Whether people react to the other worldly pull of Neptune through alcohol, drugs, martyrdom, victimization, and/or psychological disorders, or they respond to the clarion call to uplift the consciousness into the light of the Soul, depends on the degree to which they are willing to let go of the not-self.

The pathway into the higher spiritual worlds is self-generated just as that which binds the consciousness to the three planes of earth is self-generated. It is by way of people's spiritual devotion, disciplines, studies, service activities, meditations, and prayers for others that people construct the path home equipped with the skills, capacities, senses, and faculties that this journey to a far land has awakened.

The house where Neptune is located indicates the area of people's lives where the energies of Neptune slowly wear away the rigid saturnine structures that bind them to the past and to matter existence. When the spiritualizing effects of Neptune are resisted, the house where Neptune is placed indicates the area of people's lives where distortion, delusion, fantasy, and imaginings can cloud the rational mind. This is especially true for those who have yet to step upon the path.

People on the path who have dedicated themselves to their spiritual work and have successively freed their consciousness from the control that the matter forces exert upon them find the energies of Neptune to be inspiring, uplifting, and revealing. This, in turn, results in heightened spiritual aspirations and idealism.

In Jesus's chart, Neptune was placed in the last few degrees of the ninth house of religion, philosophy, and higher education. Over time this placement helped to free Jesus from the aspects of Judaism that clashed with His Piscean teachings.

In general, people who have a preponderance of planets in fire and water signs in their charts are likely to deal with the energies of Neptune better than those whose chart emphasizes the earth and air elements. (Jesus had nine astrological factors in fire and water.) People who have a preponderance of the fire and air elements in their charts tend to be more deliberative in terms of working out the spiritualization that Neptune offers. Regardless of which elements are dominant, people's ability to consciously respond to the influence of Neptune in a constructive way determines whether someone becomes a realized master or sinks deeper into the muck of maya, glamour, and illusion.

Of particular concern is whether the energies of the love petals of the Soul are able to stream along the inner petals of the etheric heart center out into people's lives. The more people love one another, the greater the amount of essential love that streams into people's lives and relationships. Over time, the energies of Neptune intensify people's devotion to the God of love and to the Masters who embody pure love-wisdom. In this way, people are slowly transformed into love itself.

Again, consciousness originates with the Soul. Over time, consciousness expands as the streams of consciousness pour through the silver cord. Lifetime after lifetime, self-consciousness is brought forth within these physical bodies, first at the physical and astral-emotional level, then at the mental level, and eventually in relation to the higher self. Where people focus their attention determines the type and quality of self-consciousness they bring forth in their lives.[68]

In general, Neptune awakens people's sensitivity toward others. Over time, it awakens people's love for humanity and brings forth a desire to help relieve the pain and suffering of others. As love for one another grows, people become less and less preoccupied with how to satisfy their own personal desires and more willing to sacrifice themselves in service to others.

This relates to the act of redemption. Through sacrifice, people are redeemed and become instruments of love and healing powers. Losing oneself in a great act of service opens the door to divine light, love, and will. This is the common experience of the mystic. An act of true martyrdom on behalf of humanity demonstrates people's ability to transcend the threefold personal consciousness and reach the summit of the mount of initiation.

Due to the attunement of the Logos of Neptune with the spiritual heart of the Solar Logos, Neptune serves as the planetary agent of absolute devotion and dedication to the purpose of the Solar Logos. This purpose involves awakening cosmic love-wisdom within and across the entire solar system.

Neptune is quite responsive to the transmission of the cosmic ray two quality of love-wisdom; however, the lowest center in the seven planes of earth that cosmic love-wisdom impacts is the fourth etheric plane of the Planetary Logos—the buddhic plane. In relation to mankind, people must generate a bridge of conscious light that links them in consciousness to their own buddhic center via the love petals of the Soul. Only then can the unifying and magnetic cosmic ray two energies begin to stream through their buddhic center into the higher mind. This begins once people approach the third initiation and begin to express unconditional love for others. When people love unconditionally,

---

[68] The seven major etheric centers, the many secondary and minor centers, plus the 960 petals of the greater crown center are all involved in the energization of the physical body. But in relation to the arising of self-consciousness within the form, the basic, sacral, and solar plexus centers are associated with the development of the four attributes of the Divine at the personal level. The heart center, throat center, ajna center, and crown center are involved in the development of the three aspects of self-consciousness in regards to the higher mind. The heart, throat, and crown centers of the greater crown center are involved in the development of the three aspects of conscious life and being of the Spiritual Triad.

the love of the Soul streams through the etheric heart center into people's surroundings to bless and uplift one another.

When people meditate and pray for the wellbeing of all sentient life, and express unconditional mercy, compassion, love, and forgiveness in their lives, the essential love of the Soul pours through the heart center. This activity strengthens the positive polarity of the heart center in relation to the negative polarity of the solar plexus center. It is at this time that the energies of Neptune awaken the innermost petals of the solar plexus. When this occurs, personal love and affections are transformed into love for all sentient life. With both the inner petals of the solar plexus center and the heart center unfolded, a channel is created in the etheric body between these two centers. It is this pathway that Neptune uses initially to nourish the Christ child on earth.

In traditional astrology, Neptune is often looked at as a beguiling force that befuddles the consciousness and obscures the light of reasoning. But from the Soul's perspective, it is the Moon that befuddles the consciousness and obscures the light. People must be ready to perceive that which Neptune reveals. Otherwise, what arises in the consciousness under the influence of Neptune will only stimulate the distorted reality that mankind clings to and perpetuates.

Until the astral body is cleansed and purified of its lower selfish emotional-desire nature, the energies of Neptune are unable to nourish the Christ child within the form. The immediate objective is for people to transform the solar plexus into the solar light that reflects the light of the Soul. This involves a shift in consciousness from the desires of the little self to the desires of the Soul.

Initially, the solar plexus reflects lunar light. This light varies in intensity, just as the light that the Moon reflects varies depending on the phase of the Moon. Once karmic patterns are met and resolved, the energies of Neptune carry the light of the Soul to the individual via the innermost petals of the solar plexus. Only then does the solar plexus reflect the solar light of the Soul instead of the lunar reflected light.

As people approach their mastery of the emotional-desire nature, the influence of the energies of the love petals of the Soul and the energies of Neptune expressing through the inner solar plexus center and the heart center help supplant the rule of Mars over the solar plexus center. This, in turn, brings about a strong devotion and dedication to the spiritual path and a desire to attain Christ consciousness.

Neptune in Scorpio

Scorpio is associated with the spiritual tests and trials that everyone on the path experiences as they work to master the three aspects of personal consciousness. In Jesus's chart, Neptune was closely related to the three water signs of the epic grand trine: Cancer, Scorpio, and Pisces. All three signs correspond to the love aspect of the Divine and to the sacrifices that are called for as people attempt to transition from the personal self to the higher self. Neptune instills the spiritual idealism necessary to attain the first three initiations.

To sacrifice through service is the essential message of the universe. The Monad, the Soul, and the personal self are each called to sacrifice themselves in one way or another. Millions of years ago, the human Monads and the Angels of the Presence freely accepted the great sacrifices they were called to make in order to unfold the three aspects of the Divine through the instrumentality of human beings.

Since Scorpio presents the different kinds of tests and sacrifices required in order for people to attain the first three initiations, it is esoterically referred to as the sign of the disciple. Most of the sacrifices mankind has endured throughout history are not the sacrifices necessary in order to attain initiation; rather, they primarily relate to the working out of natural law in relation to the evolution of human consciousness. Often, they represent karmic obligations incurred as a result of violating the law of karma. When this is the case, people have no choice. The sacrifice called for is compulsory.

The evolutionary impulses of earth obligate people to make certain sacrifices in order to attain the stage of the integrated personality. Once people have attained this stage, they can freely accept or reject the offer to make further sacrifices, without incurring karma. In the Aquarian Age, the evolutionary forces will urge people to make the sacrifices necessary to attain the first initiation. The first initiation will no longer be a matter of choice as it is today. Only when the first initiation has been achieved will humanity step from the path of probation onto the path of discipleship. Humanity will become the world disciple, regardless of religious faith, ethnicity, philosophy, or gender.

For most people, Scorpio and the energies of its co-rulers (Mars and Pluto) stimulate the instinctual aspects of the personality and the base emotions and desires. This is due to the deeply penetrating forces of Pluto which activate the instinctual-emotional nature, while the quality of the planetary forces of Mars naturally stimulates the personal desire nature.

Scorpio may seem like an unusual placement for Neptune in the chart of Jesus, since Neptune represents the urge to love, while Scorpio is associated with Pluto and with the dark precognitive instinctual region of the unconscious, the underworld. In a sense, Neptune in

Scorpio symbolically represents the duality that dominates the collective religious thought of mankind, especially in the West—heaven and hell, light and darkness.

Once people approach the third initiation, they begin to understand the true purposes of Scorpio, Pluto, and Mars. Scorpio transmits ray four and is the agent behind the tests and trials people experience on the path of initiation that require people to choose between the lower and higher expression of something. This involves the resolution of the clashes between the egocentric nature of the integrated personality and the selfless nature of the Soul. For example, as people approach the second initiation, they must choose between expressing the love aspect of the Divine as an integrated personality (which includes personal affections and conditional love) or expressing the selfless values and quality of love as a Soul. On the path, the disciple must choose between these two again and again until the selfless values of the Soul are consistently chosen.

Neptune's placement in Scorpio at the apex of the chart and one of the three points of the epic grand trine indicates that the tests and trials of initiation that Scorpio brought forth in Jesus's life involved devotion and dedication to a high ideal (devotion to the God of love). Due to the sixteen trines that formed this epic grand trine, these tests and trials were met and passed with relative ease.

Jesus didn't experience the struggle between His personal consciousness and the higher self that people usually experience when they approach the first and second initiations for the first time. This is due in large part to the trines Neptune formed to His Cancer Moon and to the planets in Pisces. Neptune helped focus the consciousness of Jesus at the level of the higher self at an early age.

Ray six Neptune in Scorpio conjunct the Mid-heaven in Jesus's chart revealed the spirituality Jesus was to strive to achieve and subsequently express in the outer world (the Mid-heaven). This involved devotion and dedication to the Father. This was possible once Jesus had unfolded the higher mind and had successfully passed a series of tests. Symbolically, these tests set His personal consciousness ablaze upon the burning ghat of spiritual life and revealed the radiant Son of God.

For Jesus, the more difficult tests that Neptune in Scorpio presented centered on the attainment of the third initiation—the sacrifice of His personal will to the will of the Soul. Here, Jesus needed to demonstrate the ability to discern between the world of the Real and the unreal, and between darkness and light. This was not easy due to the extremely subtle distinctions between the choices that are presented at the higher levels. Only by way of the intuitional mind can people determine the correct choice to make with certainty. The concrete mind is not capable of perceiving the subtle differences between the choices presented at the third initiation and higher.

Most likely Jesus demonstrated His mastery of the physical-instinctual and astral-emotional aspects of personal consciousness in His early twenties, but with the ray one ruler of Scorpio, Pluto, opposite His Sun, Mercury, and Uranus, the issues that confronted Him as He approached the third initiation were difficult. He most likely experienced conflicts within His own mind, as well as in His outer life. As He approached the third initiation, the harmony and grace that had dominated Jesus's life up to this point were greatly disrupted.

Jesus was called on to completely shift His identity away from the physical body and threefold personal consciousness. As He approached the third initiation, the clash between His personal will and the will of the Soul intensified. Again and again He was called on to choose the values and qualities of the Soul and accept the will of the Soul over a pleasant, bountiful life that was within His reach. Symbolically, Jesus stood at the edge of a great precipice immobilized by the thought of needing to leap off the ledge of personality life into the abyss.

From the perspective of the personal self, great sacrifices are called for to attain the third initiation. A series of sacrifices were required over an extended period of time as the energies of the inner sacrifice tier of petals streamed through His crown center, impacting His consciousness. As the energies of the sacrifice tier of petals stream onto the consciousness, the will of the Soul is strengthened.

As people work to attain the third initiation, they, as the dweller-on-the-threshold, come face-to-face repeatedly with the radiant Angel of the Presence. Each time they do, something of the separate self is sacrificed. This activity continues until such time when there is no more to sacrifice. All atoms of self-consciousness that bind the consciousness to the three planes of earth have been consumed by the light, beauty, and fiery radiance of the Angel.

Sacrifice is necessary upon the path up until that moment when the self as the dweller finally repudiates all perceived need for such things as personal wealth, name, fame, and power. Then, within the conscious mind, there is the realization: I am that—I am the radiant Angel.

Chapter 24

Aspects to Neptune

Although the outer planets often have a disruptive effect in people's lives, the planetary forces of the outer planets in principle, vibration, and quality are minimally important to the advancement of the personal mind and consciousness of humanity. But in terms of the spiritualization of mankind, the ray that each planet transmits is exceedingly important. By way of the ray-magnetized energies of the planets, the three aspects of the Divine are awakened within the brain consciousness, first at the level of the personality, then in relation to the Soul, and finally at the level of the Spiritual Triad.

Spiritualization begins with the unfoldment of the essential love of the Soul. It begins once the energy of the love petal of the love tier of the lotus streams into the etheric heart center and transforms the heart of the integrated personality. Technically, spiritualization takes place as the Soul energies stream through the heart and crown centers, and impact the consciousness.

The struggles of discipleship begin once the love aspect of the higher self is unfolded and sufficiently developed for people to realize the great difference in the nature, values, and qualities of the higher self in comparison to the nature, values, and qualities of the self.

Although the petals of the sacrifice tier begin to unfold on the path of discipleship, it is not until the second initiation has been attained and the will aspect of the higher self is sufficiently developed that people step upon the path of initiation. The focus of the spiritual work (study, meditation, and service activities) as people approach the path of initiation results in the transcendence of the threefold personal consciousness.

Once the third initiation is attained, an even greater spiritualization of the consciousness begins as the energies of the three planes of light start to impact the consciousness of the unified personality and Soul. The effort to link each of three light bodies to the physical body begins in earnest. This involves intensifying the light of the manasic body, the buddhic body, and much later the atmic body, and connecting each body to the physical body.

The three light bodies are created as the three types of light stream through the manasic, buddhic, and atmic permanent atoms. Just like the astral and mental bodies tied into the physical body during the early stages of development, these light bodies must tie into the physical body before the life and light of the planes of light is able to express through the refined instrument of the Soul-infused mind and consciousness.

Thus, the evolution of consciousness is an exceedingly lengthy process, especially since the spiritualization of human consciousness doesn't even begin until the energy of the second petal (the love petal) of the love tier streams into the heart center. As this quality of love impacts the consciousness, the love aspect of the Soul is slowly unfolded.

The energies of the outer planets are integral to the development of the higher self. The angular relationships that the outer planets form during their respective cycles are directly involved in the development of the three aspects of the higher self.[69] Thus, the sextile of Neptune and Pluto found in Jesus's chart should be looked at in terms of the effect it had on Him in relation to the unfoldment and development of the higher self.

In terms of this exceedingly long cycle of Neptune and Pluto, the spiritualization of the consciousness of disciples begins when Neptune forms a sextile to Pluto.

Neptune sextile Pluto (4 degrees 30 minutes)

As with all major aspects formed between one outer planet and another, Neptune sextile Pluto must be considered in relation to the divine plan that the Masters of Love-wisdom formulate and endeavor to implement on earth via their disciples and initiates. Again, the intent of the divine plan is to awaken the second aspect of the Divine (love-wisdom) within the consciousness of humanity.

The Neptune-Pluto cycle through the twelve signs of the zodiac is extremely important to the unfoldment of the divine plan on earth. Each Neptune-Pluto cycle (from one conjunction of Neptune and Pluto to its next conjunction) spans 493 years. Neptune and Pluto conjunct each other four times and occasionally five times in each sign before the conjunction takes place in the next sign of the zodiac.

---

[69] There are three major outer planetary cycles that affect the advancement of humanity as a group and the development of the higher self of the disciple. This development occurs as the outer planets form major aspects to each other: Uranus to Neptune, Uranus to Pluto, and Neptune to Pluto. As the three outer planets form a major aspect to each other, they generate ray sub-tones within an Age.

During the Neptune-Pluto cycle, impulses of the will of God, as it relates to the unfoldment of love-wisdom, are anchored in the upper mental world of the Soul. When these impulses are registered within the minds of humanity, they stimulate the unfoldment of new ideals and new forms of devotion and dedication to an ideal.

The waxing sextile formed between Neptune and Pluto in Jesus's chart represents the first major aspect of a new Neptune-Pluto cycle. This means that it was the first opportunity mankind had to conceptualize the new spiritual ideals that this particular Neptune-Pluto cycle had to offer.

The lengthy 493-year Neptune-Pluto cycle also represents an opportunity to destroy old ideals and patterns of devotion, so new, more appropriate forms of devotion and ideals can unfold. Here, the Neptune-Pluto cycle transmutes or destroys obsolete religious structures and superstitions, and sparks renewed spiritual effort. Again, the Neptune-Pluto cycle corresponds to the ongoing efforts of the Divine to bring forth love-wisdom on earth.

Each conjunction of Neptune and Pluto represents an ending of one cycle of the spiritualization of the minds of mankind and the beginning of a new cycle. Importantly, ever since Neptune formed a conjunction with Pluto in Taurus in 82 BCE, each Neptune-Pluto cycle is specifically focused on the unfoldment and development of the love aspect in relation to the Soul and the higher self. This was not the case prior to this particular cycle of Neptune and Pluto. Here, the unfoldment of the love aspect of the higher self is brought forth as the energies of ray one divine will and the qualities of ray six (devotion to an ideal) are blended and synthesized in the minds of disciples.

Since then, the waxing sextiles of Neptune to Pluto have represented an opportunity to unfold and develop a new sub-quality of the essential love of the Soul.[70] This, in turn, calls for new spiritual disciplines, methods, and techniques. Ideally, each new Neptune-Pluto cycle begins at a higher point on the evolutionary spiral than the point at which the previous Neptune-Pluto cycle began.

In relation to this lengthy Neptune-Pluto cycle, the waxing sextile represents a time when new inspired thought arises within the minds of mankind. This occurs as the impulses of love-wisdom are formulated into ideas by the Soul. Initiates, in turn, sense these new ideas and ideals and develop new systems of spiritual thought and beliefs.

The waxing sextile of Neptune to Pluto corresponds to 0 degrees Gemini (60 degrees from the 0 degrees Aries Ascendant of the chart of humanity). Since waxing sextiles are affiliated with the ray two sign of Gemini, they are conditioned with both the mutable factor of Gemini and ray two which Gemini transmits. The energies of mutable signs confer

---

[70] Most people reading this book have a waxing Neptune sextile Pluto in their charts.

openness and a willingness to accept new thoughts and ideas. As a rule, they increase people's interest in learning new things.

This reason why this sextile in Jesus's chart was so important is that the cycle of Neptune and Pluto that began in 82 BC took place at a time when the first impulses of love-wisdom were just beginning to impact mankind. The seed ideas relating to this new influx of love-wisdom onto mankind specifically advanced the divine plan that the Masters of love-wisdom had developed in order to unfold the second aspect of the Divine (love-wisdom) within the hearts and minds of humanity during the unfolding Age of Pisces.

This effort to unfold and develop love-wisdom through the instrumentality of mankind was now possible because of the great impulse of cosmic love-wisdom that was impacting the World Soul ever since Uranus formed a conjunction to Neptune in Cancer. This conjunction opened a doorway within the third planetary center—the collective minds of humanity—to love-wisdom.

Whether or not people responded to the impulses of love-wisdom depended on the extent to which the higher self was developed, the degree to which they were attuned to the Soul. It also depended on the type of aspect that the personal planets formed to this Neptune-Pluto sextile and the specific personal planets that formed an aspect to Neptune and Pluto. People need to be open to new kinds of spiritual experience, experimentation, and exploration to take advantage of the spiritual opportunities Neptune in aspect to Pluto offer. When people are not open-minded, they are unable to register these impulses of the divine mind.

Due to His advanced development and the way Neptune and Pluto tied into His personal planets, Jesus intuitively perceived the new seed ideas of love-wisdom that were being deposited in the world of Soul. The Neptune-Pluto sextile in His chart represented an opportunity for Him and His followers to create a new approach to the Divine during the Piscean Age.

This new path was a ray six path of one-pointed devotion and dedication to the God of love. With the doorway within the minds of collective humanity opening to love-wisdom for the first time, it was this sextile aspect between Neptune and Pluto two thousand years ago that offered mankind the opportunity to approach the Divine through love. Before Jesus could take advantage of this opportunity, however, He needed to first realize that the essential nature of God was love, and then lay the foundation for this new loving approach to God. Only then was He prepared to serve as the messenger of the Age of Pisces.

Throughout much of Jesus's life, Neptune and Pluto were within the orb of a sextile aspect; however, transiting Neptune and Pluto did not form an exact sextile until twenty five years after Jesus's Crucifixion (58 CE). If not for the stellium of planets in Pisces that were trine to Neptune in Jesus's chart, along with Pluto's oppositions to His Pisces planets, it is unlikely that this sextile would have had much of an effect upon the development of the higher mind of Jesus.

This sextile of Pluto to Neptune provided Jesus with a way to relieve some of the tension that Pluto's oppositions generated in His life. This relief was especially important as He approached the third initiation.

Dedicating oneself to the God of love was not a choice available to people in the western world two thousand years ago, since the mystical quality of the essential love of the Soul had yet to unfold within the consciousness of mankind. The more Jesus touched into the essential love of the Soul and realized that the nature of God is love, the easier it was for Him to embody the new divine impulses of love-wisdom that were streaming into the World Soul.

This sextile of Neptune and Pluto in Jesus's chart sensitized Him to the new impulses of love-wisdom impacting the earth. As a result of their influences, the consciousness of Jesus was transformed by love-wisdom. Now, the cycle of Neptune-Pluto always relates to the unfoldment and development of the higher self in its aspect of love and devotion. But it isn't until the third initiation is attained that people become fully responsive to the impulses of love-wisdom that pour into the world of the Soul, either by way of the Uranus-Neptune cycle or the Neptune-Pluto cycle.

The opportunity to unfold a new aspect or sub-quality of love-wisdom always begins at the waxing sextile of both the Uranus-Neptune cycle and the Neptune-Pluto cycle.

Neptune conjunct Mid-heaven (3 degrees 19 minutes)

When Jesus was born, it appeared as if Neptune was in the constellation of Scorpio conjunct the Mid-heaven. Just moments before His birth, the angle of the Mid-heaven conjoined Neptune. Though Neptune was conjunct the Mid-heaven from the ninth-house side at the time of His birth, the energies of Neptune also poured into in the tenth-house area of His life.

The Mid-heaven (cusp of the tenth house) represents the magnetized area of life where people express themselves the strongest in relation to their profession and reputation. The Mid-heaven, therefore, relates to the skills, capacities, character, knowledge, faculties, and reputation that people express professionally.

In general, people become socially and professionally significant once they have achieved the stage of the integrated personality. At this stage, people frequently become a notable force in society, for good or ill. The Mid-heaven is the summit of the mount of achievement, since it is the place where people demonstrate the skills, capacities, and abilities they have developed in their lives over many years.

Although the opposition from Pluto to the stellium of planets in Pisces, and Pluto's sextile aspects to the Moon, Neptune, and the Mid-heaven contributed a dynamic quality to Jesus's life, it was this conjunction of Neptune to Mid-heaven that determined the direction, nature, and quality of Jesus's mission.

Even though Jesus is said to have been a carpenter and helped Joseph repair farm implements in his small shop, His chart indicates that He had one calling—to demonstrate the path of initiation to mankind via the path of the heart. This involved the unfoldment, development, and mastery of the three aspects of conscious life at the level of the Soul and later at the level of the Spiritual Triad.

Neptune being the highest planetary point in the chart of Jesus indicates that the character, nature, quality, and wisdom that Neptune brings forth represented the spiritual potential Jesus could unfold in His life and demonstrate to others.

The area of the ninth house where Neptune was placed in Jesus's chart specifically relates to religion and philosophy. Here, Neptune contributed a mystical quality to the religious views, beliefs, feelings, and ideas. To Him, worshipping a transcendent God and offering animal sacrifices in the temple were not enough. He needed to experience a close relationship with His Father.

Traditional astrologers assign the father to the tenth house and the mother to the fourth house. This means that Neptune at the Mid-heaven in Jesus's chart represented that which Jesus inherited from His father and could give form to in His life: devotion and dedication to the Father. Once people begin to be influenced by their Soul charts, however, the tenth house represents that which is inherited from the mother in a psychological sense. Thus, the conjunction of Neptune to the Mid-heaven also speaks to the immense love and spiritual devotion of Mary.

The conjunction of Neptune with the Mid-heaven indicates that Jesus wouldn't have been satisfied or felt fulfilled in a traditional profession. This was especially true once He had attained the third initiation. His (social-professional) life had to reflect the psychic dynamic of Neptune—devotion to the God of love. This involved both the loving intelligence of the Divine Mother and the loving will-purpose of the Divine Father. The unification of these two principles within His mind and consciousness brought forth the only begotten, Christ consciousness.

Giving form and structure to the principle of the Christ would not have been an easy task, even for Jesus to achieve since the essential love of the Soul, along with the principles and qualities of the Age of Pisces, had yet to unfold within the consciousness of mankind.

The sure-footed and stabilizing influence of His Capricorn Ascendant, along with Saturn in His third house, contributed the concretizing factor Jesus needed to formulate the teachings of the new Piscean Age. Neptune at the Mid-heaven in Scorpio ensured that Jesus would have an opportunity to present His teachings publicly once He climbed to the summit of the mount of initiation for the third time.

Neptune, as the capstone of the epic grand trine, was the light that revealed the path of the heart to Jesus and illumined His way forward onto Christ consciousness. Christ consciousness is an all-inclusive and expansive state of mind through which the pure love-wisdom and reasoning of the buddhic-intuitional plane express freely in one's life. It is not so much a state of knowing as it is a state of unbounded wisdom. On the path of the heart, the Divine must be truly loved to be known.

Neptune trine North Node sextile South Node (47 minutes)

People must be relatively free from their past before they can achieve what the North Node represents. Freedom from one's past, especially in terms of the astral-emotional aspect of consciousness, is the evolutionary focus of each lifetime. Having unfolded and developed the concrete mind and integrated the threefold personal consciousness, people are ready to apply their soul-infused light of mind to control the physical-instinctual and astral-emotional aspects of their personal consciousness.

Since people connect to one another at the personal level via astral substances, and the Moon is associated with these substances, the quality of personal relationships formed with others involves the lunar nodes. In a sense, the nodes are magnetized fields that are sensitive to mankind's astral-emotional field of forces.

In general, it is by way of the South Node people connect with others who resonate with their past. People's karma is indicated by the hard aspects formed to the South Node and North Node. By way of the North Node, people respond to the energies of others who can help them realize their future. People who connect with them via a favorable aspect to their North Node help them achieve freedom from their past.

Since Mars, Jupiter, and Saturn did not form any aspects to the North Node in Jesus's chart, these three planets were not directly involved in His efforts to transition away from His past to His future. Although Jupiter was an exceptionally beneficial influence in Jesus's life, Mars and Saturn represented the psychic dynamics caught up in Jesus's past that needed to be modified or adjusted in some way. This involved a transformation of the beliefs, thoughts, and ideas of the past that interfered with Jesus being able to formulate the new Piscean teachings.

Aspects to Neptune discussed in earlier chapters:

Sun trine Neptune
Moon trine Neptune
Mercury trine Neptune
Venus trine Neptune
Uranus trine Neptune

Chapter 25

Pluto, the Ray One Transformer

According to myth, Pluto is the Lord of the underworld. When the young maiden Persephone plucked a narcissus from the field of flowers, the earth opened up. Pluto arose from the depths of Hades and carried off the young maiden to his lair, where he installed her as the Queen of the underworld.

The destructive power aspect of ray one that Pluto transmits can pierce the boundaries of the dark world of the unconscious and unleash the hellish torrents of selfish emotions, aggression, and the heated passions of the lower astral realm. Hatred, narcissism, and extreme egotism pull the individual into the dark underworld faster than any other traits.

There is a big difference between the destructive planetary forces emanating from Pluto that frequently impact the personal consciousness and the ray one building forces of the will. However, neither type of force is impeded by the matter substances of the three planes of earth. Ray one (will-purpose) knows no barriers. Not even the walls that Saturn builds can obstruct its movement. It is ray one in its life aspect that gives life to matter and to spirit. It therefore penetrates into the deepest levels of both consciousness and matter substances.

Pluto transmits the will-purpose aspect of the Divine as the agent of great and powerful forces that move upon and through the three planes of earth. As the agent of change, its potent influence can seem ruthless at times. This can be confusing unless the three sub-aspects of ray one are considered separately.

Most of the meanings and significances astrologers assign to Pluto pertain to the third sub-ray aspect of ray one, the destroyer sub-aspect. It is this sub-aspect of ray one that is the precipitating cause behind people's experiences of death and endings. All things on earth are vulnerable to ray one's destructive activity.

Death pertains to the death of the forms and structures both in the society and in people's lives, but it never touches the life within the form. Since Pluto is an outer planet, the processes of cyclic endings and new beginnings are best observed in relation to the structures that maintain a nation, a society, religion, or culture. These structures include their traditions, institutions, rules, and laws.

For people on the path, endings and new beginnings relate specifically to something that is obstructing the disciple's progress and must be removed in order to progress. Elements of the instinctual mind, astral-emotional desire mind, and the structures of the personal concrete mind are especially vulnerable to the power of death that Pluto wields. Through the pain people experience when something is removed from their lives, they are transformed and renewed providing they are able to let go of what has been removed.

Pluto involves the type of growth that takes place as people go through the searing pain of a loss—some forced separation or irreversible destruction of something they deeply love, e.g., a relationship, a cherished ideal, a way of life, or a core belief.

The dark, selfish emotional desire forms of the astral plane are especially vulnerable to the forces of Pluto. For this reason, the second initiation (which represents a mastery over the lower astral-emotional forces) is quite difficult. This mastery involves a large number of tests and trials that impact people's feelings and emotions. The second initiation results in freeing the consciousness from its emotional attachments to the things of earth. Only then is the essential love of the Soul able to stream onto the consciousness unhindered.

What Pluto removes from people's lives include the things of earth they are personally attached to and identify their selfhood with, since these perpetuate separatism within their consciousness. This includes their physical body, personal emotions, desires, thoughts, ideas, and beliefs.

Once the prerequisite development of the threefold personal consciousness has been achieved, ray one Pluto is involved in transforming the threefold personal consciousness. This calls for a degree of dispassion, detachment, and renunciation in relation to the things of the three planes of earth. Ray one Pluto is especially important in terms of the ongoing planetary processes to redeem and resurrect essential life from matter.

As the vehicle of transcendent will, Pluto is the agent of death of the little self. It represents the energy that carries the will of the Soul and the will and purpose of the Logos onto the individual. The force of divine will results in the elimination of the elements or factors of the personal consciousness that obstruct spiritual growth. According to the underlying laws of the evolutionary process, when factors of the personal consciousness become obsolete (in relation to the evolution of the Soul), they need to be removed. Out of the ashes of the destroyed form, a better, more refined form arises—one through which conscious life can attain a higher state.

With Pluto, the endings and new beginnings that are part of the evolutionary processes directly impact the physical-etheric body and the raw emotions. This is due to the fact that ray one easily pierces the forces of subtle matter and enters directly into the etheric body and stimulates the brain consciousness. The energies of Neptune impact the consciousness via the astral body, while the energies of Uranus impact the consciousness via the mental body.

Journeying through the dark catacombs of the unconscious and conquering its monsters (comprised of the causal atoms of one's instinctual and astral-emotional self-consciousness) is required of all people on the path. Historically, fear, hatred, and possessiveness are just a few of the emotions that have created these hideous forms within the consciousness and unconscious that mankind must conquer.

The energies of Pluto are free of all astral-emotional content, but they activate those patterns of emotions and feelings that reside deep within the unconscious that people must face and conquer. Pluto transports people into the dark recesses of their own underworld. People's awareness of the psychic monsters that dwell there prompts them to battle and conquer their demons. Only when people no longer respond to them or to their nature can they begin their work to free themselves from the patterns of behavior and emotions of the little self.

When people refuse to accept personal responsibility and project the darker elements of their nature onto others, they usually create inappropriate relations with different groups of people. This results in violations of universal law. As long as people consciously respond to their lower instinctual and astral-emotional aspects of consciousness, they will continue to exhibit negative and inappropriate behavior and actions, e.g., bigotry, hatred, envy, greed, prejudice, and manipulative, passive-aggressive behavior, etc.

Since a person's own etheric body is part of the etheric body of the planet, their primitive instinctive intelligences are both personal and collective in terms of mankind as a group-energy. All people share in this underworld of the unconscious prior to the lifting up of the vibratory rates of their subtle bodies. This uplifting of the vibratory rates of the subtle bodies takes place when the energy and light of the Soul build into, and stream through, the upper three-sub-plane levels of the respective subtle bodies.

Until people attain the second initiation, they are susceptible to the influences of the negative and emotionally charged instinctual reactions that mankind has generated throughout history. These patterns of self-centered personal consciousness have nothing to do with the evolving human soul; rather, they relate to the involutionary forces of the subtle bodies. This is one of the many reasons why the consciousness must be mentally polarized before the spiritual journey really begins. Only by way of the Soul-infused light of mind can people observe their negative patterns, gain control of them, and subsequently transmute the forces that sustain them.

People typically see the destruction of some cherished aspect of their lives or the ending of a particularly enjoyable relationship as being painful and sad. This is usually the case until people gain a better understanding of the evolutionary system of earth. For this reason, people experience an almost unending series of life lessons. Once a major lesson is learned, an old structure that limited the consciousness to a particular range or type of experiences can be eliminated.

There are no forces of evil emanating from Pluto, yet Pluto is very much associated with evil and the dark underworld. This is due to the effect the potent ray one energies have as they stream directly into the physical-etheric plane and impact the brain consciousness. This means that Pluto can stimulate what is of a lower vibratory nature and quality in the spheres of physical-etheric activity and emotional expression.

Ray one is not an energy that people have integrated into their own consciousness. It is, therefore, foreign and alien in terms of the personal consciousness and beyond people's control. It will be a long time before the whole of mankind is able to master the divine will that ray one transmits.

In relation to the evolution of consciousness, ray one corresponds to the Monad and its manifest expression as the living light of the atmic plane. Ray one is electrical in nature and, therefore, foreign to the personal consciousness. It is not soft, embracing, and unifying like the energies of the Soul. This is one of the reasons why the actions of Pluto often seem to violate people's sensitivities.

The energies of Pluto have a significant impact upon the brain consciousness and often stimulate the more primitive parts of the brain. Since plutonian energies are more potent than other energies and are relatively foreign to the psyche, they can lead to painful, frightening, and unwanted experiences and events. In those who are less evolved, the influx of the planetary forces of Pluto can result in outright hostility, malevolence, and covert aggression.

The energies of Pluto are not inherently problematic; rather, it is the effect they have on the personal mind due to what Pluto activates in the subtle bodies that is the problem. Even when people attempt to repress a tendency to lash out or they label the effects Pluto has as the influences of the devil, they can still be victimized by the patterns of forces present in the unconscious.

From the Soul's perspective, the evolutionary need is for people to eliminate the forces that the atoms of self-consciousness are attached to that vibrate at a rate below the upper three sub-plane levels of the subtle bodies. Energy at the first sub-plane level corresponds to ray one and the crown center. Energy at the second sub-plane level corresponds to ray two and the heart center, and energy at the third sub-plane level corresponds to ray three and the throat center.

The energies streaming into the upper three sub-plane levels of the mental body unfold the higher mind and self. Only by way of the energies radiating from the lotus can people unfold and develop the values, characteristics, and qualities of the Soul during incarnation. That which vibrates at the fourth sub-plane level corresponds to the four attributes of consciousness, which rays four, five, six, and seven unfold. The forces that move through the regions of the subtle bodies below the fourth sub-plane level correspond to the nature and intelligences of the vehicles, not the Soul.

The potent ray one energies of Pluto are exceedingly stimulating to all aspects of consciousness they touch. This means they can stimulate evil as well as good. Ray one should never be appropriated to satisfy personal desires, yet many people try to wield ray one for personal gain, as evidenced by the large number of despots, dictators, and tyrants throughout history. When this is the case, the destructive aspect of the forces of the will can wreak havoc in people's lives, especially in relation to the Soul's progression. Since all three outer planets represent principles that are transcendent of the personal self, their energies need to be dispersed across a group of people. Fortunately, there is a limited amount of ray one that people can successfully appropriate during this Second Solar System.

An aspect between Pluto and a personal planet often represents the need to experience lessons involving power and powerlessness, but this doesn't involve ray one as much as it involves the effects that ray one has on the emotional, desire nature. In general, dictators, despots, and tyrants have a stronger ray six egocentric desire nature than a ray one disposition. Since the consciousness of the average person is still polarized at the astral-emotional level, the aspects Pluto forms to personal planets can lead to a controlling manipulative disposition and a tendency to express hostility and personal willfulness.

When Pluto is active, its light shines upon the underbelly of mankind, especially in relation to people's selfishness and their inhumane actions toward others. Evil is still part of the dark realm of the unconscious of mankind and arises from time to time into the light of people's conscious awareness, especially in the lives of those who are selfishly preoccupied with, and strongly driven by, their need to satisfy their personal desires.

When this is the case, people are unable to hear the voices of their own Soul to perfect themselves (which Virgo, in particular, resounds). This is the message Jesus referred to when He exclaimed: "*You, therefore, must be perfect, as your heavenly Father is perfect.*"[71] This speaks to the ever-unfolding aspects of the Divine that take place within the mind and consciousness when people are on the path. As they unfold and develop the three aspects and four attributes of the Divine, they transition from step to step and stage to stage upon

---

[71] Matt. 5:48. (RSV) (italics added)

the path, eventually achieving a state of oneness with the Soul, and then a union with the Father Spirit. Ultimately, masters achieve oneness with the cosmic aspects of the Divine beyond the seven planes of the cosmic physical plane of earth.

Today, the gulf between the consciousness of the personal self and that of the Father spirit seems as great as the gulf between the instinctual intelligences of the animal and the consciousness of mankind—with one major difference. As people work to actualize their vast human potential, what they unfold, develop, and master in their lives (the various principles of consciousness, capacities, and senses) is imprinted upon the causal field of the Soul. As people actualize their potential, the perfection envisioned within the mind of God is slowly realized. Through endings and new beginnings, death and rebirth, ray one Pluto is the agent of change that offers people a way to leave the little self behind.

Pluto in Virgo

The cosmic energies of both Virgo and Pisces are magnetized by ray two and ray six; however, the symbolism of Virgo involves the gestation and birth of the Christ child, while the symbolism of Pisces involves the mature Christ.

Earthy Virgo represents the love of the Divine Mother for the different expressions of the life of earth. It represents the harvest of what has been sown in the three planes of earth. In relation to mankind, this refers specifically to the planting of the seeds of love-wisdom within the hearts and minds of mankind. Esoterically, Virgo is the sign of the Divine Mother whose seed of perfect love is planted in the soil of human consciousness once it has been sufficiently developed and purified. During the subsequent period of gestation, the Mother's seed of love is nourished by the ray two energies emanating from Jupiter, Gemini, Virgo, and Pisces.

Esoterically, Virgo represents the anchoring of love within the human forms of earth. The effect of this anchoring gives rise to the desire to perfect oneself. Initially, people apply this directive to the physical body, resulting in an interest in their physical health and appearance. When functioning at the level of personal consciousness, the urge to order and perfect oneself is applied almost exclusively to the physical body and to one's life on earth. For most people, this placement of Pluto activates life lessons that revolve around the health and fitness of the physical body and people's day-to-day work and service activities.

People also apply these inner stirrings of love to their astral-emotional nature. This results in an effort to be kind and considerate of others and their feelings. Eventually, the seed of love affects the entire threefold personal consciousness. This results in a desire to cleanse and purify oneself of negativity and to cultivate a more loving, forgiving, and sympathetic attitude toward others. Then, as the energies of the love petals of the Soul stream through the heart center onto the consciousness, people unfold the selfless and inclusive values and qualities of the Soul.

As people progress, they become more responsive to the second ray of love-wisdom and to the sixth ray of spiritual devotion and dedication that emanates from the constellation of Virgo and nourishes the seed of love-wisdom. This activity continues until the term of gestation is complete. In Capricorn (on the reversed wheel of the disciple), the Christ comes forth into the light of people's conscious awareness.

The influences of Pluto in Virgo help people detach their selfhood from the world of form, so a greater portion of love can arise within the consciousness and express through these forms of earth. As people detach themselves from the things of earth, the greater love and light of the Soul nourishes and sustains the Christ spirit until that time when the Christ child is able to step forward into the outer world of people's lives.

Pluto is always involved directly or indirectly in the processes of detachment, dispassion, and renunciation. Through detachment and renunciation, the ties that bind the atoms of self-consciousness to the things of the three planes of personal life are severed. The severance of the ties that bind people to a lower state of mind occurs over the course of people's lifetimes. People detach themselves from one thing or activity, then another, and another. The higher form of detachment that Jesus experienced relates to the complete detachment of His light and consciousness from the personality level, i.e., from the threefold personal consciousness. This higher level of detachment is necessary when Pluto is in Virgo in the eighth house opposite the Sun.

Only by way of the higher senses, faculties, and capacities that love brings forth can people sense the Father. The development of these higher senses is necessary since the faculties and senses of the personality are too coarse to even begin to sense the Father Spirit. The gate opens wide into the Father's kingdom only when the mature Christ nears its home. This occurs once the principles and unique spiritual potential imprinted upon the Soul have been actualized in one's life.

According to esoteric thought, the three forms of the Virgo Mother readies the womb of the Virgin (the purified personality) for its impregnation by the Father Spirit. The ongoing episodes of the union of spirit and matter lead to the unfoldment of love-wisdom within these human forms in terms of the three planes of earth. The three forms of the virgin Mother, who gives birth to the only begotten Son on earth, are known as Mary, Isis, and Eve. Mary relates to the physical plane and to the birth of the Christ child. Isis relates to the watery Mother matrix and to giving birth to love in relation to the astral-emotional, feeling nature.

Eve represents the birth of love in the mental matrix of the Divine Mother, i.e., giving birth to love in relation to the mind and knowledge.

Deep within the world of matter (the world where the Mother Principle expresses), love-wisdom is brought forth, first in the form of the personality and then as the divine child—the Christ child—the only begotten of the union of Father spirit and Mother matter. The Christ is nurtured and protected in the womb of human consciousness, then is born, matures, and ultimately comes forth as the mature Christ. The birthing of the Christ out of the womb of these human forms is necessary for the full flowering of Christ consciousness on earth. Thus, the three expressions of the divine Mother—Mary (Maya), Isis, and Eve—are each involved in a particular stage of transformation necessary for pure love-wisdom to manifest on earth.

Although love-wisdom corresponds to the second aspect of the Divine and to the astral aspect of the threefold personal consciousness, the principle of love is brought forth in relation to each of the three major aspects of the Monad: the integrated personality, the Soul or higher self, and the Spiritual Triad (the Real Self).

The middle petal of each of the three tiers of petals of the lotus is referred to as the love petal. Once the essential love of the Soul is brought forth in relation to the middle love petal of the intelligence tier, the three petals of the love tier, and the love petal of the sacrifice tier of petals—only then is the impersonal, unconditional essential love of the Soul anchored on earth.

This activity is prerequisite to the influx of pure love-wisdom from the buddhic center, streaming through the heart center of the greater crown center (via the middle buddhi petal of the innermost tier of petals of the lotus). The three innermost petals of the lotus (the atma, buddhi, and manas petals) conceal and protect the jewel of the lotus until the essential love of the Soul dominates the disciple's life. As pure love-wisdom streams onto the consciousness via the middle buddhi petal, the mature Christ appears on earth through these human forms of earth.

Mercury is the ruler of Virgo at the personality level, while the Moon, veiling one of the outer planets, rules Virgo at the level of the Soul. Until all elements of consciousness of the past are addressed and neutralized, the Moon blocks the influx of the energies of the outer planet it is veiling. The Moon rules Virgo at the Soul level only in the sense that it symbolically represents the ancient Mother who has taken form on earth to give birth to love-wisdom.

In Jesus's younger years, the placement of Pluto in Virgo opposite Mercury is likely to have generated conflicts in His life that pertained to His understanding of life in relation to His personal will and intellect, and the will of the Soul. As the conflicts between them were resolved, Jesus expressed greater harmony, peace, and love.

Jesus responded to the impulse of Virgo with a strong desire to heal, to teach, and to serve through love. Having expressed the Christ child in prior life times, Jesus established a course of action that sensitized Him to the influx of the energies of His Soul-centered chart when He was young. Then, as He approached the third initiation, the energies of His Soul-centered chart (of which the personality chart is a reflection) started to express through Him directly.

Again, the Soul-centered chart is a reversal of the personality chart. The planets transit the wheel of the Soul chart clockwise. The effect of the energies of the Soul-centered chart as they stream through the subtle bodies frees the atoms of self-consciousness from their imprisonment in the threefold world of earth. The usual counterclockwise movement of transits in the natal chart represents the involution of energy and planetary forces into these human forms and the unfoldment of the threefold personality in the three planes of earth.

The clockwise direction of the transits around the Soul wheel represents the evolution of consciousness out of matter. The effect of the planets transiting the Soul chart loosens the electromagnetic bond between consciousness and form, thereby liberating the self-consciousness from the three planes of earth and strengthening the bond between the mind and the Soul.

On the path, the effects that the planetary energies of the Soul chart have on the personality initially result in the blending and unification of the ray-magnetized energies of the personality chart with those of the Soul. At this point, it appears that the Nadir becomes the Mid-heaven and the Mid-heaven becomes the Nadir. This blending of energies results in the unification of the integrated personality and Soul. With each planet of the Soul chart placed in the opposite sign compared to the personality chart, the process of blending and unification involves first relating the three aspects of the Soul to the three aspects of the integrated personality. (This information provides the disciple with a major clue as to how to blend the energies of the Soul with those of the personality, which emphasizes the importance of mid-point between all oppositions where the rays are blended.)

Eventually, the psychic dynamics represented by the planets in the natal chart are uplifted and transformed by the dynamics expressed at the level of the Soul. This involves moving in consciousness to the center of the chart where the three oppositions of the signs cross. There, the ray energies blend and are subsequently unified. Slowly, the consciousness is freed from its magnetic attachment to the three planes of earth.

The superimposition of the Soul chart of Jesus onto His natal chart created a six-pointed star, the Star of David. This is indicative of the union of the threefold personality with the threefold Soul. Once the psychic dynamics represented by the epic grand trine in the personality chart were related to the psychic dynamics of the inverted epic grand trine of the

Soul chart and subsequently unified, Jesus attained the third initiation. Henceforth, Jesus's life, consciousness, and sense of the selfhood had shifted into the world of the Soul.

Even though the soul-infused integrated personality serves as an instrument of the Soul from this stage on, it is still subject to the influences of the planetary transits as they move counterclockwise through the signs of the natal chart. However, the integrated personality no longer holds the light of one's selfhood. The distinction between the evolution of the consciousness and the involutionary vehicles (including the personality) through which consciousness unfolds and advances must be kept in mind. They are not the same.

Although the personality has always been a vehicle or life form, not an evolving spirit, the illusion of being the body or the personality is completely destroyed at the third initiation. Still, the self as the Soul must continue to work through the integrated personality vehicle in order to express itself in the three planes of earth.

Pluto in the Eighth House

The house where Pluto is located represents an area of life where people experience both power and powerlessness, and where people die and are reborn in a number of ways. On the path, people repeatedly experience a series of little deaths of the personal self as the consciousness detaches itself from the things of earth.

When people are operating at the stage of personal development, it seems as if detachment from something or someone is randomly forced on them by events outside of their control. Strangely, at the point upon the continuum of the eternal-moment-of-the-now that humanity has currently reached, people seem to need pain to focus the mind. Pain seems to help people move beyond the point of evolvement they have achieved.

In the eighth-house area of life, people begin to realize that the personal ego is not really in charge of their lives no matter how strongly they insist it is. This realization arises when people look objectively at the events of their lives. Though they may do what they know to be right and appropriate, they still experience misfortune. Blaming misfortune on others or on evil influences, however, does not free them from misfortune. Nor does it free them from the forces that precipitated the misfortune. Only by searching for the cause behind the misfortune do people gain the needed understanding and learn the life lesson being presented.

The eighth house directly corresponds to Pluto, since Scorpio (which Pluto co-rules at the personality level) establishes the issues of the eighth house in the chart of humanity. This means that people's eighth-house area of life corresponds to the transforming archetype of

Pluto. In many ways, the eighth house represents the burning ghat where elements of the egocentric personal self are burned away. From the ashes of the pyre that Pluto sets ablaze, more appropriate life structures and more refined subtle bodies are brought forth. The same is true in relation to a nation or a culture.

The eighth house is also referred to as the place of dramatic collision, for this is where the will-to-love at the core of the Soul's nature enters into battle with the elements of the integrated personality—the kinsmen of Arjuna in the Bhagavad Gita. The Bhagavad Gita allegorically portrays this great battle that all people experience as they approach the second initiation. The eighth house represents the location where this battle takes place, even when other areas of life seem to be affected the most. Close relationships are almost always involved. The exact nature of the battle depends on the astrological factors conditioning the eighth house and Pluto.

Esoterically speaking, this battleground is generated by the combination of the two relatively incompatible ray energies transmitted by the two co-rulers of Scorpio: ray six Mars and ray one Pluto. This combination of ray-magnetized energies generates the battle fields of Scorpio. In its relation to the difficult second initiation, the eighth house represents the battlefield upon which the personal emotional nature (that which is loved, as well as that which is hated) and the will of the Soul are pitted against each other. The ensuing conflagration ultimately destroys the selfish emotional nature. Esoterically, it is the ensuing death by drowning in watery Scorpio that ultimately leads to the resurrection of essential life in Pisces.

In the eighth-house area of life, people face their darkness. Aggressive elements of this darkness tend to be more of a problem for men than for women, since men tend to identify strongly with the type of masculinity that Mars expresses at the personal level. Exactly what people must face depends on the type and quality of forces they personally respond to and express in their lives.

Symbolically, Pluto in the eighth house represents the doorway within the mind to the underworld. This underworld is both personal and collective in terms of people's responsiveness to the influences of the unconscious. For this reason, people with Pluto in the eighth house are bound to come face-to-face with darkness and evil at some point in their lives.

The eighth house also represents the reservoir of the psyche where all the emotional silt and dross of the past has settled to the bottom. This was especially true for Jesus since the South Node was in the eighth house conjunct Pluto. Pluto in the eighth-house area of life stirs up this silt from time to time. The eighth house represents people's encounter with both the personal and collective shadow self. Just as the solar plexus is the emotional garbage disposal of people's lives, the eighth house represents the realm of the unconscious where the masticated but undigested garbage (fears, negative feelings, and emotions) has been deposited.

By way of eighth-house experiences, selfish passions are faced and extinguished. The extinguishing of the fires of self-serving passions is necessary in order to attain the second initiation. The mastery of the astral-emotional nature that the second initiation entails cannot occur until people are no longer emotionally attached to the things of earth. Oftentimes, people lose their passion and zest for life when their selfish passions are extinguished, but this condition is temporary. The objective is not to extinguish passion, but to transform passion into a fiery spiritual zeal and aspiration—a zeal and aspiration that drives people to attain and express the higher states of mind, such as Christ consciousness, enlightenment, bliss, and at-one-ment with the Divine.

Pluto in the eighth house opposite the Sun, Mercury, and Uranus suggests that the ancient psychic patterns of the world involving murder, misuse of power, death, rebirth, and redemption needed to be addressed. With Uranus opposite Pluto in aspect to His personal planets, Jesus was tied to these ancient psychic patterns of mankind.

Some portion of the karma of mankind needed to be released from the earth to clear the path so love-wisdom could unfold within human consciousness. Thus, Jesus faced these ancient patterns of mankind in order to transmute some portion of these lower forces. This was part of His mission.

In His earlier years, however, Jesus used the energies generated by Pluto's placement in the eighth house (opposite the stellium of Piscean planets) to unfold and develop an ability to perform the works of the Father (miracles). Ultimately, this led to an ability to transform the physical body into light at His Resurrection.

Due to His level of evolvement, Jesus was not reactive to the planetary underworld. Although He did meet His old self from time to time (via this second-eighth house opposition of Pluto to His Sun and Mercury), through His great love He was able to leave behind the eighth-house consciousness of the past and immerse Himself in the ray two quality of love-wisdom that He expressed upon a ray six current of unwavering devotion to the God of love.

During His ministry, Jesus came face-to-face with the darkness and evil of humanity. As the messenger of the Age of Pisces, His planetary service involved meeting the dark, shadow self of humanity. This was triggered by His second-eighth house opposition of Pluto to Uranus. Here, too, Jesus responded with immense love for the Father and for all mankind. In effect this opposition provided Him with the opportunity to demonstrate His mastery over the lower forces of earth.

This eighth-house placement of Pluto in Jesus's chart by itself greatly intensified the dynamic of death, rebirth, and transformation in His life. For Jesus, this placement of Pluto was not to force Him to cleanse and purify the psyche or to eliminate His responsiveness to the ancient instinctual-emotional aspects of self-consciousness, as it is for most people. As the avatar of the Piscean Age, Jesus had to face the collective unconscious of mankind and respond to its hideousness and cruelty from the level of a master. He demonstrated this in a number of ways during His ministry. The way He responded to the Sanhedrin Council and to Pilate was especially telling.

The Sanhedrin decided that the teachings of Jesus were disruptive and destabilizing to the social order. Pilate concurred and imposed the death penalty on Jesus.[72] Pilate implemented the death penalty using the Roman method of nailing criminals to a crossbar by the roadside to make an example of them. (The Judean method for killing someone was by stoning.)

While hanging from the cross, Jesus exclaimed, *"Father, forgive them, for they know not what they do."*[73] Masters always respond with similar words when victimized by others, for they know that they are not the physical body. If Jesus would have felt anger or hatred toward those who advocated for His death, He would have created a karmic bond between Him and His persecutors that would have required Him to reincarnate to resolve.

Jesus's acceptance of His Crucifixion serves as an example of people's willingness to sacrifice the threefold personality to the Soul. It also represented a great sacrifice Jesus accepted on behalf of humanity. As a Planetary Server, Jesus's Crucifixion transmuted a portion of the darkness that enveloped human consciousness. This was part of His mission. Without an infusion of light into the darkness of human consciousness, the new seeds of love-wisdom could not be anchored in the hearts and minds of humanity for many, many years to come.

The path of love was not something that was available to western mankind prior to this historical period. Jesus opened the doorway within the hearts of mankind that leads onto the path of the heart. All people of good will and a kind heart are able to harvest the spiritual bounty that has unfolded as a result of the cosmic seeds of love-wisdom that Jesus helped to plant in the soil of human consciousness more than two thousand years ago.

Pluto sextile Mid-heaven (1 degree 11 minutes)

When people think of Jesus, they often think of the loving mystical side of Jesus, but His occult side was important as well. To many people, the healing and occult powers He demonstrated validated Him as the Son of God and lent credence to His Divinity. Over the

---

[72] The Sanhedrin governed Judea, but they could not impose the death penalty.
[73] Luke 23:34. (RSV) (italics added)

centuries, the miraculous works He displayed were often pointed to in an effort to convert others to the Christian faith.

> *If I am not doing the works of my Father, then do not believe me, but if I do them even though you do not believe me, believe the works, that you may know and understand that I am in the Father and the Father is in me.*[74]

This biblical verse references both the mystical realization Jesus had attained and the works He was able to perform as a result of His command of the forces of the three planes of earth. Functioning from a position of pure love during His ministry, Jesus was able to perform feats that seemed to defy the laws of nature, but they did not defy universal law. In fact, it was because of His knowledge of how things worked in heaven and on earth that He was able to perform miracles.

Though people often think of spirituality in terms of the more mystical, loving characteristics, and qualities that ray two and ray six bring forth, spirituality pertains to a progressive unfoldment of all three aspects of the Divine and their synthesis and unity at successively higher levels. Again, this involves a progressive unfoldment of the seven principles of consciousness and the actualization of the divine potential, not only in relation to the personality, but in relation to the Soul and the Spiritual Triad. This progressive unfoldment occurs as a result of the influx, blending, and synthesis of energies magnetized by the seven rays in each of the seven planes of the cosmic physical plane.

Without the ray one life-forces, there would be no life in the three planes of earth. There would be no growth in consciousness or transcendence of one state of mind and attainment of a higher state, nor could people experience at-one-ment first with the Soul and then with the Father spirit.

The ray one energies of Pluto represent the power that rejuvenates and regenerates the physical and subtle bodies. This regeneration occurs as the deep causal patterns of the un-regenerated forces (which interfere with the flow of ray one life-giving forces of the Monad) have been eliminated.

The powers Jesus demonstrated far exceeded the rejuvenating abilities common to a strong influence of Pluto in people's lives. The command over the physical forces of earth that Jesus developed was due to His mastery of the laws that govern the three planes of earth

The destroyer expression of Pluto removes the negative force patterns in the subtle bodies that block the ray one life-giving energies. These life-giving forces emanate from the Monads of both the healer and the individual being healed. When certain negative patterns of

---

[74] John 10: 37, 38. (RSV) (italics added)

force in the subtle bodies are removed, the forces of divine life are able to nourish, sustain, and vitalize the physical body.

Jesus's command of ray one power in combination with His advanced intuition, His spiritual vision, His attunement to the Divine, and His command of the healing energies of the Soul enabled Him to see the blockages of energy that resulted in ill health and remove them.

Jesus had command of all three sub-types of ray one. This is exceedingly rare for many reasons. Prior to the fifth initiation, masters are unable to command the forces of life, will, and purpose that ray one transmits. Since people no longer need to incarnate on earth after the fourth initiation, such abilities are rarely demonstrated on earth. This higher level of command calls for a perfect alignment with the Monad. This is possible only when the ray one creator energies of Vulcan have completed their work building the light bodies and the tools (faculties, skills, capacities, etc.) of the Spiritual Triad.

The sextile aspect that Pluto formed to the Mid-heaven represented an opportunity for Jesus to publically demonstrate His mastery of the forces of the three planes of earth. Although He was able to demonstrate psychic abilities and some works as He approached the third initiation, it wasn't until He had stepped upon the path of power and learned how to wield the laws that govern the forces of the three planes of earth that He was able to demonstrate many of the miracles recorded in the Bible.

By way of His command of ray one and His attunement to the Father, Jesus was able to perfect His mastery of the three sub-aspects of ray one. As a result, He was able to regenerate Himself and others, as well as cast out evil spirits, still the waters, demonstrate multiplication of substance and the transubstantiation of substance (change water into wine), and heal people of their afflictions. Overall, such powers require initiate training that usually isn't available until a master steps onto the path of power and learns how to command the forces of the three planes of earth.

This does not mean that the ray one aspect of the Divine was more important in Jesus's life than the love-wisdom or the active intelligence aspects of the Divine. In fact, Jesus had completed His development on the path of the heart before He stepped upon the path of power. The breadth of powers and extraordinary skills Jesus demonstrated represented mastery of the three aspects of the Divine at the level of the Triad. Then, as a result of the favorable aspects that a number of planets formed to the Mid-heaven, Jesus was able to publically demonstrate the skill and mastery of the Spiritual Triad during His ministry.

Pluto conjunct South Node in Virgo (3 degrees 43 minutes)

As the transmitter of the destroyer aspect of ray one, Pluto is associated with the more primitive instinctual level of the consciousness that mankind first unfolded during its ancient past.

Pluto conjunct the South Node represents a magnetic pull of the past, which people tend to express in an obsessive-compulsive way without much thought. It is possible that Jesus expressed this tendency in His early years as a driving force within Him to achieve perfection (Virgo).

It appears that Jesus had incarnated with strong psychic patterns of behavior that suppressed many of the drives and appetites of the physical body, especially in relation to His masculinity and sexuality. For lifetimes Jesus sought to be spiritually pure in His quest to be a prophet of the stature of Elijah. To Him, Elijah heard the words of the Lord and was truly the servant of the Lord. Jesus revered Him and emulated Elijah's absolute and unwavering obedience to the Lord God of Israel.

Pluto conjunct the South Node in Jesus's chart suggests that Jesus incarnated with a compulsive tendency to uphold certain astral-emotional patterns of behavior, which would have strengthened the scaffolding of His psyche, especially in relation to His personal will. Most likely, the personal willfulness of Jesus was strongest when He was defending His religious views, beliefs, opinions, and activities.

Within the symbolism of the conjunction of Pluto with the South Node is found the major life lessons that Jesus needed to address before He could move forward. First and foremost in His life, Jesus needed to learn how to wield the power of the will selflessly and to express that will in a way that led Him into the world of the Soul, the kingdom.

The conjunction of Pluto to the South Node viewed in the context of the overall tenor of the chart indicates that Jesus incarnated with an ability to control the lower forces of the three planes of matter that sought to express in His life. Only later did He develop the skills and capacities necessary to control, and then master, the three types of forces that envelop the planet.

Although control over many of the aspects of the threefold personal consciousness had been achieved prior to incarnation, Jesus still needed to fully master the will-infused mental aspect of the personal consciousness and attain the third initiation.

Once Jesus attained the third initiation, His training on how He could control the forces of the three planes of earth intensified. Eventually, the ability to wield ray one forces became as important to Him as ray two (love-wisdom) had been up to this point.

The many biblical references to Jesus as having been sent from the Father indicate that Jesus had sacrificed His personal will to the will of the Soul, and that He was fully attuned and responsive to the divine plan. The validity of this statement is further supported by the works He performed, since many of these are possible only when a master is able to wield ray one selflessly.

When Pluto is conjunct the South Node, there is nothing from the past (no emotional or mental patterns, no behavioral patterns or tendencies, no proclivities or characteristics) that can remain hidden from view. This includes the instinctual-emotional elements of the unconscious in particular. The ray one energies transmitted by Pluto enter the realm of the unconscious—the underworld of human consciousness—and activate the instinctual and lower feeling qualities and patterns hidden there. These patterns typically express in people's lives as compulsions, obsessions, selfish emotional reactions, and aggressive actions. This underworld is not the underworld of the indwelling life; rather, it is the underworld of human consciousness, darkened by the masks of ignorance.

Within this underworld, the imprints of primitive mankind still sub-stand. This relates to the ancient days of Lemuria and Atlantis, and includes patterns of behavior indicative of mankind's inhumanity to one another.

Pluto is the planetary agent offering freedom from this dark underworld of the past to those willing to face their darkness and withstand the searing fires of its destruction. Freeing emotional elements of self-consciousness from the catacombs of the underworld is necessary before people can fully gain their freedom from maya, glamour, and illusion. Again, people alone are responsible for eliminating their tendency to respond to the forces of, hatred with hatred, negativity with greater negativity, evil with evil.

Pluto conjunct the South Node in Jesus's chart was a shackle that bound Jesus to the past and blocked His movement forward until He faced this ancient past and severed all responsiveness to it. This included all imprinting of the unconscious that express in people's lives as their basic proclivities and underlying selfish tendencies, traits, and personality characteristics. Because of the difficult experiences Pluto precipitates, people often seek ways to resist and control these dark inner forces.

It is difficult to get a handle on the influences of the unconscious when people meet the present with the self of the past. When this is the case, they are unable to move forward. They usually can accept changes in some areas of life, but strongly resist making changes in other areas.

The aspects of ease formed to the North Node in the natal chart highlight areas of life and methods whereby people can easily move forward, while the challenging aspects represent issues of the past that need to be faced and resolved before they can move forward.

In general, what the Nodes represent relates to the development and advancement of the personality during a particular lifetime. But once disciples approach the third initiation, the

North Node provides clues as to the qualities, nature, characteristics, and objectives that are more in line with the planet the Moon veils.[75] The North Node then corresponds to the development and advancement of the higher self, as directed by the will of the Soul.

The past that Jesus needed to address before He was able to sacrifice His personal will to the will of the Soul and attain the third initiation included:

- The psychic dynamic of Pluto in Virgo conjunct South Node.
- Pluto in the eighth house.
- Pluto inconjunct Mars and Saturn.
- Pluto opposite the Sun and Mercury.

Jesus seems to have incarnated with a rigid pattern of obedience to the Judean standard of conduct. This rigid adherence to the past is what needed to be addressed before He could transcend the threefold personality. This includes a compulsive obedience to the Mosaic Law, commandments, dietary regulations, animal sacrifices, and social rules of conduct and behavior.

This is not to say that these commandments and rules are invalid, only that the factor of separatism that seeped into the way these rules and commandments have been interpreted and implemented often becomes problematic. The Soul has no religion; rather, its nature arises from the higher principles of universal law, not religious beliefs and dogma, which often correspond to personal and cultural preferences, not universal law.

The Judean standard of conduct called for obedience to the rules that the ancient Israelites established to govern how the tribes of the covenant community interacted with those who were Israelites and those who were not. During His ministry, Jesus challenged many of its regulations.

In relation to the past of Jesus, the Virgo archetype of the South Node, which conferred a strong desire to perfect Himself, became entangled with a compulsive need to abstain from all sin, as defined by the laws and rules that governed life in Judea. As mentioned earlier, two thousand years ago, the most effective way to free the consciousness from the drives and appetites of the physical body was by creating a harsh, religious authoritarian dynamic of the psyche that repressed the ways of the flesh (to use a Christian term).

Jesus's chart indicates that during a recent past life, the victor of this struggle between the flesh and the spirit was the Angel of the Presence, but it was a victory brought about by

---

[75] For the average person, the Moon veils the energies of Vulcan since Vulcan forges the chains of karma, but for those on the spiritual path, the placement of the Moon becomes a point through which the energies of Vulcan, Uranus, or Neptune are transmitted.

imposing harsh tactics to repress and suppress the appetites and drives of the physical body and the personal desire nature initially, not by transcending them. At that time, people on the path often engaged in severe discipline and extreme austerity, deprivation, repression, and even martyrdom, in an effort to spiritually advance. However, once the new cosmic seeds of love-wisdom started to pour onto the earth two thousand years ago, such physically punishing tactics were no longer necessary. The new approach to the Divine was through love.

The inconjunction that Pluto formed to the Mars-Saturn conjunction in Jesus's chart represents many of the mental structures and patterns of thought that were created in an effort to deny and repress the desires and appetites of the flesh. It was these patterns and habits that Jesus needed to address and eliminate in order to transcend the threefold personality.

The placement of the Mars-Saturn conjunction in the third house inconjunct the South Node and Pluto in Jesus's chart indicates that the spiritual disciplines adopted to deny and repress His basic human nature were caught up in a system of societally sanctioned thought and belief. Since people usually externalize their internal conflicts, such repression can result in an unending battle with what many think of as Satan, resulting in a failure to learn how to control the elemental lives of the vehicles themselves.

This doesn't mean there is no evil. However, the dualism indicated here is actually a conflict between the Father Principle and the Mother Principle. Often what people have historically viewed as sinful relates to this clash within the psyche between these two principles. The lack of blending and unification of these two within the consciousness of mankind has resulted in discrimination, inequality, and the domination of men over women throughout history. This is likely to continue until that time when people stop identifying their selfhood with their physical bodies and its drives and appetites.

The illusion of being separate from God and separate from all things outside of the physical body is the root cause behind the types of actions and beliefs that violate universal law and imprisons the consciousness in matter. Few people understand how the distorting, divisive influence that separatism has on their feelings, thoughts, and beliefs is a shortcoming, a sin, from the perspective of the Soul.

The effort to free oneself from the past is not easy, since the past represents the familiar and the known, while the future is unknown. It is essential to people's progression that they work to resolve the psychological characteristics and issues of the past that obstruct the path forward before they can realize the state of mind and achieve the understanding that the North Node represents. People need to understand what traits, tendencies, proclivities, and characteristics need to be modified, transmuted, or removed, and which ones need further development. This varies depending on people's point of evolvement and their Soul's evolutionary intent.

During the early years of Jesus's life, the pull of His past, as represented by Pluto's conjunction to the South Node, was strong. This was the situation Jesus was in until He learned all of the lessons and addressed the issues presented to Him by the challenging aspects Pluto formed to His personal planets. This required Him to first unfold a personality that was thoroughly infused with rays two and six.

The personality ruler of the South Node, Mercury was in Pisces opposite Pluto and the South Node, while the personality ruler of the North Node, Neptune, was trine the North Node and Mercury and sextile the South Node. This suggests that prior to His incarnation Jesus had thrown His weight, so to speak, behind the Angel of the Presence and had rejected the dweller-on-the-threshold. By the time He incarnated, Jesus was already identifying His selfhood with the Soul and its values.

Jesus had to initiate the destruction of the last few ties that bound some of His ideas and beliefs to His social and religious conditioning before He could attain the third initiation. This occurred as He responded to the spiritually transforming ray two and ray six energies of Pisces and to the sacred ray one energies of Vulcan.

Once Jesus realized the nature of God was love, there wasn't anything within His psyche that interfered with the unification of His integrated personality with the Soul. The more He embodied love, the more Jesus understood and experienced God in the second aspect, love-wisdom. This furthered His attunement and response to the divine plan.

As the magnetic pull of the past was lessened, Jesus responded more favorably to the influences, qualities, ray magnetism, and principles of Pisces. Once He was sufficiently freed from the magnetic forces of the past (via the destructive powers of Pluto), the attractive pull of His future enabled Him to achieve successively higher states of mind. The pace of His progression rapidly accelerated once He was free of the past that His South Node represented.

The methodology Jesus adopted to move beyond the old standard of conduct was through His devotion to the God of love. This involved the development of a capacity to respond to the higher expression of ray two and ray six, which Pisces transmitted. Jesus became sensitive to a much higher vibration and quality of these two rays than what anyone in the evolutionary system of earth had responded to previously.

Eventually, Jesus reached a stature in which He was governed by the Laws of the Soul, including the Law of Service and the Law of Sacrifice; rather than the social and religious laws and rules of Judea. The Laws of the Soul are not imposed upon people like the laws of society and the doctrines of religion. Obedience to the Laws of Soul arises from within and brings forth selfless values, qualities, actions, and behavior more characteristic of the Soul than the personality.

With His attainment of the third initiation, Jesus finalized the shift away from the past as represented by the Virgo South Node. At last, Jesus completed the transition of His consciousness away from the influence of the instinctual mind and the desire mind (Pluto conjunct South Node). His efforts to blend and unify the will, love-wisdom, and creative intelligence of the Soul with those of threefold integrated personality had successfully resulted in a union of the integrated personality with the Soul.

Before the forces of Jesus's past had lost all influence upon Him, however, Jesus had to reject the harsh, repressive tactics used to keep Him free from sin. This was accomplished by holding His thoughts in the light of the Soul and expressing the qualities and values of the Soul.

Initially, all of the psychic dynamics that the planets in Pisces represented were magnetized by the ray two and ray six qualities, but once the third initiation was attained, Pluto as the Soul-centered ruler of Pisces started to condition them. Though this brought in the energies of the destroyer sub-aspect of ray one, this was no longer problematic, since Jesus had transcended the personal self and wasn't susceptible to using this power selfishly and destructively. Nor were there any instinctual patterns of force that the destroyer sub-aspect of Pluto could have activated within the unconscious.

At this higher stage, Jesus used the forces of the destroyer in accordance with the divine plan to diminish the influences of the Age of Aries, so He could transition in heart and mind into the Age of Pisces. Only then could He begin to anchor the teachings of the Piscean Age on earth. This called for clearing some patterns from the collective unconscious of humanity in order to anchor the will-to-love and the will-to-build on earth.[76]

Henceforth, the exchange and interplay of energies represented by the planets in Pisces were conditioned with ray one. This influence initiated Jesus's efforts to become one with the Monad—the embodiment of divine life, will, and purpose—by advancing the development of the threefold Spiritual Triad. This resulted in His ability to express pure love-wisdom and pure reasoning under the direction of the will of the Monad, the will of God.

---

[76] Jesus's effort to anchor the will-to-create was disrupted before it could be anchored within the minds of humanity.

Aspects to Pluto discussed in earlier chapters:

Sun opposite Pluto
Moon sextile Pluto
Mercury opposite Pluto
Mars inconjunct Pluto
Saturn inconjunct Pluto
Uranus opposite Pluto
Neptune sextile Pluto

Chapter 26

Vulcan, the Builder

According to the ancient wisdom teachings, there is a very important ray one planet in our solar system that has little if any physical substance. The miniscule physical-etheric substance that the cosmic mind of Vulcan is anchored to was captured within the gravitational field of Mercury's orbit in ancient times. Astrologically, Vulcan is usually located within 3 degrees of Mercury and 8 degrees 30 minutes of the Sun.

No Planetary Logos resonated with or perceived a more accurate image of Creation that the Solar Logos envisioned than the Logos of Vulcan. Immediately, Vulcan started moving forward in life and being on the waves of the will and purpose of the Solar Logos to bring forth Creation in its sphere of influence. This image of perfected manifest life throughout the solar system represents the blueprint for awakening the heart center of the ONE.

The processes involved in the awakening of the heart center of the ONE (the solar system) involves the transmission of cosmic ray two (cosmic love-wisdom) in its seven sub-rays, which bring forth life, consciousness, and being across the entire solar system. Vulcan immediately initiated its processes to bring forth manifest Creation by awakening essential life to the will and purpose of the Solar Logos. The small, yet potent, Vulcan transmits the ray one sub-ray of cosmic ray two. (All rays that the Solar Logos transmits are the seven sub-rays of cosmic ray two, even though we refer to those sub-rays as ray one or ray two, etc.)

At this time, Vulcan transmits the second sub-ray of ray one, the builder sub-aspect. There was a time when Vulcan, like Pluto, transmitted the third aspect of ray one, the destroyer sub-aspect. This occurred at the conclusion of the First Solar System, once the purpose, goals, and objectives of the Solar Logos had been achieved. Its work to destroy the forms of the First Solar System was the last time that Vulcan transmitted the destroyer aspect of ray one. This brought an end to the First Solar System and ushered in the night of Brahma.

The evolutionary system of earth is unique in that a multitude of the life forms from the First Solar System were reawakened in this Second Solar System. The essences of the life forms of the First Solar System were brought forth on earth during the early days of the Second Solar System in an effort to generate the capacity of knowledge—to objectively know that you know—on earth, even though the focus in this Second Solar System is on manifesting the second divine aspect (love-wisdom).

Though small and obscure in relation to other planetary bodies, Vulcan is exceedingly important in terms of the spiritual path of mankind. It is the agent of the Karmic Board who fashions the tools that bind people to the wheel of karma until their debts have been paid. It is also the agent that breaks the chains that bind people to life in the three planes of earth. Disciples use the energies of Vulcan to develop certain mental tools to control, and later master, the dynamics of the three aspects of their personal consciousness.

Vulcan transmits the energies that empower the mind of the higher self. This empowerment of the mind is needed to attain the first two initiations and approach the third initiation. The energies of Vulcan are also used to forge the mental tools needed to master the forces of matter that mislead and distract life from serving the purpose of the Logos. Unless the mind is adequately infused with the quality of will, it lacks the strength to master the instinctual mind and the desire mind of these form vehicles.

Vulcan is one of the seven sacred planets of our solar system. The term sacred has to do with the level of cosmic attainment the individual Planetary Logos has achieved. The seven sacred planets include: Mercury, Venus, Jupiter, Saturn, Uranus, Neptune, and Vulcan. Each Planetary Logos that embodies a sacred planet has attained cosmic perfection.

A Planetary Logos is charged with bringing forth manifest life within its evolutionary system, while serving as a receiving-transmitting station for one of the rays of manifestation. The manifest life brought forth in an evolutionary system is initially conditioned with the ray of a Planetary Logos and the seven sub-rays of that particular ray. The Planetary Logos of each of the sacred planets are perfectly attuned to the objective that their ray serves to actualize the purpose of the Solar Logos.

The Logos of Earth is said to be relatively close to achieving the status of a sacred planet, but first, certain capacities and realizations must be achieved. Specifically, this development pertains to the awakening of a higher level of response within the life forms that constitute the personality aspect of the Logos.

People are starting to comprehend the nature of ray one in its destroyer sub-aspect that Pluto transmits, but they are far from consciously responding to the builder sub-aspect of ray one that Vulcan transmits.

The personal mind can neither perceive nor direct the building energies of ray one. In relation to the life forms of earth, this builder sub-aspect is directed from the level of the Spiritual Triad. Currently, the builder sub-aspect barely impacts mankind via the Soul. Few people are conscious of the effects that this builder sub-aspect of ray one has upon the consciousness. Yet, its effects are very real and important, especially in relation to the development of the higher self and the unification of the integrated personality with the Soul.

Vulcan is not the ruler of any of the twelve astrological signs at the personality level. The only sign it rules is Taurus at the level of the Soul. In Taurus, the energies of Vulcan are integrally involved in the attainment of enlightenment. This is due to the fact that the energies of the builder sub-aspect of ray one transform matter into light and light into matter.

According to Ancient Wisdom teachings, Mercury (at the level of the Soul) is the Messenger of God who communicates wisdom and truth. Vulcan, on the other hand, is the blacksmith of god who forges the tools of the mind that are needed to implement the ever-unfolding divine plan. These tools of the mind are the tools of power that create and transform the un-manifest (seed ideas) into manifestation. Here, light is transformed into matter and matter is transformed back into light in accordance with the Plan.

In relation to mankind, Vulcan forges the tools and instruments of the higher mind that people need for constructive, enlightened living, and divine creativity. The building energies that Vulcan transmits represent the energy of creation. This quality brings the multitude of expressions of the one life of the seven planes of the cosmic physical plane into an objective, manifest state.

Though the energies of Vulcan are not directly involved in the unfoldment and development of personal consciousness, they are definitely involved in the processes that transform the threefold personal self into the higher self. This is the result of its activity that transforms the matter substances of the threefold personal consciousness into the upper mental-plane light of the Soul. Before this is possible, the crown center must be opened to the will of the Soul. Vulcan activates the kundalini that streams up the sushumna channel and opens the crown center to the will of the Soul. At an even higher level, Vulcan opens the crown center to the living light of the atmic center, so the will of the Spiritual Triad can unfold in the master's life.

In terms of mankind, the activity of Vulcan focuses on the development of the human Monad at the level of the Soul. The building quality of ray one is used to transfer the forces (the petals) of the lower centers into the upper centers. Before the energies of Vulcan can be used to unfold and awaken the higher self, however, Pluto must destroy the elements of the personal consciousness that are divisive in nature, since they interfere with the builder's activities in the three planes of earth.

Vulcan isn't involved in the evolution of the personal consciousness, but its energies are involved in forging the chains that bind personal consciousness to the world of matter until that time when the prerequisite faculties, skills, and capacities have been developed that uplift the consciousness into the world of the Soul. People must have a basic understanding of how things work on earth before they can concentrate on their spiritual development and creativity. They gain this knowledge as they express, apply, and use different types of energy to achieve their goals and learn their life lessons.

In terms of the evolutionary system of earth, the objective of Vulcan is to supply the quality of energy needed for initiates to forge the tools (capacities, skills, faculties) that the Soul and Triad need in order to work effectively on earth to implement the Plan. Using these tools, masters learn how to transform light into matter and transform matter back into light. In so doing, masters become the co-creators of the Divine.

Before initiates can learn how to transform matter into light, they must clear the three channels of kundalini of subtle matter forces from the basic center to the crown center. This involves transforming the petals (which are etheric forces) of the seven centers into light. When cleared, the will-purpose can stream into the crown center through the sushumna onto the basic center. This results in the power to create and to transform matter into light and light into matter.

Ray one Pluto governs both the crown center and the basic center of the average person. Though Pluto still exerts a degree of influence upon the basic center of initiates, Vulcan, not Pluto, rules the crown center of initiates.

As the sushumna is being cleared of all forces of matter, the petals are burned up by the fires of essential life. When this occurs, the jewel of life-force at the center of each of the etheric centers is revealed. This occurs as a result of the actions of the Soul, not the personality. At this stage, the Soul has full command of the personality.

At this time, Vulcan's power of transformation is transmitted onto the purified integrated personality from the level of the Triad via the Soul. When the ray one energies of Vulcan stream unimpeded from the crown center to the basic center via the cleared channel of the sushumna, Vulcan serves as the agent of redemption. Redemption of essential life (the presence of God Immanent) pertains to resurrecting life from matter.

In relation to evolution of human consciousness, redemption corresponds to resurrecting essential life from the atomic forces of the physical form. This takes place at the first initiation. A much higher level of redemption takes place when essential life is redeemed from the threefold integrated personality itself. This occurs at the third initiation. In this way, essential life is transferred to the Soul, and much later transferred to the Triad.

On earth, but not throughout the solar system, the evolutionary focus of the Second Solar

System involves unfolding pure love-wisdom in these physical forms that were conceptually created during the First Solar System.

Today, the vast and powerful capacities of Vulcan help free the personal consciousness from its attachments to and identification with the elemental worlds of form-life—the created worlds. This release is necessary in order for mankind to unify the life and consciousness of the integrated personality with the Soul. Since the energies of Vulcan penetrate the matter worlds so easily, Vulcan represents the type of energy that is needed to impact the subtle matter forces in a way that frees the atoms of self-consciousness from the control and influence of the matter forces.

Since the personal mind is incapable of wielding and directing Vulcan's energies, this liberation is directed by the Soul once people on the path seek liberation from the influences and control of the forces of the physical, astral-emotional, and lower mental planes. This requires people to align and attune to their Souls in deep contemplation and meditation on a daily basis.

The transmutation of the matter forces that bind people to the things of earth begins once people step upon the path of discipleship. It is the work of the disciple to transmute the streams of matter forces that electromagnetically attach human consciousness to the substances of the three planes of earth. Symbolically, this represents the time when the Soul is said to be crucified upon the fixed cross. This means that Vulcan is active in the rebuilding of the self that takes place after the tests and trials of Scorpio that Mars and Pluto precipitate.

All people are subject to the pain and sorrow of human life, but only when they are on the path do the experiences of searing pain and sorrow have anything to do with the tests and trials of initiation. Prior to this time, the loss of what people desire (whether of a material or a relational nature) represents the working out of natural law and karma.

During the early stages of human development, free will is limited to a relatively small range of possibilities, but it is not inviolable. Here, the forces of evolution slowly move people forward, regardless of their personal wishes and desires, though the pain and sorrow that accompanies the loss of something or someone who is cherished, but here is little growth. At this early stage of human development, few people learn the evolutionary lessons behind the losses they experience.

The forces of Vulcan move people's evolution forward at the personal level. Not until people approach the third initiation can they begin to consciously and constructively respond to, and direct, the energies of Vulcan. People's sensitivity and mental response to the energies of Vulcan strengthen the ability to renounce the things of earth, once dispassion and detachment have sufficiently loosened the consciousness from the chains that bind it to the three planes of earth. Only then can Vulcan transform the matter forces of the petals of the five etheric centers into light. Physical prana continues to vitalize the physical body, but essential life has been freed from the atomic forces of the three planes of matter. (Spiritual prana emanating from the Monad also continues to stream into the etheric body onto the physical body.)

During the phase of unification, when the integrated personality and Soul are being merged, the tools Vulcan forges are referred to as spiritual virtues and values, e.g., mercy, unconditional love, compassion, forgiveness, generosity, and a deep concern for the health and well-being of others. Such values and virtues represent just a few of the tools that the energies of Vulcan help disciples forge in their lives in an effort to liberate the indwelling life from its imprisonment.

These qualities are referred to as the tools of the Soul when they are used on behalf of others without reference to oneself. When this is the case, the selfless expression of such qualities transforms the threefold personal consciousness into the light of the Soul. This transformation of subtle matter into light is accomplished by way of the energies of Vulcan.

By way of Vulcan, the will of the Soul is slowly integrated into people's conscious lives. This occurs once people have advanced the loving intelligence of the Soul. Until this time, people are oblivious to the will of the indwelling life that Vulcan expresses. They are oblivious to the effects that Vulcan has on them, even though its forces have carried them down the path of evolution for lifetimes, while their eyes were closed to the light.

As the transmitting agent of sacred life and purpose, Vulcan permeates the densest matter and informs the intelligences found there that they, too, are divine. Vulcan is associated with the mineral kingdom in particular. Mankind has repeatedly sacrificed the elemental lives of the mineral kingdom through its production of tools to aid in the construction and destruction of the life and forms of earth. Though the energies of Vulcan are not directly involved in the unfoldment of human consciousness until people approach the third initiation, they are active in people's lives from the moment of individuation to the moment of the master's ascension.

In general, humanity has yet to reach the point of evolvement wherein people are consciously responsive to the quality of energies that Vulcan transmits. As with the outer planets, the energies of Vulcan cannot be integrated into the consciousness in a way that allows people to apply and implement them in their lives until they approach the third initiation. A sufficient amount of energy from the will tier of the lotus must stream through the crown center and impact the brain before mankind becomes consciously responsive to the ray one qualities of life in its sub-aspect of love (the builder sub-aspect).

Vulcan was quite active during Jesus's adult years, especially during the years of His ministry. Because of the influences of Vulcan, Jesus was able to perceive the divine purpose of the Father spirit and was attuned to the divine plan that the Masters of love and wisdom had developed to work out divine purpose on earth.

Once Jesus attained the third initiation, the close conjunction of Vulcan with His planets in Pisces and its opposition to Pluto intensified the potency of the ray one influence. After the third initiation, the heightened ray one influence helped Jesus to better attune Himself with the will of the Father and the will-purpose of the Logos as it pertained to the unfolding Age of Pisces. Only when the builder and the destroyer sub-aspects of ray one are related to each other can people accurately perceive an aspect of the divine plan, depending on the ray their Soul is on. (Each of the ashrams is charged with developing the divine plan as it relates to their particular ray.)

Upon transcendence of the integrated personality at the third initiation, Jesus's responsiveness to the higher expression of ray six and cosmic ray two, which Neptune receives and transmits, was also intensified. This, in turn, sensitized Him to the cosmic love-wisdom that emanates from the heart center of the Solar Logos. This intensified His unwavering love and devotion to the God of love.

As the disciple approaches the third initiation, Vulcan forges the keys that unlock the chains of the mind that bind the consciousness to the lower mental level of the personality. Later, it forges the keys that unlock the chains that limit the expression of life to the range of the higher mind. This occurs at the fourth initiation. The energies of Vulcan are, therefore, quite active at both the third initiation and the fourth initiation.

At the fourth initiation the causal body of the Soul is shattered and the Soul is transcended. For Jesus, this occurred once His capacity to love exceeded the causal body's capacity to contain it. This moment when the Soul is transcended, is very different from any moment of life up to this point. A feeling of being utterly alone and bereft of all life initially consumes the fourth-degree initiate. At the fourth initiation, the causal force field that has constrained the Angel of the Presence for millions of years is shattered, freeing the Angel from its service to the Planetary Logos.

Initially, this event is discouraging, due to the release of the Angel. Even in the midst of a crowd, the sudden departure of the Angel causes the new master to feel alone and forsaken. But this sense of being forsaken is only temporary. Once the new fourth-degree masters steps through the portal of the cardinal cross (where the two crossbars meet), they enter the immense light of buddhic plane.

It is by way of Pisces that the master reaches the final step of the path of the heart, achieves Christ consciousness, and begins to serve humanity as the world Savior. (It is by way of Aquarius that the initiate steps upon the final step of the path of the mind and becomes the World Server.) As the World Savior, Jesus served as a blacksmith to the Logos, a divine co-creator, having mastered ray one in its builder aspect.

Jesus became the fashioner of a new image of God—the loving Father. In so doing, He forged the tools mankind needed in order to achieve freedom from the three planes of earth. This refers to the new tools of the heart that Jesus developed and anchored as part of His mission and service to God and mankind.

Vulcan in Pisces and Its Aspects

Again, Pisces represents the synthesizing phase of the evolution of consciousness. During this phase, the understanding garnered and the development achieved in the preceding eleven signs is synthesized and its essence extracted. As a result of the processes of synthesis, people's identification with certain elements of the not-self are eliminated. The consequence of no longer responding to, or expressing, certain patterns of thought and behavior is growth and transformation. In this way people outgrow certain characteristics, tendencies, and traits. On the path, this leads to a greater alignment with, and attunement to, the Soul and an increase in the unifying and attractive qualities of the essential love of the Soul, which, in turn, build into the manifest conscious life and being of the higher self.

The energies of Pisces always carry a person away from the material world. A negative reaction to this influence can result in a downward spiral into the confusion and chaos of drugs and alcohol, whereas a positive reaction results in an uplift of the consciousness into the higher planes. When the latter is the case, the energies of Pisces accelerate the pace at which people assume the values and qualities of the selfless Soul and fulfill the charge of the Soul to manifest love-wisdom on earth.

The divine power of love and devotion is greater with this placement of Vulcan than it is with any other placement. It is the vulcanized power of uplifting love that knows no distinction or differentiation, only ever-expanding inclusiveness. This leads people to renounce their identification with the personality characteristics that are contrary to the selfless nature and values of the Soul.

In a number of ways, Jesus's chart suggests that He had renounced materiality in past lives and was detached from the things of earth. Much of what usually interferes with people's ability to express divine love was eliminated prior to incarnation. However, the influences of the unconscious that expressed via His personal will and affected the quality of some of His thoughts and beliefs still needed to be modified before Jesus could express Christ consciousness and implement the divine plan free of distortion. Only when the blocking energies of the threefold personal consciousness and ego have been eliminated do the energies of Vulcan forge a powerful link between the brain, personal mind, mind of the Soul, and the divine plan.

In Jesus's chart, Vulcan was closely conjunct the Sun, Mercury, and Uranus and was trine the Mid-heaven, Neptune, and Moon. It also opposed Pluto and the earth. Vulcan was integrally tied into both the epic grand trine and the kite configuration of planets.

The close conjunction of Mercury, the Sun, Uranus, and Vulcan, along with their trine to Neptune, suggest that Jesus was on the path of initiation (as defined two thousand years ago) prior to His incarnation. Once He fully sacrificed His personal will to the will of the Soul, the integrated personality became one with the Soul. This unification requires an even higher degree of detachment, dispassion, and renunciation in order to free the consciousness from the conditioning of the past.

The interplay of the energies of Vulcan with Neptune, Uranus, the Sun, and Mercury strengthened and intensified Jesus's attunement to the will and purpose of the God of love. He innately responded to the building energies of the divine will.

The interplay, exchange, and synthesis of the energies of Vulcan and Pluto resulted in an exceptionally potent influence of ray one in Jesus's life. This means that the teachings He brought forth were infused with power of the divine will and purpose, especially in relation to the incoming Age of Pisces and its conditioning ray of manifestation—ray six.

The close conjunction of Vulcan to Mercury, Uranus, and the Sun in Jesus's chart meant that their energies were regularly drawn on to rebuild His life and being at successively higher levels. Their energies were also drawn upon to rebuild the integrated personality once the light of the personal self was absorbed into the light of the Soul. With a close conjunction of His Piscean Sun to Vulcan, it was the will-purpose of the Logos in its aspect of the builder that Jesus came to identify His selfhood with, not the destroyer sub-aspect that Pluto transmits.

The Vulcan trine Moon aspect heightened Jesus's sensitivity to His Soul purpose and intensified His sensitivity to the divine plan of the Spiritual Hierarchy. Neptune's Soul-centered ruler-ship of the Moon and the veiling of Uranus by the Moon both contributed potent energies from the higher planes of light that enhanced Jesus's intuition and sensitivity, especially in relation to the divine plan and His mission.

Initially, the interplay of the energies of the Vulcan-Mercury conjunction helped Jesus forge the keys that unlocked the chains that had limited His consciousness, first as a personality and then as a Soul. As an initiate, the interplay of energies between Vulcan and Mercury enabled Jesus to ideate His teachings in relation to the path of the heart and people's approach to the Divine through loving devotion.

During His ministry, the ray one energies transmitted by the sacred planet Vulcan blended with those of the Sun, Mercury, and Uranus in a way that empowered the teachings that Jesus brought forth, sanctifying His mission at the highest level. The favorable influences of Mercury, Uranus, and Neptune with Vulcan all contributed to Jesus's ability to awaken love-wisdom within the hearts and minds of humanity.

The energies of Vulcan blend well with the energies of the synthesizing planet Uranus. The blending of these two types of energies sensitized the consciousness of Jesus to the new spiritual archetypes and seed ideas emanating from the planes of light via the mind of the Soul during the early days of the Piscean Age.

More so than any other combination, this Uranus-Vulcan interplay of energies attuned Jesus to the divine plan and awakened the intuitional mind of divine ideation. This occurred once Jesus generated the rainbow bridge of light that linked His higher mind to the spiritual mind of the Triad (via the petals of the lotus). The fact that Uranus and Vulcan are conjunct in Jesus's chart is especially auspicious.

Vulcan conjunct Uranus strengthened the relationship between ray one and ray seven in Jesus's life. This intensified the energy necessary to clear the sushumna and link the crown center to the basic center. This clearing of the sushumna channel between the basic center and crown center had to occur before Jesus could fully conceptualize the new principles, spiritual ideas, and archetypes of the Piscean Age.

Such a potent interplay of ray one and ray seven energies in the lives of initiates often brings forth a social, political, or religious revolutionary who challenges the culture in a way that transforms it into a vehicle that better represents the divine plan. Revolutionary-minded initiates plant the seeds of new spiritual paradigms within the collective minds of humanity. Overtime these seeds come to fruition through the thoughts and ideas of the advanced members of society. Jesus accomplished this when He planted the principle of pure love-wisdom on earth.

The combination of Uranus and Vulcan represents the power to create. The blending of these two energies in the life of Jesus enabled Him to envision the seed ideas that the Spiritual Hierarchy projected and enabled Him to construct the foundation upon which the spiritual teachings for the Piscean Age were built.

The opposition of Vulcan to Pluto was initially an outside force that acted upon Jesus during His younger years. Both in past lives and during His younger years, Jesus most likely experienced the potent destructive forces of Pluto as the all-powerful Satan. This belief needed to be mitigated, however, before Jesus could transcend the personality. Jesus accomplished this by gaining power over the Satan of the Senses—the instinctual, emotional, sensory nature—as He approached the third initiation.

The opposition of Pluto to the Sun, Mercury, and Uranus, and its inconjunction to Mars and Saturn may explain why the concept of Satan played an important role in Jesus's life. Before His ministry started, however, Jesus had gained command of the World Satan. This doesn't occur when people assign the activity of their own instinctual-emotional atoms of self-consciousness to the influences of Satan. If Jesus wasn't willing to accept the changes Pluto brought forth in His life, it would have been difficult for Him to take command of the forces that precipitated the events and actions on earth that were deemed to be the work of Satan.

The concept of a good God and a bad god which Zoroastrianism contributed to Judaism, provided people with a reasonable explanation for the difficulties they experienced. For millennia, people were unaware that much of what they thought of as evil arose because of the nature of the physical body and their own instinctual-emotional atoms of self-consciousness. The development of such concepts as Satan and Lucifer is understandable, since the instinctual and often destructive lower emotional aspects of personal consciousness operate below the light of people's conscious awareness. From the dark recesses of the mind, they affect people's lives in important ways.

Pluto opposite Vulcan represents the primordial conflict between good and evil. For this reason, the will-to-destroy often arises when Vulcan and Pluto are opposite each other. The effect that the will-to-destroy has on people and on the society depend on whether it is the personal self or the higher self that is expressing this force. When it is the personal self, the release of this energy can have disastrous consequences.

For Jesus, the effects of the opposition of Pluto to Vulcan during His younger years most likely expressed as a clash between His personal will and the will of the Soul, especially as He was approaching the second initiation. Due to the heightened potency of ray one, these two dynamics of the psyche represent the greatest extremes that human consciousness can fathom. Pluto symbolizes the forces of darkness and destruction, while Vulcan represents the forces of light and creation. These two needed to be related to each other within the mind of Jesus.

The etheric body that the Soul of Jesus appropriated for His incarnation did not have the channel of the sushumna fully cleared from the basic center to the crown center. Such clearing is necessary in order to link the basic center to the crown center. The opportunity to clear the sushumna channel and relate the crown center to the basic center is what the conjunction of Vulcan and Uranus and their opposition to Pluto offered.

Once the basic center and crown center are linked and the sushumna is cleared of all obstructions, Pluto and Vulcan start to work together, resulting in the complete sacrifice of the personal will to the will of the Soul. The combination of the energies of Pluto and

Vulcan represent the most forceful expression of the divine will and power available to mankind at this time. This power is esoterically referred to as the will-to-good which is both miraculously creative, as well as destructive of all that blocks the path of divine ideation and creation.

Only the fourth-degree initiate is capable of expressing the will-to-good without distortion, due to the intense dynamism that the combined forces of Pluto and Vulcan represent. The ability to will absolute good into the manifest world of earth is possible once all of the apparent oppositions within the mind and consciousness have been resolved. This includes the apparent opposition between light and darkness, good and evil. Again, as people approach the third initiation, the clash between good and evil involves the resistance of the dweller-on-the-threshold to the Angel of the Presence. For the most part, good and evil are conditions of the active intelligence and do not necessarily represent some entity.

Jupiter's placement in Taurus (which Vulcan rules at the Soul level) helped Jesus attain enlightenment. This placement strengthened Jesus's access to divine will and greatly enhanced the unfolding dynamic within Him that is referred to as the will-to-love. This represents a combination of the building aspect of ray one forces and enlightened pure love-wisdom that ushered forth as a result of Vulcan's ruler-ship of Taurus. By the beginning of Jesus's ministry, the will of the Father which He expressed as the will-to-love was no longer transcendent; rather, Jesus freely expressed it on earth via the instrumentality of the purified integrated personality.

Jesus sacrificed the will of the Soul to the divine will at Gethsemane, shortly before His arrest. This, along with His responses to the Sanhedrin and to Pilate, demonstrated Jesus's attunement to the will of the Father and confirmed His willingness to sacrifice all that He was not (through the death of the physical body), so He could more fully express that which He truly was.

His ability to resurrect the physical body is emblematic of the power of ray one in its builder sub-aspect. Jesus was able to transmute His physical cellular form into a body of light. This transubstantiation was possible as a result of His command of the sacred ray one forces in its builder aspect. With the ability to command the builder quality of ray one, Jesus was able to accelerate the vibrations of the light of the cells. This acceleration burned up the cellular forces, transforming the matter of His body into light. Jesus was the first person to express the light of resurrection on earth.

In the early days of the Aquarian Age, the Christ will be returning on the builder sub-aspect of ray one to build the kingdom of heaven on the earth—the world of the Soul. This feat will involve transforming the light of the kingdom into a planetary body of exceedingly refined substance. This does not mean that all people will be functioning as a Soul at that time. Most will not.

The kingdom already exists in the planes of light, but not until the Christ reappears will the work begin to transform the matter of earth into the light of the world of the Soul. This work will continue throughout the Aquarian Age. The incarnation of the Christ is required to anchor the world of the Soul on earth. This doesn't mean that the Christ will necessarily take physical incarnation. The overshadowing Christ operating from the upper mental realm could anchor and manifest on earth the kingdom through the instrumentality of the initiates on earth. Just like the overshadowing Soul brings forth the higher mind in these forms of earth.

The Coming One will incarnate on this builder sub-aspect of ray one and begin the work necessary to create a new heaven and a new earth. Until there are enough people who function as a Soul, however, there is no need for Him to incarnate. This transformation of heaven and earth will require a substantial number of initiates and masters who have learned how to wield ray one in its expression as the builder. The training to learn how to wield the laws that govern ray one in its builder sub-aspect begins soon for advanced disciples and initiates.

Chapter 27

Earth, the Blue Star of the Heavens

Within the light and forces of planet earth, people move forward from step to step and stage to stage, from initiation to higher initiation. Slowly humanity achieves successively higher states of mind and consciousness as gods-in-the-making of the evolutionary system of earth.

The effects that the planet earth has on people must also be considered in this treatise on the evolution of consciousness. The earth doesn't rule any of the twelve signs of the zodiac at the personal level. However, it is the ruler of Sagittarius at the Soul level. This means that people are not consciously sensitive to the uplifting influences of the Logos of Earth until they have transcended the personality and attained a union of the integrated personality and the Soul.

Under no circumstances should Sagittarians begrudge the fact that the earth is the Soul-centered ruler of Sagittarius. Though the earth has yet to attain the status of a sacred planet, it offers the training for seven spiritual initiations, plus the two threshold initiations for a total of nine primary initiations (twenty-seven ray initiations).

The earth offers training for human beings at each stage of development. These stages represent the unfoldment, development, and mastery of the seven principles of consciousness, which human beings actualize in relation to the seven planes of the cosmic physical plane of earth. It also provides the initial training that ascended masters need in order to step upon one of the seven cosmic paths that lead away from the cosmic physical plane. Once the ninth initiation is attained, ascended masters transcend the cosmic physical plane, continuing their development and service either in the cosmic astral plane or cosmic mental plane.

Most evolutionary systems are limited in the training they offer, since the human beings of these evolutionary systems are at a similar point of development. The earth is one of the few multidimensional evolutionary systems in which individuals who have yet to attain the first initiation and ascended masters exist simultaneously in the same system.

The energies of Sagittarius relate to vision and the inner mind's eye. This pertains to that faculty of vision that allows people to perceive a personal objective or goal to achieve. Symbolically, the archer of Sagittarius, with intense one-pointed focus, withdraws an arrow from its quiver and shoots toward its target. It is the ray-two magnetically attractive forces of Jupiter (the exoteric ruler of Sagittarius) that help people achieve the goals they personally establish for themselves.

There is a point in the personality life of the advanced Soul, however, when the things of earth lose their luster. People's drive to satisfy their personal desires and achieve self-serving personal goals and objectives diminishes as a result of the spiritual vision that the energies of Sagittarius bring forth. Spiritual vision is not seen by the two physical eyes; rather, spiritual vision is seen only by way of the third eye—the ajna center—once it is constructed in the etheric body via intense concentration and one-pointed focus.

By way of spiritual vision, the mount of initiation is seen in the distance. The Logos of Earth shines its sublime light upon the mount of initiation, illumining the path that leads the disciple higher. This light cannot be perceived with the physical eyes. Only the single eye focused upon the sublime light can pierce the fog of personal glamour and illusion and see the mount of initiation that rises up from the plains of personal life.

Blending the ray-magnetized energies and qualities with their individually unique energies, people construct their path home. By way of their utilization of different types and ray qualities of energy, people attain successively higher states of mind, consciousness, life, and being on earth.

Being the focal point of ray three energies in our solar system, the Logos of Earth works to bring forth a unique expression of active intelligence—one that is conditioned with love. Initially, this involves the manifest development of the four attributes of consciousness of the Divine. These four attributes of consciousness are brought forth as a result of people's utilization and experimentation with the energies magnetized by one or other of the seven rays, especially rays four, five, six, and seven initially.

This manifest development of the active intelligence of the Logos is taking place on earth during the Second Solar System. During this Second Solar System, life across the solar system in all planes is unfolding and developing the seven sub-ray qualities of cosmic ray two ushering from the heart center of the Solar Logos. In other words, the active intelligence of earth is an aspect of cosmic love-wisdom. For this reason, the objective set before humanity is to unfold loving creative intelligence.

The earth's astrological placement in a person's natal chart is an important factor that is often overlooked. The sign and house placement of the earth offers clues as to how people are likely to use the energies impacting them and reveals the underlying theme that runs through people's lives. The earth is the place where the Divine treads the pathways of mankind.

In relation to the evolution of human consciousness, the earth is located 180 degrees opposite the Sun. The opposition of the earth to the Sun represents an opportunity to establish a relationship between the consciousness (which originates with the Soul) and the human form. As a result of the interplay of energies between the earth and the personality, which the Sun represents, successively greater expressions of self-consciousness are brought forth within the physical body.

Year after year, lifetime after lifetime, people become self-conscious: first in relation to the physical body and the three aspects of personal consciousness, then in relation to the Soul, and eventually in relation to the Spiritual Triad. Slowly, people attain progressively higher states of mind and consciousness within the body of the Logos of Earth, who bathes all life of the seven planes of earth in its ray light, life, and being.

The astrological factors associated with the earth (the sign and house placement and the planetary aspects formed to the planet) indicate the ease or difficulty people have unfolding new atoms of self-consciousness, as they move forward in life upon their own unique life path.

In Jesus's chart, the earth is located in the sign of Virgo. Of the three signs conditioned by the element earth, Virgo transmits the most nourishing and nurturing energies in relation to the indwelling life of human consciousness. The esoteric symbolism of Virgo relates to the processes that bring forth self-consciousness within the physical body in relation to love.

Symbolically, Virgo magnetizes the physical-etheric body in a way that enables the brain consciousness to receive the seeds of essential love from the Soul. It also represents the energies that protect these seeds of love until they are ready to manifest as new expressions of self-consciousness. Initially, self-consciousness arises within the brain consciousness mainly in relation to the lower mental aspect of personal consciousness when the planet is under the influence of Virgo, but later Virgo brings forth self-consciousness in relation to the loving intelligence of the higher self.

Once the higher mind is brought forth, Virgo represents the Virgin Mother (the purified threefold personality vehicle) which, when united with the Father spirit, is impregnated with the seeds of cosmic love-wisdom—the seeds that bring forth Christ consciousness. Within the womb of the form-world of mankind, the seed of love-wisdom is nourished and protected until it is safe to manifest within the human consciousness as the Christ child. The Soul endures hundreds of lifetimes before an integrated personality is brought forth that is advanced enough to register the qualities that express Christ consciousness.

Virgo brings in the energies of ray four Mercury at the personality level and reveals the duality—the conflicts that exist within the personal consciousness. For disciples, Virgo shines a light upon the personal mind and contrasts it with the Soul and its qualities of essential love. In this way, the faculty of discrimination is developed.

At the personal level, Mercury always reveals duality—the apparent oppositions or conflicts—that exist within the personal consciousness, so they can be harmonized (via the energies of Venus) in relation to each other and then unified. The forms of duality found in the astral-emotional and lower mental aspects of consciousness do not exist at the level of the Soul, since they relate only to the threefold form consciousness caught up in illusion, glamour, and maya.

For people on the path, Virgo and Scorpio (where Neptune was located in Jesus's chart) are the two signs most frequently associated with the processes that unfold Christ consciousness. Both signs represent critical moments in the Soul's progression and are integrally involved in people's efforts to attain a union of the integrated personality with the Soul.

The ray four Moon rules Virgo at the Soul level. This reference to the Moon's ruler-ship of Virgo has nothing to do with the Moon in the sky or to its decaying planetary forces. Instead, the Moon outwardly conceals a center through which a sub-quality of the energies of Uranus, Neptune, or Vulcan advances one of the three aspects of the higher mind.

Once Jesus attained the third initiation, the energies of Uranus (conditioned with ray six Neptune) poured through the Moon's position in the natal chart. Since Neptune rules Cancer at the Soul level, the Moon's placement at 9 degrees Cancer 15 minutes in Jesus's chart became a center where the ray six energies of Neptune were combined with the ray seven energies of Uranus. This greatly intensified the importance of the spiritualization of Jesus that the Uranus trine Neptune aspect offered Him.

As the interplay of energies represented by the conjunction of Uranus and the Sun in His chart impacted Jesus at the Soul level, He was able to create a channel that linked His mind to the intuitional mind via the abstract mind. This enabled Jesus to touch into the reservoirs in the planes of light, where many of the principles and seed ideas of the Age of Pisces were deposited by the Masters of the Spiritual Hierarchy. Unquestionably, the refined qualities of Uranus significantly impacted the path work of Jesus across all stages of His life.

The earth in Jesus's chart was placed in the eighth house, the house of transmutation and transformation, endings and new beginnings, death and rebirth. This represents the area of life where people die to a lower state of mind in order to attain a higher state. Scorpio and its rulers Pluto and Mars establish the life lessons and issues of the eighth house. These issues involve the transmutation of the obsolete patterns of the emotional-desire nature, resulting in significant personal transformation.

Both Pluto and the eighth house correspond to the transformation of human consciousness and to the ray one aspect of the will of the Divine, especially its destroyer sub-aspect. The eighth house is therefore the house of liberation, whose energies can be used to free people from their past. Since the destroyer sub-aspect of the will is a ray three aspect of ray one, the energies of Pluto and the eighth house naturally resonate with the evolution of consciousness on earth, since the earth is a ray three planet.

With Leo on the eighth-house cusp in the chart of Jesus (Virgo was intercepted in the eighth house), the first and fifth rays were also involved in the eighth-house issues that Jesus faced. Leo on the eighth-house cusp strongly emphasized the fires of purification that destroy that which interferes with people's efforts to express the divine will.

This placement of the earth suggests that Jesus's life path involved periods of rather intense transformation in His life, consciousness, identity, and selfhood. As a result, Jesus was able to attain successively higher initiations in a relatively short period of time. The speed with which He experienced these initiations was accelerated by the conjunction of Pluto to the earth.

Jesus moved quickly along the path of the heart onto the path of power. This shift onto the path of power enabled Him to demonstrate the works of the Father. This does not mean that He had left the path of the heart. At this advanced stage, the buddhic-plane quality of love-wisdom was part of His very nature. Prior to stepping upon the path of power, Jesus had attained Christ consciousness and became the very embodiment of pure love-wisdom. Symbolically speaking, *"And the Word became flesh and dwelt among us."*[77]

An eighth house earth forming a conjunction to Pluto indicates Jesus often experienced endings and new beginnings, sacrifice, death, and rebirth. All who have stepped upon the path are called to sacrifice, i.e., to die in consciousness to the form nature and be reborn as spirit. People must first die to selfishness at the physical, astral-emotional, and lower mental levels in order to salvage the Soul from its imprisonment in the caverns of the underworld. (Jesus was ultimately called on to sacrifice not just the physical body and threefold personal self, but the Soul as well.)

On earth, the salvaging of life goes on continually. The hawks and maggots devouring the flesh of a carcass, and the termites and beetles devouring the wood—all are salvaging essential life from the world of form. The salvation of life takes place as the mineral kingdom sacrifices its forms to the plant kingdom, the life forms of the plant kingdom are sacrificed to the animal kingdom, and the life forms of the plant and animal kingdoms are sacrificed to human beings. Human beings, in turn, sacrifice the personality to the Soul. A life form is always sacrificed to a higher form of life.

The essence of the work of World Saviors is to salvage essential life from the life

---

[77] John 1:14. (RSV) (italics added)

forms of matter. In this way, the Soul is freed from its imprisonment in the three planes of earth. Planetary Saviors demonstrate the highest form of sacrifice currently known to mankind.

Planetary Aspects Formed to the Earth

The earth is a major receiving and emanating planetary center in the solar system. Within this center, there are billions of major and minor reception and transmission centers of energy. The most important centers of the planet are referred to as the planetary head center (Shamballa), the planetary heart center (the Spiritual Hierarchy), and the planetary throat center (humanity).

The earth is where a small portion of the different types and qualities of energies and forces that stream through the ethers of earth impacts the physiology and consciousness of people via the seven etheric centers of the planet. Universally, the personal self (the overarching dynamic of the psyche which the Sun represents) slowly becomes responsive to the different types and qualities of energies that stream from these planetary centers into the receptive centers in people's own etheric bodies. In this way, people slowly unfold loving intelligence as creative gods-in-the-making.

The earth is where energy involutes into the world of matter and expresses on earth via the forms of earth. Consciousness, on the other hand, is evolutionary. The earth is where the path begins for a multitude of Souls, but it is not where the path ends.

The placement of the earth at 14 degrees Virgo 28 minutes positions the earth opposite Uranus, the Sun, Mercury, North Node, and widely opposite Venus in the chart of Jesus. Along with Pluto, the earth divided the western side of the epic grand trine in half. This further intensified the dynamism of the compelling kite configuration of planets in the chart of Jesus. The dynamism that these oppositions contributed to Jesus's life cannot be underestimated. They, along with the inconjunctions of Pluto and the earth to Mars and Saturn, were responsible for systematically transforming the life, mind, and consciousness of Jesus, propelling Him forward from initiation to initiation onto His Crucifixion, Resurrection, and Ascension.

The placement of the Sun opposite the earth in Jesus's chart had ramifications and significances that far exceeded the effects that this opposition usually has. To the average person, this opposition of the Sun to the earth relates to the efforts of the Soul to bring forth self-consciousness within these physical bodies of earth. This involves the unfoldment and development of the three aspects of personal consciousness.

Lifetime after lifetime, the Sun and the earth are opposite each other. This presents people with the opportunity to relate consciousness (which originates with the Soul) to the brain, resulting in self-conscious life forms on earth. For this reason, incarnation on earth is necessary to unfold the creative potential of both the integrated personality and the higher self.

For people on the path, the opposition of the Sun to the earth corresponds to the long-term efforts of the Soul to consciously relate the crown center to the basic center. This pertains to the evolutionary objective to relate the Divine to the physical world of mankind, i.e., to relate God to mankind. By way of resolving the opposition of the Sun to the earth (spirit and matter, the Soul and the personality, light and darkness), conscious life is brought forth within the human forms of earth. For people on the path, this opposition of the earth to the Sun corresponds to the effort of the Soul to spiritualize human consciousness by unfolding the human spirit in and through these forms of earth.

The placement of the earth in Jesus's chart strongly linked the ray energies and forces of the planets of the epic grand trine with those of the earth. For most people, the opposition of the earth to a stellium of planets indicates the presence of major conflicts within the psyche. Such conflicts make it difficult to proceed forward until they are resolved. Having resolved such conflicts prior to incarnation, Jesus wasn't confronted with such issues on a personal level as most people are.

Since Jesus had, for all practical purposes, mastered the three aspects of personal consciousness prior to His incarnation, the oppositions of the planets in Pisces to the earth represented the oppositional forces Jesus encountered as the voice for the changes impacting the consciousness of mankind as the earth was transitioning into the Age of Pisces. The conjunction of the earth and Pluto and their oppositions to the planets in Pisces in the chart of Jesus also represented the social-religious opposition Jesus encountered as He attempted to anchor love-wisdom on earth and present the new teachings of the Age of Pisces.

The Pisces-Virgo opposition involved two very different sub-qualities of ray two energies that (when harmonized with each other) uplifted the consciousness of Jesus into a higher quality of the essential love of the Soul, and later uplifted the consciousness into the buddhic-plane of pure love-wisdom. During His ministry, the planetary oppositions to the earth in Jesus's chart were more representative of the clashes He encountered anchoring the principle of love in the consciousness of mankind than conflicts within His own psyche.

By way of the energies of Virgo, the seeds of love-wisdom are first anchored in these forms. By way of the energies of Pisces, these seeds bear the fruit of love and wisdom. The planting takes place in Virgo. The harvest takes place in Pisces.

The earth's opposition to Mercury and Uranus in Jesus's natal chart precipitated the type of experiences Jesus needed in order to unfold the intuitional mind and subsequently intuit the new ideals, principles, and teachings of the Piscean Age.

The earth is frequently opposite Mercury, since Mercury is never far from the position of the Sun. This opposition typically relates to the forces of evolution that compel people to unfold and develop the concrete mind, intellect, and rational thought. At the higher levels, however, this opposition impels the unfoldment of the faculties and capacities needed in order to create a relationship between the intuitional mind and the concrete mind.

Again, Mercury is a focal point for the energies magnetized by ray four: (harmony through conflict). The opposition of the earth to Mercury for the average person relates to the processes involved in becoming consciously aware of the many forms of duality that exist in the personal consciousness, so that the apparent oppositions can be related to each other and subsequently harmonized. When functioning at the Soul level, however, the interplay and exchange of the ray energies of this Mercury-earth opposition help unfold the pure reasoning and wisdom of the buddhic intuitional plane. As a result of this opposition between ray four (Mercury) and ray three (earth), the intuitional mind of Jesus was linked to the refined concrete mind.

Once Jesus had resolved the differences between the teachings of the Age of Pisces and the Age of Aries within His own consciousness, the opposition of Uranus to the earth represented the societal forces of opposition Jesus encountered as the voice of the Piscean Age. It is not that it was difficult for Him to comprehend the path of the heart or to accept the ideals of the Piscean Age; rather, the difficulties He encountered were due to the ingrained societal forces of resistance to the Piscean teachings. The resulting clash was intensified by Pluto's conjunction to the earth and its opposition to Uranus.

Though Jesus envisioned a new heaven and a new earth and was able to perceive the truth that He was to teach, the entrenched social, political, and religious authorities of Judea and the Roman Empire worked hard to disrupt and even destroy His teachings.

There was a mere 1 degree 38 minutes of separation between Pluto and the earth. This means that Jesus was confronted with the ray one power of Pluto throughout much of His life. If Jesus hadn't gained control of this power, it would have killed Him before it was His time to pass from the earth. It also means that when Jesus incarnated, He was ill-disposed (in consciousness) toward the material world of earth, especially in terms of the drives and appetites of the physical body.

Historically, people have often looked at the events and experiences in their lives that Pluto precipitates as the work of the devil. Jesus most likely did as well—at least initially. However, because of Pluto's conjunction to the earth and its opposition to the stellium of planets in Pisces, Jesus was able to work through these forces and gain command of them. This He did by sacrificing His personal will to the divine will and learning how to consciously apply the power of the divine will to the forces of the three planes of earth.

Both the earth and Pluto served as the focalizing lens through which the ray energies of the epic grand trine expressed in Jesus's life. Since the midpoint of the conjunction of the earth and Pluto was 15 degrees 17 minutes Virgo, Mercury at 15 degrees 48 minutes Pisces represented the psychic dynamic that received the greatest concentration of ray energies transmitted by the planets of the kite configuration. This accelerated and intensified the development of, first His intellect and then His abstract mind and intuitional mind.

Throughout His ministry, Jesus expressed a power and spiritual authority that far exceeded anything previously seen in the West. Due to the spiritual mastery He had attained and the influences of ray one Pluto, combined with ray three influence of the energies of the earth, Jesus not only spoke with great authority, but was able to heal the sick, return sight to the blind, and even resurrect the dead as in the case of Lazarus. It is not surprising that some people thought Jesus was Elijah, while others thought He was Beelzebub.

The ray one energies of Pluto are able to pierce through the substances of the three matter planes and reveal people's hidden resources and capacities, as well as reveal the destructive, instinctual-emotional patterns of the unconscious. Such patterns are often unintegrated fragments of self-consciousness that people have rejected, but not transmuted or transformed.

Often these fragments are limiting and negative feelings and patterns of behavior that can adversely impact people's lives, no matter how deeply people have buried them. Pluto throws these patterns into the light of people's awareness so they can be observed and addressed. This conjunction of the earth and Pluto sensitized Jesus to the presence of darkness and evil in the world. In fact, His energies at times reflected people's darkness and evil back to them. With Pluto, no emotions can remain hidden in the catacombs of the unconscious for long. In the midst of evil, Jesus gained command over the forces of earth, both good and evil. Within this field of intense ray one forces, Jesus had to learn how to command them before He could work out His progression and attain Christ consciousness, resulting in His ability to anchor love-wisdom on earth.

The close conjunction of Pluto to the earth meant that Jesus would either gain command over the negative and dark forces present on earth or be victimized by them. Through His unwavering dedication to the will of God, Jesus brought forth the skill and power to see through the densest forms of matter and defeat the forces of darkness and evil that resided behind the masks of form-life. The fact that Jesus could perceive what people concealed from others was especially troubling to many.

The earth was also opposite Vulcan—the builder. This brought forth an urge to create new capacities, skills, faculties, and other tools to demonstrate the enlightened will of the Father on earth. This aspect relates specifically to the unfoldment of an ability to command the forces of the physical plane: to heal, to still the waters, and so forth. Many of His works involved His command of the forces of the mineral kingdom (which Vulcan rules), resulting in unusual powers over the physical substances of earth. This opposition of the earth to Vulcan indicates that Jesus needed to harmonize ray one power with rays two and three before He could relate the forces of destruction to the forces of creation.

During His ministry, Jesus used the destroyer sub-aspect of ray one along with the builder sub-aspect of Vulcan to present new principles and ideals that could free the minds of humanity from obsolete practices, beliefs, and superstitions that arose during the Age of Aries. By way of the interplay and exchange of the energies between the earth, Pluto, and Vulcan, Jesus was able to transmute many of the lower planetary forces and bring about a degree of transformation of the earth. This allowed greater light to stream into the upper sub-plane levels of the three planes of earth. By the time of His crucifixion, there was greater light on earth than there was before He incarnated.

The opposition of the earth to His planets in Pisces also suggests that Jesus had to relate and subsequently master the threefold personal consciousness and then the threefold Soul, while in the midst of the travails of life on earth. He could not remove Himself from society like many of the mystics did who came before Him.

By way of the spiritual training that He received, once He attained the third initiation, Jesus learned how to command the forces of the three subtle bodies of the planet. Although this training by the masters started once He attained the third initiation, Jesus did not complete His transition from the path of the heart to the path of power until the climaxing moments of His mission.

The sextile of the earth to Neptune and to the Moon provided Jesus with a way to constructively relieve the tension generated by the earth's opposition to the planets in Pisces. Since both the Moon and Neptune were trine the stellium of planets in Pisces, the tension and stress generated by the oppositions led to the blending and harmonization of the ray energies of the earth and Pluto with the ray energies of the epic grand trine.

Collectively, the planets of the kite configuration transmitted all seven rays. Pluto, along with the Masters of Hierarchy, focused the seven rays into one intense beam of light that impacted the mind of Jesus, the consequence of which was to bring forth Christ consciousness in relation to all seven rays. Only the avatar of an Age can serve as a messenger of the divine plan in relation to all seven rays. Jesus became an agent of the seven ray ashrams of the

Spiritual Hierarchy. Usually a master is an agent of just one ray ashram, e.g., the Ray Two Ashram or the Ray Six Ashram, but rarely an agent for all seven ray ashrams.

As an initiate, Jesus became the instrument through which ray one (Vulcan), ray two (the Sun), ray three (the earth), ray four (Mercury and the Moon), ray five (Venus), ray six (Neptune), and ray seven (Uranus) were blended and synthesized in relation to each other as a result of the interplay and exchange of energies of the kite configuration of planets.

In this way, all seven aspects of the divine plan were interlinked and unified. People's favorable response to love-wisdom over the past two thousand years has brought the Logos of Earth ever closer to achieving the cosmic initiation that will transform the earth into a sacred planet.

With the earth sextile the Moon in His chart (and the Moon trine the Sun), Jesus had an interesting relationship between His past and His path work in this life. Since there was little from His past (no patterns of personal behavior or feelings) that needed to be addressed, Jesus had an opportunity at a young age to draw on the spiritual development and mastery that had been achieved in prior lifetimes. This, in conjunction with the sextile of the earth to Neptune, brought forth a strong sense of spiritual duty and responsibility and an all-consuming desire to serve God and to heal those who were suffering.

From an early age, Jesus was sensitive and responsive to the cosmic love-wisdom radiating from the spiritual heart center of the Solar Logos. This was greatly intensified as a result of the blended synthesis of the ray energies of the planets with the cosmic ray two energies of the Sun, once He attained the third initiation.

Most people are unable to integrate the energies of the earth and Neptune without creating distortion, illusion, and confusion. Since Neptune represents the highest expression of devotion—a devotion to love-wisdom in its purest sense—only those whose consciousness is polarized at the level of the Soul or higher are able to fully utilize Neptune's ray six energies as an emanation of cosmic ray six and cosmic ray two energies that emanate from the heart center of the Solar Logos.

Neptune sextile the earth in the chart of Jesus represented an opportunity to transform the ideals of the Age of Aries into the ray six ideals of the Age of Pisces. This involved blazing a new path that allowed people to connect to the heart of God. This activity has been ongoing throughout the Age of Pisces.

Jesus utilized the exchange and interplay of the ray three energies of earth and the ray six energies of Neptune to formulate the principle of love-wisdom on earth and to teach humanity how to approach the Divine through loving devotion. This represents the first part of His mission. The second part will work out when the Christ reappears in the three planes of earth to build a new heaven and a new earth. Details about this event will be decided in the centennial conclave of the Masters, in consultation with the Buddha, at Wesak 2025.

Earth, the blue star of the heavens, revolves around a seemingly minor sun located in one of the many outer spirals of the great galactic chakra of life and being called the Milky Way, yet it has an exceedingly important and bright future. Toward the end of the Second Solar System, the Logos of Earth will achieve a level of perfection that attracts its cosmic twin flame from a region in the Pleiades.

The union of these two great cosmic ones will instantaneously transmute the matter of all seven planes of the cosmic physical plane into cosmic light—not just in relation to the earth but in terms of the entire solar system. In this way, the heart center of the ONE is awakened and the firmament of this remote spiral of the Milky Way will be illumined. Henceforth, the blue star once known as the earth will stand as the brilliant jewel of cosmic life at the core of the cosmic heart center of the ONE.

Addendum

Addendum

Why Was December 25, 1 AD, Chosen?

Could Jesus have been born on a day other than December 25, 1 AD? This was one of the first questions I asked myself when the birth chart of Yeshua first appeared. I had no desire or intention to present an alternative date for the birth of Jesus. I love Christmas. Without it, Christianity would be missing something of great value. This is true even though Christmas has become exceedingly materialistic and, therefore, antithetical to the teachings of Jesus.

Theological scholars universally agree that Jesus was born on a day other than December 25, 1 AD. In fact, there isn't any historical evidence to support that He was born on December 25, 1 AD. Even the early church fathers had proposed a number of different dates.

December 25, 1 AD, was selected as the day to celebrate the birth of Jesus for a number of reasons that had nothing to do with the day He incarnated. The date of His birth was never recorded. Nor was there a historical year one or a year one hundred for that matter.

As is commonly known, the Gregorian calendar used today was created in 525 AD by the Scythian monk Dionysius Exiguus. Dionysius was repulsed by the idea that the church continued to date the important celebrations of the church using a calendar based on the accession of the Roman Emperor Diocletian. After all, Diocletian had persecuted the early Christians. Dionysius proposed a new calendar, the Gregorian calendar. All historical events prior to 525 AD were backdated.

Dionysius prefaced the table he had developed for dating Easter with a statement that it had been 525 years since the birth of Jesus. This statement alone was accepted by the church to indicate the year Jesus was born, yet there isn't any historical record to support his statement.

Even more glaring is the reason why December 25 was selected as the day of Jesus's birth. There is little doubt that once the Roman Empire had adopted Christianity, December

25 was selected in an effort to supplant the raucous final day of the Roman Festival of Saturnalia.

There are so many theological studies and investigations that refute December 25, 1 AD, as the actual birthday of Jesus that discussing this topic further is meaningless. It is more difficult to prove December 25, 1 AD, was the date of His birth than it is to suggest that Jesus was born on some day other than December 25, 1 AD.

Biblical scholars also doubt the historical accuracy of the birth story as discussed in the books of Matthew and Luke. It appears that this nativity story started to circulate through some of the Christian communities of the Mediterranean region after the books of Matthew and Luke were written. This hypothesis is based on the fact that the two books of the Bible that have the nativity story do not refer back to this auspicious event.

Biblical scholars believe that the books of Matthew and Luke were both written between 80 and 85 AD, while the book of Mark was written sometime between 65 and 70 AD (at least thirty-two years after the death of Jesus). In the book of Mark, the nativity story is noticeably absent.

Prior to 65 AD, the words of Jesus were orally transmitted. Except for a small theorized document referred to as Q, it is believed that His teachings were not written down prior to the book of Mark. This is understandable, since the early followers of Jesus believed that He would be returning soon. By 65 AD, many of the Apostles and the early followers of Jesus had died. Only then did the followers of Jesus see a need to write down His teachings.

The place where Jesus was born is just as much a mystery as His date of birth. The book of Matthew indicates that Jesus was born in Bethlehem and implies that Mary and Joseph resided there. According to the book of Luke, Mary and Joseph resided in Nazareth and traveled to Bethlehem to be enrolled in the census when Jesus was born. (Historically, this census took place in 9 AD.)

Many biblical scholars believe Jesus was born in Nazareth since He was referred to as the Nazarene. According to Jewish tradition at the time, it is unlikely that Jesus would have been referred to as a Nazarene unless He was born in Nazareth. Referring to someone by the place of their birth continues today in much of the Middle East.

My recollection is that the chart that first appeared on the dot matrix printer in 1987 had a birth place of Nazareth. I remember being baffled when I saw the Nazareth birthplace, since I had been entering Bethlehem as His place of birth.

From an astrological perspective, it doesn't matter whether Jesus was born in Nazareth or Bethlehem. Both charts have the planets in the same signs and houses. There is a slight difference between the two charts, however, in the degree and minute of the signs on the cusps of the twelve houses. The Ascendant for the Nazareth chart is 25 degrees Capricorn 57 minutes, while the Ascendant for the Bethlehem chart is 26 degrees Capricorn 33 minutes. This represents a difference of a mere 36 minutes.

This slight difference between the two Ascendants is significant only for dating events that involve the Ascendant. There is only one instance in which this slight difference between the two charts is significant. This involves dating when the ministry of Jesus started and how long it lasted.

If Jesus was born in Bethlehem, His ministry is likely to have spanned a little over a year before He was crucified. The Nazareth natal chart, on the other hand, suggests that His ministry spanned approximately three years before His Crucifixion. Since the synoptic Gospels suggest His ministry lasted anywhere from a little over a year (book of Mark) to three years (book of Matthew), the Gospels cannot be used to definitively establish when His public ministry started.

Table One

Rays That the Signs and Planets Transmit

Sign	Ray	Traditional Ruler	Ray	Soul-centered Ruler	Ray
Aries	1, 7	Mars	6	Mercury	4
Taurus	4	Venus	5	Vulcan	1
Gemini	2	Mercury	4	Venus	5
Cancer	3, 7	Moon	4	Neptune	6
Leo	1, 5	Sun	Rays 1-7	Sun	Cosmic Ray 2
Virgo	2, 6	Mercury	4	Moon	4
Libra	3	Venus	5	Uranus	7
Scorpio	4	Mars Pluto	6 1	Mars	6
Sagittarius	4, 5, 6	Jupiter	2	Earth	3
Capricorn	1, 3, 7	Saturn	3	Saturn	3
Aquarius	5	Saturn Uranus	3 7	Jupiter	2
Pisces	2, 6	Jupiter Neptune	2 6	Pluto	1

Printed in the United States
By Bookmasters